AGAINST POPERY

Early American Histories

DOUGLAS BRADBURN, JOHN C. COOMBS, AND S. MAX EDELSON, EDITORS

Against Popery

BRITAIN, EMPIRE, AND ANTI-CATHOLICISM

Edited by Evan Haefeli

UNIVERSITY OF VIRGINIA PRESS
Charlottesville and London

UNIVERSITY OF VIRGINIA PRESS

Printed in the United States of America on acid-free paper

First published 2020

1 3 5 7 9 8 6 4 2

Library of Congress Cataloging-in-Publication Data

Names: Haefeli, Evan, editor.
Title: Against popery : Britain, empire, and Anti-Catholicism / edited by Evan Haefeli.
Description: Charlottesville : University of Virginia Press, 2020. |
Includes bibliographical references and index.
Identifiers: LCCN 2020020096 (print) | LCCN 2020020097 (ebook) |
ISBN 9780813944913 (hardcover) | ISBN 9780813944920 (epub)
Subjects: LCSH: Anti-Catholicism—Great Britain. | Anti-Catholicism—United States. |
Religious tolerance—Great Britain. | Religious tolerance—United States.
Classification: LCC BX1766 .A33 2020 (print) | LCC BX1766 (ebook) | DDC 305.6/8241—dc23
LC record available at https://lccn.loc.gov/2020020096
LC ebook record available at https://lccn.loc.gov/2020020097

Jacket art: Sawneys Defence against the Beast, Whore, Pope, and Devil, etc., print, 1779.
(Prints & Drawing Division, © The Trustees of the British Museum)

For Martha Elena Rojas,
who agreed that anti-Catholicism mattered

CONTENTS

ILLUSTRATIONS

ACKNOWLEDGMENTS

EDITED VOLUMES HAVE THEIR own special sorts of debts, beginning with the gratitude of the editor for the long-suffering patience and cooperation of the contributors. The idea for this volume began with the excellent conference "Anti-Popery: Fears of Catholics and the Transatlantic Experience, c. 1530–1850," held at the University of Pennsylvania, September 18–20, 2008, and sponsored by the McNeil Center for Early American Studies, the Omohundro Institute of Early American History and Culture, Catholic University, and Columbia University. I thank Brendan McConville and Owen Stanwood for their thoughts about this volume at an early stage and their encouragement. However, only some of these essays began as papers presented at the conference, and I am grateful for everyone who has agreed to join this enterprise since then. I would also like to thank Martin Burke for his encouragement of the project and his thoughts on Ireland and anti-Catholicism, Ted McCormick for reading an early draft of my Irish chapter, and my colleague Brian Rouleau for reading my chapter on the British colonies.

Publishing a collection of essays is especially challenging these days, with few presses willing to take on such projects anymore. Consequently I am very grateful to the series editors Douglas Bradburn, John C. Coombs, and S. Max Edelson who accepted the manuscript, and especially Dick Holway, the press editor who shepherded it through to the final stage, and the two anonymous reviewers for their vital feedback. Since Dick retired, Nadine Zimmerli has done an excellent job of seeing the book through the final phase of publication with the editorial assistance of Helen Chandler, Ellen Satrom, Charles Bailey, and the copyeditor, Marilyn Campbell. I am also very grateful to the various institutions that loaned the images and gave us the permission to use them, namely the British Museum, the John Carter Brown Library, the Beinecke Library at Yale University, the Folger Shakespeare Library, the Parliamentary Art Collection, the Yale Center for British Art, the Tate, the

Norton Simon Art Foundation, the Pennsylvania Academy of the Fine Arts, and the Victoria and Albert Museum.

Finally, I would like to thank my parents, Richard T. and Nancy Crowell Haefeli, whose support and assistance was essential in navigating the final technicalities of pulling this volume together.

AGAINST POPERY

INTRODUCTION

Anti-Catholicism, Anti-Popery, and the British-American World

Evan Haefeli

UNDERSTANDING AMERICAN REVOLUTIONARIES' IDEAL of liberty has puzzled people since the days of the Imperial Crisis, when Samuel Johnson famously wondered, "how is it that we hear the loudest yelps for liberty among the drivers of negroes?" The slaveholder George Washington certainly feared that the "Invasion of our Rights and Priviledges by the Mother Country" meant the British government was "endeavouring by every piece of Art and despotism to fix the Shackles of Slavery upon us" and "make us as tame and abject slaves as the blacks we rule over with such arbitrary sway." John Adams meanwhile insisted that the American patriots were not "Negroes" but people "as handsome as old English folks, and so should be as free." However, his explanation of English liberty, coming in the form of a *Dissertation on the Canon and Feudal Law,* struck his otherwise sympathetic London editor as "very curious." For Adams, English liberty was a Protestant value that had emerged out of centuries of resistance to the "ecclesiastical and civil tyranny" of "the Romish clergy" and "the Princes of Europe," both driven by "the same purposes of tyranny, cruelty and lust."[1]

Before we can answer Samuel Johnson's question, we must realize neither George Washington nor John Adams were being hypocritical. Instead they were voicing a centuries'-old and pervasive Anglo-American tradition of anti-popery, a still poorly understood dimension of the revolutionaries' ideal of liberty. Although originating in early modern England, whence it was carried to America by the first colonists, by the late eighteenth century anti-popery's hold on Britain had weakened—hence the British elites' puzzlement at the revolutionaries' pronouncements. Anti-popery is related to, and often hard to distinguish from, anti-Catholicism. The boundaries between them are fuzzy, not least because the rhetoric, literature, and ideas overlap. However, where anti-Catholicism is often regarded as a religious prejudice, an animus to Roman Catholics and their religion, scholars of early modern England have been arguing that anti-popery was an ideology deriving from hostility to the religious *and* political example of the Roman Catholic papacy. By drawing on this concept of anti-popery, the present volume not only seeks to expand our approach to what is often called anti-Catholicism, but also to demonstrate that it was even more important than we realize. Between the sixteenth and nineteenth centuries anti-popery was inseparable from British and American understandings of liberty and slavery, justifying the hegemony of Protestants on both sides of the Atlantic up through the American Revolution, when its logic helped inspire the fatal split between British Protestants. Scholars of early America have largely missed anti-popery's importance because they tend to treat religion as distinct from political ideology and to study slavery with little reference to the religious-political culture of the enslavers. Samuel Johnson we can understand; George Washington and John Adams pose more of a challenge.[2]

Early Americans' anti-popish worldview has been obscured by the rise of anti-Catholicism as a category of analysis. A growing number of studies rightly insist on its importance. The literary scholar Elizabeth Fenton has recently argued that it was essential to "U.S. conceptions of religious pluralism and its corresponding 'right of conscience'" as well as "U.S. political culture's notions of individual freedom and national pluralism." By studying anti-Catholicism we can see the "symbiotic relationship between liberal democracy and Protestantism."[3] More recently, Maura Jane Farrelly has given us a survey of early American anti-Catholicism from the seventeenth century to the mid-nineteenth-century riots against Irish Catholic immigrants.[4] However, in a modern America proud of its tolerance, where Roman Catholics are an accepted presence at the highest levels of government, anti-Catholicism is generally dismissed as the "prejudice that rarely utters its name," an "ugly little secret" of discrimination against ethnic Catholics, a "persistent prejudice" against their religion, or the "last acceptable prejudice" of American liberalism.[5] A noted Protestant scholar of Christianity, Rodney Stark, has recently published a book "debunking" various anti-Catholic "myths," from the idea of the so-called Dark Ages to exaggerations of the Inquisition's cruelty. His challenge to these and other misconceptions has rightly earned praise from the Catholic press for its "honest recognition" of historical facts. Like many others, he classifies anti-Catholicism as one of several examples of irrational religious intolerance, like anti-Semitism.[6] Over the last two decades it has become common to link anti-Catholicism to anti-Islamism, seeing in the Catholic experience a precedent for the victimization of other religious minorities.[7]

The habit of describing anti-Catholicism as "paranoid," "virulent," "bigoted," and "unhinged," reinforces the impression that it is more a problem to be overcome than a phenomenon to be analyzed. It also suggests the degree to which many of us still rely on the framework of "the paranoid style" developed by Richard Hofstadter and David Brion Davis in the 1960s. They grouped nineteenth-century

American anti-Catholic, anti-Masonic, and anti-Mormon sentiment together as examples of the countersubversion deployed by conservative Anglo-Americans to oppose perceived threats to the dominant Protestant social and political order.[8] Anti-Catholicism was thus not really about Catholics per se so much as conservative Protestant fears. They felt their hegemony threatened by non-Protestant immigrants, secret societies, and religions.

Influential as the paranoid style framework has been, a growing number of scholars are finding it inadequate. On the one hand some, like Kyle Haden, want to overcome anti-Catholic bias by moving beyond descriptions of "the symptoms of anti-Catholic animus" to uncover "the underlying anthropological source of anti-Catholic hostility." Haden believes "human identity needs theory" can help us understand the deeper roots of conflict "beneath the surface of rationalizations and ideological justifications."[9] Steven Conn, on the other hand, wants to take its political dimensions seriously and to sideline the assumption that anti-Catholicism is primarily about "ethno-religious bigotry and economic anxiety." He claims the marginalization of religious history within the historical profession makes that difficult because it allows Catholics to police any history involving their ancestors. Their tendency to insist that "any criticism of Catholicism or the Church *ipso facto* amounts to anti-Catholic bigotry" has discouraged exploration of "the contours of anti-Catholic debate." The result is "a wall of separation between religious ideologies and the rest of our political discourse" that prevents us from accounting for resistance "to the Pope as a political leader." For that, Conn proposes the concept of "ideological anti-Catholicism."[10]

Conn's "ideological anti-Catholicism" sounds very similar to the concept of anti-popery. Anti-popery represents a mix of political and religious concerns that can be traced back to the earliest days of the Reformation. In 1549, Thomas Cranmer, the first Protestant archbishop of Canterbury, insisted that the pope's so-called "holy decrees" were mere inventions created "more than a thousand years after the faith of Christ was full, and perfect!" He and his fellow reformers believed they were liberating Europeans from the "bishop of Rome's ordinances and laws" which were "so wicked, so ungodly, so full of tyranny, and so partial, that since the beginning of the world were never devised or invented the like."[11]

Anti-popery and anti-Catholic religious prejudice overlapped in many ways, but anti-popery does a better job of suggesting the link between Protestantism and liberty that existed in the minds of many an anti-Catholic bigot. Cotton Mather traced the problem of popery, the antithesis of Protestant liberty, back to the fall of the Roman Empire when, surrounded by invading Germanic tribes, the once pure "Christian Church" fell into "Apostacy." Then, "a little Priest" managed "to establish himself with a mixt Religion among those Barbarous Nations, and then there appeared openly in the Temple of God that ANTICHRIST." Indeed, "whoever calls himself, or desires to be call'd by others, The UNIVERSAL BISHOP, is the FORE-RUNNER of ANTICHRIST." The "Satanical Spirit, working in the Bishop of Rome" allowed "a crafty Clergy" to unite "under one spiritual Monarch" and become "the Conquerors of the Pagans, from whome they had been conquered." The pope imposed "a Christianity disguised with Paganism, and a Doctrine of Daemons" that included "Miracles, and Austerities of forbidding to marry, and commanding to abstain from Meats to render the Cup of their Abomination the more inebriating." When the papacy dominated Christianity, "Idolatry, Persecution, and all mysterious Iniquity" were promoted in a worship full of "external Pomp, agreeable to carnal minds, meretricious Allurement, under the pretence of Decency, and all the Pagaentry of Ceremonies, Vestments, Gesturs, Musick, Painting," and rituals. The essence of popery lies in this association of false religion with political tyranny. Mather bitterly recalled the "Devilism" of the "vile Man sitting in his Pontifical Chair," who had "blasphemously usurped" his position and now "was with infinite Blasphemy adored as the Lord God."[12]

Britain's struggle with popery did not end with the abandonment of the Roman Catholic religion. The Reformation unleashed an apocalyptic radicalism that, already in the 1540s, was encouraging some English Protestants to denounce the "popery" of the Church of England.[13] Cotton Mather was part of this tradition. The main target of his anti-popish account was not the Church of Rome but the Church of England, which was threatening Protestant Dissenters. Mather reminded his readers that his puritan ancestors had fled "into a Wilderness" to escape "the Persecutions of Ceremony-Mongers, that ever were, and ever will be Enemies to all the true Interests of the Nation." Linking his religious and political critique to the language of liberty, he defended the Dissenters as not just pious individuals, but as "Freemen" of "the brave English Nation" whose watchwords were "LIBERTY and PROPERTY" as they resisted the efforts of an "illegal, despotick, and arbitrary Government" to forcibly impose "Rites" that violated "the scruples of their tender Conscience."[14]

Anti-popery thus did not just oppose a foreign, Catholic danger: it also confronted the potential popish danger from within. A few early American historians have begun to pick up on this subversive aspect of anti-popery and the ways it could divide Protestants against each other rather than unite them against a foreign Catholic threat.[15] This volume builds on such work and suggests the complexity of early American anti-popery by situating it within the broader context of early modern English, Scottish, and Irish history. The British-American world, for purposes of this book, is a shorthand meant to comprise Britain (England, Scotland, and Wales), Ireland, and the British colonies, including those that later made up the emergent United States. For a variety of professional and intellectual reasons these places are generally studied in isolation, but for the period covered by this volume such an approach makes little sense. Much more is gained by bringing them together. This volume's geographically broad and chronologically deep approach reveals strong continuities as well as important changes over time and space, showing how a shared culture of anti-popery could manifest rather differently depending on local context. Anti-popery adapted to a remarkable range of environments, from Scotland to South Carolina; political cultures, both monarchical and republican; and figured in a wide series of different situations, from sexuality and art to diplomacy. *Transnational* is a rather anachronistic term for this period, but our approach complements the current trend in studies of modern anti-Catholicism to emphasize international and transnational links.[16]

Juxtaposing studies of Britain, Ireland, and early America over three centuries also helps overcome the currently fragmented state of the scholarship, which primarily exists in isolated articles and essays. Even the few available books on the topic are restricted to a particular time, place, theme, or set of sources. To overcome this fragmentation, we have assembled a group of leading authorities and emerging scholars from both sides of the Atlantic working in several different disciplines to present the story of anti-popery and anti-Catholicism *before* massive immigration from Ireland and other Roman Catholic countries introduced sizable numbers of Catholics into the Protestant majority polities of Britain and the United States in the mid-nineteenth century. In this formative period of Anglo-American anti-Catholicism, anti-popery operated in a world where actual Roman Catholics were few, outside of Ireland of course.

Pulling together the disparate and widely scattered and interdisciplinary body of work on anti-popery and anti-Catholicism in the early modern history of America, Ireland, Britain, and its empire for the first time, this volume conveys the dynamic, yet paradoxical, role anti-Catholicism and anti-popery played in events and processes both large and small. To suggest something of how they evolved over these three centuries, the book is divided into three chronological sections. The first, "Foundations," focuses on the sixteenth- and seventeenth-century origins in Britain, Ireland, and America. Surveying the historiography of early modern England, Tim Harris probes the complex relationship between anti-popery and anti-Catholicism, arguing that the two closely related phenomena are distinct and that anti-popery was certainly an ideology, not just a religious prejudice. In a case study on the anti-popish origins of Virginia, the first permanent English colony in America, Cynthia Van Zandt firmly situates the emergence of Anglo-America within the broader struggle against popery at home and abroad, while Craig Gallagher does much the same with the rather different case of Scotland, where the Reformation had suppressed Roman Catholicism much more radically and effectively than in England. With Presbyterianism dominant, anti-popery figured more in struggles over the character of the established church than in struggles against Roman Catholics. The Catholic-majority kingdom of Ireland, on the other hand, was a recurring obsession of British-American anti-popery. Sitting at the heart of the British-American world, it figures at least briefly in most of this book's essays. Taking a long view, I show how the widespread fear of Irish Catholic barbarism and insurgency gave anti-popery a distinct inflection when it came to dealing with Ireland or the Irish. Since Ireland also contained the full diversity of anti-popish valences available in the British-American world, thanks to its potent mix of confrontations between not only the country's Protestant minority and its Catholic majority but also the various sectarian differences between Protestants, Ireland's anti-popery forged a special link between Britain and America up through the Revolution.

The second section, "Hegemony," examines some of the cultural facets of anti-popery in these years. Andrew R. Murphy, Gregory Smulewicz-Zucker, and Susan P. Liebell show how playing cards offered more than just bigoted fun. They also served as a source of popular political theorizing—playing with the cards produces a range of different narratives confirming various anti-popish conspiracy theories. Laura Stevens examines the British Protestant appropriation of the Virgin Mary. Traditionally an effective symbol for the messy bodies of women, her image was transformed by misogynistic Protestant desires into a clean and clear model of Protestant conduct and piety. Clare Haynes's review of Benjamin West's transatlantic career, in a field still dominated by Roman Catholic works, is a brilliant case study of anti-popery's ability to change and adapt in a world that was never entirely British or Protestant.

The third section, "Transformations," illustrates anti-popery's role in the dramatic political and religious changes on both sides of the Atlantic during the Age of Revolutions. Surveying anti-popery across the empire, but especially in British North America, I show how it connected colonists to the political culture of Britain notwithstanding their great distance from the metropole. In addition to uniting Britons against their French and Spanish Catholic rivals, the persistent question of how to include or exclude Roman Catholics within the empire repeatedly divided colonists as well as their fellows in England—up through and including the Declaration of Independence in 1776. Brendan McConville then shows how the unfolding course of the Revolution pushed anti-popery into the unusual role of actually ameliorating conditions for Roman Catholics once the Revolution's leaders realized they needed to ally with France, the once hated enemy. Here, the Revolution's leaders overcame the Francophobic anti-Catholic predispositions of their followers but could not supplant them. The American Revolution was a major turning point for British anti-popery as well. Isolated and without allies, the empire turned to its Catholic subjects for help, alienating a significant portion of the population who made their outrage felt in the notorious 1780 Gordon Riots in

London. As Peter Walker shows, the loyal performance of Roman Catholics in the Revolution contrasted sharply with the disloyalty of both American Protestants and the rioters, and facilitated the gradual move toward tolerating Catholics. Even as the rhetoric of anti-popery remained the same, this very different context allowed it to contribute to religious liberty for both Roman Catholics and Protestant Dissenters—without requiring a deeper change of mindset. Consequently, although religious liberty came to prevail in both the United States and Britain in the nineteenth century, anti-popery and anti-Catholicism remained very much a part of both societies.

The final two chapters address the persistence of anti-Catholicism and anti-popery into the modern era. The brief conclusion emphasizes some of the key points raised by this volume and sketches out their connection to the better-known anti-Catholicism of the nineteenth century. It also highlights a few additional interpretive challenges—not least of which is the persistence of the polemical priorities from the early modern period in how we continue to study this phenomenon. How far can we extricate ourselves from the dilemmas and struggles of the past? Finally, Anthony Milton offers an epilogue that wisely reminds us of how complex and varied anti-Catholicism is and has been. He ends by cautioning against using anti-Catholicism as an easy way to interpret complex events that were never exclusively or even primarily about Roman Catholicism. Finding anti-Catholicism should, he insists, be the beginning of our analysis, not its culmination.

The early modern period is emphasized here not just because it was foundational, but also because it is the period where the best scholarship on anti-popery has been developing. Until the mid-1970s, British historians treated anti-Catholicism largely as an irrational religious bigotry. In 1971, Carol Weiner described anti-Catholicism in the Elizabethan and early Jacobean periods as a combination of "wishful thinking" and "mistaken judgment." The British blamed Jesuits and the papacy for all sorts of problems and produced a "distorted perceptions of events" that filled people with "an almost insuperable anxiety."[17] Subsequent studies examined anti-Catholicism's role in fueling hostility to Spain (often through the "Black Legend" of Spanish cruelty in America)[18] and France.[19] Thanks to the Stuart Pretender's religion, allies, and residence abroad, the Jacobite threat after 1688 was easily linked to this foreign Catholic threat.[20] Linda Colley capitalized on this trend in her influential 1992 book on British nationalism, which argued that roiling anti-Catholicism played a crucial role in uniting Britain's ethnically diverse people into a new nation between the Union of Scotland and England in 1707 and the Reform Acts of the 1830s.[21] The development of more personal contacts with foreign Roman Catholic people, places, and cultural artifacts did little to diminish these prejudices. As the British began to travel around Europe as tourists, art collectors, and scholars in the eighteenth century, they largely confirmed the anti-Catholic observations of their ancestors. Clare Haynes's essay on Protestant artists like Benjamin West studying while resisting Italian Catholic high art is a brilliant illustration of how British-American culture could absorb Catholic influence without giving up on its anti-Catholic prejudices.[22]

However, there is much that anti-Catholicism alone cannot account for and, as Tim Harris shows, in the mid-1970s scholars began to wonder why it could pit English Protestants of different religious inclinations against one other. They realized anti-popery had intellectual coherence—indeed, as Peter Lake argued, it "provided the central organizing principle for a whole view of the world." That worldview also meant it did not always operate in a strictly nationalist or simply anti-Catholic fashion. Lake noticed that the "supposedly nationalist nature of English anti-popery" was "conspicuous by its absence" in his 1980 study of William Whitaker, a Cambridge professor who educated many leading puritans. Stressing the importance of theology (particularly the identification of the pope with Antichrist), Lake found that Whitaker instead prioritized pure doctrine over the specific canons of the Church of England, taking an international Protestant position that favored a pro-Protestant, anti-Catholic foreign policy regardless of immediate national interests. Alternating in his writings "between fear of the strength and power of" Antichrist "and an almost overweening confidence in the certainty of eventual victory," Whitaker created a "dialectical relationship between anxiety and assurance" that had "a remarkable structural similarity to the basic mechanism or dynamic of the puritan view of election." Rather than the "self-satisfied complacency" of assurance about one's salvation, it instead fostered an anxious, "frenetic activity" that encouraged Whitaker to assimilate the positions of his opponents within the Church of England with those of "the papists and when challenged to justify the severity of his response he invoked the threat of popery." Here we see the religious roots of the more radical form of anti-popery and its ambivalent relationship to fellow Protestant countrymen and national institutions like the established church.[23]

Early modern English historians are acutely aware that anti-Catholicism did not knit the British together quite as easily as Colley and others have claimed, for they need to explain how a sentiment that should have united Protestants against Catholics instead divided them to catastrophic effect in the English Civil Wars of the 1640s and then again during the Glorious Revolution of 1688–89. In these and other cases, anti-popery varied depending on an individual's particular religious commitments. Puritans, as Lake suggests, can be identified by their "attitude to the Church of Rome, with its concomitant commitment to a vision of a godly community and commonwealth, freed from the taint of popery." More moderate members of the Church of England, who defended the role of bishops or certain ceremonies, preferred more nuanced images of Roman Catholicism. It was wrong but not completely steeped in error. Archbishop William Laud, the great foe of puritans, deliberately avoided accusing the pope of being Antichrist or condemning his religion as utterly false.[24]

Probably the most influential essay for studies of anti-popery has been Peter Lake's 1989 "Anti-Popery: The Structure of a Prejudice." Working from the puritan tradition of anti-popery, he first defines popery as "an anti-religion, a perfectly symmetrical negative image of true Christianity." The pope, as Antichrist, "was an agent of Satan, sent in to the Church to corrupt and take it over from within." Unlike "an overt enemy like the Turk," the pope had risen to power "by stealth and deception, pretending piety and reverence while in fact inverting and perverting the values of true religion." At the same time, since every negative value assigned to Roman Catholics implied its positive corollary among Protestants, "the Protestant negative image of popery can tell us a great deal about their positive image of themselves." Anti-popery drew on the general early modern "process of binary opposition, inversion or the argument from contraries" that was common "in both the learned and popular culture of early modern Europe." The world was divided up into positive and negative "characteristics" that provided "a symbolic means of labeling and expelling" threatening "trends and tendencies," many of which came from within the Protestant community. In "situations in which values central to" Protestants' "self image came under threat," anti-popery could thus serve as a "'rational response.'" Often, the hostility to Roman Catholics was less about sheer hatred than a way "to play down the significance of the internal divisions among English Protestants," who disagreed both on what constituted popery and when and how to deploy it. Presbyterians, who "saw the rule of one minister over another as a direct emanation of the pope's tyrannical rule over the Church," used anti-popery "to emphasize the need to extend the process of reformation from the sphere of doctrine to that of discipline." Episcopal conformists invoked it "to underwrite the essential soundness of the régime which had stood so long in the breach against Rome." As Craig Gallagher shows in his chapter, this divide is key to understanding anti-popery in early modern Scotland.[25]

Since the struggle against popery was so central to the puritan cause, from Presbyterian Scotland to Congregational New England reformed Protestants tended to produce more, and more thorough, works of anti-popery, giving them a broad, lasting influence over the idea of popery even among those who were not as committed to the reformed cause. For example, Andrew Willet, who taught at Cambridge before becoming a clergyman, published a synthesis of anti-papal thought, *Synopsis Papismi,* in 1592 that served as a standard reference guide for all sorts of Protestants engaging in religious controversies with Roman Catholics for the next two centuries. In this vein, the connections between English and American anti-popery also could be surprisingly direct and personal. Willet's son Thomas is likely to have carried his ideas, if not his book, to America where he became first a Plymouth colonist and then New York's first mayor. William Whitaker taught a number of important emigrants to New England and had a son who served as a minister in Virginia. Cynthia Van Zandt's essay shows just how personal the connection between English and colonial anti-popery could be.[26]

Texts, both new and recycled, were crucial to spreading anti-popery around the British-American world and studies of print culture remain crucial to scholarship on anti-popery. Few were more important than John Foxe's *Book of Martyrs*, republished in New York in 1794 in an edition that had been "revised and corrected, with additions and great improvements" including "elegant copper plate engravings."[27] In this volume, Murphy, Smulewicz-Zucker, and Liebell treat anti-popish playing cards as texts meant to instructing illiterate masses about popish threats through play. Other studies also have documented how elite anti-popish arguments could penetrate into the less literate masses, for example in the case of the "Spanish Match" of the early 1620s. However, controlling the message has always been a challenge. A recent study of early Tudor anti-Catholicism argues that the print revolution actually permitted anti-Catholic pamphlets to move quickly beyond the official message as they became cheaper and more widespread, presenting "many paradoxes and contradictions" to those who sought to establish an official anti-Catholic message. In a particularly well documented case from the reign of King James I, when the overcrowded chapel of the French ambassador suddenly collapsed during a sermon by a visiting Jesuit, leaving dozens dead and injured, we can see writers leaping to the presses to ensure their audience interpreted the incident properly: as a judgment of divine providence against Roman Catholicism and not just a tragic accident. People were not always so easily manipulated, however. Efforts to present the Thirty Years' War as an international Catholic campaign against Protestantism did not completely succeed. Archbishop of Canterbury George Abbot tried to discourage King James I from negotiating with Catholic powers by discrediting their religion through the publication of tell-all books by Catholic converts, but failed. On the other hand, Oliver Cromwell's Western Design against Spanish America was in no small part inspired by the work of the Catholic apostate Thomas Gage, who claimed the Spanish represented "Jesuiticall policy meeting with Antichrists policy and Ambition" to fill "the Infantile Church or Asia and America with troopes of" missionaries who, "under pretence of salvation," were actually bringing "damnation and misery to their poor and wretched souls."[28]

Given the importance of texts to Anglo-American anti-Catholicism, it is no surprise that scholars of literature have been prominent in stressing its cultural importance. They have been particularly important in drawing attention to issues of gender and sexuality.[29] Laura Stevens's essay shows how gender helped mark the difference between Protestant and Catholic attitudes towards the Virgin Mary. Regarding Mary Queen of Scots, Ann McLaren has argued that an "antipathy to

THE VERY

Beggars PETITION

Againſt POPERY:

Wherein they lamentably complain to King *Henry* the VIII. of the CLERGY;

1. Of their abominable Covetouſneſs and Oppreſſion, in ſeveral Particulars, from §3. to §13. 2. Of their Inſatiable Letchery, *being Devils at women:* and how they apply themſelves by all Slights they may, to have to do with every Mans wife, Daughter, and Maid, (*as well Ladies as meaner Perſons, when they come in their way*) from §13 to 17. 3. They brought in Theft with them, and nouriſhed it under them; §17. 4. That they baffled all Laws, that none could take hold of them, tho they raviſhed men's Wives and Daughters, (*which that curſt Crew would be at again, tho not in that ſeeming holy Method, but now in an open, odious debauched Way, like infernal Incubuſſes, who now have naturalized Succubus's for their turn,* &c.) For the Law was too weak to hold them; they making ſuch as begin with them quickly to ceaſe proſecuting them, §18. 5. An Example hereof, ſee in the Bp. of *London.* §19. 6. Tho the Statute of *Mortmain* was made to prevent giving them any more, yet ſtill they got more than any Duke, §20, & 21. 7. Their yearly Exactions came by curſed pretenſions of praying peoples Souls out of Purgatory, *&c.* §22. 8. This Doctrine of Purgatory was alwaies oppoſed by godly learned men, §23, & 24. 9 Their Helliſh Policy in not ſuffering the New Teſtament to be tranſlated in the Mother-tongue, leſt their Hypocriſy and Cheating ſhould be diſcovered §25, 26. 10. The Impudence of Dr. *Allen* and Dr. *Horſey*, fined to the King, but afterwards therefore amply rewarded by the Clergy, §27. 11. The Reaſon of this was becauſe the Chancellor was one of them, *viz.* a Clergy man, §28. 12. The Cheat of giving Lands or Money to the Church for the Poor or Maſſes, §30. 13. They Petition to turn theſe Blood-ſuppers out to labor, and get them wives of their own, §31. 14. The Benefits and Advantages of ſo doing, *&c.* §31, 32. *Theſe Arguments and the like, prevailed with this King to caſt off the Popes Authority, and why any ſhould be ſo fooliſhly wicked, as to think to return us to it, I know not, moſt certainly they will find themſelves deceived with a vengeance, &c.*

Preſented to King *Henry* VIII. in the 29 Year of his Reign, *An.Dom.* 1538. 8 years before his Death: And Now Printed *verbatim* from a very old Copy, only mending the Authograpy, for the eaſe of the Reader, making the ſeveral Sections, and Collecting the foregoing Contents. *Worth peruſing by both Papiſt and Proteſtant, for the one to ſee how his Forefathers and he have been and are gull'd; and the other to ſee how he is like to be eternally abuſed, if he either through Fear of Death, or otherways embrace Popery,* 1680.

Simon Fish, *The Very Beggars Petition against Popery: wherein they lamentably complain to King Henry the VIII. of the Clergy,* 1680. (Courtesy of the Folger Shakespeare Library)

First published in Antwerp in 1529 by the humanist Simon Fish, this faux petition complained the clergy took alms away from the genuinely needy, among other misdeeds. This edition added the picture of Henry VIII and wondered "why any should be so foolishly wicked, as to think to return us to" the Roman Church he abolished.

female rule" was "central to the orchestrated anti-Catholic campaign" Protestant propagandists launched to delegitimize her claim to the English throne in the years 1568–72. Linking her Catholicism to her allegedly sexually promiscuous and tyrannical behavior, these men suggested her rule would lead to immorality and disorder. In its place, they imagined a "xenophobic, misogynist" and "virulently anti-Catholic" nation, a constitutional state "in which ideological conviction, in the last resort, counted for more than blood claims to political authority."[30]

Anti-popery involved action as well as theory, and here its capacity to divide Anglo-American Protestants is clearest. In his examination of "practical antipapistry," Michael Questier found zealous magistrates of not particularly elite background gaining the courage to challenge their social superiors in a struggle against not just Roman Catholicism but also a "more general corruption and slackness in the provinces." His 1997 case study of Elizabethan priest hunters in the North of England rejects Catholic martyrologists' portrayal of them as "essentially irrational" persecutors of pious individuals. Instead, they had "a political ideology that extended beyond the bounds of simply hating the Roman Catholic Church." Some priest hunters sought to suppress corruptions beyond Roman Catholic religious practice, such as customs fraud and government venality, bringing them into conflict with local elites. Their anti-popery certainly reinforced their commitment to suppressing Roman Catholicism in England, but from the state's perspective anti-popery was an unreliable ally, offering "by turns sometimes a legitimation of the regime and, at other times, a bitter criticism of it." Since the anti-popish magistrates identified their opponents as papists regardless of their actual religious affiliation, anti-popery clearly could justify aggression against local elites in the name of the interest of the state and its church. This quality made it "potentially a disruptive and even oppositional set of ideas."[31]

Anti-popery's interest in conspiracy had the virtue of being able to explain political conflicts that were not supposed to happen, such as those between loyal Protestant subjects and the agents of their monarch or even the monarchy itself. Brendan McConville's essay addresses this problem for the American Revolution. For the English Civil War, Peter Lake found that as relations between the early Stuarts and their Parliaments broke down anti-popery provided "an unimpeachably 'other,' foreign and corrupt origin and explanation for conflict" in a political system "still predicated on the need for agreement and the existence of ideological consensus." Combining "a number of disparate phenomena" into "a unitary thing or force" associated with the Antichrist, it made all those "not directly implicated in the problem (popery)" implicitly "part of the solution (non-popery)." At the popular level, anti-popery "was crisis-related." Crises gave "the most committed Protestants" a chance "to lead bodies of opinion far broader than those normally deemed Puritan," including anti-popish rioters whose violence was directed at "ritually impure or threatening objects." At the elite level, puritans could acquire power and influence by uniting "evangelical Calvinist thought . . . with native traditions of representative government, centered on Parliament, and concepts of active citizenship based on essentially classical models which members of the ruling class had encountered during their years at university." Their views "of the effects of popery on the Church" thus acquired a "basic structural similarity" to political thinkers' views "of the effects of corruption on the commonwealth."[32]

Anti-popery could make sense of otherwise perplexing political processes and social changes because it had a sociocultural theory about how the progression from corruption to tyranny happened. The culprit was mankind's sinful and sensual nature. Human failings could explain everything from the apostasy of the Church of England to the fragile quality of liberty in the British-American world. Unfortunately, this theory left people with an acute awareness that they were constantly in danger of being corrupted. And once they became corrupt, the fall into popish despotism was inevitable. One had to be constantly vigilant, and that vigilance inspired a variety of subversive and even revolutionary actions designed to stop the apparent progress of popery before it was too late. The revolutionary propaganda of the Civil War of the 1640s, the Glorious Revolution of 1688, and even America's Declaration of Independence all reflect this theory. When the Declaration denounced the "repeated injuries and usurpations" committed by King George III and claimed that his "long train of abuses and usurpations, [were] pursuing invariably the same Object," namely to "reduce" the colonists "under absolute Despotism" and establish "an absolute Tyranny over these States," it was not saying something new but rather applying the centuries'-old logic of anti-popery.[33]

Still, as even Lake admits, the anti-popish conspiracy theory of corruption within the church and state is not enough to explain the outbreak of open conflict on its own. In the case of the English Civil War, conflict erupted only after it was mirrored by an anti-puritan conspiracy theory. This theory held that puritans resented monarchy and refused to be properly governed by it. For those at the beleaguered center of British politics and church government, like King Charles and Archbishop Laud, puritanism explained the baffling popular resistance to their policies. In 2006, Lake described anti-puritanism as, like much of anti-popery, not always a "coherent ideological" position, but rather a group "of ideas, attributes, and narratives" that could be arranged, synthesized, and articulated in the service of a range of political objectives. In this case it buttressed elitist, antidemocratic tendencies. In a world divided into these "two parallel but mutually exclusive conspiracy theories," contemporaries were confronted, not with "an irrational panic or knee-jerk response to a non-existent popish threat," but rather "with a choice between two competing sets of social and political, as well as religious, priorities and values." That is when the fighting began.[34]

Like anti-popery, anti-puritanism reflected the religious commitments of those espousing it. It can be traced back to the sixteenth-century Roman Catholic polemicists who first coined the term "puritans." To discredit the character and loyalty of the hotter sort of Protestants, these Catholics emphasized how puritans' emphasis on scripture and disregard for established authorities led them to disorder and disobedience. Conservative conformists then picked up on these ideas to defend the established church against puritan criticisms. By the second half of the seventeenth century, anti-puritanism was being directed at Dissenters, but most especially to Presbyterians, whose association with feisty Scots, the regicide, and Cromwellian revolution, together with their comparative strength in numbers "attracted far more vitriolic reactions than all other Dissenting denominations put together." Where reformed Protestant commitments were strong, as in Scotland or America, anti-puritanism had little purchase. However, one can find it even there, whether in Scottish Episcopalian complaints about their Presbyterian countrymen or Catholic Marylanders' denunciations of their Protestant critics. In Ireland, as Evan Haefeli's essay suggests, one can see anti-Presbyterianism gaining ground as attitudes toward Catholics ameliorated. These ideas and attitudes were relational and are best considered in a broader context rather than isolation.[35]

Recognizing the diversity of anti-Catholic views, in 1999 Anthony Milton urged a mitigation of the idea that "papophobia" was rampant. In an essay on the "Limits and Ambiguities of Early Stuart Anti-Catholicism," Milton pointed out that not all anti-Catholic writers relied "on the simple representation of popery as a satanic inversion of normative Protestant values." Indeed, few of even the most violently anti-Catholic writers lived a relentlessly anti-Catholic existence. From the international stage to the immediate family, cross-confessional cooperation and interaction was often the norm. Diplomacy required respect for the leading kingdoms of France and Spain. Sometimes foreign policy interests limited the enforcement of anti-Catholic legislation within Britain. Protestants read and engaged with a wide variety of Catholic works on everything from intellectual culture to devotional literature, biblical commentary, and of course the arts. Rare was the puritan library with no Catholic books, or the puritan family without some Catholic relations. At the local level, the "practical compromises and adaptations" evident in "anti-Catholic discourse, intellectual scholarship, and politics," extended to the treatment of Catholic individuals. Social codes of respect, honor, and neighborliness often trumped confessional concerns in personal interactions, including the enforcement of the penal laws. Then, of course, there were the ancestors, all of them Catholic. In Britain and Ireland there were also many physical remains of Catholic material culture, including the churches where anti-Catholic sermons were preached. In truth, "early modern English men and women were used to disregarding confessional divisions on a fairly systematic basis." In fact, at the local level, the tendency to portray Catholics as an alien, foreign, and demonic force actually made the suspension of anti-popery easier. Recusants one knew and recognized did not cause much concern. Instead, "popular opprobrium" tended to be directed at distant, unknown foreigners. It was "strangers," whether out-of-town visitors or Irish soldiers, "who most often generated the local 'popish scares'" in times of crisis. Milton expands on these important cautions and qualifications in his epilogue to this volume, urging us not to see anti-popery as an easy explanation for all sorts of complex conflicts.[36]

Clearly, not all anti-popery is the same. Lake insists the ideology he identified was relevant only for the early Stuart period. While it still resonated in later periods, especially among reformed Protestants, it changed and adapted to the new circumstances brought on by civil war and revolution. During the English revolution, Anglican royalists used it to attack puritan revolutionaries. Thereafter, they deployed it against the expanding challenge from other Dissenters, like Quakers, who had not existed before. Puritan revolutionaries and Anglicans, meanwhile, both accused England's major colonial and commercial rival, the Protestant Dutch Republic, of seeking a popish "universal monarchy" through their monopoly on international trade.[37]

During the Restoration period (1660–88), a "Protestant opposition to anti-popery," developed, becoming strongest after the Roman Catholic James II became king. Scott Sowerby boils this "anti-anti-popery" down to "two main types." One "was articulated by Anglican Tories who supported the king's policies because they believed it was their duty to do so." The other "was articulated by dissenters and Whigs who supported those policies because they believed it was in their interest to do so." The second form was newer than the first. It represented the views of people from the radical anti-popish tradition for whom the Church of England's repression of Protestant Dissent was now the greater threat. Again, the quality of their anti-popery derived from their religious commitments. Both portrayed anti-popery as mere "fears and jealousies" but they addressed this problem in different ways. Tories sought to redirect the old fears away from Catholics and toward the new conservative fear: antimonarchical revolution. For the formerly anti-popish Whigs, the primary enemy was persecution. Roman Catholics, now a harmless minority in the country, were no longer the persecutors. The real threat came from those who opposed James II's agenda for religious tolerance.[38]

The Glorious Revolution of 1688 eased these bewildering contortions by straightening out the crossed circuitry between domestic and foreign popery. Roman Catholics were definitively excluded from the throne—to the hearty delight of most colonists, for who anti-popery became a cornerstone of their loyalty to the empire, as my essay on British America shows. Within Britain, however, anti-popery continued to fracture. In a society that still considered party politics illegitimate, its conspiratorial discourse saturated the language of party politics during the unseemly competition for power between Tories and Whigs. While it "certainly overlapped with the oppositional, republican, or civic humanist critique," Mark Knights points out the "fear of corruption went much wider." The once vehemently anti-popish Whigs now advocated "an ideal of a politer, more rational, though inherently less inclusive form of politics."[39] Colin Haydon, in a series of studies of mid-eighteenth-century anti-popery, has shown how the British consensus on anti-popery withered. Although a significant number of Protestants retained the older anti-popish attitudes that remained current in the colonies, metropolitan elites began to look more favorably upon Roman Catholics and their religion. The greater threat to the eighteenth-century empire, as with the mid-seventeenth-century monarchy, seemed to come from the radical anti-papists. This discrepancy had fatal consequences for the British Empire, and ultimately eroded the official anti-Catholic apparatus on both sides of the Atlantic. Peter Walker's essay shows how the rise in anti-puritan sentiment ironically collaborated with anti-popish priorities to end the penal regime against Catholics and Dissenters that had been created in seventeenth-century England.[40]

By combining new approaches along with overviews of current scholarship, we hope this volume will serve as a common reference point for future work within and between the usually separate fields of early modern British, Irish, and American studies. One point emerges clearly from this joint effort. The principles, prejudices, and language of anti-popery and anti-Catholicism have no intrinsic loyalty to any particular nation or sociopolitical order. Through kingdoms, empires, and republics, they helped knit the Protestant British-American world together—and tear it apart.

Notes

1. Samuel Johnson, *Taxation no Tyranny* (London, 1775), 79, 89; *George Washington: A Collection*, ed. W. B. Allen (Indianapolis: Liberty Fund, 1988), 31, 39; *The True Sentiments of America* (London, 1768), 114, 115, 117, 118; T. H. Breen, "Ideology and Nationalism on the Eve of the American Revolution: Revisions Once More in Need of Revising," *Journal of American History* 84, no. 1 (June 1997): 13–39, esp. 29–38, which includes the Adams quote. Breen's discussion of the revolutionaries' fears of slavery ignores anti-popery.
2. *A Companion to the American Revolution*, ed. Jack P. Greene and J. R. Pole (Oxford: Blackwell, 2004), has a whole section discussing fourteen key concepts, including liberty, republicanism, virtue, and interests, but no entry for anti-popery or anti-Catholicism. Michael Guasco, *Slaves and Englishmen: Human Bondage in the Early Modern Atlantic World* (Philadelphia: University of Pennsylvania Press, 2014), likewise ignores the discourse of popery. The essays in Jack P. Greene, ed., *Exclusionary Empire: English Liberty Overseas, 1600–1900* (Cambridge: Cambridge University Press, 2010), treat liberty as essentially a secular abstraction, albeit one that—especially in Ireland—happens to favor Anglo-Protestants. For a similar criticism,

see Carla Gardina Pestana, "Protestantism as Ideology in the British Atlantic World," in *The World of Colonial America: An Atlantic Handbook*, ed. Ignacio Gallup-Diaz (New York: Routledge, 2017), 263–79.

3. Elizabeth Fenton, *Religious Liberties: Anti-Catholicism and Liberal Democracy in Nineteenth-Century U.S. Literature and Culture* (New York: Oxford University Press, 2011), 4.
4. Maura Jane Farrelly, *Anti-Catholicism in America, 1620–1860* (Cambridge: Cambridge University Press, 2018). Concentrating mostly on Maryland and New England, she keeps the story closely tied to the history of actual Roman Catholics in America.
5. Stephen Kenny, "A Prejudice That Rarely Utters Its Name: Historiographical and Historical Reflections upon North American Anti-Catholicism," *American Review of Canadian Studies* 32, no. 4 (December 2002): 639–72; Andrew M. Greeley, *An Ugly Little Secret: Anti-Catholicism in North America* (Kansas City: Sheed Andrews and McMeel, 1977); Michael Schwartz, *The Persistent Prejudice: Anti-Catholicism in America* (Huntington, IN: Our Sunday Visitor, 1984); Mark S. Massa, S.J., *Anti-Catholicism in America: The Last Acceptable Prejudice* (New York: Crossroad Publishing Company, 2003); Philip Jenkins, *The New Anti-Catholicism: The Last Acceptable Prejudice* (New York: Oxford University Press, 2003). For Canada, see J. R. Miller, "Bigotry in the North Atlantic Triangle: Irish, British, and American influences on Canadian anti-Catholicism," *Studies in Religion/Sciences Religieuses* 16, no. 3 (Summer 1987): 289–301.
6. Rodney Stark, *Bearing False Witness: Debunking Centuries of Anti-Catholic History* (West Conshohocken, PA: Templeton Press, 2016); Carl E. Olson, "The Protestant Debunking of Anti-Catholic History," *Catholic Answer* 30, no. 4 (2016): 35. Anti-Catholicism is also included in John Corrigan and Lynn S. Neal, eds., *Religious Intolerance in America: A Documentary History* (Chapel Hill: University of North Carolina Press, 2010).
7. For example, Andrew Hamilton, "Anti-Islam is the New Anti-Catholicism," *Eureka Street* 24, no. 18 (September 2014): 5–6. Yvonne Maria Werner notes parallels between controversies over "women's issues" among Catholics and Muslims in "'The Catholic Danger': Anti-Catholicism and Swedish National Identity in a Nordic Perspective," *Scandia* 81, no. 1 (January 2015): 1–13, quote on 11. Scott C. Alexander connects nineteenth-century anti-Catholicism with current Islamophobia and debates about white privilege and nationalism in "Seasons of Our Discontent: Anti-Catholicism, Islamophobia, and Systematic Racism in the United States," *Religion and Culture Forum*, April 14, 2017, http://voices.uchicago.edu/religionculture/2017/04/14/summers-of-discontent-title/. Christopher C. Lund, "The New Victims of the Old Anti-Catholicism," *Connecticut Law Review* 44, no. 3 (2012): 1001–20, looks at cases involving Muslims, atheists, evangelical Protestants, and Wiccans, to argue that these religious minorities are suffering from the same discriminations nineteenth-century Catholics had endured.
8. David Brion Davis, ed., *The Fear of Conspiracy: Images of Un-American Subversion from the Revolution to the Present* (Ithaca, NY: Cornell University Press, 1971); Richard O. Curry and Thomas M. Brown, eds., *Conspiracy: Fear of Subversion in American History* (New York: Holt, Rinehart, and Winston, 1972).
9. Kyle E. Haden, OFM, "Anti-Catholicism in U.S. History: A Proposal for a New Methodology," *American Catholic Studies* 124, no. 4 (Winter 2013): 27–45, quotes on 28, 30.
10. Steven Conn, "'Political Romanism': Re-evaluating American Anti-Catholicism in the Age of Italian Revolution," *Journal of the Early Republic* 36, no. 3 (Fall 2016): 521–48, quotes on 523, 533, 542, 545–48. Timothy Verhoeven's recent call for a transnational approach to American anti-Catholicism also finds the "insularity" of the field "both frustrating and puzzling," "Transatlantic Connections: American Anti-Catholicism and the First Vatican

Council (1869–70)," *Catholic Historical Review* 100, no. 4 (Autumn 2014): 695–720, quote on 698.

11. Newton Key and Robert Bucholz, eds., *Sources and Debates in English History, 1485–1714* (Oxford: Blackwell, 2004), 64–65; Richard Bauckham, *Tudor Apocalypse: Sixteenth-Century Apocalypticism, Millenarianism, and the English Reformation, from John Bale to John Foxe and Thomas Brightman* (Abingdon, Oxon.: Sutton Courtenay Press, 1975).
12. Cotton Mather, *Eleutheria: or, An Idea of the Reformation in England* . . . (London, 1698), 4–6, 11, 20–21.
13. Karl Gunther, *Reformation Unbound: Protestant Visions of Reform in England, 1525–1590* (Cambridge: Cambridge University Press, 2014).
14. Mather, *Eleutheria*, 59–60, 76.
15. For example, Owen Stanwood, "The Protestant Moment: Antipopery, the Revolution of 1688–89, and the Making of an Anglo-American Empire," *Journal of British Studies* 46 no. 3 (July 2007): 481–508.
16. Timothy Verhoeven's "Introduction" to the special issue "Transnational Approaches to the History of Anti-Catholicism in the Modern Era," *Journal of Religious History* 39, no. 2 (June 2015): 175–81; Marjule Anne Drury, "Anti-Catholicism in Germany, Britain, and the United States: A Review and Critique of Recent Scholarship," *Church History* 70, no. 1 (March 2001): 98–131; Yvonne Maria Werner and Jonas Harvard, eds., *European Anti-Catholicism in a Comparative and Transnational Perspective* (Amsterdam: Rodopoi, 2013).
17. Carol Z. Wiener, "The Beleagured Isle: A Study of Elizabethan and Early Jacobean Anti-Catholicism," *Past & Present* 51 (May 1971): 27–62, quotes on 29, 33, 36.
18. On the Black Legend, see Benjamin Keen, "The Black Legend Revisited: Assumptions and Realities," *Hispanic American Historical Review* 49, no. 4 (November 1969): 703–19; and William S. Maltby, *The Black Legend in England: The Development of Anti-Spanish Sentiment, 1558–1660* (Durham, NC: Duke University Press, 1971). On the politics of anti-Spanish sentiment, see Thomas Cogswell, *The Blessed Revolution: English Politics and the Coming of War, 1621–1624* (Cambridge: Cambridge University Press, 1989); and Nicole Greenspan, *Selling Cromwell's Wars: Media, Empire, and Godly Warfare, 1650–1658* (Abingdon, Oxon.: Pickering and Chatto, 2012). Julian Lock, "'How Many Tercios Has the Pope?' The Spanish War and the Sublimation of Elizabethan Anti-Popery," *History* 81, no. 262 (April 1996): 197–214, argues that the focus on the Spanish enemy in the 1590s overrode (for some) earlier ideas of an international Catholic conspiracy directed by the pope. Anthony Milton denies there is any evidence for this. On the contrary, "it merely reflected the capacity of a simply binary opposition to coexist with a more informed and discriminating perception of political divisions among Roman Catholic countries," "A Qualified Intolerance: The Limits and Ambiguities of Early Stuart Anti-Catholicism," in *Catholicism and Anti-Catholicism in Early Modern English Texts*, ed. Arthur F. Marotti (New York: St. Martin's Press, 1999), 96–97, 113n35.
19. Jeremy Black, "The Catholic Threat and the British Press in the 1720s and 1730s," *Journal of Religious History* 12 (December 1983): 364–81; J. F. Bosher, "The Franco-Catholic Danger, 1660–1715," *History* 79, no. 255 (February 1994): 5–30.
20. Susannah Abbott, "Clerical Responses to the Jacobite Rebellion in 1715," *Historical Research*, 76, no. 193 (August 2003): 332–46, demonstrates the importance of anti-popery to anti-Jacobitism. Raymond D. Tumbleson, *Catholicism in the English Protestant Imagination: Nationalism, Religion, and Literature, 1660–1745* (Cambridge: Cambridge University Press, 1998), argues that elites deliberately manipulated popular anti-Catholic and anti-Jacobite fears.
21. Linda Colley, *Britons: Forging the Nation, 1707–1837* (New Haven: Yale University Press, 1992). Similarly, Jonathan Scott links domestic and foreign anti-popish concerns in *England's*

Troubles: Seventeenth-Century English Political Instability in European Context (Cambridge: Cambridge University Press, 2000); while Michael M. Clarke, "Charlotte Brontë's *Villette,* Mid-Victorian Anti-Catholicism, and the Turn to Secularism," *English Literary History* 78, no. 4 (Winter 2011), 967–89, argues that Charlotte Brontë employed anti-Catholicism in the cause of religious reconciliation and modern secularism.

22. Morgan Strawn, "Pagans, Papists, and Joseph Addison's Use of Classical Quotations in the *Remarks on Several Parts of Italy,*" *Huntington Library Quarterly* 75, no. 4 (December 2012), 561–75; Clare Haynes, "'A Trial for the Patience of Reason'? Grand Tourists and Anti-Catholicism after 1745," *Journal for Eighteenth-Century Studies* 33, no. 2 (May 2010): 195–208; Clare Haynes, *Pictures and Popery: Art and Religion in England, 1660–1760* (Burlington, VT: Ashgate, 2006).
23. Peter Lake, "The Significance of the Elizabethan Identification of the Pope as Antichrist," *Journal of Ecclesiastical History* 31, no. 2 (April 1980): 161–78, quotes on 161, 162.
24. Lake, "Elizabethan Identification," 171, 178; Anthony Milton, *Catholic and Reformed: The Roman and Protestant Churches in English Protestant Thought, 1600–1640* (Cambridge: Cambridge University Press, 1995); and Timothy H. Wadkins, "The Percy-'Fisher' Controversies and the Ecclesiastical Politics of Jacobean Anti-Catholicism, 1622–1625," *Church History* 57, no. 2 (June 1988): 153–69.
25. Peter Lake, "Anti-Popery: The Structure of a Prejudice," in *Conflict in Early Stuart England: Studies in Religion and Politics 1603–1642,* ed. Richard Cust and Ann Hughes (New York: Longman, 1989), 72–106, quotes on 73, 74, 77, and 79.
26. Randall J. Pederson, "Andrew Willet and the *Synopsis Papismi,*" *Puritan Reformed Journal* 1 (January 2009): 118–39; Anthony Milton, "Willet, Andrew (1561/2–1621), Church of England Clergyman and Religious Controversialist," and Robert C. Ritchie, "Willet, Thomas (1610/1–1674), Mayor of New York City," in *Oxford Dictionary of National Biography,* online edition, consulted July 7, 2019 (henceforth *ODNB*). On Whitaker, see Francis J. Bremer, *Congregational Communion: Clerical Friendship in the Anglo-American Puritan Community, 1610–1692* (Boston: Northeastern University Press, 1994), chap. 1. For his son, see Harry Culverwell Porter, "Alexander Whitaker: Cambridge Apostle to Virginia," *William and Mary Quarterly* 3rd ser. 14, no. 3 (July 1957): 317–43.
27. Paul Wright, *The New and Complete Book of Martyrs . . . Being Foxe's Book of Martyrs* (New York, 1794). On the origins and significance of this crucial text, see Elizabeth Evenden and Thomas S. Freeman, *Religion and the Book in Early Modern England: The Making of Foxe's 'Book of Martyrs'* (Cambridge: Cambridge University Press, 2011).
28. Thomas Cogswell, "England and the Spanish Match," in *Conflict in Early Stuart England: Studies in Religion and Politics, 1603–1642,* ed. Richard Cust and Ann Hughes (New York: Longman, 1989), 107–33; Leticia Álvarez-Recio, *Fighting the Antichrist: A Cultural History of Anti-Catholicism in Tudor England,* trans. Bradley L. Drew (Brighton: Sussex Academic Press, 2011), 1, 2; Alexandra Walsham, "'The Fatall Vesper': Providentialism and Anti-Popery in Late Jacobean London," *Past & Present* 144 (August 1994): 36–87; Leticia Álvarez-Recio, "Anti-Catholicism, Civic Consciousness, and Parliamentarianism: Thomas Scott's *Vox Regis* (1624)," *International Journal of English Studies* 13, no. 1 (2013): 133–47; Robert von Frideburg, "The Continental Counter-Reformation and the Plausibility of the Popish Plot, 1638–1642," in *England's Wars of Religion, Revisited,* ed. Charles W. A. Prior and Glenn Burgess (Burlington, VT: Ashgate, 2011), 49–73; Michael C. Questier, "John Gee, Archbishop Abbot, and the Use of Converts from Rome in Jacobean Anti-Catholicism," *Recusant History* 21, no. 3 (May 1993): 347–60; Allen D. Boyer, "Gage, Thomas (1603?–1656)," *ODNB;* Thomas

Gage, *The English-American His Travail by Sea and Land; or, A New Survey of the West Indias* (London, 1648), 3.

29. Frances E. Dolan, *Whores of Babylon: Catholicism, Gender, and Seventeenth-Century Print Culture* (Notre Dame, IN: University of Notre Dame Press, 1999); Arthur F. Marotti, *Religious Ideology and Cultural Fantasy: Catholic and Anti-Catholic Discourses in Early Modern England* (Notre Dame, IN: University of Notre Dame Press, 2005); Bianca Brigitte Bonomi, "'How Might I See / The Thing, That Might not be, and yet was Donne?' (I.VI.39): Seeing, Believing, and Anti-Catholicism in Book One of Spenser's *Faerie Queene*," *Reformation and Renaissance Review* 7, nos. 2–3 (2005): 163–87; John McTague, "Anti-Catholicism, Incorrigibility, and Credulity in the Warming-Pan Scandal of 1688–9," *Journal for Eighteenth-Century Studies* 36, no. 3 (September 2013): 433–48; Gerhardt Schuette, "Edmund Spencer's Anti-Catholicism: Duessa's Part in It All," *Michigan Academician* 42 (September 2015): 108–18; Devori Kimbro, "'A cardinalles red-hat, and a kings golden crowne:' Pamphlet Anti-Catholicism and Fabricated Authority in Thomas Milles's *The Misterie of Iniquitie* (1611)," *Prose Studies* 37, no. 3 (2015): 181–99. Going against this trend, Philip Goldfarb, "The Devil, Not the Pope: Anti-Catholicism and Textual Difference in *Doctor Faustus*," *Renaissance Papers* 53 (2014): 47–58, argues that Christopher Marlowe's play was less anti-Catholic than has been thought, being instead an argument for religious unity.
30. Ann McLaren, "Gender, Religion, and Early Modern Nationalism: Elizabeth I, Mary Queen of Scots, and the Genesis of English Anti-Catholicism," *American Historical Review* 107, no. 3 (June 2002): 739–67, quotes on 743, 767. See also Kristen Post Walton, *Catholic Queen, Protestant Patriarchy: Mary, Queen of Scots, and the Politics of Gender and Religion* (New York: Macmillan, 2007).
31. Michael Questier, "Practical Antipapistry during the Reign of Elizabeth I," *Journal of British Studies* 36 (October 1997): 371–96, quotes on 371–73, 396.
32. Lake, "Anti-Popery," 82, 89.
33. "Declaration of Independence: A Transcription," https://www.archives.gov/founding-docs/declaration-transcript, consulted July 4, 2019. Michelle Orihel, "'All Those Truly Acquainted with the History of Those Times': John Adams and the Opposition Politics of Revolutionary England, ca. 1640–1641," *New England Quarterly* 86, no. 3 (September 2013): 433–66, demonstrates Adams's engagement with that earlier English history.
34. Lake, "Anti-Popery," 94, 97; Peter Lake, "Anti-Puritanism: The Structure of a Prejudice," in *Religious Politics in Post-Reformation England*, ed. Kenneth Fincham and Peter Lake (Woodbridge: Boydell, 2006), 80–97, quotes on 84, 96; Peter Lake, "Post-Reformation Politics, or on Not Looking for the Long-Term Causes of the English Civil War," in *The Oxford Handbook of the English Revolution*, ed. Michael J. Braddick (Oxford: Oxford University Press, 2015), 21–41. Laud seems to have been especially prone to conspiracy thinking. Jason Peacey says he had difficulty distinguishing between "personal opposition to him and opposition to the institution he headed," "The Paranoid Prelate: Archbishop Laud and the Puritan Plot," in *Conspiracies and Conspiracy Theory in Early Modern Europe: From the Waldensians to the French Revolution*, ed. Barry Coward and Julian Swann (Burlington, VT: Ashgate, 2004), 113–34, quote on 115. Anti-puritanism has not received anything like the level of attention devoted to anti-popery, but see Jennifer L. Andersen, "Anti-Puritanism, Anti-Popery, and Gallows Rhetoric in Thomas Nashe's *The Unfortunate Traveller*," *Sixteenth Century Journal* 35, no. 1 (Spring 2004): 43–63.
35. Patrick Collinson, "Antipuritanism," in *The Cambridge Companion to Puritanism*, ed. John Coffey and Paul C. H. Lim (Cambridge: Cambridge University Press, 2008), 19–33; Antoinette Sutto, *Loyal Protestants and Dangerous Papists: Maryland and the Politics of Religion in*

the English Atlantic, 1630–1690 (Charlottesville: University of Virginia Press, 2015), 17, 69, 75–76, 129; Jan Albers, "'Papist Traitors' and 'Presbyterian Rogues': Religious Identities in Eighteenth-Century Lancashire," in *The Church of England, c. 1689–c. 1833: From Toleration to Tractarianism*, ed. John Walsh, Colin Haydon, and Stephen Taylor (Cambridge: Cambridge University Press, 1993), 317–33, quote on 322.

36. Anthony Milton, "A Qualified Intolerance: The Limits and Ambiguities of Early Stuart Anti-Catholicism," in *Catholicism and Anti-Catholicism in Early Modern English Texts*, ed. Arthur F. Marotti (New York: St. Martin's Press, 1999), 85–115, quotes on 88, 99, 105; George Hilton Jones, "The Irish Fright of 1688: Real Violence and Imagined Massacre," *Historical Research* 55, no. 32 (November 1982): 148–53.
37. Steven Pincus, *Protestantism and Patriotism: Ideologies and the Making of English Foreign Policy, 1650–1668* (Cambridge: Cambridge University Press, 1996); Steven Pincus, "Popery, Trade, and Universal Monarchy: The Ideological Context of the Outbreak of the Second Anglo-Dutch War," *English Historical Review* 107, no. 422 (January 1992): 1–29. For earlier manifestations of anti-Catholicism and anti-Spanish sentiment in Anglo-Dutch relations see Kimberly J. Hackett, "The English Reception of Oldenbarnevelt's Fall," *Huntington Library Quarterly* 77, no. 2 (Summer 2014): 157–76.
38. Scott Sowerby, "Opposition to Anti-Popery in Restoration England," *Journal of British Studies*, 51, no. 1 (January 2012): 26–49, quotes on 34–35.
39. Mark Knights, "Faults on Both Sides: The Conspiracies of Party Politics under the Later Stuarts," in *Conspiracies and Conspiracy Theory in Early Modern Europe: From the Waldensians to the French Revolution*, ed. Barry Coward and Julian Swann (Aldershot-Burlington, VT: Ashgate, 2004), 153–72, quote on 168. See also Susannah Jane Abbott, "Anti-Catholicism and Anti-Popery: Religion and Language in English Politics, 1678–1720" (PhD diss., University of Reading, 2004).
40. Colin Haydon, *Anti-Catholicism in Eighteenth-Century England, c. 1714–80: A Political and Social Study* (Manchester: Manchester University Press, 1993); Colin Haydon, "'Popery at St. James's': The Conspiracy Theories of William Payne, Thomas Hollis, and Lord George Gordon," in *Conspiracies and Conspiracy Theory*, ed. Coward and Swann, 173–95; Colin Haydon, "Eighteenth-Century English Anti-Catholicism: Contexts, Continuity, and Diminution," in *Protestant-Catholic Conflict from the Reformation to the 21st Century: The Dynamics of Religious Difference*, ed. John Wolffe (New York Palgrave Macmillan, 2013), 46–70.

PART I

Foundations

Anti-Catholicism and Anti-Popery in Seventeenth-Century England

Tim Harris

ANTI-CATHOLICISM AND ANTI-POPERY WERE not the same thing. It is a point that should perhaps be unnecessary to make, given the extensive historiography that now exists on anti-Catholicism and the fear of popery in early modern England. Our current understanding is heavily indebted to two pioneering articles that appeared in *Past and Present* in 1971, one an investigation of Elizabethan and early Jacobean anti-Catholicism, the other an examination of the popular fear of Catholics during the English Revolution.[1] Several other important works appeared in the 1970s and early 1980s documenting the role that fear of popery or of a popish plot played in the origins of the English Civil War.[2] Restoration scholars were not far behind. In 1973 John Miller outlined the contours of the anti-Catholic tradition and showed how a hostility toward popery came to divide Protestants over the course of the seventeenth century, with rival Protestant factions accusing each other of being popishly affected or papists in masquerade.[3] Building on Miller's insights, in the mid-1980s I documented how the language of anti-popery could be used by Protestant nonconformists to condemn the reestablished Anglican Church, by Whigs to condemn Tory opponents of Exclusion, and by Tories and high church Anglicans to condemn Whigs and Dissenters.[4] Peter Lake's deservedly renowned article of 1989 on "Anti-Popery: The Structure of a Prejudice" was a relatively late intervention—and one with an ironic title, since it argued that anti-popery was less a prejudice or irrational passion than a species of ideology, a bearer of distinct and distinctive religio-political values and agendas, which had the potential to divide Protestants among themselves.[5] Since then, there has been much excellent work shedding further light on various aspects of anti-Catholicism and anti-popery in early modern England. Indeed, it is impossible to write about the political and religious upheavals of the seventeenth century without coming to terms with English people's fears of Catholicism and popery at this time.[6]

As a result, we have come to develop quite a sophisticated understanding of the complexities of anti-Catholicism and anti-popery as ideological constructs and societal prejudices in Stuart England. This very complexity, however, can prove confusing. It does not help that contemporaries themselves were sometimes confused. Popery could mean different things to different people, and what it meant was contested. There was a certain degree of terminological confusion, for although contemporaries recognized there was a distinction between a hatred of popery and a hatred of Catholics, they did not always use vocabulary that made that distinction clear. Sometimes contemporaries simply misunderstood each other, or chose to pretend they misunderstood each other. The purpose of this chapter, therefore, is to offer an overview of the phenomena of anti-Catholicism and anti-popery in seventeenth-century England (though with some glances back to the sixteenth), sketching out the basic contours of these overlapping but ultimately discrete ideologies/prejudices, with the aim of providing further clarification and addressing some remaining misconceptions. The rhetoric of anti-popery could be deployed by English Protestants to defend "true" religion in opposition to the Roman Catholic faith as well as the interests of the Protestant nation against perceived threats posed by supporters of the Church of Rome. It also emerged as a powerful oppositional ideology, used to criticize official policy in the English Church and state that was deemed (in various ways) to be popish. At the same time, it was embraced by those who sought to defend the established church and the crown from those very attacks (and was thus directed against Protestant critics who themselves were raising alarms about the threat of popery). A fear of popery could involve hostility to Roman Catholicism and to practicing Roman Catholics. Yet, it could also lead to concerns about the direction the Protestant Church was taking in England and about what fellow Protestants were up to. During the political and religious upheavals of the seventeenth century, the fear of popery divided the English as much as united them.

Let me start with anti-Catholicism. The concept itself is really a modern one. In the seventeenth century the English did on occasion use the term *Catholic* with reference to the Church of Rome. Yet for them, *catholic* still predominantly carried the meaning of universal, and thus some held that the Protestant Church in England was the true "catholic" church. English people were more likely to call adherents of the Roman Catholic faith "papists," and thus to talk of papistry and papistical when referring to the Roman Catholic religion, although they did also use the term *popery* to refer to the Roman Catholic faith, a terminological ambiguity that muddies the waters. In modern-day parlance, anti-Catholicism can mean either an antipathy toward the Roman Catholic religion or an antipathy toward those individuals who practice that religion. The former was undoubtedly widespread in early modern England. A hatred of the Roman Catholic faith, however, did not inevitably translate into a hatred of actual Roman Catholics.

Anti-Catholicism was both a religious and a political ideology. Protestants condemned the Catholic Church as erroneous, heretical, and apostate. They saw the pope as the Antichrist (the servant of Christ's greatest adversary the devil), regarded certain key practices and beliefs encouraged by the Church of Rome as superstitious and idolatrous, and condemned the Catholic clergy as corrupt and hypocritical.[7] The Elizabethan writer on witchcraft Reginald Scot equated what he saw as the superstitious elements within Catholicism—such as pilgrimages, the veneration of saints, transubstantiation, exorcism, and the acceptance of papal authority—with the tricks played by conjurors.[8] An anonymous "Church of England" author of 1641 thought the notion "that the Bread and wine in the Sacrament should be transubstantiated into the Body of Christ" was "a mere invention of latter times" and "diametrically opposite to reason and nature"; "the elevation of the Host by the Papists" he viewed as "rank idolatry."[9] The early Tudor evangelical polemicist John Bale associated papistry with sexual disorder and thought all papists were sodomites. The puritan minister James Cranford, writing in the aftermath of the Irish Rebellion of 1641, argued that the popes included among their ranks "ten Sodomites, fourteene infamous for adulteries, nine Simoniacks, twelve Tyrants, [and] three and twenty Necromanticks."[10]

The struggle for the Reformation in England was also a struggle for England's—and the English crown's—control over its own Church, involving a rejection of papal supremacy in ecclesiastical affairs and an affirmation that the king of England was sovereign in both temporal and spiritual matters. The pope, however, claimed the right to depose monarchs who were in schism with the Church of Rome—in 1570 Pope Pius VI issued a bull excommunicating Elizabeth, releasing all her subjects from obedience, and excommunicating those who obeyed her orders—while a number of Catholic writers (many of them Jesuits) published works arguing that it was legitimate for subjects to resist heretical (i.e., Protestant) rulers. Catholic rulers, so it seemed to English Protestants, ruthlessly persecuted their Protestant subjects, as the history of Mary Tudor's reign (1553–58), when just under 300 Protestants were burned at the stake for their beliefs, and the practices of various Catholic states in continental Europe seemed to attest—the Saint Bartholomew's Day massacre of several thousand Protestants in France in 1572 being a particularly poignant example. Catholicism, therefore, came to be associated with a threat to the sovereignty of the English crown, conspiracy against the English state, tyrannical rule, brutal persecution, and even mass slaughter—a threat not just to the true religion, but also to English people's lives, liberties, and properties.

This perception of Catholicism was reinforced by developments under Elizabeth: note the various Catholic plots and conspiracies, such as the Northern Rebellion (1569), the Ridolfi Plot (1571), the Throckmorton Plot (1583), and the Babington Plot (1586), and note also the Spanish Armada of 1588, Philip II of Spain's foiled attempt to launch a coastal attack on England. The fact that England was at war with Catholic Spain from 1585 to 1604, and that the Spanish lent support to the Catholic Irish in their revolt against the English crown in the 1590s, meant that anti-Catholicism became by the later sixteenth century an intrinsic aspect of English patriotic identity. The Catholic threat, because it came ultimately from Rome and (at this time) from Spain, was seen as foreign, as un-English and anti-English—and this was true even when that threat was from Catholic conspirators within England.

Historical developments over the course of the seventeenth century further served to reinforce the perception of Catholicism as a political threat to England's national interests and internal security, the freedoms and securities of Protestants in England, and the Protestant cause across Europe. Here we might note the Gunpowder Plot of 1605 (the Catholic conspiracy to blow up James I and other members of the royal family and the English political establishment when the king came to open Parliament on November 5); the furor over the proposed match between Prince Charles and the Catholic infanta of Spain in the late 1610s and early 1620s; England's wars with Catholic Spain and Catholic France in the late 1620s; and the Thirty Years' War, which engulfed most of Europe between 1618 and 1648 (with English Protestant opinion particularly concerned about the brutal atrocities supposedly committed by Catholic forces against Protestant civilians in the German-speaking lands of central Europe). The Catholic threat to the English state hit home in late 1641 with the bloody uprising of Irish Catholics against the English Plantation of Ireland, in which several thousands of English Protestants lost their lives. Then there was the Great Fire of London of 1666, which was widely blamed on Catholics at the time: indeed a Frenchman named Robert Hubert confessed to having started the fire while acting as an agent of the pope and was duly tried and executed as a result, though Hubert's confession was undoubtedly false.

This history was reinforced in the public memory by a combination of print, sermons, and public commemoration. John Foxe's famous martyrology, his *Actes and Monuments* of 1563, which went through several editions and became the best-selling book in English after the Bible, graphically documented the trials and tribulations of those who had suffered for the "true" faith at the hands of the Catholic Church.[11] Protestant preachers fulminated against the teachings and deeds of the Catholic Church from the pulpit, as they sought to guide their own flocks onto the true path to salvation. The anniversary of Elizabeth's accession—November 17—came to be commemorated as the day that saw England's deliverance from Catholic tyranny following the demise of Mary Tudor: officially under Elizabeth, then revived unofficially under the Stuarts. In January 1606 Parliament passed legislation stipulating that November 5 be observed annually as day of thanksgiving for the failure of the Gunpowder Plot: each year on this day parishioners would attend church to hear a suitably rousing anti-Catholic sermon and to thank God for delivering them from "Popish treacherie" and "Popish superstition and tyrannie," before returning to their neighborhoods to commemorate that deliverance with bonfires and fireworks.[12]

As a result, English men and women came to see Catholicism as a political threat and as a religion of brutality. "A Romanist is such an other thing / As would with all his hart murther the King," ran one rhyme from the early 1620s.[13] English pamphleteers writing about the Gunpowder Plot cast it as the latest in a long line of Catholic conspiracies against the Protestant states of Europe, in the process often recapitulating a long history of alleged Catholic atrocity: the sacking of cities, deflowering of virgins, and slaughtering of innocents. Recalling the horrors of the Saint Bartholomew's Day massacre in France, one author in 1606 rhymed,

> There Papists tossed harmeles babes,
> upon their speares sharpe point:
> Then did their wombs eviscerate,
> and teare them joynt from joynt,

and invited readers to imagine "dismembered corps" and "dissevered" limbs lying "mangled every where" if the Gunpowder Plot had succeeded.[14] Yet, as another author put it at the time, "the mischeife plotted against us" was not just "bodily"; it was also "spirituall," since the aim was to reduce all our posterity "to the former bondage of popish blindnes, superstition, and Idolatry."[15] In 1624 the Scottish-born religious controversialist Alexander Leighton pointed to "the belluin rage and cruelty, executed upon the Germanes and Bohemians" by Catholic soldiers during the Thirty Years' War, such as "the ripping up of women, the shamefull abusing of them . . . the torturing of men with new devised torments; the bashing in the bloud of inoffensive children," and "the cruel murthering of Gods Ministers."[16]

English pamphlets published about the Irish Rebellion of 1641 carried similar depictions of Catholic brutality: "putting men to the sword, deflowering Women . . . and cruelly murdering them, and thrusting their Speeres through their little Infants before their eyes, and carrying them up and downe on Pike-points." Although much of this literature was pure invention, it nevertheless served to perpetuate the view in the minds of English Protestants that Irish Catholics (and Catholics more generally) were capable of the most inhumane acts.[17] Whig authors revived this imagery during the Exclusion Crisis of 1679–81—the crisis over whether the Catholic heir, James, Duke of York, should be excluded from the succession—which

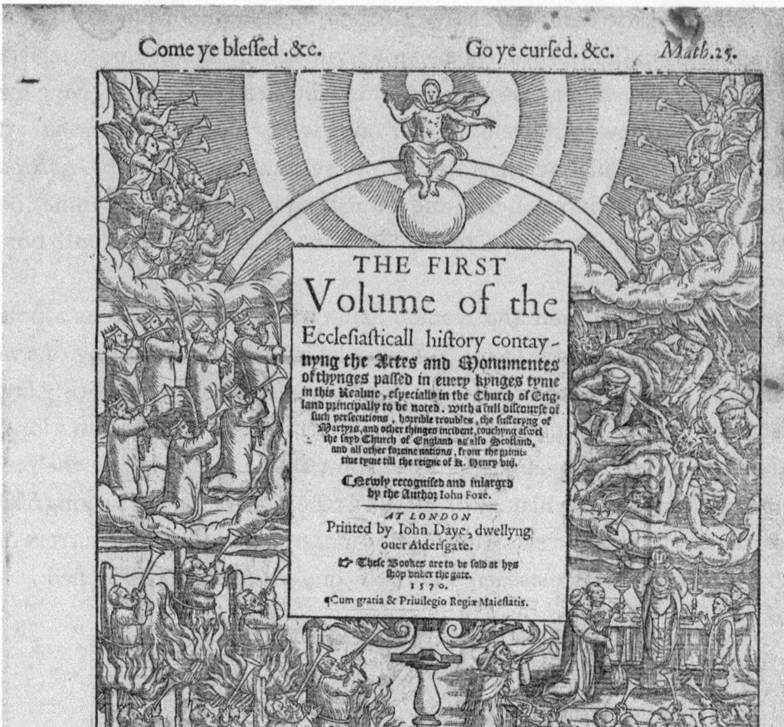

John Foxe, *The First Volume of the Ecclesiastical history contayning the Actes and Monumentes of thynges passed in every kynges tyme in this Realme*, 1570. (Courtesy of the Folger Shakespeare Library)

The ways of the "persecuted Church," whose "blessed" members are admitted by Jesus into the Kingdom of Heaven, are contrasted in stages, from worship services to the afterlife, with the "persecutyng Church" of the "cursed" banished to Hell. This famous cover illustration was used into the nineteenth century.

followed in the aftermath of the revelations by Titus Oates of yet another supposed Catholic conspiracy against the English state. "Imagine you see the whole Town in a flame," Charles Blount urged his readers in 1679, "occasioned this second time, by the same Popish malice which set it on fire before." "Fancy, that amongst the distracted Crowd, you behold Troops of Papists, ravishing your Wives and Daughters, dashing your little Childrens brains out against the walls, plundering your Houses and cutting your own Throats, by the name of Heretick Dogs." Or, "casting your eye towards Smithfield," he continued, alluding to the site in London where many Protestants had been executed in Mary Tudor's reign, "imagine you see your Father, or your Mother, or some of your nearest and dearest Relations, tyed to a Stake in the midst of flames."[18]

To what extent, then, did this antipathy toward the Catholic religion translate into a hatred of actual Catholics? In practice, English Protestants usually found it easy to live in peace with their Catholic neighbors.[19] Indeed, English Protestants often protested that they felt no antipathy toward individual adherents of the Catholic faith. Barnabe Rich, the Essex-born soldier who spent much of his adult life in Ireland, recalled in a tract published in 1612 "the persecutions, the tortures and torments" periodically "prosecuted by poplings, against the true professors of the Gospell," and proceeded to condemn papists as "blind and out of their wits" and the Catholic religion as nothing "but Idolatry, superstition and hypocrisie."[20] Yet just two years earlier he had pronounced how he pitied papists rather than harbored malice toward them, and indeed that he loved many papists in Dublin, "for, may not a man love a papist, as hee loveth a friend that is diseased?"[21] Sir William Pelham, writing to Secretary Edward Conway in February 1624, when England was gearing up for war with Spain, insisted that although he thought papists were not true subjects he "love[d] many of theyr persons and hate[d] none."[22] In parts of the country where Catholics were a sizable presence, community solidarity could sometimes lead Protestants to side with their Catholic neighbors against overly zealous government agents seeking to enforce the recusancy laws.[23]

For many Protestants the ideology of anti-Catholicism in itself dictated that they should be tolerant toward individual adherents of the Catholic faith. As far as Protestants were concerned, only the Church of Rome persecuted people for their religious beliefs; if Catholics, or other religious minorities, fell afoul of the law in England it was for committing crimes against the state, not for heresy. The Church of England clergyman Robert Abbot, preaching in 1625 on the *Danger of Popery*, could plead: "God forbid we should delight to imbrue our heads or hands in the blood of any [papists]. The cruelty of their false religion and the mercy of ours is well enough known."[24] The November 5th sermons, the puritan minister Matthew Newcomen pointed out in a sermon delivered before the Commons in 1642, were intended "not so much to inrage you against their persons [Catholics], as against their

Religion. . . . Not to study revenge upon the Papists, so much as upon popery."[25] The Solemn League and Covenant of 1643, its defenders insisted, was a covenant "not against papists but Poperie, not the men but the Errors."[26]

It was not quite that simple, however. Not all Protestants thought the same way and Protestant thinking was not always consistent. For many, it was a logical inference to draw that individual Catholics themselves must be suspect by dint of the fact that they adhered to the Catholic faith. The bishop of Gloucester, Godfrey Goodman, in his retrospective history penned in the 1650s, observed how toward the end of Elizabeth's reign "the common people" switched from hating "the Welsh, the Scots, or the Spaniard, and the French upon occasion" to hating Catholic recusants above all others.[27] Charles Blount, writing in 1679 at the height of the Popish Plot scare, tarnished all Catholics with the same brush, imploring his readers that if Charles II were murdered they should arm themselves and avenge

Faiths Victorie in Romes Crueltie, engraving, 1670s? First printed c. 1630. (Courtesy of the Folger Shakespeare Library)

Recounting the final moments of these victims of "bloody Jesuites, Preists, Friers, liers-all" and "Christian Champions of our English nation," this broadside reproduces for inspiration their last words spoken as they, "Like sacred Swans singing most sweetly," died "In Christ couragious, when theire flesh was frying."

their sovereign's death, "both upon his Murtherers, and their whole Party," for in Blount's opinion there was "no such thing as an English Papist who is not in the Plot, at least in his good wishes."[28]

Nevertheless, acts of aggression toward individual lay Catholics were not common. Catholic clergy could sometimes incur the wrath of the local populace. One Catholic apologist, writing in 1604 at a time when English Catholics were busy petitioning James I for toleration, noted how "the Godly and zealous Artisans and Prentises of London, and other places" would raise "alarmes of Stoppe the Traytor, when they see an Innocent Priest passe their streets."[29] There were attacks on Catholic chapels from time to time, but the objective was to stop Catholic worship, not to beat up individual Catholics: people vented their fury in the main against symbols of the Catholic religion, although sometimes also against officiating clergy. Thus, when a Catholic chapel opened in Lime Street in London on Sunday April 18, 1686, at a time when the Catholic James II was encouraging his coreligionists to celebrate their faith openly, a crowd of apprentices followed the priests to mass and threatened to "break their crosses and juggling-boxes down." In the ensuing fracas, the youths pulled one of the priests out of the chapel and dragged him through the gutter. Of course, once a demonstration has turned into a riot, there is the risk that people not initially targeted by the crowd might get caught up in the melee. It would certainly be naïve to assume that, as passions became inflamed, protestors would continue to reserve their anger for the clerics and refrain from targeting lay worshippers. When youths returned to besiege the Lime Street chapel the following Sunday, the authorities ended up making a total of twenty arrests, some of whom turned out to be Catholics—presumably worshippers who had become caught up in the fighting.[30]

There can be no denying that a visceral hatred toward individual Catholics could at times manifest itself. That is why anti-Catholicism still needs to be seen as a prejudice, an irrational passion, as well as a species of ideology. A revealing insight is provided by the response of Londoners to a tragedy that happened at Blackfriars on October 26, 1623, when a garret adjacent to the French ambassador's residence used for celebrating mass suddenly collapsed, killing the preacher and some hundred worshippers and injuring many more. The noise of the building collapsing quickly drew a huge crowd, and while some rushed to offer first aid and assistance to the survivors, others—"puritans" according to their critics—gave vent to their outrage at this illicit Catholic conventicle by slinging mud and stones, hurling insults, and even attacking the wounded as they were being carried away for treatment.[31] Yet even this particular incident is complicated by the fact the chapel belonged to the French ambassador: in other words, this was foreign Catholic worship in the heart of the city, even if many of those who frequented this foreign chapel were in fact English.

By and large, during the outbursts of anti-Catholic rioting that occurred at various times of political crisis during the seventeenth century, such as on the eve of the English Civil War or of the Glorious Revolution, crowds, if they did target individuals, tended to target specific Catholics—known political enemies or those associated with unpopular governmental policies—rather than random Catholics. For example, in the early summer of 1640, mutinous troops who had been pressed into service to fight against the Scots in the Second Bishops' War murdered two army officers who were suspected of being papists. Similarly, following the outbreak of the Civil War, parliamentarian crowds attacked various prominent Catholics believed to be supplying arms to Charles I's army. In late 1688, as James II's regime began to collapse in the wake of William of Orange's invasion, crowds directed their anger against high-profile Catholic supporters of the king and the places where Catholics in England worshipped.[32]

So far, my discussion has focused on anti-Catholicism in the sense of antipathy either to the Catholic faith (papistry) or to practicing Catholics (papists). Anti-popery was something slightly different. As mentioned already, contemporaries did use the word "popery" to refer to the religion practiced by Catholics. When Gilbert Burnet wrote during James II's reign of "the late Apostates to Popery," he was clearly thinking of Protestants who had converted to Rome, albeit that elsewhere he referred to practicing Catholics as papists.[33] Similarly, during the Exclusion Crisis, the Catholic heir was consistently referred to as the "popish" successor. The words papistry and popery, papistical and popish, then, were at times used interchangeably by contemporaries and frequently seen as synonymous. Yet this laxity in word usage should not obscure the fact that contemporaries often made it clear that what they understood by popery was something more than simply papistry. Popery was anything associated with what the pope or the Church of Rome stood for. A type of religious practice could be popish, as too could an idea. Popery could also be advanced by people who saw themselves as committed Protestants and who were even recognized by those who criticized them for promoting popery as being Protestants.

The rhetoric of anti-popery was invoked to criticize the established church in England: initially by puritans, who thought the Elizabethan Settlement of 1559–63 had been a compromise and that the English Church still needed to be purged of popish remnants, and then after 1662 by Protestant Dissenters, who found they could not conform to the Restoration Church because they believed it contained too many relics of popery. Thus, puritans and nonconformists regarded certain ceremonies retained in the prayer book, such as kneeling for communion or using the sign of the cross in baptism, as popish because they lacked scriptural foundation and were instead inventions of the papacy in the early Middle Ages. Images in churches, stained-glass windows, and objects such as crucifixes could all be seen as popish in the sense of encouraging idolatry. Consequently, those who promoted such ceremonies and practices were, in the eyes of their critics, guilty of promoting popery. Most controversial in this respect were the efforts of Archbishop William Laud and the Arminian faction in the Church of the 1630s to enforce stricter ceremonial conformity, to beautify English churches, and to move the communion table to the east end of the church, position it altar-wise, and rail it in (even adorning it with an altar cloth, candlesticks, and crucifixes). To many English Protestants (and not just puritans), this was popery. Yet it was not necessarily papistry, nor were the people promoting it necessarily thought to be papists.[34]

Once again, a certain caution is necessary here. Laud was not a papist by any stretch of the imagination. Neither were the overwhelming majority of Arminians, although a small number did convert to Rome after the collapse of the Caroline regime. Many Laudians were in fact strident in their condemnation of the errors of the Church of Rome.[35] Yet while most contemporaries would have recognized the distinction between being an actual papist and being a Protestant who was guilty of promoting popery, many likely would have felt that in *practice* there was no difference. Critics thought that Laud and his supporters, by reintroducing popish practices, were effectively compelling English Protestants to engage in Catholic worship.[36] And some doubtless truly believed that Laud and the Arminians were Catholics. For example, in May 1634 London apprentice Richard Beaumont alleged that Laud "had a crucifix in his howse and manye other pictures, and mayntayned poperie."[37] The issue is further confused by the fact that for tactical reasons critics of Laud often deliberately sought to collapse any distinction between popery and papistry. The framers of the Long Parliament's Grand Remonstrance, which was presented to Charles I on December 1, 1641, for example, alleged that there was a plot by "the Jesuited Papists," "the bishops, and the corrupt part of the clergy," and evil "counsellors and courtiers" to subvert the government and religion of the kingdom, which involved cherishing "the Arminian Party in those points wherein they agree with the Papists" and introducing opinions and ceremonies that were "fittest for an accommodation with Popery."[38] Root-and-branch reformers in the early 1640s denounced the institution of episcopacy as anti-Christian because the bishops had sided with the Laudian project for the advancement of popery. The Church of England cleric and future royalist Thomas Swadlin, preaching in London in the summer of 1642, could agree that the Jesuits had plotted "to usher in Arminianisme, that in the end they might bring in Papisme into the Church."[39]

Nonetheless, even though there was perceived to be a corrupt party within the English Church who agreed with the papists on many points, and who seemed to be advancing popery (and thereby either wittingly or unwittingly helping to advance the cause of Rome), the language that critics of the Laudians used suggests that they recognized that papistry and popery were different things. Preaching before the Commons on December 22, 1641, for example, Stephen Marshall saw the recent sufferings of the Protestants in Ireland as a warning from God for the English to mend their ways, pointing in particular to the prevalence of the sin of idolatry. Not only did England have an "abundance of Idolatrous Papists," he intoned, but also an "abundance of Popish idolatrous spirits, superstitiously addicted." To Marshall, and presumably also to many of his auditory, "idolatrous papists" and "popish idolatrous spirits" were not the same.[40]

In similar fashion, during the Exclusion Crisis of 1679–81 Whigs used the rhetoric of anti-popery to condemn those Protestants who supported the Duke of York's right to the throne. When Whigs accused the English bishops and the Tory clergy of being popishly affected, it was in part because these clerics supported the Catholic heir; yet it was also because they upheld church ceremonies that many Whigs and Protestant nonconformists regarded as popish and because they backed the persecution of Protestant Dissenters (persecuting people for their religious beliefs being a popish principle). It was not that those who made these charges thought the Tory clergy literally were Catholics. However, when we are dealing with the language of politico-religious abuse in a highly charged polemical atmosphere, we inevitably see slippage and a blurring of terminological distinctions. Thus, the Whigs tended to castigate all supporters of York's right to the succession, lay and clerical, as papists in masquerade. Doubtless, in the minds of many who favored Exclusion, to all intents and purposes they were.[41]

It has been suggested that after the Restoration—and especially from the 1670s, with growing concerns about the prospect of a popish successor in England and the expansionist ambitions of Louis XIV of France—the fear of popery became more of a political than a religious concern. As Steven Pincus has put it, "by the later seventeenth century most English people understood popery as a means of instituting arbitrary government."[42] There is much to be said for this view. Certainly during the Exclusion Crisis, Whig writers and politicians, in their efforts to rally public support for their campaign to exclude the Duke of York, tended to put the stress on the political nightmare that would befall England should a Catholic succeed to the throne. As the Earl of Shaftesbury put it in a speech in the House of Lords in March 1679, "popery and slavery" went "hand in hand."[43] Thus the Whigs predicted that a Catholic king would set himself up as an absolute monarch, do away with parliaments, rule with a standing army, impose heavy taxes, and persecute Protestants. In short, a Catholic king would be a threat to lives, liberties, and estates.[44]

The Catholick Gamesters or a Dubble Match of Bowleing, engraving, 1680. (Courtesy of the Folger Shakespeare Library)

England's Catholic peers seem too busy playing nine-pins to participate in the unfolding Popish Plot but, in the ballad below, they claim to have been scheming for the last "fifty Years" against the "Protestant Int'rest," causing the Civil War, the burning of London, and "much more" to serve our "Mother-Church, that Whore."

However, we should resist the temptation to see the ideology of anti-popery as becoming more secular over time. On the one hand, as we have seen, anti-popery had always had a political as well as a religious dimension from the very beginning. On the other hand, Whig propagandists during the Exclusion Crisis repeatedly emphasized how they wanted to preserve "our Religion from Popery," as well as "our Liberty and Property."[45] Cruder forms of Exclusionist propaganda often indulged in traditional satirizing of Catholic religious practices. One work of 1679, set as a dialog between the devil and the pope, has the former thank the latter for fighting all his battles, telling him how his "fi'ry Bulls, and bloody Inquisition," "Feign'd Purgatory . . . false Tradition, Beads, Images . . . Relicks, Crucifix, Indulgence, Pardons, and such taking-tricks" had "more augmented" the devil's "Infernal Host, Than Pagan-Rome," and "dam'd more Souls, than Hereticks e're lost."[46]

Moreover, our impression of the relative importance of political versus religious anxieties depends on where we look. Pamphlets aimed at convincing members of Parliament, the electorate, or the broader public that it would be a bad idea to have a Catholic ruling the country inevitably tended to focus on the political threat of popery—on the tyranny that would follow should the Catholic heir be allowed to succeed. So too did sermons delivered on political anniversaries. Preaching on the anniversary of the regicide in 1681, one cleric, after first reminding his auditors of the "blot cast on England" on this day, then launched an attack on Catholicism as a religion that rejoiced in the sin of murder, and warned that "If popery [were to] prevayle," English Protestants would be burned or hanged, "the pavements sprinkled with childrens blood, and walls besmeared with enfants brains."[47] By contrast, regular Sunday sermons tended to focus more on Catholicism as a false religion. For example, in 1678 Philip Taverner, the minister of Hillingdon, Middlesex, preached how "the popish religion" (which he also referred to as "popery") was "wholly A Stranger" to "The Principles of the true Christian Religion." In his view this was because it owned "blaspheming in its very foundation," maintained "Idolatrous worship to Be lawfull," taught "the doctrine of Divells" in forbidding priests to marry or prohibiting the consumption of meat at certain times, claimed that there were "more Mediators . . . between God and man" than Jesus Christ, and owned "prayer in an unknown tongue, not understood by him who prayes," among other things: Taverner listed twelve reasons altogether. At number eight, however, he condemned the popish religion because it maintained "it selfe by Force of armes, yea by murder and cruelty . . . and Massacres of Protestants."[48] Clearly, contemporaries did not neatly segregate the religious and political dangers of Catholicism; for most, they were part and parcel of the same package.

Even works that emphasized the political dangers of allowing York to succeed nevertheless tended to stress that the reasons why a Catholic heir could not be trusted to rule other than in an arbitrary way were related to religious belief. Take

Elkanah Settle's *Character of a Popish Successor*, published just before the meeting of the Oxford Parliament in March 1681, for example. Seeking to expose the fallacy of Tory arguments that York, once king, would nevertheless continue to protect the Church of England as by law established, Settle insisted that if York were in fact to do so he would be conferring "his Favours . . . on those very Men, whom (by the Fundamentals of his own uncharitable Persuasion, which dooms all that dye out of the Bosom of the Romish Church to a certain state of Damnation) he cordially believes do preach and teach, and lead his Subjects in the direct way to Hell." In short, the reason why a Catholic king could not be trusted was fundamentally tied to Catholic teachings on how one attained salvation. Settle went on to ridicule the Tory argument that a king's religion was irrelevant and that "a zealous Prince of any Religion" might out of "tenderness" and a "sense of his Peoples Peace . . . continue the Administration of Laws and Devotion in the same Channel he found them": "Alas! alas! If he's a Bigot in Religion, all his Morals are Slaves to his Zeal."[49]

Likewise after the accession of the Duke of York as King James II in 1685, English Protestants continued to be concerned about the religious as well as the political implications of Catholic rule. As James began to use the dispensing power to allow his coreligionists to hold office in violation of the Test Act, a group of Anglican clergy—led by the London-based divines John Tillotson, Edward Stillingfleet, Thomas Tenison, and William Sherlock—orchestrated a press and pulpit campaign to defend their version of the true religion and to condemn the errors of the Church of Rome. James responded by issuing a Declaration to Preachers in March 1686 ordering clergy to avoid religious controversy and to concentrate on practical and moral divinity. Many clergy ignored the order, insisting that they could not properly fulfill their pastoral role if they were not allowed to address their parishioners' concerns about the right path to salvation. This concern with religious matters can also be seen further down the social scale. For instance, the crowd that attacked the Catholic chapel in Lime Street, London, in April 1686, not only wanted to stop a religious meeting that they believed was in violation of the law; they also broke the priests' crucifixes, proclaiming "they would have no wooden gods worshipped there." Similarly, at Bristol in late May of that year, in protest against the opening of a Catholic chapel near the Custom House, the "lower orders" staged a public procession "in Scoff of Popery," "carrying before them a piece of Bread with much ceremony," while a couple dressed up as the Virgin Mary and a monk began fondling each other "very rudely and immoderately." This was a satire of what was perceived to be a false and hypocritical religion.[50]

We have seen, then, how anti-popery emerged as a powerful oppositional ideology under the Stuarts. However, the language of anti-popery was also invoked by progovernment polemicists, and even by the crown itself, to condemn Protestants who were critical of government policy in Church and state—to condemn, that is, those very Protestants who had accused the government of promoting popery. Thus, the charge of popery was leveled against Protestant religious and political radicals: Presbyterians (both English and Scottish), puritans, separatists, and those whom contemporaries thought of as being antimonarchical. The argument here worked partly by analogy: political and religious radicals, by seeking to undermine the Protestant monarchy and the established Church of England, were in fact seeking the same ends as the pope, whether wittingly or not. Yet the argument was also made that the ideas advanced by religious and political radicals were Catholic in the literal sense that they were taken from Catholic writers, with resistance theory being the classic example.[51]

This pro-establishment strand within anti-popery emerged early. In response to the Marprelate pamphlets of 1588–89 condemning the English ecclesiastical hierarchy and church service as popish, for example, the canon of Westminster Richard Bancroft likened Presbyterians to Catholics because both claimed a jurisdiction above that of the monarch.[52] In 1605, at a time when the government was cracking down on puritan nonconformity, the Church of England cleric Oliver Ormerod produced a lengthy tract lambasting English puritans for attacking the Church of England, undermining the authority of the crown, and stirring up the masses against the state, and for thus being as bad as or worse than Catholics: just "as there was a day when Herod and Pilate were made friends," Ormerod pronounced, so too there is a day "when Papists and Puritanes are made friends."[53] Some contemporaries even used the occasion of the Gunpowder Plot to attack puritans and Scottish Presbyterians. Preaching at Saint Paul's Cross on November 10, 1605, the bishop of Rochester, William Barlow, warned that there were "some among us" (i.e., in England) who came "very neare to the same dangerous position" of the Catholics in making "Religion the stawking-horse for Treasons," and recalled how Scotland had bred the likes of John Knox and George Buchanan (Presbyterians who were famous for their advocacy of resistance theory).[54] James I expressed similar views. Writing in 1609 in defense of the new Oath of Allegiance imposed on English Catholics, he condemned Jesuits for their opposition to episcopacy and alleged that in this regard they were "nothing but Puritan-papists."[55] In a speech before the English Parliament in May 1610 relating to the controversy over impositions, James admonished MPs for daring to dispute the royal prerogative, warning them not to "set such laws as make the shadows of kings and dukes of Venice," since only "papists and puritans were ever of that opinion."[56] "As Papistrie is a disease in the minde," he told the Scottish bishops in August 1621, shortly after the Scottish Parliament's ratification of the controversial Five Articles of Perth, "so is puritanisme in the brain"; the best remedy for both, James thought, was "a grave, settled, uniform and well ordered Church."[57]

Identifying puritan radicalism with the threat of popery was thus a fundamental aspect of what we might term conformist Protestant or Anglican-royalist thinking. Such arguments tended to be advanced most forcibly at times of crisis, when critics of royal policy in Church and state were themselves trying to exploit fears of popery to inflame opinion against the government in the hope of building pressure for change. Yet it would be wrong to see conformist Protestant anti-popery as purely reactive, as a cynical tactical ploy to divert criticism by throwing the charge of popery back against one's opponents. It also reflected what such Protestants genuinely conceived of as constituting popery.

For instance, when the Scottish Covenanters in 1638–40 accused Charles I and his Laudian allies of trying to foist a popish prayer book on Scotland, and when John Pym and the English parliamentarian-puritan alliance of 1640–42 alleged that Charles I had fallen victim to a popish plot to subvert the true Protestant religion, defenders of royal policy responded in kind by accusing the Scottish Presbyterians and English puritans of advancing popery. Yet in doing so they were drawing on a preexisting intellectual paradigm, not fabricating new ideological tools to meet the situation. Preaching at Durham Cathedral in 1639, at the time of the First Bishops' War, the bishop of Durham, Thomas Morton, claimed that although Roman Catholics and Scottish Covenanters disagreed "in Religion," they nevertheless agreed "in this one Conclusion of professing violent Resistance, for defence of Religion"; it was almost as if the Covenanters "meant to be the Disciples of Papists."[58] Others condemned the Covenanters' maxims as being "the same with the Jesuites" because they thought that "the King's authority [was] of humane institution . . . and not from God."[59] Likewise, on the eve of the English Civil War, the Cheshire royalist Sir Thomas Aston claimed that the Presbyterians and separatists agreed with "the Jesuites" in insisting on "the subjection of Prince and people to the tyranny of their Discipline."[60] The royalist poet John Taylor equated "The Papist and the Schismatique" because "both grieve[d] The Church."[61]

Writing from royalist Oxford in 1643, after Civil War had broken out, the Church of England cleric Edward Symmons identified multiple ways in which the supporters of Parliament against Charles I were in effect working to "introduce Popery." These included advancing "the Doctrine of resisting Princes" and "of calling Kings to account by the Subjects"; claiming to be able to absolve men from their oaths of allegiance, insisting that no faith was to be kept with malignants as papists did with regard to heretics; offering salvation to those who died in the cause and damnation "to the contrary parties"; urging men to break the laws of God in zeal for the cause, and offering violence and cruelty to their enemies; and defaming honest men who differed from themselves in points of judgment.[62] Symmons's list was long, but it was not miscellaneous; the charges were ideologically quite specific. In 1644 the former Scottish and now Church of Ireland bishop John Maxwell, also writing from royalist Oxford, not only insisted that the "Puritan and Jesuite" concurred in robbing "Kings of their Sacred and divine Right and Prerogative: making them derivatives from the people," but also alleged that "like Herod and Pilate" they were "reconciled to crucify the Lords anointed." Thus "our Sectaries," Maxwell continued, despite "pretending such a zeale against Popery," did nevertheless "joyne with the worst of Papists" in borrowing "their great ordinance of batterie against Soveraignty, from the Jesuits magazen."[63] Preaching at Breda in 1649, shortly after the regicide, the Church of Ireland bishop Henry Leslie (another transplanted Scot) pointed out that the "doctrine of opposing, deposing, and killing of Kings . . . was first brocht in the Court of Rome a thousand years after Christ, to maintain the Popes faction against the Emperour, and other Princes," and had been "since hotly defended by the Jesuites, and others of the Popes parasites." "What they have spued out of their mouth," Leslie bemoaned, "the Puritanes have licked up, borrowing all their arguments."[64]

Royalist polemicists tended to blur the distinction between puritans and separatists, often using the terms interchangeably, so as to tar the former with the sins of the latter. Yet it is important to recognize that moderate puritans, those who wanted to reform the Church from within, were also critical of separatists and likewise compared them to papists in terms of being a threat to the unity of the Church. For instance, a manuscript work of 1620 condemning the proposed Spanish Match—allegedly written by one Thomas Alured but likely drafted by the puritan divine John Preston—compared Christ's Church to a closely woven coat: although currently "at peace within it selfe," the author warned, "some itching Seperatists" sought "to make a hole in our coate and Church, which the Papists labour[ed] to rent worse, and the desperate Jesuit" to make "past mending."[65] Puritan polemicists helped to perpetuate this argument against the radical sects during the 1640s and 1650s. The Presbyterian Thomas Edwards, in his *Gangraena* of 1646, adduced a mass of evidence to show how "the Sectaries and the Jesuits agree in many things."[66] The anti-Laudian campaigner William Prynne came to believe that Jesuits and Catholics, having first sided with the court in their campaign to subvert Protestant liberties in England, switched sides at the end of the Civil War and began to infiltrate the parliamentary army. Thus, Prynne condemned Pride's Purge of December 1648 and the subsequent actions against the king as being "the designs and projects of Jesuits, Popish Priests, and Recusants," whom he claimed bore "chiefe sway" in the "Councels" of the newly purged Parliament, to "destroy and subvert our Religion, Lawes, Liberties, Government, Majestracy, Ministry, the present and all future Parliaments, the King, his Posterity, and our three Kingdoms." Prynne later accused the purged Parliament of playing "Popes and Jesuites" in deposing and beheading Charles I.[67] He also subsequently alleged that Quakers were "but the Spawn of Romish Frogs, Jesuites and Franciscan Fryers, sent from Rome to seduce the intoxicated Giddy-headed English nation." The puritan divine Richard Baxter similarly blamed the Jesuits for the regicide and believed that the Quakers upheld "Poperie."[68] Quakers, on the other hand, who came to be excluded from the Cromwellian toleration under the terms of the Humble Petition and Advice of 1657, accused the puritans of abandoning their former principles and embracing "the spirit of popery" in allowing themselves to "be drawn to persecute."[69]

When the Tories during the Exclusion Crisis accused the Whigs and Protestant nonconformists of popery, then, they were tapping into an ideological framework that had deep roots. Since this is a subject I have discussed extensively elsewhere, I shall simply outline the logic of the Tory case here.[70] The Tories claimed that the Whigs were at heart republicans and nonconformists who wanted to destroy the monarchy and the established church in England. The pope and the Catholic powers of Europe had long tried to do the same, but had always been frustrated. The republicans and nonconformists, on the other hand, had tried just once—in the 1640s—and succeeded. The Whigs were therefore working for exactly the same ends as the pope. "What is term'd Popery? . . . To Depose a King," one broadside asked; and "What's true Presbytery? . . . To Act the thing."[71] By arguing that nonconformists should be granted liberty of conscience, moreover, the Whigs, Tories alleged, would let popery in by the back door of toleration.

The Tories did not think the Whigs and the Protestant nonconformists actually were Catholics, although they sometimes suggested that they were not simply helping the papists unwittingly but working in alliance with them. Yet they did repeatedly insist—quite accurately—that Whig arguments for popular sovereignty and justifications of resistance were Catholic in origin. As one clergyman, preaching in 1679 on the anniversary of the regicide, put it: "let presbyterians remember this," that their doctrine "that Kings were to give an account to the people . . . is from the Pope, and let us know that all popery is not only among them that call themselves papists, but that such among us as doe inveigh most bitterly against the name, doe as hotly own the thing as anyone bred all his lifetime at the Pope's feet."[72] The Anglican divine Edward Pelling, preaching on the same anniversary three years later, documented in detail how the arguments deployed by opponents of Charles I in the 1640s "were once the Proper Creed of the Jesuites," "Originally . . . taught by Mariana, by Bellarmine, by Azorius, and divers Jesuites more."[73]

It is true that the Tories set out quite self-consciously to turn Whig arguments against their authors. Given that the Whigs had stirred up considerable public anxiety about the threat of popery and arbitrary government, Charles II and his supporters recognized that it would not work simply to deny that there was any such threat; instead those opposed to Exclusion set out to convince people that if they were worried about popery and arbitrary government they needed to stop the Whigs.[74] Yet the tactic could work only because accusing Protestant critics of the English Church and monarchy of popery was already a credible argument to make, and one that had been being made for a century. Tory anti-popery was an Anglican-royalist argument before it was an anti-Whig argument. It was also an anti-Country party argument before it was an anti-Exclusionist argument. Thus Roger L'Estrange, the government's surveyor of the press from 1662 to 1679 and a key government propagandist during the Exclusion Crisis, revamped the traditional Anglican-royalist line of puritan popery in 1678—before Titus Oates's revelations of the Popish Plot—in his answer to Andrew Marvell's famous *Account of the Growth of Popery and Arbitrary Government* of 1677. In an attack on Presbyterians whose title said it all—*Tyranny and Popery Lording It Over the Consciences, Lives, Liberties, and Estates Both of King and People*—L'Estrange pondered what difference there was, "more than in the Name," "betwixt the Papal Tyranny . . . and the Presbyterial?" What power was "more Absolute, Or what Decrees more Infallible, than That of Presbytery, Which . . . Over-rules Laws, sets up Othes of Treason against Othes of Allegiance; and covers the Crime of Rebellion with the Title of Virtue."[75]

In endeavoring to provide a framework for thinking about anti-Catholicism and anti-popery in seventeenth-century England, I have not sought to assess the extent to which English Protestant characterizations of early modern Catholicism or Catholics—or the various harbingers of popery, for that matter—were fair or accurate. We are clearly dealing with distortions and misrepresentations. In outlining the ideological constructions of seventeenth-century actors my intention has not been to endorse or validate them.[76]

Moreover, my focus here has been on England. As will by now be clear, context is crucial to understanding how the ideologies of anti-Catholicism and anti-popery were articulated and mobilized in any given time or place, and the other essays in this volume set out to explore the appropriate contextualizations for other parts of the British-American world across the early modern period. For the same reason I have touched only briefly on anti-Catholicism and anti-popery as relating to Ireland and Scotland. It is probably fair to say that the Anglo-Protestant ideologies of anti-popery in Ireland were similar to those in England, because those ideologies were English, whether conformist Church of England or puritan/nonconformist. Yet the context was crucially different. On the one hand, the Protestant Church of Ireland in the early seventeenth century was not as contaminated by what puritans would have regarded as popery as the Church in England was. It thus made less sense than it did for England to structure a Protestant critique of the established church in Ireland at this time in the language of anti-popery. Even as Lord Deputy Thomas Wentworth and Bishop John Bramhall endeavored to bring the Church of Ireland into closer conformity with that in England in the mid-1630s, they found it impossible to introduce the full Laudian agenda: when new Irish canons were introduced in 1635 the provisions in the English canons for cathedral clergy to wear copes when administering communion, for using the sign of the cross in baptism, for bowing at the name of Jesus, and for kneeling at communion were omitted.[77] On the other hand, the fact that the vast majority of the population of Ireland remained Catholic throughout the seventeenth century—75 to 80 percent, compared to perhaps only 3 percent for England—meant that fear of popery in Ireland was more closely bound up with concerns about what actual Catholics were doing.

Moments of intense politico-religious crisis in Ireland could thus give rise to a level of sectarian violence not seen in England.[78] We also need to recognize that the attitudes of Protestants in Ireland—whether of English or Scottish descent—toward the Catholics of Ireland could be different from those of Protestants in England, depending on circumstances: the reality of having to get by in a majority Catholic country might at times serve to mitigate Protestant fears of Catholicism, though at others (especially times of crisis) serve to heighten them. To complicate matters further, what English, Anglo-Irish, or Scots-Irish Protestants thought of the Catholic inhabitants of Ireland was also crucially shaped by the degree to which the Irish threat was seen as rooted primarily in ethnicity or religion—and again, this was something that changed over the course of the early modern period.[79]

The contexts for Scotland were different yet again. There were clearly overlaps between Scottish and English anti-Catholicism and anti-popery (the views of Scottish Episcopalians were similar in this regard to those of Anglicans), and there were similar anti-Catholic riots and demonstrations north of the border at times of political crisis (such as the Exclusion Crisis or the Glorious Revolution). However, the distinctive nature of the Scottish Reformation—which was carried out in opposition to the crown rather than by it (as had been the case in England)—meant that there was a powerful anti-Erastian streak to the Scottish ideology of anti-popery. For Scottish Presbyterians in particular, the royal supremacy over the Church was seen as popish, whereas in England anything that threatened the royal supremacy tended to be seen as popish.[80]

Even with regard to England my analysis has not been exhaustive. Such was the richness of anti-Catholicism and anti-popery as ideologies that more could be said to add nuance to the account offered here. Anti-popery is complicated not only because it was a species of ideology, and a multivalent ideology at that, but also because it remained at some level a prejudice—that was why the ideology had so much purchase—and when people give voice to their prejudices they tend not to think in logically consistent ways. Thus, as we have seen, some of the analytical distinctions historians would like to make often do not transfer neatly into the lived experience of the past. There was terminological confusion and slippage. The capacity to distinguish from where, or from whom, the true threat of popery came could break down at times of intense crisis or emotional stress. People could realize there was a difference between popery and papistry but speak as if there was none and at times act as if they had given up believing there was any.

There was, then, an emotional, even irrational aspect to the English fear of Catholicism and of popery. Nevertheless, anti-Catholicism and anti-popery were also ideologies, in the sense that they were reasoned religious and political positions that possessed their own logic, at least for the early modern English Protestant mindset. They were ideologies, however, that served to divide English Protestants among themselves. The fact that English Protestants could disagree so fundamentally among themselves about their anti-Catholicism and anti-popery at one level reinforces the notion that a hostility to papistry and to popery was a key defining characteristic of English national identity: the English were all, by definition, against both. At the same time anti-popery was not, at this time, an ideology that could unite the nation. This was, after all, a century of revolution.

Notes

1. Carol Z. Wiener, "The Beleaguered Isle: A Study of Elizabethan and Early Jacobean Anti-Catholicism," *Past and Present* 51 (1971): 27–62; Robin Clifton, "Popular Fear of Catholics during the English Revolution," *Past and Present* 53 (1971): 23–55. See also Robin Clifton, "Fear of Popery," in *The Origins of the English Civil War,* ed. Conrad Russell (London: Macmillan, 1973), 144–67.
2. Brian Manning, *The English People and the English Revolution, 1640–1649* (London: Heinemann, 1976), esp. chap. 2; Anthony Fletcher, *The Outbreak of the English Civil War* (London: Edward Arnold, 1981); Caroline Hibbard, *Charles I and the Popish Plot* (Chapel Hill: University of North Carolina Press, 1983); Michael G. Finlayson, *Historians, Puritanism, and the English Revolution: The Religious Factor in English Politics before and after the Interregnum* (Toronto: University of Toronto Press, 1983).
3. John Miller, *Popery and Politics in England 1660–1688* (Cambridge: Cambridge University Press, 1973), chap. 4. See also K.H.D. Haley, "'No Popery' in the Reign of Charles II," in *Britain and the Netherlands,* Vol. 5: *Some Political Mythologies: Papers Delivered to the Fifth Anglo-Dutch Historical Conference,* ed. J. S. Bromley and E. H. Kossmann (The Hague: Martinus Nijhoff, 1975), 102–19.
4. Tim Harris, "Politics of the London Crowd in the Reign of Charles II" (PhD diss., Cambridge University, 1985); Tim Harris, *London Crowds in the Reign of Charles II: Propaganda and Politics from the Restoration until the Exclusion Crisis* (Cambridge: Cambridge University Press, 1987).
5. Peter Lake, "Anti-Popery: The Structure of a Prejudice," in *Conflict in Early Stuart England: Studies in Religion and Politics 1603–1642,* ed. Richard Cust and Ann Hughes (Harlow: Longman, 1989), 72–106. See Lake's characterization of this article in his "Anti-Puritanism: The Structure of a Prejudice," in *Religious Politics in Post-Reformation England,* ed. Kenneth Fincham and Peter Lake (Woodbridge: Boydell Press, 2006), 81, 83.

6. The works are too numerous to list here, but especially worthy of mention are Anthony Milton, *Catholic and Reformed: The Roman and Protestant Churches in English Protestant Thought, 1600–1640* (Cambridge: Cambridge University Press, 1995); and the brief though highly insightful discussion in Conrad Russell, *The Causes of the English Civil War* (Oxford: Clarendon Press, 1990), 75–82.
7. For Protestant views of the Catholic Church as a corrupt and corrupting institution, see also Mark Knights, "Religion, Anti-Popery, and Corruption," in *Popular Culture and Political Agency in Early Modern England,* ed. Michael Braddick and Phil Withington (Woodbridge: Boydell Press, 2017).
8. Reginald Scot, *The Discoverie of Witchcraft* (London, 1584), 433; James A. Sharpe, *Instruments of Darkness: Witchcraft in Early Modern England* (Philadelphia: University of Pennsylvania Press, 1997), 54.
9. *A Dialogue betwixt Three Travellers* (London, 1641), 5.
10. James Cranford, *The Teares of Ireland* (London, 1641), sig. A3v.
11. Elizabeth Evenden and Thomas Freeman, *Religion and the Book in Early Modern England: The Making of John Foxe's "Book of Martyrs"* (Cambridge: Cambridge University Press, 2011).
12. *Prayers and Thankesgiving to Be Used by all the Kings Majesties Loving Subjects, For the Happy Deliverance of His Majestie, the Queene, Prince, and States of Parliament, from the Most Traiterous and Bloody Intended Massacre by Gunpowder, the 5 of November 1605* [London, 1606?], sigs. D2r–v, D3; David Cressy, *Bonfires and Bells: National Memory and the Protestant Calendar in Elizabethan and Stuart England* (London: Weidenfeld and Nicolson, 1989), chaps. 8, 9.
13. [Thomas Scott], *The Interpreter* ([Edinburgh?], 1622), 15.
14. I. H., *The Divell of the Vault* (London, 1606), sigs. B2v, C2v; Jason White, *Militant Protestantism and British Identity, 1603–1642* (London: Pickering and Chatto, 2012), 26.
15. *Certaine Arguments to Perswade and Provoke the Most Honorable and High Court of Parliament* (London, 1606), 23.
16. A[lexander] L[eighton], *Speculum Belli Sacri* (London, 1624), 182.
17. *Bloody Newes from Ireland* (London, 1641), title page; Joseph Cope, *England and the 1641 Irish Rebellion* (Woodbridge: Boydell Press, 2009), chap. 4.
18. [Charles Blount], *An Appeal from the Country to the City* (London, 1679), 2.
19. Anthony Milton, "A Qualified Intolerance: The Limits and Ambiguities of Early Stuart Anti-Catholicism," in *Catholicism and Anti-Catholicism in Early Modern English Texts,* ed. Arthur F. Marotti (Basingstoke: Macmillan, 1999), 85–115; Alexandra Walsham, *Charitable Hatred: Tolerance and Intolerance in England, 1500–1700* (Manchester: Manchester University Press, 2006), 208–9, 273–75.
20. Barnabe Rich, *A Catholicke Conference* (London, 1612), sigs. A3v, C2, D3v, E2.
21. Barnabe Rich, *A New Description of Ireland* (London, 1610), sig. Bv.
22. The National Archives of the UK (TNA), Public Record Office (PRO) SP 14/159, fol. 37v.
23. Michael J. Braddick, *State Formation in Early Modern England, c. 1550–1700* (Cambridge: Cambridge University Press, 2000), 305–6, 325; Walsham, *Charitable Hatred,* 273–74.
24. Robert Abbot, *The Danger of Popery; or, A Sermon Preached at a Visitation at Ashford in Kent* (London, 1625), 23.
25. Matthew Newcomen, *The Craft and Cruelty of the Churches Adversaries, Discovered, In a Sermon Preached at St. Margarets in Westminster, before the Honourable House of Commons Assembled in Parliament, November 5, 1642* (London, 1643), 62.
26. "Answers to Quaeries touching the Covenant," EL 7732, Huntington Library, San Marino, California.

27. Godfrey Goodman, *The Court of King James the First,* ed. John S. Brewer, 2 vols. (London, 1839), 1:86–87.
28. [Blount], *Appeal,* 4.
29. John Lecey, *A Petition Apologeticall* (London, 1604), sig. Aiiv.
30. Tim Harris, "London Crowds and the Revolution of 1688," in *By Force or By Default? The Revolution of 1688,* ed. Eveline Cruickshanks (Edinburgh: John Donald, 1989), 47–48; Tim Harris, *Revolution: The Great Crisis of the British Monarchy, 1685–1720* (London: Allen Lane, 2006), 200–201.
31. Alexandra Walsham, "'The Fatall Vesper': Providentialism and Anti-Popery in Late Jacobean London," *Past and Present* 144 (1994): 36–87; Tim Harris, *Rebellion: Britain's First Stuart Kings* (Oxford: Oxford University Press, 2014), 219.
32. Mark Charles Fissell, *The Bishops' Wars: Charles I's Campaigns against Scotland 1638–1640* (Cambridge: Cambridge University Press, 1994), 278–83; Clifton, "Popular Fear of Catholics"; John Walter, *Understanding Popular Violence in the English Revolution: The Colchester Plunderers* (Cambridge: Cambridge University Press, 1999); Harris, *Revolution,* 290–303; Steve Pincus, *1688: The First Modern Revolution* (New Haven: Yale University Press, 2009), 256–57; Scott Sowerby, *Making Toleration: The Repealers and the Glorious Revolution* (Cambridge, MA: Harvard University Press, 2013), 242–44.
33. [Gilbert Burnet], *The Ill Effects of Animosities among Protestants* ([London?], 1688), 13, 14.
34. Harris, *Rebellion,* 300–321; Milton, *Catholic and Reformed,* 60–92.
35. Miller, *Popery and Politics,* 82; Michael Questier, "Arminianism, Catholicism, and Puritanism in England during the 1630s," *Historical Journal* 49 (2006): 57–60.
36. Russell, *Causes,* 78–79.
37. TNA, PRO SP 16/267, fol. 192.
38. *The Parliamentary History of England from the Earliest Period to the Year 1803,* ed. William Cobbett, 36 vols. (London, 1806–20), 2:946–47.
39. Thomas Swadlin, *The Soveraignes Desire Peace: The Subjects Dutie Obedience* (London, 1643), 14.
40. Stephen Marshall, *Reformation and Desolation* (London, 1642), 45.
41. Harris, *London Crowds,* chap. 5.
42. Steven C. A. Pincus, "From Butterboxes to Wooden Shoes: The Shift in English Popular Sentiment from Anti-Dutch to Anti-French in the 1670s," *Historical Journal* 38 (1995): 351.
43. *Parliamentary History,* 4:1116.
44. Tim Harris, "'Lives, Liberties, and Estates': Rhetorics of Liberty in the Reign of Charles II," in *The Politics of Religion in Restoration England,* ed. Tim Harris, Paul Seaward, and Mark Goldie (Oxford: Basil Blackwell, 1990), 221–23; Tim Harris, *Politics under the Later Stuarts: Party Politics in a Divided Society 1660–1715* (London: Longman, 1993), 85–86.
45. Philolaus, *A Character of Popery and Arbitrary Government* (London, 1681), 7.
46. [John Oldham], *Tom Tell-Troth; or, A Dialogue between the Devil and the Pope, About Carrying on the Plot* (London, 1679), 1–2.
47. Folger Shakespeare Library, V.a.403, 137–39.
48. Folger Shakespeare Library, V.b.313, 6, 8–10.
49. [Elkanah Settle], *The Character of a Popish Successor* (London, 1681), 2–3, 4.
50. Harris, "London Crowds and the Revolution of 1688," 47–48; Harris, *Revolution,* 197–202. For the Anglican clergy's response to James II's attempts to promote Catholic toleration, see also Brent S. Sirota, *The Christian Monitor: The Church of England and the Age of Benevolence, 1680–1730* (New Haven: Yale University Press, 2014), chap. 1.

51. The Catholic roots of Protestant resistance theory are traced in Quentin Skinner, *The Foundations of Modern Political Thought*, 2 vols. (Cambridge: Cambridge University Press, 1978).
52. Richard Bancroft, *A Sermon Preached at Paules Crosse, the 9 of Februarie, Being the First Sunday in the Parleament, Anno 1588* (London, 1588[/9]); Mary Morrissey, *Politics and the Paul's Cross Sermons, 1558–1642* (Oxford: Oxford University Press, 2011), 208–13.
53. Oliver Ormerod, *The Picture of a Puritane*, 2nd ed. (London, 1605), sig. M4v.
54. William Barlow, *The Sermon Preached at Paules Crosse, the Tenth Day of November* (London, 1606), sig. E3v.
55. James I, *An Apologie for the Oath of Allegiance . . . Together with a Premonition* (London, 1609), 44.
56. *Proceedings in Parliament, 1610*, ed. Elizabeth Read Foster, 2 vols. (New Haven: Yale University Press, 1966), 2:103.
57. Quoted in David Calderwood, *The True History of the Church of Scotland* ([Edinburgh?], 1680), 784–85.
58. Thomas Morton, *A Sermon Preached before the King's Most Excellent Majestie, in the Cathedrall Church of Durham* (London, 1639), 3–4, 9.
59. [Walter Balcanquhall], *A Large Declaration Concerning the Late Tumults in Scotland* (London, 1639), 3; John Corbet, *The Ungirding of the Scottish Armour* (Dublin [i.e., London], 1639), 29.
60. Thomas Aston, *A Remonstrance against Presbytery* (London, 1641), sig. G2v.
61. John Taylor, *Mad Fashions, Old Fashions, All Out of Fashions* (London, 1642), sig. A4.
62. Edward Symmons, *A Loyall Subjects Beliefe, Expressed in a Letter to Master Stephen Marshall* (Oxford, 1643), 85–89.
63. [John Maxwell], *Sacro-Sancta Regum Majestas* (London, 1644), 3, 133.
64. Henry Leslie, *The Martyrdom of King Charles* (The Hague, 1649), 32.
65. Thomas Alured, *Coppie of a Letter* (London, 1642), 6.
66. Thomas Edwards, *The First and Second Part of Gangraena* (London, 1646), 40; Ann Hughes, *Gangraena and the English Revolution* (Oxford: Oxford University Press, 2004).
67. *Mr Prynne's Demand of His Liberty* (London, 1648); William Prynne, *The Substance of a Speech* (London, 1649), 80 (misnumbered p. 48).
68. William Prynne, *The Quakers Unmasked* (London, 1655), title page; Richard Baxter, *The Quakers Catechism* (London, 1665), sig. C2v; Miller, *Popery and Politics*, 85–86; William M. Lamont, *Marginal Prynne* (London: Routledge and Kegan Paul, 1963), chap. 6; William M. Lamont, *Richard Baxter and the Millennium* (London: Croom Helm, 1979), 109–13; Ian Y. Thackray, "Zion Undermined: The Protestant Belief of the Popish Plot during the English Interregnum," *History Workshop Journal* 18 (1984): 28–52; Stephen A. Kent, "The Papist Charges against the Interregnum Quakers," *Journal of Religious History* 12 (1982–83): 180–90.
69. Isaac Pennington, *The Axe Laid to the Root of the Old Corrupt-Tree* (London, 1659), sig. A4.
70. Harris, *London Crowds*, 133–44; Harris, *Politics under the Later Stuarts*, 98–100; Tim Harris, *Restoration: Charles II and His Kingdoms, 1660–1685* (London: Allen Lane, 2005), 237–52. See also Jacqueline Rose, "Robert Brady's Intellectual History and Royalist Antipopery in Restoration England," *English Historical Review* 122 (2007): 1287–1317 (though her claim on 1287 that this strand of Restoration Royalist polemic has been "hitherto largely overlooked" is puzzling).
71. *Interrogatories; or, A Dialogue between Whig and Tory* (London, 1681).
72. Bodleian Library, MS Rawlinson E 134, p. 325.
73. Edward Pelling, *A Sermon Preached on the Anniversary of That Most Execrable Murder of K. Charles the First Royal Martyr* (London, 1682), 13–14.

74. This strategy was articulated by Sir Francis North in a memo written at the time of the Exclusion Crisis about how to undeceive the people concerning the Popish Plot: British Library, Add. MSS 32,518, fols. 144–52.
75. Roger L'Estrange, *Tyranny and Popery Lording It Over the Consciences, Lives, Liberties, and Estates Both of King and People* (London, 1678), 91.
76. See the warnings voiced by Jeffrey Collins, "Restoration Anti-Catholicism: A Prejudice in Motion," in *England's Wars of Religion, Revisited*, ed. Charles W. A. Prior and Glenn Burgess (Farnham: Ashgate, 2011), 281–306.
77. Harris, *Rebellion*, 352–53.
78. Most famously at the time of the 1641 Irish rebellion, of course, for which see Nicholas Canny, *Making Ireland British, 1580–1659* (Oxford: Oxford University Press, 2001), chap. 8; Eamon Darcy, *The Irish Rebellion of 1641 and the Wars of the Three Kingdoms* (Woodbridge: Royal Historical Society / Boydell Press, 2013). For other examples of sectarian violence across the seventeenth century see Alan Ford and John McCafferty, eds., *The Origins of Sectarianism in Early Modern Ireland* (Cambridge: Cambridge University Press, 2005); Harris, *Rebellion*, 151–53, 167–68, 348–49, 433–43; Harris, *Restoration*, 383; Harris, *Revolution*, 112–14, 122–24, 428–29.
79. Tim Harris, "Hibernophobia and Francophobia in Restoration England," *Restoration: Studies in English Literary Culture, 1660–1760* 41, no. 2 (Fall 2017): 5–32.
80. Russell, *Causes*, 34–35; Harris, *Restoration*, 187–88, 198–99; Harris, *Revolution*, 149–53, 157–58, 372–78, 385. For Scotland, see the chapter by Craig Gallagher in this volume.

The Gunpowder Plot, Anti-Popery, and the Establishment of Virginia

Cynthia J. Van Zandt

EARLY SEVENTEENTH-CENTURY ENGLISH COLONIZATION of North America took place in a context infused by anti-popery. Some of the people involved in Virginia colonization had long been associated with repressive measures against English Catholics and with deep suspicion of papal intrigue. Many of them had ample reasons to distrust the papacy, the Jesuits, and European Catholic kingdoms, especially Spain. It is not surprising, then, that English colonization was in part a reaction to Spanish and Catholic power. And yet, the earliest decades of English exploration and colonial experimentation were not exclusively Protestant. For twenty years before the founding of the Virginia Company, English Catholics had imagined North America as a place where they might be free of persecution, while remaining loyally English and observantly Catholic. Several plans moved forward, raising money, lobbying for crown permission, buying ships, and entering into agreements with sea captains and explorers.[1] Alongside more widely studied Elizabethan ventures such as Roanoke, these early colonial schemes illustrate efforts by Protestant officials, as well as Catholic elites, to address the problems raised by the ongoing presence of a Catholic minority in a Protestant kingdom, particularly during the long years of war with Spain. Early ideas about English colonization in America contained a far wider range of possibilities than would eventually develop, especially in the wake of the Gunpowder Plot of 1605, which simultaneously provided an additional stimulus to English colonization plans and eroded support for allowing English or Irish Catholics to emigrate to North America.

In Jacobean England, anti-popery and hatred of Spain involved a complex web of fears, with some elements rather than others coming to the fore at particular times. Invariably, they combined fears of the subversion of English order and government by crypto-Catholics in English society and of Spanish desire for popery and universal monarchy.[2] The plot by English Catholics to blow up the king and Parliament that was exposed on November 5, 1605, confirmed the worst of anti-popish fears.

The scope of the plot was shocking. The plotters were not satisfied with the idea of regime change—they also wanted to punish the entire Protestant power structure of the kingdom. As James I pointed out, the plot "was not only for the destruction of my Person, nor of my Wife and Posteritie only, but of the whole Body of the State in generall; wherein should neither haue been spared, or distinction made of yong nor of olde, of great nor of small, of man nor of woman." It aimed at the "Subuersion of the State," by cutting out at one stroke, not only the monarch, but also his heirs, and much of the political and social leadership and structure on which seventeenth-century English government depended. Had it succeeded, the plotters would have blown up the "whole Nobilitie, the whole Reuerend Clergie, Bishops and most part of the good Preachers, the most part of the Knights and Gentrie." In fact, James claimed, it would have taken away the "whole Iudges of the land, with the most of the Lawyers and the whole Clerkes."[3] Writing a generation after the event, George Hakewill proclaimed that, "for myne owne part I thinke that no true English heart can seriously think, or tongue speake, or hand write of it without some kind of horrour & astonishment."[4] If such a thing were possible in London, at the center of English government, then how much more opportunity would enemies have to conspire in English colonies so far from home?

The plot was all the more shocking given James Stuart's interest in peaceful relations with Spain. His peaceful intent was evident even before he became king of England upon Elizabeth's death in March 1603, and gave some people hopes that perhaps conditions for Roman Catholics within Britain might ease under his rule. English Catholics had put out a series of feelers to try to lobby James VI of Scotland in favor of milder policies toward recusants once it became clear he would accede to the throne. After he acceded to the throne as James I of England, he acted quickly to end England's war with Spain. The 1604 Treaty of London ended almost twenty years of conflict, creating a peace that lasted until the end of James I's reign.[5] English Roman Catholic hopes at home, however, were disappointed. Combined with resentment at having a Scottish king, this sense of grievance helped inspire a handful of them to devise the radical scheme to blow up the king together with his Parliament.[6]

The Gunpowder Plot of 1605 reoriented the direction of English colonization of North America to exclude English Catholics. A number of the men most involved and most influential in chartering the Virginia colonies, including James I, Robert Cecil, earl of Salisbury, Sir John Popham, Popham's son Francis, and Edwin Sandys, were keenly and directly aware of the extraordinary threat posed by the plot, as it had personally threatened them.[7] Still, their subsequent promotion of colonial settlement labored under a peculiar tension. Anti-Catholic feeling was high, and anti-Spanish sentiment persisted, especially as Spain maintained its claim to all of the Americas. That was one concession James had not made in his peace with

Spain.[8] Thus, in the early seventeenth century, the Elizabethan goal of countering Spanish power in the New World, with all its anti-popish overtones, persisted alongside the pro-Spanish Jacobean foreign policy, and the deep mistrust and justifiable fear of English Catholic treachery. The resulting tension wove anti-popery into the culture of English America from the beginning, leaving an especially strong mark on early Virginia.

While scholars of England have begun reassessing the nature and influence of the Gunpowder Plot, it still has not received as much attention from early American historians. However, contemporaries recognized the irrevocable way the Gunpowder Plot had shifted the ground of English politics, and England's first permanent North American colonies emerged within a framework forged in part by it. The

Video Rideo, text in Latin, English, and Dutch, engraving, 1621. (© The Trustees of the British Museum. All rights reserved.)

"I see and smile" says Jehovah, whose Hebrew name is radiated by the sun, revealing the Gunpowder Plot and scattering the Spanish Armada. Published at the height of the Spanish Match negotiations, this influential print designed by a militant Protestant links the incidents as a combined threat to divinely protected England.

plot galvanized plans for some colonies, even as it began closing off possibilities for others. The first two Virginia colonies were the primary beneficiaries of the impulse to go forward. Both had already been in the works; indeed, at the same time the plotters were forging their scheme, the founders of the Plymouth and Virginia Companies' were planning their colonies.[9] James I granted the letters patent for the two Virginia colonies on April 10, 1606, a mere five months after the plot. Only nine months after the plot, in August of 1606, two ships sailed on behalf of the Plymouth Company to scout an appropriate location for a northern colony.[10] Just over a year after the Gunpowder Plot, in December 1606, colonists set out on behalf of the Virginia Company. The continuing efforts by Salisbury and others of the King's Council to track down those English conspirators who remained in Europe stretched well into 1610, covering the first years of Virginia's existence.[11] For King James and his ministers, uncovering the Gunpowder Plot remained as much at the fore of their concerns as colonization. Indeed, some of the same people were involved in both enterprises.

Initially, Sir John Popham had envisioned the Virginia colony as a place where England's poor could find refuge, and where England could find a solution to some worrisome changes brought on by the peace with Spain. Writing in late 1605 or early 1606, Sir Walter Cope told the Earl of Salisbury of Popham's great interest in North Virginia, because "in the experyence of hys place The Infynite numbers of Cashiered Captaines & Soldyers, or pore artezan that would, & cannot worke, & of Idell vagrants that maye & will not worke, whose Encrease threateneth the state, ys affectionately bent to the plantation of Virginia, in the which he hathe allredye taken greate paines."[12] The "Infynite numbers of Cashiered Captaines & Soldyers" were men who were being released from military service after the peace treaty between England and Spain. Significantly, many were English Catholics who had spent years in the military service of Spain. Now in peacetime they were due to come home, and England was not entirely sure it wanted them.

The prospect of hundreds of soldiers released from service, many even from the service of the Spanish king, prompted rival colonization schemes involving Catholics. George Waymouth's expedition to the northern part of Virginia between March and July 1605 had two distinct groups of supporters with very different goals. One group of supporters from Devon wanted to find expanded fishing grounds south of the Newfoundland cod fishery. Sir Thomas Arundell, an English Catholic, led the other group of supporters, sending at least two men on the expedition to scout out a location in North Virginia for a colony of English Catholics.[13] Arundell's plan, like Popham's, involved the possibility of using veterans of the long English-Spanish war as colonists; however, Arundell wanted to use English Catholics recently released from the Spanish army. Unfortunately, the plan did not get crucial support from within the English Catholic community. The prominent

Jesuit Robert Parsons refused to support the plan, arguing that Spain would surely kill any English who tried to settle in the Americas. He felt English Catholics had a duty to stay in England to fight for the faith. If English Catholics were given permission to emigrate to North America, with freedom of conscience and the right of return to England, then, he feared, Catholicism would not survive in England.[14] At the same time, Parsons's opposition reveals why early seventeenth-century plans to create English Catholic colonies in North America might have had a real chance of moving forward. Giving English Catholics a haven safely outside the kingdom could have weakened the push for toleration of Catholics at home. Until November 1605, the very thing Parsons opposed had real appeal for English Protestants.

However, the idea of a colony for English Catholics became politically untenable after the Gunpowder Plot. After November 1605, colonies that had been planned for English Catholics were pushed aside. Another plan to establish an English Catholic colony in North Virginia emerged as the successor to Arundell's, but it never got off the ground. Sir John Zouche, working with Weymouth, had begun plans for a Catholic colony before the fall of 1605 but stopped after the Gunpowder Plot. Several months later, Zouche was apparently told he would be given permission and did receive a passport in the summer of 1606, but his ships never actually left England.[15] The combination of poor timing and an old rivalry with Sir John Popham got in the way.[16] The Gunpowder Plot had changed the idea of America as a place where problematic groups could be sent to reduce the problems they caused at home. The idea itself did not go away, resurfacing most famously with separatist and puritan colonization of New England a generation later, but for English Catholics the door closed—for a time. Virginia's 1609 charter required colonists to take the Oath of Supremacy, and its 1612 charter gave colonial officials the right to require the Oaths of Supremacy and Allegiance to anyone coming to the colony, both of which were designed to exclude Roman Catholics from settling within the colony. However much some English Catholics hoped to send Catholics to Virginia, it was not a viable option.[17]

In addition to concerns about English Catholics, fear of Spain, and the desire to compete with its claims in the Americas, remained an important factor in inspiring colonial enterprises.[18] The Gunpowder Plot increased the sense of urgency of those who saw colonies as a weapon against Spain.[19] The firmly Protestant Virginia Company launched two colonies in 1606: Sagadahoc and Jamestown. One of the most important sponsors of Sagadahoc was Sir John Popham, who had little sympathy either for Spain or for English Catholics.[20] As chief justice of the King's Bench, he almost certainly would have been killed in the blast if the Gunpowder Plot had succeeded. As lord chief justice, he presided over the trial of the Gunpowder conspirators. His support for the Plymouth Company and the short-lived colony of Sagadahoc in Maine (his nephew and son-in-law had prominent roles in voyages there) was such that Sagadahoc is often referred to as "Popham's colony," but he also lent extensive support to the founding of the Virginia Company and probably drafted the charter of both companies.[21] John Farrar, another important figure in the Virginia Company, drafted a manuscript map of North America that represented both Virginia colonies as significant English bulwarks against Spain. Referencing the charters of both colonies, rather than the actual arrival of colonists, he portrays them both as having been founded at the same time in 1606, highlighting the fact that both moved forward a few short months after November 1605.[22]

Anti-Spanish colonial promoters had to proceed very carefully, however. Their king was determined to keep the peace with Spain, and he rejected the conspiracy theories that suggested a foreign power had played a role in the Gunpowder Plot.[23] For him to do otherwise would almost surely have led to war, a war he could ill afford, and which would close off foreign trade opportunities he was working to open after the Treaty of London.[24] The king was so keenly aware of the cost of making such a claim that his public pronouncement about the Gunpowder Plot forbade his subjects from talking about rumors that foreign powers were behind the plot. Still, as his prohibition makes clear, the rumors were already circulating.[25]

Yet there was an element of truth to the rumors about the Spanish. Although neither the Spanish crown nor its ministers seem to have supported the Gunpowder Plot actively, they did back a number of other tactics to help English Catholics and to try to return a Catholic monarch to the throne of England. Some of the individual conspirators, for instance, had previously been in the pay of Spain. They had been part of a group of English émigrés, Catholic and Protestant, who sought opportunity in the wars of the continent and fought as soldiers in the Spanish Netherlands against the Dutch, many of them in Sir William Stanley's famous company of English Catholic expatriates. Guy Fawkes, the most famous of the Gunpowder plotters, was closely associated with Sir William Stanley. Fawkes had also fought in defense of Jesuits in the Spanish Netherlands in the 1590s. He and fellow plotters Robert Catesby and Christopher Wright had all negotiated for Spanish help. They wanted Spain to fund the plot, and hoped to use Stanley's company for a Catholic invasion of England in the wake of the destruction they planned for November 5. There is no clear evidence that the Spanish court either knew the details of the plot or actively supported it. However, the fact that Englishmen tried to get Spanish support for the conspiracy raised fears that did not go away—and which carried over to Virginia.[26]

Spanish power remained a force with which to be reckoned in Virginia's early years. That threat was reinforced by the fate of the *Richard,* one of the first ships sent out by the Virginia Company. Departing in 1606 to explore the northern coast of Virginia (what later came to be called New England), the *Richard* was captured by a Spanish fleet in November, after months at sea. The ship and its crew were taken to Spain, where they were held as prisoners. John Stoneman, the *Richard*'s pilot, was questioned about the Virginia coast and asked to draw maps of the region. Fortunately for him, he managed to escape and eventually found his way back to Cornwall in late 1607. Only nine months after the Gunpowder Plot was discovered and before either Virginia colony ever had colonists, Spain had already threatened them.[27]

Both Sagadahoc and Jamestown were set up with one eye always on the threat of Spain.[28] The colonies' fear that Spanish ships might appear at any time was a constant concern. At Sagadahoc, the first thing the colonists did after choosing a location for the colony was to listen to a sermon, choose leaders, read out the laws of the colony, then begin "to entrench and make a fort."[29] As for Jamestown, its supporters declared the colony would "provide and build up for the publike *Honour* and *Safety* of our *Gratious King* and his *Estates*," advising its colonists "may be seated as a Bulwarke of defence, in a place of advantage, against a stranger enemy," that is, Spain.[30]

This concern about the military power of Spain was integrally connected to another: the question of whether or not Spain could somehow weaken them from within while waiting to invade from without. Historians are familiar with the terrible struggles that characterized Virginia's earliest years. Indeed, food shortages, disease, conflict with Indigenous peoples, and quarrels over what should be done and by whom beset both colonies. Severe weather played its part too—drought at Jamestown and a harsh Little Ice Age winter at Sagadahoc. At Sagadahoc, terrible relations with the Etchemins, the lack of clear leadership after the death of George Popham, the loss of financial support after the John Popham's death in 1607, combined with the toll of a severe winter proved fatal to the colony.[31] In Jamestown, fear of the enemy without and within threatened to undo the colony, as the early controversy coalescing around the colony's first president, Edward Maria Wingfield, reveals.[32]

Wingfield was one of Captain John Smith's most hated adversaries. Surrounded by hardship, Smith and many colonists came to the conclusion that their troubles were the result of an insider's deliberate sabotage. Interpreting what was happening to them through the lens of anti-popery, their suspicions spared neither social rank nor colonial position, and increasingly widely held rumors of the most damaging kind focused on Wingfield. Colonists charged that he hoarded food, starving them and keeping the best rations hidden for himself. Early accounts from Jamestown, as well as recent archaeological evidence, demonstrate beyond any doubt that the early Jamestown colonists suffered terribly. After several months, the colonists deposed Wingfield and gleefully watched him return to England with Christopher Newport and Gabriel Archer (another enemy of Smith's) in 1608.[33]

In an effort to clear his name with the company, Wingfield wrote a passionate defense that reveals a key reason why colonists thought he was such a bad leader: they believed he was part of a popish Spanish plot to destroy the colony. Wingfield's account, "A Discourse of Virginia," was intended for a small audience; he made it clear that he sought to repair his reputation with his social equals, humbly craving "some patience to answere many scandlus imputacions, which malice, more than malice hath scattered upon my name." Explaining that his fellow colonists resented his efforts to be an impartial leader, as well as his breeding and manners, Wingfield gives the impression that he was a poor choice for president of the colony, or at best, a well-intentioned but hapless failure. The charges of hardship and starvation occupy the bulk of Wingfield's "Discourse," and have been thoroughly explored by scholars. Yet one of the most intriguing accusations against him has received considerably less attention. In the final section of his "Discourse," Wingfield confronted the most damaging charges lodged against him: "it is noysed that I Combyned with the Spanniards to the distruccion of the Collony: That I ame an Athiest because I Carryed not a Bible, with me, and because I did forbid the preacher to preache, that I affected a Kindome."[34]

Anti-popery was a political tool designed to ferret out the political disloyalty of someone who was doubly faithless. If Wingfield were a Spanish spy and agent, it followed that he was neither a faithful Protestant nor a faithful English subject. Just as the English Gunpowder plotters were suspected of working on behalf of Spain to destroy England's Protestant power structure and facilitate a Catholic takeover, so Wingfield was suspected of being a traitor who appeared to be one of them but who was not. Wingfield seems to have decided that the best approach was to use a touch of ironic humor in countering this charge. "I Confesse I have always admired any noble vertue & prowesse as well in the Spanniards (as in other Nations) but naturally I have always distrusted, and disliked their neighborhoode." His humor was meant to highlight the absurdity of the charge, but the fact that he felt compelled to confront the accusation against him reveals how seriously he and others took it.[35]

Wingfield was comparatively lucky. Another colonist accused of being a Spanish agent, Captain George Kendall, was arrested for conspiring against the colony and then executed for treason.[36] The charge of being an atheist was just as serious. The term "atheist" was used in more than one way in the sixteenth and seventeenth centuries. It did at times carry the modern meaning of someone who denied the existence of God; however, it also often meant someone who "is an enemy to the Gods."[37] It is in this sense that "atheist" served at times as an interchangeable charge with "papist," for Protestants had no doubt that the pope and all Roman Catholics were enemies to true religion. To colonists who had begun to suspect that they were starving because Wingfield was keeping rations from them, the fact that he had brought no Bible to the colony was thus a damning piece of evidence. Significantly, Wingfield did not attempt to make light of this charge. He took it so seriously that his explanation carries the excessive detail of someone in near panic. He describes sorting through his books and sending many of them, including a Bible, to London in a trunk with various foodstuffs. He then says he left his trunk in Mr. Croft's house in Ratcliff. Somehow the trunk was never sent to Virginia. Wingfield suspected Croft of stealing many of his things, even giving some of the evidence for his suspicion, though noting he did not know what happened to his Bible. He meant to take it, but it was lost along the way with other of his belongings.[38]

Not only did the president of the council have no Bible, but also he allegedly cancelled sermons. According to Wingfield, his accusers claimed he "did forbid the preacher to preache, that I affected a Kindome." The charge that he sought a kingdom, that he sought to obtain power by placing his authority over the minister's, was part of the larger accusation that he worked to subvert the colony from within to help Spain, because he was not a true Protestant Christian. He admitted that there were occasions when he suggested the minister should skip his sermon, but not in the way the other colonists claimed. According to Wingfield, the Algonquian enemy, not the Spanish one, was to blame for the missed sermons. "Twoe or three sundayes morninges" he reported, "the Indians gave us allarums at our Towne, by that tymes that they were answered, the place aboute us well discovered, and our devyne service ended, the daie was farr spent." Wingfield argued that it had not been his idea; instead, the minister had raised the issue. When the "preacher did aske me if it weare my pleasure to have a sermon," Wingfield replied "that our men weare weary, and hungry, and that hee did see the tyme of the daie farr past (for at other tymes hee never made such question but the service finished he began his sermon) & that if it pleased him wee would spare him, till some other tyme." The charge that he "affected a Kingdome" by not allowing the minister to preach, he insisted, was wrong: "My mynde never swelled with such ympossible mountebanck humors, as could make me affect any other Kingdome then the kingdome of heaven." Yet the decision to postpone the sermon fueled his opponents' suspicions that he was working to undermine the colony.[39]

Wingfield concluded his defense against the charge of popery by stressing his own spiritual diligence and Christian humility in listening to his minister's sermons. "I never failed to take such noates by wrighting out of his doctrine as my Capacity could Comprehend," he wrote, "unlesse some raynie day hindred my indeavour." He insisted that his choice of a minister for the colony was evidence of his good intentions and of his loyalty to king and Protestantism. His "first worke," he claimed, "was to make aright choise of a spirituall Pastor." He appealed for help to the archbishop of Canterbury, "who gave me very gracious audience in my request. And the world knoweth, whome I tooke with me; truly in my opinion a man not any waie to be touched with the rebellious humors of a popish spirit, nor blemished with the least suspition of a factius scismatick."[40]

Wingfield's troubles reveal how influential anti-popery was in the lives of the early Jamestown colonists. It could be overtly political, sometimes apocalyptic, and sometimes more nuanced, and people on both sides of the Atlantic used it to marshal support and guide the direction of English colonization during the early years of the Virginia Company. Sermons to the Virginia Company repeatedly emphasized the necessity of being vigilantly anti-popish to have good governance. William Symonds, preaching in 1609, repeatedly warned against the dangers of popery. The colony would be successful, he said, as long as "such as doe manage the expedition, are carefull to carry thither no Traitors, nor papists that depend on the Great Whore." In the post–Gunpowder Plot world, the company must avoid the complacency of thinking that fellow Englishmen were trustworthy.

To those who protested that they could trust their kin and fellow countrymen, Symonds replied, "for any thing that I can see, since ATHEISTS and PAPISTS, haue gotten out of their serpents holes, and conuersed with men, they haue sowed such cockell among our wheate, that in many places a man is in no such peril to be cheated and cosoned, if not murthered & poisoned, as among his own kindred that are affected that way." As a "true Hearted Protestant," Symonds then answered the main argument against attempting American colonies, that "Papists that shall come on the backe of us" (in other words, Spain and France would attack Protestant English colonies), by pointing out that Catholics had few successes of which to boast in their quest for world domination. "Though their industrie hath bene nothing inferior to the divuels, that came from compassing of the earth, to and for; yet they may cast a wofull accompt." Nonetheless, to be overconfident could prove the undoing of the Virginia Company. The papist enemy, after all, was dangerous and subtle. "The onely peril," he cautioned, "is in offending god, and taking of Papists in to your company: if once they come creeping into your houses, then looke for mischiefe: if treason or poison bee of any force: know them all to be very Assasines, of all men to be abhorred." Righteous, anti-popish leadership was required: "hope in God that hee, that hath sent you abroad, will also send you such gouernours, as will cast out the leaven out of your houses."[41]

Although William Symonds's sermon focused on atheists and papists, a warning about Spain lay between the lines—of necessity given the king's peace policy toward Spain. However, no one sailing to the Americas could forget about the Spanish threat. The instructions to Sir Thomas West were explicit about both sets of problems. West was ordered "not to lande or touche upon anye of the Kinge of Spaine his dominions" on his voyage to Virginia. If he should get caught in a storm and forced to anchor in Spanish territory, then he was directed to call a meeting with all of the Spanish officials and read James I's commission, so that the Spanish would know that England was planting a colony in Virginia and to prove that this was not piracy or a formal act of war. At the same time, the instructions emphasized that Virginia was to be a Protestant colony in every way, noting, "your Lordship is to take principall order and care for the true worship and service of God as by havinge the Gospell preched, frequent prayers and the sacraments often administred as becommeth Christians." West needed to ensure regular Christian practice and enforce conformity "with the counsel of your said prechers and ministers." As needed, he was to "proceede in punishinge of all atheisme, prophanisme, popery and schisme by exemplary punishment to the honor of God and to the peace and safety of his church over which in this tenderness and infancy your Lordship must be especially solicitous and watchfull."[42]

Fears of subversion from within and of the power of Spain come up explicitly toward the end of West's instructions. He was ordered to "take especiall care what relacions come into England and what letters are written & that all things of that nature may be boxed up and sealed and sent first to the Counsell here." Whenever ships arrived, he was to "endeavor to knowe all the particular passages and informacions given on both sides and to advertise us accordingly."[43] Some of this was no doubt an effort to try to prevent bad publicity, but another motivation was to keep Spain from getting the information.[44] The company continued to worry about a Spanish invasion. In the face of such fears, some urged the company to press ahead as much as possible in order to forestall a Spanish attack. Lord Chancellor Egerton reportedly said that "the proper thing is to fortify ourselves all at once, because when they will open their eyes in Spain they will not be able to help it, and even tho' they may hear it, they are just now so poor that they will have no means to prevent us from carrying out our plan."[45]

It is unclear if the threat to Virginia was entirely external. The charges against Wingfield, his defense against them, the execution of George Kendall, Symonds's warning not to harbor "Papists," and the concerns in Governor West's instructions are especially intriguing in light of archaeological findings by the Jamestown Rediscovery team. They have uncovered a significant number of Catholic worship materials at the Jamestown site. In addition to rosary beads and a crucifix, archaeologists have uncovered a silver reliquary with bone inside, found in the grave of Gabriel Archer, who had returned to Virginia in 1609 only to die during the starving time of 1610. Much remains unclear about how to interpret the physical evidence of Roman Catholic artifacts in early Jamestown. Protestant colonists may have carried pre-Reformation family artifacts with them across the Atlantic. It may be that there was a group of colonists who were secret Catholics; it may be that some colonists were in the pay of Spain. More work remains to be done; however, the archaeological discoveries are particularly suggestive in light of the documentary evidence from people inside and outside the colony.[46]

The Jamestown colony continued to struggle into the 1620s. By the end of James's reign, it was not clear what its fate would be. Despite many efforts, the scandal of the colony's failure to flourish continued to grow after the investigations that followed news of the devastating 1622 Powhatan attack. The company found itself very much on the defensive, with a deeply anti-Spanish faction accusing some within it of being pro-Spanish at worst, and hapless tools of Spanish interests at best. Their fears increased after James I decided to marry the Prince of Wales to the Spanish infanta. Negotiations began as early as 1613, as the original plan had been to marry Prince Henry and the Infanta Maria. After Henry's death, negotiations continued, but this time shifted to have Henry's younger brother Prince Charles marry the infanta. The negotiations reached their height in 1622–23 before collapsing when Prince Charles and the royal favorite, the Duke of Buckingham, turned against the failed scheme.[47]

English subjects rejoiced at the removal of the Spanish and papist threat to the monarchy, but the bitterness of the struggle over the Virginia Company persisted. The anti-Spanish faction within the Virginia Company feared that the Spanish ambassador and his agents who had worked to promote the Spanish Match were laboring to break up English Protestant power in the colonies. In the summer of 1624, James I had a special commission created to resolve the situation. It included several of James's most powerful ministers, including Privy Council Secretary George Calvert: a conforming Protestant who came from a Catholic family in Yorkshire, and thus was seen by many as a crypto-Catholic. The commission made the decision to dissolve the Virginia Company. After James I's death in March 1625, the colony reverted to royal control under his son Charles.[48]

Anti-popery persisted in Virginia after the dissolution of the company, as evidenced by an event that took place five years later. Colonists in Jamestown watched with dismay as George Calvert, now Lord Baltimore, arrived in the Chesapeake looking for land. Calvert had been one of those closest to James who advocated in favor of the Spanish Match. The failure of the Spanish Match had marked the end of his career in court: he retired, embraced the Catholicism of his family, and refused to take service under Charles, who still regarded him as trusted servant. King James had granted Calvert a Newfoundland colony, Avalon, but by 1629, Calvert had decided to give up on that cold, expensive, and difficult endeavor. With Charles's support, this former member of the Privy Council and of the commission that had dissolved the Virginia Company was searching for another setting for his colony.[49] The combination of his Catholic faith and opposition to the Virginia Company made him deeply unwelcome in Virginia. His arrival at Jamestown was greeted with open hostility.

Governor John Pott refused to allow Baltimore to stay unless he took the Oath of Supremacy and the Oath of Allegiance. It was both a militantly Protestant and startlingly vindictive move, draped in the guise of loyalty to the king and to earlier colonial instructions. It was also a clever move; the likelihood of Virginians being punished for requiring anyone to take the oaths was almost nonexistent, since it was the law according to the colonial charter. The fact that they might take particular pleasure in turning away one of the commissioners, who had dissolved the Virginia Company in such humiliating fashion, was an added bonus. It was an act of revenge infused with anti-popery.[50]

The Catholic question was part of English colonization from the beginning of Elizabethan efforts to establish English colonies in North America. Between 1582 and 1606, there were repeated schemes to settle hundreds of English and Irish Catholics in North America. The sudden intervention of the Gunpowder Plot both choked off this possible path for colonization and strengthened the hand of anti-popish and anti-Spanish colonizers—even as England upheld its peace with Spain. Consequently, the plot both brought the possibility of using American colonies as a way to solve the challenges of England's Catholic minority to an abrupt end and provided a strong impetus to make English colonization both Protestant and anti-Spanish. Additionally, the fallout from the plot gave anti-popery an especially acute edge in early Virginia's political culture, to occasionally divisive and deadly effect. Controversy over the role of Spain and Catholics within England and the colonies persisted into the 1620s, contributing to the downfall of the Virginia Company. However, into the 1630s colonial Virginians firmly upheld the Protestant vision of English colonization that had been forged in the wake of the notorious Gunpowder Plot.

Notes

I presented an earlier version of this paper at the conference, "Antipopery: The Transatlantic Experience c. 1530–1850" at the McNeil Center for Early American Studies in 2008. I am grateful to the participants in that conference and especially to Evan Haefeli and to the anonymous readers for the University of Virginia Press for their suggestions as I revised this material.

1. On Elizabethan Catholic colonization schemes, see David Beers Quinn, "The English Catholics and America, 1581–1633," in his *England and the Discovery of America, 1481–1620, From the Bristol Voyages of the Fifteenth Century to the Pilgrim Settlement at Plymouth: The Exploration, Exploitation, and Trial-and-Error Colonization of North America by the English* (New York: Alfred A. Knopf, 1974), 364–97; and Donald F. X. Connolly, "A Chronology of New England Catholicism before the Mayflower Landing," *Records of the American Catholic Historical Society of Philadelphia* 70, no. 3–4 (1959): 88–108.
2. See, e.g., David Harris Sacks, "Discourses of Western Planting: Richard Hakluyt and the Making of the Atlantic World," in *The Atlantic World and Virginia, 1550–1624*, ed. Peter C. Mancall (Chapel Hill: University of North Carolina Press for OIEAHC, 2007), 419.

3. *His Majesties Speech in This Last Session of Parliament, as Neere His Very Words as Could Be Gathered at the Instant* (London, 1605), B2 v.
4. George Hakewill, *A Comparison between the Dayes of Purim and That of the Powder Treason for the Better Continuance of the Memory of It* (Oxford, 1626), 29–30.
5. For a useful discussion of these points, see, W. B. Patterson, *King James VI and I and the Reunion of Christendom* (Cambridge: Cambridge University Press, 1997). The treaty agreement was reached in August 1604, and ratifications were exchanged in June 1605; see Quinn, "English Catholics and America," 384.
6. Jenny Wormald, "Gunpowder, Treason, and Scots," *Journal of British Studies* 24 (1985): 141–68. Mark Nicolls, *Investigating Gunpowder Plot* (Manchester: Manchester University Press, 1991), argues that the evidence supports interpretations that the Gunpowder Plot was a full-blown conspiracy, not just something fabricated by James I and his ministers. For an opposing view, see Francis Edwards, S.J., "Still Investigating Gunpowder Plot," *Recusant History* 21 (1993): 305–46. See also James Sharpe, *Remember, Remember: A Cultural History of Guy Fawkes Day* (Cambridge, MA: Harvard University Press, 2005); and for particular treatment of the Jesuit mission in England, see Alice Hogge, *God's Secret Agents: Queen Elizabeth's Forbidden Priests and the Hatching of the Gunpowder Plot* (New York: HarperCollins, 2005).
7. Some of them also had long experience in diplomatic and intelligence activities against both Spain and the papacy. During Elizabeth's reign, for example, Robert Cecil had used a network of intelligencers to monitor the activities of Jesuits and other priests in England, as well as the activities and plans of the papacy. He well understood the challenges England faced as a Protestant kingdom that refused to grant toleration to its Catholic subjects. Robert Cecil and Sir John Popham had tried to negotiate papal withdrawal of the Jesuits from England in 1601 during the Appellant Priests controversy. See Patrick Martin and John Finnis, "The Secret Sharers: 'Anthony Rivers' and the Appelant Controversy, 1601–2," *Huntington Library Quarterly* 69, no. 2 (June 2006): 195–238; see 205–6 for the 1601 negotiations for the withdrawal of the Jesuits.
8. England and Spain devoted considerable energy to negotiating this point during discussions for the Treaty of London. On the role of the Americas in the treaty negotiations, see, e.g., David B. Quinn, *Explorers and Colonies: America 1500–1625* (London: Hambledon Press, 1990), 325–28. For an important discussion of differences in English and Spanish interpretations of the treaty, see William S. Goldman, "Spain and the Founding of Jamestown," *William and Mary Quarterly* 68, no. 3 (July 2011): 431–32.
9. On the timing of the planning of the Virginia Company and colony, see Warren M. Billings, John E. Selby, and Thad W. Tate, eds., *Colonial Virginia: A History* (White Plains, NY: KTO Press, 1986), 12.
10. Contemporary accounts such as William Strachey's discuss the beginnings of both colonies as being nearly simultaneous, though in fact the ships bound for the southern colony left a few months before the ships bound for the northern colony. See, e.g., William Strachey, *The Historie of Travaile into Virginia Britannia: Expressing the Cosmographie and Comodities of Country Togither with the Manners and Customes of the People Gathered and Observed as Well by Those Who Went First Thither as Collected by William Strachey, Gent. First Secretary of the Colony*, ed. R. H. Major (London: Hakluyt Society, 1959), 162.
11. A. H. Dodd, "The Spanish Treason, the Gunpowder Plot, and the Catholic Refugees," *English Historical Review* 53 (1938): 646–50, for a discussion of efforts by Salisbury and other of the king's ministers to bring émigrés like Hugh Owen, Baldwin, and Charles Bayley to trial in England for conspiracy and treason in the Powder Plot.

12. "[December 1605 or January 1606], Sir Walter Cope to the earl of Salisbury," in David B. Quinn and Alison M. Quinn, *The English New England Voyages, 1602–1608* (London: Hakluyt Society, 1983), 378.
13. Quinn and Quinn, *English New England Voyages*, 56–70; Quinn, "English Catholics and America," 389–90.
14. For a copy of Parson's letter, see, Quinn and Quinn, *English New England Voyages*, 242–47; Quinn, "English Catholics and America," 384–85.
15. The Zouche project had supporters at court. In June 1606 William Udall wrote to the earl of Salisbury assuring him of English Catholics' loyalty and support for expelling the Jesuits from England. See "19 June 1606. William Udall to the earl of Salisbury," in Quinn and Quinn, *English New England Voyages*, 318.
16. David and Alison Quinn noted Zouche's "plan aborted, at least partly owing to administrative obstruction at a high level," *English New England Voyages*, 313.
17. There was a project to send several ships of Catholic veterans of the Nine Years' War from Ireland as colonists to Virginia in 1606, which was loosely associated with Zouche's proposal to settle Irish Catholics in Maine/Norumbega or elsewhere in the northern part of Virginia. The venture fell apart, and before another project could replace it, a rival solution replaced it. Lord Arundell headed up a new regiment of Catholic soldiers in the Low Countries, taking with him many of the otherwise idle combat veterans of the Irish and Spanish wars. In 1609, Lord Arundell did try one more time to propose to send 500 English men, probably Catholics, and 500 Irish Catholics to North America to help defend English colonial possessions. The Spanish ambassador worried they would go to Jamestown, but Arundell's focus may have been on the threat posed by New France. See Quinn, "English Catholics in America," 391–92. Lord Baltimore's future Catholic ventures in Newfoundland and the Chesapeake would go against this grain, but they were treated with suspicion and hostility outside court.
18. For example, David Quinn notes the English learned that Spanish ships had seized the English ships the *Castor* and *Pollux*, in April 1606, as the Virginia Company received its first charter. James I sought peace with Spain and had it, but he also moved ahead with Protestant expansion into North American territories; see David B. Quinn, "James I and the Beginnings of Empire in America," in *Explorers and Colonies: America, 1500–1625* (London: Hambledon Press, 1990), 321–40. For recent works touching on the continuing influence of Spain, see, e.g., Carla Gardina Pestana, *Protestant Empire: Religion and the Making of the British Atlantic World* (Philadelphia: University of Pennsylvania Press, 2009); J. H. Elliott, "The Iberian Atlantic and Virginia," in *Atlantic World and Virginia*, ed. Mancall, 542, 548–49; Audrey Horning, *Ireland in the Virginian Sea: Colonialism in the British Atlantic* (Chapel Hill: University of North Carolina Press, 2013); Goldman, "Spain and the Founding of Jamestown," 427–50.
19. Douglas Bradburn has pointed out that "peace with Spain at the accession of King James VI of Scotland to the throne of England was not the end of anti-Spanish sentiment or of firm belief in the Protestant cause, but it did break up the dominance of the anti-Spanish block at the center of English court politics." He also discusses the ways in which Henry Stuart formed an informal court "as the center of opposition to official government policy" "as early as 1606," and that Henry was staunchly anti-Catholic. Douglas Bradburn, "The Eschatological Origins of the English Empire," in *Early Modern Virginia: Reconsidering the Old Dominion*, ed. Douglas Bradburn and John C. Coombs (Charlottesville: University of Virginia Press, 2011), 28.
20. For an extensive discussion of Popham's attitudes and activities, including his proposals for colonization, see Douglas Walthew Rice, *The Life and Achievements of Sir John Popham*

1531–1607 Leading to the Establishment of the First English Colony in New England (Madison, NJ: Fairleigh Dickinson University Press, 2005).

21. His nephew, George Popham, was the first president of Sagadahoc, and his son Francis was also a director of the company. See Strachey, *Historie of Travaile into Virginia Britannia,* 172–79, for a discussion of George Popham's election as president, his role in the colony, and his death. Billings, Selby, and Tate, *Colonial Virginia,* 12, note that Popham may have gotten assistance from Attorney General Sir Edward Coke, Solicitor General John Doddridge, and Salisbury himself in drafting the Virginia Company charter. On Salisbury's and Popham's interest in colonization, see also Alexander B. Haskell, *For God, King, and People: Forging Commonwealth Bonds in Renaissance Virginia* (Chapel Hill: University of North Carolina Press, 2017), 139–40.
22. The sketch map was the basis for Farrar's better-known 1650 published map, and it differs from the later published versions in significant respects. Farrar's manuscript map is reproduced in W. P. Cumming, R. A. Skelton, and D. B. Quinn, *The Discovery of North America* (Winter Park, FL: American Heritage Press, 1972), 268, "Ould Virginia, 1584, now Carolana, 1650, New Virginia, 1606, New England, 1606," map by John Farrar, 1650. An original is in the New York Public Library, I. N. Phelps Stokes Collection, Addenda Map 9. The published version of Farrar's map appeared in Edward Williams, *Virgo Triumphans; or Virginia Richly and Truly Valued* (London, 1650). Robert Beverley's *History of the First Settlement of Virginia* (1705) sees the two Virginia colonies as linked, noting that James I issued a charter for "two distinct Companies to make two separate Colonies," and he goes on to describe the men in charge of the first (Jamestown) and second (Sagadahoc) colony.
23. The court quickly embarked on a public relations campaign to quash speculation about Spanish involvement. On December 1, the Earl of Salisbury wrote to the Earl of Dumfermline, lord chancellor of Scotland, about the plot, and Cecil's letter states that "no foreign prince" was involved in the plot, "James I: Volume 17, December, 1605," in *Calendar of State Papers Domestic: James I, 1603–1610,* ed. Mary Anne Everett Green (London, 1857), 265–77. *British History Online* http://www.british-history.ac.uk/cal-state-papers/domestic/jas1/1603-10/pp265-277, accessed July 27, 2018.
24. The Spanish Company was chartered on May 31, 1605, to encourage English trade with merchants in Spain and Portugal. The company had received earlier Tudor charters, but it was revived under James I after the Treaty of London.
25. See, for instance, *His Majesties Speech in This Last Session of Parliament, as Neere His Very Words as Could Be Gathered at the Instant* (London, 1605), C2v–C3r. For additional discussion of this point see Nicolls, *Investigating Gunpowder Plot,* 37.
26. Dodd, "The Spanish Treason," 627–50.
27. "The Fate of the Richard, Henry Challons Captain, on Her Voyage to Mawooshen, 1606," in *New American World: A Documentary History of North America to 1612,* ed. David B. Quinn, with the assistance of Alison M. Quinn and Susan Hillier, 5 vols. (New York: Arno Press, 1979), 2:403–19; Henry O. Thayer, *The Sagadahoc Colony, Comprising the Relation of a Voyage into New England; (Lambeth Ms)* (Portland, ME: Gorges Society, 1892), 10–11; Strachey, *Historie of Travaile into Virginia Britannia,* 163.
28. France was a significant threat to Sagadahoc as well; the colonial settlement of Port Royal was founded in 1605. For additional discussion of the threat Spain presented to England's colonies, see also, Gerald P. Fogarty, *Commonwealth Catholicism: A History of the Catholic Church in Virginia* (Notre Dame, IN: University of Notre Dame Press, 2001), 8, 196; Emily Mann, "To Build and Fortify: Defensive Architecture in the Early Atlantic Colonies," in

Building the British Atlantic World: Spaces, Places, and Material Culture, 1600–1850, ed. Daniel Maudlin and Bernard L. Herman (Chapel Hill: University of North Carolina Press, 2016), 33.

29. Strachey, *Historie of Travaile into Virginia Britannia*, 173. Christopher Bilodeau and Alfred Cave also have pointed out the speed with which the colonists aggressively antagonized the Etchemins with catastrophic consequences: Bilodeau, "The Paradox of Sagadahoc: The Popham Colony, 1607–1608," *Early American Studies* 12, no. 1 (Winter 2014): 18.

30. Lord De la Ware, Sir Thomas Smith, Sir Walter Cope, and Master Waterson, *A True and Sincere Declaration of the Purpose and Ends of the Plantation Begun in Virginia* . . . (London, 1610), 3–4. The full sentence is: "but by this provision they may be seated as a Bulwarke of defence, in a place of advantage, against a stranger enemy, who shall in great proportion grow rich in treasure, which was exhausted to a lowe estate; and may well indure an increase of his people long wasted with a continual war, and dispersed uses and losses of them: Both which cannot choose but threaten us, if we consider, and compare the ends, ambitions and practices of our neighbor countries, with our owne."

31. Sir Ferdinando Gorges, a member of the Council for the North Virginia Colony, described competition for leadership and infighting among the Sagadahoc colonists in a December 1607 letter to the earl of Salisbury, in Quinn and Quinn, *English New England Voyages*, 332–33, 450. On the hardships caused by the severe winter, see, e.g., Quinn and Quinn, *English New England Voyages*, 334.

32. Wingfield was one of the men chosen by the Virginia Company to serve on the colony's council, which chose him as president in May 1607. John Smith clearly despised Wingfield and delighted in thwarting him at every turn. Wingfield, who had ordered Smith placed in irons for conspiracy to mutiny, returned the sentiment with gusto.

33. Edward Maria Wingfield, *A Discourse of Virginia*, in *Captain John Smith: Writings with Other Narratives of Roanoke, Jamestown, and the First English Settlement of America*, ed. James Horn (New York: Library of America, 2007), 962. Wingfield's account was not published until the nineteenth century. William M. Kelso, *Jamestown, the Buried Truth* (Charlottesville: University of Virginia Press, 2006), 187, offers a recent summary of the charges against Wingfield. The work of Kelso and his colleagues at the extraordinary Jamestown Rediscovery archaeology center has confirmed textual accounts of the terrible mortality in the early years.

34. Horn, ed., *Captain John Smith*, 963. See also Cynthia Kierner, *Inventing Disaster: The Culture of Calamity from the Jamestown Colony to the Johnstown Flood* (Chapel Hill: University of North Carolina Press, 2019), 28. I thank Karen Kupperman for suggesting I consider charges that Wingfield was a crypto-Catholic. Some popular histories insist that Wingfield was a Catholic, or a crypto-Catholic, pointing to his middle name "Maria" as evidence of his belonging to a Catholic family. His father's middle name also was Maria, so the use of the name dated from the period before England's split with Rome. I have found no evidence of Wingfield being a recusant or a crypto-Catholic, other than the accusations of his fellow colonists at Jamestown. See, e.g., R. C. Simmons, "Wingfield, Edward Maria (*b.* 1550, *d.* in or after 1619)," in *Oxford Dictionary of National Biography*, ed. H.C.G. Matthew and Brian Harrison (Oxford: Oxford University Press, 2004); online ed., ed. David Cannadine, October 2007, http://www.oxforddnb.com/view/article/29735, accessed August 15, 2016.

35. Horn, ed., *Captain John Smith*, 963. On the centrality of Protestantism in early Jamestown and the interconnected relationship of governance and religious belief, see Brent Tarter, "Evidence of Religion in Seventeenth-Century Virginia," in *From Jamestown to Jefferson: The Evolution of Religious Freedom in Virginia*, ed. Paul Rasor and Richard E. Bond (Charlottesville: University of Virginia Press, 2011), 17–42. Wingfield's almost lighthearted effort to

counter accusations that he worked for Spain is particularly interesting given Sir Walter Raleigh's inability to exonerate himself of such charges.

36. Kelso, *Jamestown, the Buried Truth,* 40.
37. See, *Oxford English Dictionary,* s.v. "atheist."
38. Wingfield's description is almost painful to read, given the seriousness of the charge and the string of circumstances out of his control that he claims led to it, Horn, ed., *Captain John Smith,* 963.
39. Horn, ed., *Captain John Smith,* 963.
40. Horn, ed., *Captain John Smith,* 965–66.
41. William Symonds, "The Epistle Dedicatorie," in *Virginia: A Sermon Preached at White-Chapel* (London, 1609), A3v, 19, 43–46.
42. Virginia Council, "Instructions, Orders and Constitucions . . . to . . . Sir Thomas West, Knight, Lord La Warr," in *The Three Charters of the Virginia Company of London with Seven Related Documents; 1606–1621,* Jamestown 350th Anniversary Historical Booklet Number 4 (Williamsburg: Virginia 350th Anniversary Celebration Corporation, 1957), 71, 73. Item eight ordered him to work to convert the natives to Christianity, which, I would argue early seventeenth-century English people also saw as an important blow to popery.
43. *Three Charters,* 74.
44. There is ample evidence that Spain received intelligence reports about Virginia. J. H. Elliott notes that Philip III never acted on them, because his main objective was to deal with the revolt of the Spanish Netherlands. However, it would not have been clear in the early seventeenth century that Spain would not take military action against the Virginia Colony, and the evidence I present here suggests the possibility that Philip III did indeed try to plant agents inside the Jamestown colony. On Spanish policy, see Elliott, "Iberian Atlantic and Virginia," 549–50. For additional material about Spanish views of Jamestown as a threat, and of English perceptions of the Spanish threat, see Goldman, "Spain and the Founding of Jamestown"; and Christopher Andrew, "The Decline of Early Stuart and Spanish Intelligence, and the Rise of the French Cabinet Noir," in *Secret World: A History of Intelligence* (New Haven: Yale University Press, 2018), 191–213.
45. See Wesley Frank Craven, *The Virginia Company of London, 1606–1624.* Jamestown 350th Anniversary Historical Booklet Number 5 (Williamsburg: Virginia 350th Anniversary Celebration Corporation, 1957), 15.
46. Kelso, *Jamestown, the Buried Truth,* 187, notes that, while the construction of the church shows the colonists' commitment to their faith, "it is curious, however, that almost all the religious artifacts in the Rediscovery collections are Catholic." See also the Jamestown Rediscovery website, where the archaeology team posts regular updates about their excavations. For Catholic worship items, including the crucifix, see historicjamestowne.org/collections/selected-artifacts/religion-2/; for the reliquary found on Captain Gabriel Archer's grave, see historicjamestowne.org/archaeology/chancel-burials/archaeology/reliquary/. For a popular account of the chancel burial and reliquary discovery, see Adrienne Lafrance, "A Skeleton, a Catholic Relic, and a Mystery about American Origins," *The Atlantic,* July 28, 2015. For Gabriel Archer, see http://www.EncyclopediaVirginia.org/Archer_Gabriel_ca_1574-ca_1610.
47. For a summary of the negotiations over the Spanish Match, see Patterson, *King James VI and I and the Reunion of Christendom,* 314–38.
48. For a thorough discussion of the role and membership of the commission, see Wesley Frank Craven, *Dissolution of the Virginia Company: The Failure of a Colonial Experiment* (Oxford: Oxford University Press, 1932), 326–27. Marvin Arthur Breslow, discussing puritan English writers who insisted that Spain and Catholic were synonyms, and that Spain represented

the great threat to England, argues that the emphasis on Spain became publicly and widely held by 1624, Marvin Arthur Breslow, *A Mirror of England: English Puritan Views of Foreign Nations, 1618–1640* (Cambridge, MA: Harvard University Press, 1970), 49–57. William Goldman, in "Spain and the Founding of Jamestown," argues that a Spanish faction was in fact laboring to destroy English Protestant power in North America, but that it was outmaneuvered by a different faction.

49. Calvert may well have regarded his efforts to establish a colony for English Catholics, first at Avalon and then at Maryland, as a continuation of Lord Arundell's 1605 plans. George Calvert's son, Cecilius, married Arundell's daughter Ann. For further discussion, see David Beers Quinn, *England and the Discovery of America, 1481–1620* (New York: Alfred A. Knopf, 1974), 396n7.

50. John D. Krugler, *English and Catholic: The Lords Baltimore in the Seventeenth Century* (Baltimore: Johns Hopkins University Press, 2004), 105, also suggests that Virginia was especially hostile to Calvert because of his role on the commission appointed to deal with the troubled colony. For a summary of the different affirmations that were required in the Oath of Allegiance of 1606 and a discussion of why the pope and Roman Catholics found the oath to be incompatible with Catholicism, see Patterson, *James VI and I and the Reunion of Christendom*, 76, 79–80. For additional discussion of Calvert, see, Robert Emmett Curran, "'To Sew the Holy Faith in His Land': The Calverts and the Beginnings of Catholic Settlement," in *Papist Devils: Catholics in British America, 1574–1783* (Washington, DC: Catholic University of America Press, 2014), 21–20.

Kirk and Crown

SCOTTISH PRESBYTERIAN ANTI-POPERY, 1550–1690

Craig Gallagher

LIKE THEIR PROTESTANT CONTEMPORARIES in England, Ireland, and colonial America, early modern Scots spent a lot of time worrying about popery. From almost the moment that the Scottish Reformation was secured, leading reformers like John Knox and George Buchanan had warned against Catholic plots to subvert their hard-won liberties and to reestablish popish tyranny. Oddly, though, historians of early modern Scotland have barely acknowledged anti-popery as an influence on the nation's history. Indeed, apart from recent scholarship on Scottish Catholics, there has been little work done on Protestant ideas about popery or Catholics more broadly in the century-and-a-half following the Scottish Reformation.[1] In general, early modern Scottish historians have touched on popery only to downplay its influence, because most have regarded contemporary fear of Catholics to be hyperbolic in a kingdom whose Catholic population was statistically insignificant between the Reformation and the mid-nineteenth-century influx of Irish immigrants associated with *An Ghorta Mor* (the Irish Potato Famine).[2] Scottish historians have thus assumed that anti-popery and anti-Catholicism required a tangible Catholic minority against which Protestants could direct their anger and anxiety to be credible. This view, however, has restricted detailed analysis of anti-popery in Scotland to works focusing on the nineteenth and twentieth centuries.[3]

What this narrow interpretation of anti-Catholic fears has obscured, however, is that in early modern Scotland, the majority of anti-popish concerns were directed at fellow British Protestants rather than Roman Catholics. Unlike the English, Scottish reformers had secured their Presbyterian Reformation in the teeth of determined royal opposition from Mary, Queen of Scots, in the 1560s. With English support, the Protestant Lords of the Congregation defeated and dethroned Mary, and then launched a Reformation that proved far more efficient than that of England in changing the religious affiliation of their countrymen and women. For many Scots, however, the precarious nature of their victory despite royal resistance instilled a constant fear that their nation might backslide once more into popish tyranny. That anxiety inspired a deep-seated suspicion among Scottish Presbyterians that their Stuart monarchs might be closeted papists.

Combined with their staunch anti-Erastian and anti-Episcopal beliefs, this mix of religious and political concerns gave Scottish anti-popery a particularly radical flavor in the seventeenth century. Most of those concerns emerged in defense of the Kirk that Knox, Buchanan, the earl of Moray, and the Lords of the Congregation had established in 1560—a mostly, but before 1690 not entirely, Presbyterian church governed by the General Assembly of Presbyterian ministers.[4] Unlike England, where royal supremacy was exercised through powerful bishops and archbishops, these Scots insisted that the highest ecclesiastical authority in the kingdom was the General Assembly, giving Scottish anti-popery a distinctly Presbyterian quality. In his seminal essay, Peter Lake carved out a special exception for Presbyterians, who embodied a radical populist strand of anti-popery because they "saw the rule of one minister over another as a direct emanation of the pope's tyrannical rule over the Church." Popes and bishops were proscribed as usurping agents of Antichrist whose claims to authority over individual ministers was a threat to their efforts to save souls. The Kirk recognized the suzerain authority of Mary's son, the young King James VI, after his coronation in 1567 but was careful to avoid declaring him to be the head of the national church because all Scots were equally part of Christ's earthly kingdom. As the Presbyterian rector of Glasgow University, Andrew Melville, reminded James VI in 1584, "Thair is Chryst Jesus the King, and his Kingdome the Kirk, whase subject King James the Saxt is, and of whose kingdome [he is] nocht a king, nor a lord, nor a heid, b[u]t a member!"[5] This aversion to episcopal and lay authority over the Kirk pulled Scottish Presbyterians into a long struggle between 1560 and 1690 to defend their Reformation that had, at its heart, a fundamental political rejection of the divine right of kings. Considered ungovernable radicals by several Stuart monarchs, Scottish Episcopalians, and even many of their fellow reformed Protestants, Scottish Presbyterians nevertheless stood firm against what they saw as the growing specter of absolutist, popish tyranny in Britain.

When early modern Scottish Presbyterians warned about popery, then, they were not usually pointing to a tangible threat posed by a minority Catholic population or rival Catholic empire. Instead, they were often talking about fellow Protestants, ranging from King Charles I to Archbishop James Sharp, whose episcopal or Erastian beliefs they considered dangerous.[6] Like many English and colonial American puritans, they were mistrustful of ecclesiastical hierarchies and quick to spy tyrannical intentions behind reforms that strengthened bishops or introduced new liturgies or ceremonies that deviated from scripture. But the peculiar national context of the Presbyterian Church of Scotland gave Scottish Presbyterian warnings about popery a political character that was more radical than English anxieties about a Catholic succession to the throne or a French invasion.[7] They believed the Kirk was a law unto itself in ecclesiastical affairs, and brooked no interference even from monarchs raised in their own confession, like James VI and I, or William III. Yet they also thought about popery as a global threat to Protestantism and carried the fight abroad in Europe during the Thirty Years' War, to England and Ireland during the Civil War, and to the Americas during the Restoration era. In short, Scottish Presbyterians sought to turn their own nation into an anti-popish example for all of Christendom, and aspired to remake Britain and its expanding global empire along the same lines.

Three flashpoints in the long post-Reformation struggle between Kirk and crown for control of Scottish religious affairs illustrate how Scottish Presbyterians moved from seeing anti-popery as a national cause to one with British, and then global and imperial implications. The political backlash to James I's Five Articles of Perth in 1618, the Covenanter rebellion against Charles I in 1638, and the creation of a Presbyterian exile community following the Restoration of Charles II in 1660 reveal the persistence and radicalness of Scottish Presbyterian anti-popery. Even their English, Dutch, French, and Swedish religious brethren believed their obsession with popery made them seem like radical zealots who sought to overturn the political and social order in the British realms. Nevertheless, as these events show, Scottish Presbyterians did not seek to reinvent British society so much as they sought to return it to the religious establishment they had created in their homeland at the beginning of their Reformation. Only such a Kirk could best protect Protestants from overreaching royal tyrants at home and abroad.

The Scottish Reformation began in kirk sessions and parish presbyteries that kept the wheels of local justice turning while the royal judiciary lay moribund under Queen Mary's regent, Mary of Guise, in the 1540s. In the course of the 1550s, Scottish reformers like John Knox and James Stewart, 1st Earl of Moray, succeeded in persuading most of their countrymen and women to reject their old beliefs and to embrace their strict Calvinist theology. When, in 1560, the Scottish Estates of Parliament voted to transform the Kirk from a Catholic to a Calvinist ecclesiastical polity, it merely established de jure what reformers had already de facto achieved. Building on the premise that the crown could not manage the affairs of the parish, Scottish Protestants had built their Reformation up from these local sources to create a Kirk that English puritans would envy. Altars and images were banished from the churches. Ministers did not wear the priestly garments, like the surplice, required for their English Protestant colleagues. Church services were based on sermons and Bible-reading. Popish holidays like Christmas were abolished. Parish

The Royall Orange Tree, Or a thankfull remembrance of Gods mercifull Deliverance of these three Kingdomes of England Scotland and Ireland from Popery and Slavery by the Prudent conduct of his Illustrious Highness the Prince of Orange now our Gracious King, engraving, 1691.

The tree grows out of portraits of King William and Queen Mary. Its individual "oranges" represent incidents from the Glorious Revolution, from King William's landing in England through his pacification of Scotland to the final Irish surrender at Limerick.

kirk sessions closely monitored individual's behavior within the community. After 1572, church members had to give a confession of their faith. Although the office of bishop was not yet abolished, the Presbyterian system replaced its role in administering the church. Having created this Kirk without royal input, Presbyterians intended to preserve it from royal interference.[8]

Presbyterian reformers owed much of their extraordinary success to a royal power vacuum. Between 1548 and 1584, their monarch was either absent or a minor or both. After the ouster of Mary, Queen of Scots in 1567, John Knox, George Buchanan, and the Lords of the Congregation were determined to secure the Scottish Reformation by ensuring that her son and heir, James VI, was raised as a staunch Protestant. Having battled against one Stuart monarch to secure religious reforms, Scotland's Protestant leaders sought to avoid doing battle with another. In the wake of the assassination of the king's uncle and regent, the Earl of Moray, Buchanan, the kingdom's most eminent historian and theologian, was appointed preceptor to the king in 1570. His responsibility was to educate James VI in matters of the law, statecraft, and religion, and to impress upon him that his royal title did not give him the authority to interfere with the autonomous General Assembly of the Kirk.

For Buchanan, the law, statecraft, and religion were fundamentally intertwined issues rooted in questions about whence the legitimate authority of a king derived. In 1579, he published *De Jure Regni apud Scotos* [The law of kingship among the Scots], which presented a debate over the source of royal authority Buchanan was purported to have had with Thomas Maitland of Lethington, a Catholic loyalist to Queen Mary who had died in 1572. As part of his provocative argument that the source of royal authority was the will of the people, he issued a diatribe against "the immoderat power, and unbridled Tyranny of the pope of Rome." Buchanan invoked the papacy as the original source of political usurpation in contemporary Europe, and he pointed to its arbitrary appointment of bishops over churches and parishes in Europe as its exemplary offense. He exclaimed to Maitland that, according to biblical law, "a Bishop must be the husband of one wife," by which Christ meant one church. Yet the pope had usurped the critical link between minister and church to enrich and empower tyrannical prelates across Europe. These bishops, by usurping Christ's authority within a parish, became irreligious tyrants akin to overreaching magistrates and kings in sixteenth-century Europe who ignored the will of the people as expressed through their ministers and presbyteries. The lesson, as Buchanan outlined in the book's dedication to his student, James VI, was that "A Kingdome is a principality of a Free man among free men: Tyranny is a principality of a Master over his slaves. For defence of a Kings safety the subjects watch and ward, For a Tyrant forrainers do watch to oppress the Subjects. The one beareth rule for the Subjects welfare, the other for himself." In other words, to avoid becoming a tyrant, the young King James ought to heed the settled ecclesiastical will of the people's tribunes, the ministers of the General Assembly.[9]

Buchanan, then, used anti-popish tropes to instill in Scotland's first Protestant monarch the belief that the Kirk and the crown were two separate pillars of Scottish institutional and theological life. To infringe on the former would be an act of despotism and tyranny by the latter akin to the worst crimes the pope had committed throughout Europe. Scottish Presbyterians were trying to raise a properly Presbyterian king aware of his ecclesiastical standing as another of Christ's subjects under the ministers in the General Assembly, which would preside alongside the king over an autonomous Kirk. James VI, it was hoped, would set the template for godly kingship for his successors and ensure that Scotland became a Protestant and Presbyterian example to all Christendom. To drive the point home, in 1581, they pressured the young king into signing the Negative Confession. Sometimes known as the first National Covenant, it repudiated papal and prelatical influence over the Kirk entirely. The following year, under the sway of the Presbyterian royal chaplain, John Craig, James assented to the Scottish Parliament's formal abolition of Episcopacy. These actions appeared to demonstrate the proper confessional humility Buchanan expected from the king. As it turned out, however, James soon came to resent the influence of Presbyterians on his education and developed his own sophisticated views on kingship that rejected these Presbyterian premises, and much of the anti-popery that went with it.[10]

Soon after assuming full control of his court in 1583, James VI began to demonstrate a clear preference for Scottish Episcopacy over Presbyterianism. He sought to install bishops and make himself the supreme royal governor of the Kirk in the same manner as his older cousin Elizabeth I ruled in England. James cultivated a power base among northeastern Scottish noblemen. They helped him promote an episcopal version of the Kirk in the Highlands and Islands. By capitalizing on the enduring loyalty of many Gaelic clansfolk to his dynasty, James undercut Presbyterian efforts to proselytize in these regions, promoting Episcopalian missionaries in their stead. Despite the counter-efforts of Scottish Jesuits, they rooted Catholicism out of all but the most remote Hebridean islands of Scotland.[11] By the time he inherited the English throne twenty years later, James VI had helped transform Scotland into the most thoroughly Protestant nation in Europe, as measured by how few Catholics remained. Yet he also ensured that Scotland was increasingly divided between two competing forms of Protestantism, the Episcopal and the Presbyterian. While individuals favoring either form of Kirk could be found across the country, the divide had a strong geographical dimension: Episcopalians were strongest in the northeast, thanks to the many conservative graduates of Aberdeen University; Presbyterians were strongest in the southwest, thanks partly to the more radical influence of Glasgow University.[12]

King James' efforts to claim some control over the Church of Scotland began in 1584, when he introduced legislation to the Scottish Parliament to affirm royal authority over the Kirk, partly by restoring royally appointed bishops to its government. These reforms came under heavy criticism from Presbyterians like James Craig and Andrew Melville, who labeled them the "Black Acts." From their pulpits, they railed against them as popish usurpations. Melville, called before a courtroom by the King's Bench to answer charges of sedition, "answered that he would not be [j]udged by the king & counsaile, because he had spoken the same in pulpit, which pulpit in effect he alleged to be exempted from the [j]udgement & correction of princes." Melville spoke for many ministers across Scotland when he argued that the Kirk was under attack by a lay authority who had no right to interfere in religious affairs. By rejecting religious hierarchy and the role of the crown in ecclesiastical affairs, he made popery a matter of the crown's prerogative powers and how they ought to be limited.[13] Nevertheless, Presbyterians did manage to compromise with the king by permitting two royal bishops who were to be subordinate to the General Assembly, a body whose ecclesiastical authority James VI thereafter dedicated himself to reducing.[14]

James was troubled by what he regarded as a challenge to his authority as king. For him, some of the most radical Presbyterians seemed as potentially threatening to monarchy as the Jesuits. While he famously claimed that he was "loath to be thought a Persecutor," he increasingly associated Presbyterians with "the *Puritans*, and *Novelists*" he encountered in England after assuming its throne. They were, he said in his first speech to the English Parliament in 1603, "a *Sect* rather than a Religion" since they "do not so far differ from us in points of Religion, as in their confused form of policy and parity, being ever discontented with the present Government, and impatient to suffer any superiority, which maketh their sect insufferable in any well-governed Commonwealth."[15] At the root of his contempt for Presbyterians, then, was their respective contempt for his claim to royal authority over ecclesiastical affairs.

A year later, during the debates over English Church policy at Hampton Court Palace, James made his most famous pronouncement about the connection between church and state: "No Bishop, No King."[16] Thereafter he began clamping down on Presbyterian dissent in his homeland and promoting Episcopal bishops committed to upholding the royal supremacy. In 1618, a heavily Episcopal General Assembly of the Church of Scotland agreed to the Five Articles of Perth, which created the Court of High Commission in Edinburgh, an ecclesiastical council composed of Scotland's bishops and the king's privy counselors. The commission, in turn, (re)introduced reforms to the Scottish liturgy that included kneeling at communion, setting aside the observance of holy days, and empowering bishops to ordain parish ministers.[17]

The commission also reduced the legal powers of local kirk sessions, which outraged many Presbyterians as this eliminated the source of their confessional power. Many parishes refused to comply with these mandates, including in the commission's own Edinburgh neighborhood, where every attempt to force through reforms was blocked by intransigent parish ministers unwilling to cede power from their local presbytery to a diocesan bishop. When combined with the general furor instigated by the Spanish Match—King James's attempt to marry his son and heir, Prince Charles, to the Infanta Maria Anna of Spain—it became clear to Scottish Presbyterians that James VI's delicate balance between Episcopalian and Presbyterian interests had given way to a policy of confessional uniformity across his three kingdoms.[18]

The reaction of leading Scottish Presbyterians to the Five Articles was predictably fierce. Beyond instigating local resistance to diocesan reforms, Presbyterian ministers and theologians raised a hue and cry about the tyrannical authority granted to the king's high commissioners. David Calderwood, a minister from Jedburgh in southern Scotland, spoke for many in 1621 when he lambasted the Court of High Commissioners as a cabal of "usurping Prelates" who "tyrannize over loyall subjects, faithfull Patriots, [and] conscientious professours" of the Presbyterian faith through Scotland. "What is this [council] but the Spanish inquisition?" he asked, rejecting the theological basis of the commission and its various mandates. Calderwood went so far as to use this Protestant Episcopalian council, one modeled on a comparable Anglican body which had succeeded in securing Protestantism in England, to raise the specter that, because the commission "sit[s] at the rudder, and may turn religion as it pleaseth them," then "Satan shall set up Papistry, or any other religion whatsoever in short processe of time" in Scotland.[19] For Calderwood, the practice of episcopal governance introduced the possibility that Catholicism would soon return in Scotland through the nefarious actions of a body that had usurped the political authority of the clergy.

Rather than associate with such impurity, parishioners began avoiding what was increasingly regarded as an "English" liturgy. In groups small and large they met to worship in homes, barns, fields, and valleys. Some of those gathering adopted a distinctively Scots Presbyterian custom of large, public, semi-annual communion festivals known as Holy Fairs, whereby hundreds of people from miles around would gather for three or four days of prayers, sermons, and intense religious experiences culminating in the breaking of bread at long tables at which men and women sat by the dozens to receive communion. Probably developed in the southwestern counties in the 1590s, they had become an important part of the region's Protestant culture by the 1610s, were carried over to Ulster in the 1620s, and eventually made their way to America along with Ulster Scots emigrants in the eighteenth century. These communal outdoors experiences had great appeal in rural areas, but also challenged the Jacobean Kirk by disregarding both the boundaries of parishes and the authority of bishops. It was also in the southwest that minister Samuel Rutherford elicited from a dying nobleman, John Gordon, in 1634 the admission that he believed the ceremonies introduced by the reforms of James and Charles were "plain Popery," "Idolatrous and Antichristian, and come from Hell." Only those "who are nick named Puritans," Gordon confessed, gave "comfort to my soul."[20]

This fundamental rejection of the royal levers of ecclesiastical power was more than a religious dispute for the Presbyterians. As the reign of James I's son Charles would show, the political stakes were high. Soon Scotland would set an example to the rest of Christendom in its quest to liberate Protestants from tyranny worldwide.

On February 28, 1638, five years after King Charles I had been crowned king of Scotland at Holyrood Palace in Edinburgh, an assembly of Scottish nobles, gentry, burgesses, and clergy gathered about a mile away in Greyfriars Kirkyard to rebuke him. These Scottish Presbyterians convened in opposition to reforms introduced over the past year by Charles and the archbishop of Canterbury, William Laud, imposing ecclesiastical and liturgical conformity with the Church of England on the Kirk. The assembled crowd affixed their signatures to the *National Covenant*, a document that repudiated King Charles's agenda and committed its subscribers to foreswear "the practice of all [in]novations already introduced in the matters of the worship of God" in Scotland. These Covenanters—as the subscribers would become known to history—expressed their firm belief that imposing Anglican conformity on Presbyterians could only "sensibly tend to the re-establishing of the popish religion and tyranny, and to the subversion and ruin of the true reformed religion, and of our liberties, laws, and estates." They accused their Protestant prince and his advisors of trying to usurp their religious liberties and imposing an arbitrary and tyrannical church government on them by dragooning them into performing "superstitious rights and ceremonies papistical," under the guidance of anti-Christian bishops reading from a Scottish *Book of Common Prayer* with no foundation in scripture. The accusation that Charles I sought to impose popish tyranny on his Scottish subjects was at the heart of the document that committed them to war with their own sovereign to defend what they saw as their rightful Presbyterian privileges.[21]

Charles I had wasted little time pushing for ecclesiastical convergence across his three British kingdoms following his ascension to the throne after the death of his father in 1625. In tandem with his archbishop of Canterbury, William Laud, the king had taken steps to concentrate political and religious authority in the crown in both Scotland and England, where he ruled by Privy Councils and High Commissions rather than by Parliaments or General Assemblies. In Scotland, his political reforms had ranged from reductions in the power of nobles over judicial matters in their lands to the empowerment of the Episcopal High Commission to act as a Privy Council in its own right. Liturgical reforms, meanwhile, included relatively innocuous changes such as the requirement that clerics in Scotland wear white rather than black robes, to transformational innovations like the introduction of a Scottish *Book of Common Prayer* that broke with the practice of strict Bible worship established in the Kirk at the Reformation.

The introduction of a Scottish *Book of Common Prayer* provoked widespread rioting in many Scottish towns on the day it was introduced in 1637, leading to the formation of a Presbyterian organization known as "The Tables" that pledged to restore Scottish Presbyterianism to its Reformation-era precedents. One of the leaders of the Tables was George Gillespie, a private chaplain to the staunchly Presbyterian Earl of Cassilis who would go on to help write the Westminster Confession. Gillespie decried the introduction of "English-popish ceremonies" in Scottish worship, and pledged that the Tables would fight "for the Trueth of God against the errors of men, for the purity, of Christ against the corruptions of Antichrist" amid royal efforts to usurp their Protestant liberties.[22] Although the Tables would be roundly rejected as a confessional body by the king, they provoked a furious conversation among Scottish Protestants about the proper relationship between their monarch and matters of faith.

By early 1638, with the signing of the *National Covenant*, the widespread discontent with the Caroline reforms had become an open rebellion. The General Assembly gathered in November 1638 to complain of "the many and great innovations and corruptions lately by the Prelats and their adherents intruded into the doctrine, worship, and discipline of this Church, which had beene before in great puritie to our unspeakable comfort established amongst us." It then declared the Church of Scotland to be a Presbyterian church and abolished episcopacy.[23] In order to justify their repudiation of the king's policies, the Covenanters were careful to accuse his advisors—and chiefly Laud—of being "the authours of our novations, and the arch-enemies of reformation, [who] have labored to poison his Majesties sacred Ears." They argued that the king had to conform to the tenets staked out in the *National Covenant* and recognize he had no right to arbitrarily interfere in Scottish ecclesiastical matters without the consent of the Kirk and Parliament.[24] Many leading Covenanters were careful to stake out legal justifications for their rebellion that held Episcopacy to be an affront to divine law, to which civil law must remain subject.[25] King Charles, of course, did not agree and went to war to enforce his edicts in his northern realm. But the Scottish Army of the Covenant, which drew upon veterans of the Thirty Years' War who had rallied to the Protestant standard of King Gustavus Adolphus of Sweden in 1630, defeated his royal army. An aborted royal invasion of Scotland in 1639 was followed in 1640 by Covenanter victories in northern England that led to the Scottish occupation of Newcastle. Charles I was forced to repeal his ecclesiastical reforms and to turn to the English

Parliament for money to continue fighting the Scots. But English politicians were quick to use their newfound leverage against him. Within a few years, the Long Parliament had taken up arms against the king as well.[26]

In the 1640s, what began as a rebellion to restore the gains of the Scottish Reformation and Scotland's status as a Protestant example to all Christendom transformed into a grand campaign to entirely root out popery from the three British kingdoms. Emboldened by their victories in the Bishops' Wars, Scottish Presbyterians seized the political and ecclesiastical levers of power in their homeland and restored the Kirk to its proper Presbyterian settlement. They then turned to exporting their confession abroad. In 1642, they sent an army to Ulster to help defend their Presbyterian cousins from the Catholic Confederate uprising in Ireland. Reformed Protestants in the other Stuart realms lauded the Covenanters for this intervention. One English commentator commended their efforts to relieve "the extreame misery, and calamity that the Protestants in Ireland are daily involved in," which he credited to their "owne, free, and spontaneous will . . . to goe Voluntarily in Ireland to helpe and relieve the said poore Protestantes."[27] In 1643, meanwhile, they struck a deal with the English Parliamentary forces to intervene against royal troops in England, where they played a critical role in the Parliamentary victory at Marston Moor in 1644. Their intervention was especially welcome among the majority Presbyterian faction at Westminster, whom Edward Bowles spoke for when he declared the English and Scots unified to refute "the jealousie that Parliaments and Puritans are Enemies to [Charles I's] Prerogative and Power." They were instead "defending our-selves against the confederacie of Papists, Prelates, Court Parasites, and their Adherents, whose endeavours of introducing Popery and Tyranny, are farre beyond jealousie."[28] Together with English and Irish Presbyterians, the Covenanters sought to defeat the embodiments of popery throughout Britain and Ireland.[29]

The alliance between the Covenanters and other Presbyterian factions across Britain was set out in the *Solemne League and Covenant*, the formal agreement they signed with English Parliamentarians in 1643. In return for Scottish assistance against the king, the English Parliament committed to establishing Presbyterianism in the Churches of England and Ireland. Their collective ambition was for Britain as a whole to become a bastion against popery at home and abroad. The *Solemne League*'s preamble declared its subscribers to be for "the Extirpation of Popery, Prelacy, [meaning] Church government by Archbishops, Bishops, their Chancellors and Commissaries, Deans, Deans and Chapters, Archdeacons, and all other Ecclesiastical Officers depending on that hierarchy; Superstition, Heresie, Schisme, [and] Prophaneness." They targeted ecclesiastical hierarchy as a popish affront to the authority of the clergy, and likened it to the same schismatic heresy practiced by Anabaptists, Quakers, and Fifth Monarchists. And while the subscribers to the *Solemne League* did not repudiate monarchy, they did declare the king's prerogative powers to be forfeit, and expressed hope that this measure might give "encouragement to the Christian Churches groaning under, or in danger of the yoke of Antichristian Tyranny" elsewhere in Europe.[30] Although the *Solemne League* did not survive the rise of Oliver Cromwell and his New Model Army, it nevertheless served as a rallying cry for Scottish Presbyterians who sought to resist and undo popish tyranny across Britain for the next half-century.

Despite the early successes enjoyed by the Covenanters during the Wars of the Three Kingdoms, their ambition to create an anti-popish Presbyterian British realm lost steam during the late 1640s. The Covenanters began to lose their military and political advantages after leading Scottish Presbyterians extracted a commitment from Charles I to embrace their confession should they help restore his authority. This futile Engager cause contributed to the Second Civil War, which led to Charles I's execution in 1649. Leading Covenanters then blackmailed his son and heir, Charles II, into the same promises in return for restoring him to his English and Irish thrones. Charles II subscribed to the Covenants, an oath many would later hold against him after the Restoration when he followed his father and grandfather in supporting Episcopacy in Scotland. This second attempt to restore the Stuarts to the throne also failed, and Oliver Cromwell toppled the Covenanters from power in Scotland in 1651. Nevertheless, Scottish Presbyterians had convinced two monarchs to give their cause legitimacy, strengthening their broader argument that Presbyterianism was the rightful system of church government for the British kingdoms. Their unwavering faith in their cause would sustain a simmering resistance to Charles II's regime after he finally regained his crown in 1660. Eventually it would inspire widespread Scottish support for the Glorious Revolution in 1688.[31]

Following two decades of devastating civil warfare, the Stuart monarchy had emerged stronger than ever in its ancestral homeland. Upon his Restoration to the throne in 1660, Charles II entrusted his government in Scotland to the former Covenanter-turned-royalist John Maitland, 2nd Earl of Lauderdale. As royal commissioner, Lauderdale's determination to defend the royal prerogative was matched only by his zeal for suppressing the king's critics. In 1661, the king instructed Lauderdale to ensure that the Scottish Parliament disestablished Presbyterianism in the Kirk and restored Episcopacy once more, albeit in a form reminiscent of the restrained Jacobean Kirk of the late sixteenth century rather than the High Anglican Episcopate his father had instituted. Lauderdale also restored the royal supremacy over ecclesiastical affairs in Scotland to ensure that Charles II had greater control over Scottish confessional and political life than either his father and grandfather had enjoyed.[32]

Even in the war-weary years of the early Restoration era, however, Scottish Presbyterians remained determined to challenge the king's sweeping new powers as popish usurpations of their rights. Many were particularly embittered by the punitive measures Lauderdale embraced to enforce conformity with the new Church order, including fines levied on anyone who was absent from Episcopal services on Sundays, and a demand that any minister who sought to retain his parish repudiate the Covenants and the Presbyterian establishment. Ministers who refused to conform again took to preaching to their congregations in secluded fields and vales. To crack down on these open-air services known as conventicles, Lauderdale's regime set out to defrock any minister who refused to swear oaths to the crown and renounce the Covenants, including many in the Presbyterian heartlands of southwestern Scotland. He also recruited Highland soldiers who remained loyal to Scottish Episcopacy and quartered them in the homes of suspected Presbyterian dissidents.

Violent incidents between Lowland Presbyterians and Highland troops steadily increased after 1662, until tensions boiled over into an uprising against Lauderdale in 1666. Recalling that Charles II had subscribed to the Covenants in 1651, two and a half thousand Scots took to the Pentland Hills near Edinburgh in an attempt to force the king to hold to his promise "att his coronation [to] engadge to rule the nation according to the revealed will of God in scripture [and] to prosecute ye [rules] of ye nationall and Solemne League and covenants and [to] fullie to establish presbitourial government." They complained of specific popish abuses committed by Lauderdale, such as "Greivous fines, Sudden Imprisonments, vast quarterings of Souldiers, [and] cruell Inquisitions by ye High Commission of ye false Kirk."[33] Unfortunately, few Protestants elsewhere in the Stuart realms offered them much support, as many were weary of war after two decades of conflict. The brief rising achieved little more than solidifying the king's civil authority and painting Scottish Presbyterians as seditious and ungovernable troublemakers.[34]

The failed Pentland Rising precipitated a widespread royal crackdown on Scottish Presbyterians, especially those who still adhered to the tenets of the Covenants or had been involved in previous rebellions against the crown. Rather than face imprisonment or forcible conversion, many chose exile, fleeing to nations and colonies overseas where they expected a warmer welcome. A number went to the Dutch Republic, where exiles of all stripes tended to find refuge, or Dutch colonies abroad like New Netherland and Suriname. The Dutch protected the king's most vociferous Scottish critics from extradition to Britain on charges of sedition. These included John Livingston, a former Covenanting leader, and James Stuart of Goodtrees, a radical lawyer who argued for a right to resist monarchs. As a result, the Scottish exile community grew in Amsterdam, Rotterdam, and Utrecht in the 1670s and 1680s, as Scots sought out ministerial and mercantile career opportunities that were denied to them at home.[35] In New Netherland, the Dutch had close relations with their puritan neighbors in New England. This allowed young Scots such as John Borland to leave Scotland to pursue their careers abroad in places like Boston. John and his brother Francis—an aspiring Presbyterian minister—benefitted from the patronage of the Livingston family and a Scottish Rotterdam merchant, Andrew Russell, who helped them forge ties to elite Boston puritans like Cotton Mather and Samuel Sewall. These ties were rooted in their mutual mistrust of the Restoration monarchy and their aversion to popery and tyranny in the wider British Empire. Later Scottish Presbyterian exiles favored English colonies like Pennsylvania, the Carolinas, and East New Jersey, where concerns about popery suffused local debates over proprietary rights, royal influence, the spread of Anglicanism, and even commercial regulation. The militancy of Scottish Presbyterian anti-popery fit comfortably in these environments where French allied with Native Americans taught by Jesuit missionaries loomed over New England and New York's northern frontier, while Spanish Florida threatened Carolina in the south. Robert Livingston's lamentation that "a cloud of popery hangs over our heads" echoed the fears of many English Americans.[36]

A shared aversion to popery and arbitrary government in civil and ecclesiastical affairs forged bonds between Scottish Presbyterians, Dutch Calvinists, and English puritans and gave Scots a welcome in the English empire decades before the British Union of 1707. Overseas, the radical anti-popish beliefs of Scottish Presbyterians seemed mainstream. Their inherent suspicion of the prerogative powers claimed by the Stuarts found common cause with other British Protestants following the revelations known as the "Popish Plot" in 1678. Although Titus Oates had invented the conspiracy to murder Charles II, the problem that it posed—the succession to the throne of the King's Catholic brother, James, Duke of York—was acute and stirred significant anti-popish feeling across the three kingdoms and the colonies. Amid the subsequent political battle over the succession that came to be known as the Exclusion Crisis, the newly ennobled duke of Lauderdale took steps to head off Presbyterian unrest in Scotland by hiring more Highland militias to police the countryside. In response to further violence, a group of disaffected Presbyterians assassinated the archbishop of St. Andrews, James Sharp, in May 1679. His murder sparked a second Presbyterian rebellion against Lauderdale. Attendees at an illicit conventicle at Loudon Hill near Ayr attacked a royal brigade after its commander, John Grahame of Claverhouse, demanded they disperse. Their disdainful quip in response to the royalist's order gained them some notoriety: "Farts in the Kings Teeth, and the Counsell, and all that h[a]s sent you, For wee appear her for the King of H[eaven]."[37] Although the uprising was ultimately crushed at Bothwell Brig a month later, it brought about the downfall of Lauderdale in Scotland. It also provoked a turn toward more repressive martial government by the Restoration regime.[38]

The Tory reaction that followed the rebellion in 1679 left Scottish Presbyterians as far from their goal of a godly Presbyterian realm as they had been since the Reformation. The Duke of York was appointed as Lauderdale's replacement in 1680 to keep him out of the public eye in London, where the Exclusion Crisis still raged. His regime deported Presbyterian dissidents to the colonies, particularly to those like East Jersey and Pennsylvania whose proprietors, such as Robert Barclay of Urie or William Penn, were his personal friends. Worse, York sought to promote tolerance for Catholics in Edinburgh (against the advice of his Episcopal advisors on the Privy Council).[39] Both approaches to confessional justice appalled Protestant onlookers in Scotland, England, and abroad, who feared such things would become official policy once York became king.

Their fears were prescient. Despite a joint rebellion by Protestant noblemen, the Duke of Monmouth in England and the Duke of Argyll in Scotland, to prevent his coronation, King James II ascended to his throne upon his brother's death in 1685. As king, James II continued to promote Catholic toleration in Britain and the colonies. His rule confounded Scottish Presbyterians, however, for despite being a "profest papist" who claimed an "arbitrary despotic power" over his subjects, he also extended toleration to them in the form of indulgences to return to Scotland and take up parishes in the Kirk.[40] His olive branch fractured the community between those who accepted it and those who condemned them as "Confederating with Malignant Usurpers."[41] These reactionaries feared that the indulgences undermined their claim to sole religious legitimacy in Scotland by normalizing toleration as a confessional policy throughout the three kingdoms.[42] The king's indulgences may have allowed Presbyterians to practice their religion openly for the first time since the Restoration, and thus to become ecclesiastical rivals to Scottish Episcopalians, but James II remained as far from their ideal monarch as it was possible to be.[43]

Nevertheless, the rise of a Catholic heir to the British thrones validated a century of warnings issued by Scottish Presbyterians about the ever-present specter of popery. Their reputation *rose* among their fellow British Protestants. In the colonies, English governors were eager to welcome Scottish Presbyterian subjects as a bulwark against their French and Spanish rivals. Joseph Morton, for example, struck a deal with Lord Cardross to settle a Covenanter colony near modern day Port Royal, South Carolina.[44] In the Netherlands, meanwhile, leading exiles like the minister William Carstares joined the court of William of Orange, husband to Mary Stuart, the eldest daughter of James II. As William's personal chaplain, Carstares played a leading role in the Dutch invasion of England in the fall of 1688 that caused James to flee the country and be replaced by William III and Mary II as co-monarchs.[45] Carstares was then instrumental in securing a Presbyterian settlement for the Kirk at the Glorious Revolution. The Presbyterian cause was aided by the refusal of leading Scottish Episcopal bishops to foreswear James II while he still lived. A sizable moderate faction quelled efforts by Alexander Shields and others to resubscribe to the Covenants and launch another campaign to expand their faith throughout Britain, but Presbyterians finally had the ecclesiastical and political autonomy they had long craved. Their warnings about a popish threat to the British throne had come true, and in the wake of British Protestants uniting to defeat it in 1688, they had once more claimed the mantle of a Presbyterian and reformed example to all Christendom.[46]

The insistent anti-popery of Scottish Presbyterians brought on decades of suffering through rebellion, exile, and emigration, but would ultimately see them redeemed as pillars of the anti-popish empire by 1690. Their once radical stance against religious and political tyranny became a broadly held consensus in Britain and British America. Even then, however, Scottish Presbyterians stood out as particularly radical compared to their peers, as other historians of anti-popish Protestants around the British world have pointed out.[47] However, by placing Scottish anti-popery in the context of scholarship on early modern England and colonial America, which has demonstrated anti-popery's efficacy as an ideological and political impetus of reformed Protestants to push for, or to resist, reforms to civil and ecclesiastical institutions at both the local and the imperial level, Scottish Presbyterians clearly fit well within a broader pattern—albeit in the extraordinary circumstances of Scotland.

Scotland achieved a Reformation that was as thorough as any in Europe in the mid-sixteenth century, in terms of Catholics left unconverted in its wake, but at the expense of driving a wedge between its monarch and the Presbyterian Kirk. Their Reformation had been more radical than the English one, taking root despite the opposition of a Catholic monarch. It then had two decades to consolidate while James VI was still a child, allowing it gain maturity without significant royal influence. Thereafter, Protestant monarchs wary of the Kirk's independence, up through and including William III, favored some sort of role for bishops in the national church. As a result, whenever Scots sought to either advance or defend their Presbyterian faith between the Reformation in 1560 and the Treaty of Union in 1707, they came into conflict with their monarch over confessional conformity, ecclesiastical hierarchy, and the extent to which infringing on the autonomy of the clergy represented popish tyranny.

Despite the fact that the pope held little sway in political matters within early modern Britain and there were few Catholics present in Scotland who presented a tangible threat, anti-popish beliefs justified Presbyterians' refusal to compromise. In the Jacobean era they stood alone as radicals because they believed the monarch's preference for bishops would lead to obtain arbitrary and tyrannical authority akin to what they believed the pope wielded over Catholic worshippers. Presbyterianism, they insisted, was the only viable bastion against such designs. It was the only mainstream confession that rejected prelacy and modeled church government to empower individual clergy according to what they saw as the original wishes of Christ. Embracing the Covenants between 1638 and 1643, Scottish Presbyterians then became committed to building a Protestant redoubt throughout the three kingdoms, to serve as the ultimate anti-popish example to all Christendom. Although they were defeated and forced into exile between 1651 and 1688, leaving their prospects for Presbyterian supremacy hanging by a thread, events conspired to make their aversion to popery ever more compelling to British Protestants. At their political nadir, Scottish Presbyterians suddenly could claim *bona fides* as anti-popish, anti-Stuart activists that earned them friends and patrons in Europe and North America. Their ultimate victory following the Glorious Revolution reduced the immediate popish threat and allowed Scottish Presbyterians to build on these links over the next century. But their descendants and heirs kept alive the memory of their struggle. Especially in the New World, they stood vigilant against the prospect that the British monarchy might overreach into their affairs once more in 1776.

Notes

1. See, for example, Allan I. Macinnes, "Catholic Recusancy and the Penal Laws, 1603–1707," *Records of the Scottish Church History Society* [hereafter *SCHS*] 23 (1987): 27–63; Michael A. Mullett, *Catholics in Britain and Ireland, 1558–1829* (New York: St. Martin's Press, 1998), 102–19; and R. Scott Spurlock, "'I Do Disclaim Both Ecclesiasticke and Politick Popery': Lay Catholic Identity in Early Modern Scotland," *SCHS* 38 (2008): 5–22.
2. See the otherwise robust works by Arthur Williamson, "Scotland, Antichrist, and the Invention of Great Britain," in *New Perspectives on the Politics and Culture of Early Modern Scotland*, ed. John Dwyer, Roger A. Mason, and Alexander Murdoch (Edinburgh: John Donald, 1982), 34–58; David George Mullan, *Scottish Puritanism, 1590–1638* (New York: Oxford University Press, 2000), 1–12; Alasdair Raffe, "The Restoration, the Revolution, and the Failure of Episcopacy in Scotland," in *The Final Crisis of the Stuart Monarchy: The Revolutions of 1688–91 in Their British, Atlantic and European Contexts*, ed. Tim Harris and Stephen Taylor (Woodbridge: Boydell Press, 2013), 87–108.
3. See, for example, the collected the essays in Raymond Boyle and Peter Lynch, eds., *Out of the Ghetto? The Catholic Community in Modern Scotland* (Edinburgh: John Donald, 1998); and T. M Devine, ed., *Scotland's Shame?: Bigotry and Sectarianism in Modern Scotland* (Edinburgh: Mainstream, 2000).
4. The capitalized word Kirk is a colloquial term for the established Presbyterian Church of Scotland, "kirk" more generally meant a church in early modern Scotland (and northern England).
5. Quoted in a diary written by his nephew, James Melville. See Robert Pitcairn, ed., *The Autobiography and Diary of Mr. James Melvill, with a Continuation of the Diary* (Edinburgh: Wodrow Society, 1848), 370.

6. On anti-Erastian ideas among Scottish Presbyterians, see Colin Kidd, "Conditional Britons: The Scots Covenanting Tradition and the Eighteenth-Century British State," *English Historical Review* 117, no. 474 (2002): 1147–76.
7. On anti-popery among other British Protestants, see J. F. Bosher, "The Franco-Catholic Danger, 1660–1715," *History* 79, no. 255 (1994): 5–30; Brendan McConville, *The King's Three Faces: The Rise and Fall of Royal America, 1688–1776* (Chapel Hill: University of North Carolina Press, 2006), 105–41; Owen Stanwood, *The Empire Reformed: English America in the Age of the Glorious Revolution* (Philadelphia: University of Pennsylvania Press, 2011), 1–23.
8. On the Scottish Reformation see, among others, Gordon Donaldson, *The Scottish Reformation* (Cambridge: Cambridge University Press, 1990); Clare Kellar, *Scotland, England, and the Reformation, 1534–1561* (Oxford: Oxford University Press, 2003); Alec Ryrie, *The Origins of the Scottish Reformation* (Manchester: Manchester University Press, 2010). On kirk sessions and the Scottish Reformation, see Michael F. Graham, *The Uses of Reform: "Godly Discipline" and Popular Behavior in Scotland and Beyond, 1560–1610* (Boston: Brill, 1996), 130–62; and Margo Todd, *The Culture of Protestantism in Early Modern Scotland* (New Haven: Yale University Press, 2002), 1–23, 361–412.
9. George Buchanan, *De Jure Regni apud Scotos; or, A Dialogue, Concerning the Due Priviledge of Government in the Kingdom of Scotland, betwixt George Buchanan and Thomas Maitland* (Edinburgh, 1680), 45, 46, 67.
10. On the early political wrangling around the Jacobean Kirk, see Alan R. MacDonald, *The Jacobean Kirk, 1567–1625: Sovereignty, Polity, and Liturgy* (Brookfield: Ashgate, 1998), 6–29.
11. On the sixteenth-century Highlands and Islands, see Jane Dawson, "Calvinism and the *Gaidhealtachd* in Scotland," in *Calvinism in Europe, 1540–1620*, ed. A. C. Duke, Gillian Lewis, and Andrew Pettegree (New York: Cambridge University Press, 1994), 231–53; and Allan I. MacInnes, *Clanship, Commerce, and the House of Stuart, 1603–1788* (East Linton: Tuckwell Press, 1996), 1–30. On James VI's ecclesiastical policies in both regions, see Fiona A. MacDonald, *Missions to the Gaels: Reformation and Counter-Reformation in Ulster and the Highlands and Islands of Scotland* (Edinburgh: John Donald, 2006), 11–54. On Jesuit attempts to revitalize Catholicism in Scotland, see Mullett, *Catholics in Britain and Ireland*, 33–54.
12. Gordon Donaldson, "The Emergence of Schism in Seventeenth-Century Scotland," and "Scotland's Conservative North in the Sixteenth and Seventeenth Centuries," in his *Scottish Church History* (Edinburgh: Scottish Academic Press, 1985), 191–203, 204–19; David George Mullan, *Episcopacy in Scotland: The History of an Idea, 1560–1638* (Edinburgh: John Donald, 1986).
13. Quoted in Christopher Studley, *Treason pretended against the King of Scots by certaine lordes and gentlemen, whose names hereafter followe; With a declaration of the Kinges Maiesties intention to his last acts of Parliament: which openeth fully in effect of all the saide conspiracy; Out of Skottish into English* (London: 1585), f. 4.
14. On the "Black Acts" and ecclesiastical compromise in the 1580s, see W. B. Patterson, *King James VI and I and the Reunion of Christendom* (New York: Cambridge University Press, 1997), 1–30; MacDonald, *Jacobean Kirk*, 50–100; and Tim Harris, *Rebellion: Britain's First Stuart Kings, 1567–1642* (Oxford: Oxford University Press, 2014), 45–62.
15. Charles Howard McIlwain, ed., *The Political Works of James I* (Cambridge, MA: Harvard University Press, 1918), 276; Arthur Wilson, *The History of Great Britain, Being the Life and Reign of King James the First* (London, 1653), 18–19; Peter Lake, "The King (the Queen) and the Jesuit: James Stuart's *True Law of Free Monarchies* in Context/s," *Transactions of the Royal*

Historical Society 14 (2004): 243–60; Pauline Croft, *King James* (Houndsmills, Basingstoke, Hants.: Palgrave Macmillan, 2003), esp. 10–47.

16. William Barlow, *The Summe and Substance of the Conference . . . at Hampton Court* (London, 1604), F2v, Mv.
17. On James and the Scottish Kirk, see Macdonald, *Jacobean Kirk*. On the Five Articles, see John D. Ford, "Conformity in Conscience: The Structure of the Perth Articles Debate in Scotland, 1618–38," *Journal of Ecclesiastical History* 46, no. 2 (1995): 256–77.
18. On the fallout among Presbyterians, see Laura A. M. Stewart, "The Political Repercussions of the Five Articles of Perth: A Reassessment of James VI and I's Religious Policies in Scotland," *Sixteenth Century Journal* [hereafter *16CJ*] 38, no. 4 (2007): 1013–36.
19. David Calderwood, *The altar of Damascus or the patern of the English hierarchie, and Church policie obtruded upon the Church of Scotland* (Edinburgh, 1621), 38–39.
20. Anon., *The Last and Heavenly Speeches, and Glorious Departure of John Viscount Kenmuir* (Edinburgh, 1649), 15, 18; Leigh Eric Schmidt, *Holy Fairs: Scottish Communions and American Revivals in the Early Modern Period* (Princeton, NJ: Princeton University Press, 1989), 21–32. John Coffey, *Politics, Religion, and the British Revolutions: The Mind of Samuel Rutherford* (Cambridge: Cambridge University Press, 1997), 17–25, discusses the applicability of the term "puritan" in the Scottish case.
21. There were many copies of the *National Covenant* printed after its initial signing. For the version consulted and quoted from for this chapter, see "National Covenant [copy]," Huntly Papers, Adv.MS.20.6.15, National Library of Scotland [hereafter NAS].
22. Quotes from George Gillespie, *A Dispute against the English-Popish Ceremonies, Obtruded Vpon the Church of Scotland Wherein Not Only Our Ovvne Argumemts against the Same Are Strongly Confirmed, but Likewise the Ansvveres and Defences of Our Opposites, such as Hooker, Mortoune . . . Forbesse, &c. Particularly Confuted* (Leiden: W. Christiaens, 1637), 11–12. On popular opposition to Charles I's reforms in Scotland, see Laura A. M. Stewart, *Rethinking the Scottish Revolution: Covenanted Scotland, 1637–1651* (New York: Oxford University Press, 2016), 29–86.
23. *The Protestation of the Generall Assemblie of the Church of Scotland, and of the Nobleman, Barons, Gentlemen, Borrowes, Ministers, and Commons* (London, 1638), A2r–v; Allan I. Macinnes, *Charles I and the Making of the Covenanting Movement, 1625–1641* (Edinburgh: John Donald Publishers, 1991), 49–213.
24. Quote from the General Assembly of the Kirk, *An Information to All Good Christians Vvithin the Kingdome of England, from the Noblemen, Barrons, Borrows, Ministers, and Commons of the Kingdome of Scotland, for Vindicating Their Intentions and Actions from the Unjust Callumnies of Their Enemies* (Edinburgh, 1639), 4.
25. Robert Baillie was one such minister. See F. N. McCoy, *Robert Baillie and the Second Scots Reformation* (Berkeley: University of California Press, 1974), 1–12. Samuel Rutherford was an exception to this, because he valued natural law, as befit his scholastic training, to justify religious rebellion. See Coffey, *Mind of Samuel Rutherford*, 1–29.
26. On Scottish veterans from the Swedish campaign, see Steve Murdoch, "Beating the Odds: Alexander Leslie's 1640 Campaign in England," in *Fighting for Identity: Scottish Military Experience, c. 1550–1900*, ed. Andrew MacKillop and Steve Murdoch (Boston: Brill, 2002), 33–60.
27. Quotes from Anon., *A glorious victory obtained by the Scots against the rebels in Ireland Shewing in a very true, and warrantable relation how the Scots to the number of two thousand five hundred and fifty went voluntarily into Ireland vnder the command of Colonell Hayse to relieve the poore distressed Protestants there the last day of Decem. 1641. With the number of those rebels that they*

slew, and the names of some townes where they pillaged the same, wherein the rebels inhabited, and had first taken from the Protestants (London, 1642), 21.

28. Quotes from Edward Bowles, *The mysterie of iniqvity yet working in the kingdomes of England, Scotland, and Ireland, for the destruction of religion truly Protestant discovered, as by other grounds apparant and probable, so especially by the late cessation in Ireland, no way so likely to be ballanced, as by a firme union of England and Scotland, in the late solemne covenant, and a religious pursuance of it* (London, 1643), 4.
29. On the Scottish Covenanters and their engagement with Ireland and England in the early 1640s, see Allan I. MacInnes, *The British Revolution, 1629–1660* (Basingstoke: Palgrave Macmillan, 2005), 111–92; and Stewart, *Rethinking the Scottish Revolution*, 171–213.
30. As with the *National Covenant*, many extant copies of the *Solemne League and Covenant* exist. For the copy consulted for this piece, see *A Solemn League and Covenant, for Reformation, and Defence of Religion, the Honor and Happinesse of the King, and the Peace and Safety of the Three Kingdoms of England, Scotland and Ireland. Together with a Preamble, Made by a Worthy Member of the House of Commons, to Invite All Good Christians to the Constant Keeping of It* (London, 1643), 7.
31. On the Engagement to restore Charles I, and the subsequent effort to restore Charles II, see MacInnes, *British Revolution*, 152–92. The Engagement was a formal political event whose adherents were known as the Engagers. See here for the basics: https://en.wikipedia.org/wiki/Engagers.
32. As Tim Harris has argued, the Scottish civil law system gave Charles II more latitude to impose royal reforms in his northern realm than he enjoyed in England, and thus he came closer to being a de jure absolute monarch in Scotland than anywhere else. See his *Restoration: Charles II and His Kingdoms, 1660–1685* (New York: Penguin, 2006), 85–135; and also Clare Jackson, *Restoration Scotland, 1660–1690: Royalist Politics, Religion, and Ideas* (Woodbridge: Boydell Press, 2003), 14–44.
33. Quotes from a handwritten copy of the "Declaration by the Pentland Rebels," dated November 1666, Lauderdale Papers, vol. XIII, Add MS 23125, 198, British Library [hereafter BL].
34. On the ambivalence of other Protestants to Covenanter rebels after 1660, see Jackson, *Restoration Scotland*, 104–30.
35. On the Dutch Republic's extradition policy toward the government of Charles II, see James Walker, "The English Exiles in Holland during the Reigns of Charles II and James II," *Transactions of the Royal Historical Society* 30 (1948): 111–25. On the Scottish community in the Netherlands more generally, see Ginny Gardner, *The Scottish Exile Community in the Netherlands, 1660–1690: "Shaken Together in the Bag of Affliction"* (East Linton: Tuckwell Press, 2004); and Esther Mijers, *"News from the Republick of Letters": Scottish Students, Charles Mackie, and the United Provinces, 1650–1750* (Boston: Brill, 2012).
36. Quoted in Robert Livingston to Andrew Russell, July 23, 1683, RH15/106/494/30, NAS. On concerns about popery in the colonies during the reigns of Charles II and James II, see Stanwood, *Empire Reformed*, 85–112.
37. Quote from Claverhouse's report on the skirmish, entitled "Lasmahago, a Good Accompt of the Action There to Yt the Rebel Compny," dated August 1, 1679, Lauderdale Papers, vol. XXVIII, Add MS 23243, ff. 34–35, BL.
38. On the Bothwell Brig uprising and the royal reaction to it, see Elizabeth Hannan Hyman, "A Church Militant: Scotland, 1661–1690," *16CJ* 26, no. 1 (1995): 49–74; and MacInnes, *Clanship, Commerce, and the House of Stuart*, 130–38.
39. On the Duke of York's governance of Scotland between 1680 and 1685, see Harris, *Restoration*, 329–76. On his sponsorship of Scottish settlements abroad, for which he provided

indentured colonists for his proprietor friends, see Ned Landsman, "William Penn's Scottish Counterparts: The Quakers of 'North Britain' and the Colonization of East New Jersey," in *The World of William Penn,* ed. Richard S. Dunn and Mary Maples Dunn (Philadelphia: University of Pennsylvania Press, 1986), 241–57; and David Dobson, "Seventeenth-Century Scottish Communities in the Americas," in *Scottish Communities Abroad in the Early Modern Period,* ed. Alexia Grosjean and Steve Murdoch (Boston: Brill, 2005), 105–33.

40. Quotes are from James Stuart of Goodtrees, in Gardner, *Scottish Exile Community,* 199.

41. Quote from Alexander Shields, *A Hind Let Loose; or, An Historical Representation of the Testimonies of the Church of Scotland for the Interest of Christ with the True State Thereof in All Its Periods* (Edinburgh, 1687), 87.

42. On this normalization of toleration, and the decline in support for persecution as a legitimate confessional objective, see Mark Knights, "'Meer Religion' and the 'Church-State' of Restoration England: The Impact and Ideology of James II's Declarations of Indulgence," in *A Nation Transformed: England after the Restoration,* ed. Alan Houston and Steven Pincus (Cambridge: Cambridge University Press, 2001), 41–70.

43. On this renewed ecclesiastical rivalry, see Alasdair Raffe, *The Culture of Controversy: Religious Arguments in Scotland, 1660–1714* (Woodbridge: Boydell Press, 2012), 208–33.

44. Lord Cardross and his involvement in the Stuart's Town settlement is detailed in the "Alexander Dunlop Memorandum Book" (1686), Manuscripts M-2318, William L. Clements Library, University of Michigan, 1–5.

45. On the involvement of Scots in the Netherlands in the Glorious Revolution, see Gardner, *Scottish Exile Community,* 178–93.

46. On Scottish Presbyterians and the Revolution settlement, see Jeffrey Stephen, *Defending the Revolution: The Church of Scotland, 1689–1716* (Burlington, VT: Ashgate, 2013).

47. Peter Lake, "Anti-Popery: The Structure of a Prejudice," in *Conflict in Early Stuart England: Studies in Religion and Politics, 1603–1642,* ed. Richard Cust and Ann Hughes (New York: Longman, 1989), 72–106, quote on 77; David W. Miller, "Religious Commotions in the Scottish Diaspora: A Transatlantic Perspective on 'Evangelicalism' in a Mainline Denomination," in *Ulster Presbyterians in the Atlantic World: Religion, Politics, and Identity,* ed. David A. Wilson and Mark G. Spencer (Dublin: Four Courts Press, 2006), 22–38; Katherine Carté Engel, "Connecting Protestants in Britain's Eighteenth-Century Atlantic Empire," *William and Mary Quarterly* 75, no. 1 (2018): 37–70.

Barbarians and Papists

IRELAND, ANTI-POPERY, AND BRITISH AMERICA, 1536–1775

Evan Haefeli

BRITISH COLONIES WERE HAUNTED by fear of the "Barbarous Irish." Seventeenth-century Barbados was rife with rumors of Irish servants joining "in Rebellion" with enslaved Africans. On Montserrat—where Irish made up a majority of the colonists—a wealthy English planter in 1654 accused the governor, an Irish Protestant, of leaving the island "Prey to the next Invader" by arming the "Barbarous Irish and their Abetters" and letting a "Papist" serve as their officer. In 1741, New Yorkers were told that a massive slave conspiracy of "negro confederates" aided by "many of the Irish catholics" serving in the colony's garrison "was conceived to destroy this city by fire, and massacre the inhabitants" on "St. Patrick's night." A priest, allegedly baptizing the black insurgents, told "them he made them Christians, and forgave them all their sins, and all the sins they should commit about the plot." In 1758, a Congregational minister in western Massachusetts rounded out a winter of anti-Catholic sermons with an extended account of "ye horrid massacre of Ireland, set on foot by ye pope & his clergy & car[ri]ed on in a most inhumane & barbarous" manner. Four years later, a Virginia farmer's son sailing to England fell into lugubrious reflection upon catching sight of the Ulster coast. This "place rendered famous in history, by the massacre of one hundred thousand Protestants, in the reign of King Charles the first . . . made such a deep impression on my heart, as is not easily described."[1]

These reactions reflected a "specifically Irish tradition of anti-Popery" that, as John Gibney describes it, "derived its potency from the structural reality that Protestants in Ireland remained a minority." Into the 1770s, this "virulent" anti-Catholicism served as "the anti-type of all that Protestants professed to believe and value" as well as a "way of explaining and understanding what the Protestants took to be their precarious yet privileged position in Ireland," confirms Toby Barnard.[2] However, Irish anti-popery also differed from generic anti-Catholicism in the way it included anti-Irish prejudices dating back at least to twelfth century. Ironically, the trope of Irish barbarity had Roman Catholic origins connected to the papal propaganda justifying the Anglo-Norman conquest of the 1170s. Bernard of Clairvaux had criticized "the wild, barbaric nature of the people," who drove Saint Malachy, archbishop of Armagh, "out of his own diocese and country" for advocating the reform of the Irish church along papal lines. Adrian IV, the one and only English pope, laid the legal groundwork for the eventual invasion with his 1155 papal bull *Laudabiliter* claiming the Irish were incapable of reforming themselves. Finally, one of the conquerors, Gerald of Wales, wrote an influential book about Ireland that sealed the Irish reputation as "a barbarous people, literally barbarous" who, judging by "modern ideas," were clearly "uncultivated" and retained the "habits of barbarians." These stereotypes persisted over the next three and a half centuries until the Protestant Reformation combined them with anti-Catholicism, creating a potent anti-Irish anti-Catholicism that reached a peak in the 1640s.[3]

The overseas legacy of this savage anti-Irish anti-Catholicism underscores how Irish anti-popery was about more than what was taking place within Ireland but also shaped attitudes toward Irish people across the British-American world. Sympathy for Irish Protestants became such an integral part of British Protestant patriotism that Americans only relinquished it with much regret after their confrontation with Parliament descended into armed conflict in 1775. Within Ireland, however, the story was far more complex. Beginning with the Irish Parliament's renunciation of its ties to the pope in 1536, Irish anti-popery developed a mix of moderate and radical positions. At one end, Anglo-Irish Catholics sustained the ancient trope of Gaelic barbarity to distinguish themselves from the excessive devotion to the papacy of their neighbors. Meanwhile, after 1641 intra-Protestant anti-popery grew along with Protestant religious diversity. Especially after the decisive Williamite victory of the 1690s left Irish Catholics disenfranchised and impoverished, it sometimes seemed like other Protestants posed the greater popish threat. For a brief time in the 1790s Irish Catholics even seemed like reliable allies for Ulster Scots Presbyterians against the Anglican Ascendancy, long the real force for "compulsion in religion" and the most threatening "instrument of antichristian tyranny." Their neighbors' Roman Catholicism, on the other hand, seemed doomed to wither away in "the final triumph of rational, reformed Christianity" heralded by the United Irish movement. In North America, however, where even the Ulster Scots were characterized as barbarians, fear of the "Wild Irish" remained strong well into the nineteenth century.[4]

Reconstructing this history of Irish anti-popery confronts several challenges. On the one hand, anti-Catholicism was largely imported. Indeed, it was so intrinsic to British colonization that, in most accounts, it hardly merits singling out as a distinct object of study. The few studies that exist generally focus on Ulster, where the confrontation between Protestants and Catholics was, and remains, most extreme.[5]

Elsewhere, scholars have come to minimalize the story of anti-Catholicism as part of a broader rejection of the old habit of interpreting Irish history primarily through the Catholic-Protestant divide. They point to the complex combination of ethnic, political, and economic rivalries among and between Protestants and Catholics. As Tim Harris points out, "tensions that on the surface seem to be rooted in divided confessional loyalties appear in reality to be far more complex" and "about much more than just religion." Situating Ireland within the wider conflicts of the British-American world, Harris shows how the duke of Argyle's 1685 rebellion against King James II in Scotland led Catholics in Ireland to fear the Ulster Scots would support it while Ulster Scots feared their English Protestant neighbors would unite with Irish Catholics against them. For these and other reasons, some scholars believe anti-Catholic prejudice can and should be separated out from its anti-Irish counterpart. However, from the broader perspective of the long term across the British-American world, it seems more valuable to emphasize how these elements were combined—and recombined—into a distinctive and persistent Irish anti-popery.[6]

Ethnic difference was an issue in Ireland long before the advent of the Reformation. The largest and most ancient group on the island was the Gaels, or "Old Irish." Despite an ethno-linguistic affiliation with the rest of Celtic Britain, the life of Saint Patrick illuminates how weak the Celtic fraternity was, both within Ireland and across the British Isles. The Reformation exacerbated those divisions. Whereas most Welsh and Scottish Gaels converted to Protestantism, few Gaelic Irish did. As the single largest body of Roman Catholics within the British-American world, the Gaelic Irish then contributed decisively to the revival of Catholicism within it, beginning in the late sixteenth century when the close relationship between the MacDonnells of Ulster and the MacDonalds of the Western Isles and Highlands facilitated Roman Catholicism's return to Scotland.[7] In the seventeenth century, Gaelic Irish immigrants began carrying Catholicism to America, helping it grow into one of the major religions of the United States. By the mid-nineteenth century, Irish Catholics were also establishing communities up and down Britain's west coast from Glasgow to Wales. The subsequent burst of anti-Catholic agitation on both sides of the Atlantic was equally anti-Irish and anti-immigrant.[8]

The second significant group of Irish Catholics, the "Old English," represented the first non-Gaelic community to colonize the island. Distinguished by language and culture from their Gaelic neighbors, their roots extend back to the ninth century, when Norse and Danish Vikings settled on the coast. After the Anglo-Norman conquest, their port towns of Dublin, Wexford, Waterford, Cork, and Limerick formed entry points for English immigrants colonizing the surrounding countryside. Anglo-Norman dynasties presided over the lordship of Ireland on behalf of

England's monarch, with *Laudabiliter* as their charter for social and political dominance. However, they never controlled all of Ireland. At the dawn of the sixteenth century, an Old English gentleman felt compelled to draw a distinction between this "land of peace" dominated by the English, especially the Pale of Settlement around Dublin, and the "land of war" belonging to the "wyld Irishe." The Old English, like the Old Irish, mostly stayed loyal to Catholicism after the Reformation, and insisted that the line between civilization and savagery was an ethnic one between themselves and the Gaels, not a religious one between Catholics and Protestants. In the 1550s an agent of the Catholic Queen Mary described Irish Gaels treating their churches more as "stabells for horses and herdhowses for cattell, than holly places" and their priests as "common spyes and messengers of myschefs."[9]

The Old English desire for supremacy within Ireland occasionally muddled their enthusiasm for the papacy. For example, Thomas Fitzgerald, son of the lord deputy and 9th Earl of Kildare, once criticized a rival for being overly attached to the pope. Only in 1534, when King Henry VIII's reforms threatened his family's control over the lord lieutenancy, did he launch a revolt by publicly declaring his allegiance to the papacy and denouncing the king as a heretic. However, the less exalted Old English families who dominated Ireland's Parliament remained loyal, helped suppress Kildare's revolt, and then in 1536, at the urging of the Englishman who succeeded Kildare as lord deputy, passed an Act of Supremacy rejecting papal authority. The eagerness with which they grabbed up church properties suggests they had some sympathy for religious reform, at least as long as they could profit from it.[10]

Six years later, in 1542, the Crown of Ireland Act abolished the lordship and declared Ireland a kingdom. For the first time, all its inhabitants, Gaelic and English, became equally subjects of England's monarch. The political and religious reforms that followed introduced a new ethnic group: the "New English," generally referred to as the Anglo-Irish by the eighteenth century. Like the "Old English," they were not all originally English. A number had Welsh, Huguenot, Dutch, and German origins. Technically, their Protestantism distinguished them from the "Old English," but not always. Until the creation of the penal regime in the 1690s, Ireland was by many measures the least onerous place for Catholics to live in the British Isles. Some of the New English (and, later, Scots) immigrants were Catholic. Meanwhile, some Old English and even a few Gaels became Protestant. Nevertheless, the exceptions to the general pattern of ethno-religious allegiance were few.[11]

The New English imported anti-Catholicism to Ireland, pioneered through the work of John Bale. A major proponent of England's Reformation, in 1553 Bale took up the post of bishop of Ossory in the cathedral town of Kilkenny, a proud bastion of the Old English order. His account of his brief tenure there is the first important text of Irish anti-popery. Arriving in Ireland, he was struck by its "many abhomynable ydolatryes." Religious services were "like a popysh masse," he complained, "with the olde apish toyes of Antichrist, in bowyinges and beckynges, knelinges and knockings." By preaching the Gospel, Bale "sought to distroye the ydolatries & dissolve the hypocrites yockes." He urged his priests to follow his example rather than "occupie so muche of the tyme in chauntynge, pypynge, and syngynge." His Protestant experiment attracted some sympathizers, but ended abruptly when Mary became queen a few months later. Bale was dismissed. Powerless, he watched as a procession paraded "most gorgeously, all the town over" and "chattered" and "chaunted" the Latin liturgy "with great noyse and devocion." He grumbled that Irish priests would make "ye witlesse sort believe yt they can make every daye newe goddess of their little whyte cakes," and claim "yt they can fatche their frindes sowles from flaminge purgatory if nede be." Now, "without checke," they would also "have other mennes wives in occupienge, or kepe whores in their chambers, or els play the buggery knaves, as they have done always, and be at an utter defiaunce with marriage." Sin meant little to such men, content in the knowledge that "confession was able to burnish them agayne, and to make them so white as snowe, though they thus offended never so oft." How long would this "tirannie against" God's "manifest truthe" last?[12]

Bale's accusations of idolatry and sexual deviancy were the common stuff of anti-Catholicism, but his concern that priests would absolve all sins soon became a crucial explanation for Irish Catholic resistance to Queen Elizabeth's reforms, as illustrated by John Derricke's 1581 poem *The Image of Irelande.* His depiction of a small rebellion involving minor Gaelic chieftains and their warriors, or, "wantone Irishe wilde Woodkarne," is dedicated to the Protestant poet and national hero Sir Philip Sidney. One of the last books produced by John Day, publisher of John Foxe's *Acts and Monuments,* it has beautiful woodcuts providing unrivaled illustrations of sixteenth-century Gaelic life, which Derricke characterizes as "more brutishe" than all beasts, "more bloudier then the wolfe, or savage beare." While he says little about Roman Catholic religion, Derricke blames the "friers" as "the cause . . . of hurleburles in this lande." Priests caused the woodkerns "to rebell / against their (soveraigne quene)" by persuading them "that it is almost deede to God / to make the English subiectes taste / the Irishe Rebells rode." After battle, friars used the "Apeishe toies" of "booke, the Candell and the Bell" in vain attempts "remission to obtaine" for the warriors' sins, reassuring them that if their "soules should chance in hell," they could "bryng them quicklie out." "Beholde," Derricke concluded, "the plaguy counsell of a pockie frier, the very frutte of Papistrie."[13]

The rebellion described by Derricke was just one of a long series that began with Kildare's revolt and ended with the Nine Years' War (1593–1603). Blaming Irish priests helped account for the failure of reformers like Sir Henry Sidney, father of Sir Philip Sidney, who spent thirteen years between the 1550s and 1570s (eight of them as lord deputy) struggling to get Irish aristocrats to cooperate and

Engraving of Irish fighting the English, from John Derricke, *The Image of Ireland with a discoverie of woodkarne, wherin is moste lively expressed, the nature, and qualitie of the saied wilde Irishe woodkarne*, 1581. (Courtesy of the Folger Shakespeare Library) Illustrates the role of Irish Catholic priests in Irish Gaelic rebellions. They absolve the rebels of their sins before they go to war and then mourn when the English kill these "Devills sonnes."

Irish clergymen to renounce their papal affiliation, with limited success. His son defended him by explaining that the Irish had a "revengefull hate to all englishe as to their only conquerours, and that which is most of all with so ignorant obstinacy in papistry, that they doe in their sowles deteste the presente government." Irish resistance blunted the New English reforms, but ultimately failed to prevent the loss of ever more lands to Protestant "plantation." The colonization process that began in County Down in the 1560s–1570s expanded into Munster in the 1580s, and was implemented to most drastic effect in Ulster after 1603, dispossessing far more Irish than it converted or "civilized."[14]

Nevertheless, there was some truth to the claim that Irish Catholics had a special attachment to the papacy. After the Anglo-Norman conquest, the papacy had gained a largely positive reputation by overseeing Ireland's church in a remarkably evenhanded fashion, effectively mediating between Irish Gaelic and English interests. After the Reformation, it openly supported Irish rebels on several occasions. In 1572 the papacy sent troops to support the so-called Desmond Revolt in Munster. In the 1640s it sent two envoys to support the uprising. Papal support could justify a break with England just as it had once justified the invasion of Ireland. The Old English aristocrat James Fitzmaurice Fitzgerald, cousin of the earl of Desmond, argued that England's Reformation broke with *Laudabiliter:* the Irish could now choose a new monarch. In the 1640s, Gaelic Franciscans argued they were waging a holy war and Gaelic elites contemplated transferring their obedience to either the pope or the Spanish Hapsburgs, suggesting the accusations that they were more were loyal to the pope than their British Protestant monarch were not always incorrect.[15]

Irish resistance also prevented the Church of Ireland from becoming the church of all the Irish. Officially Protestant ever since the Irish Parliament's second Act of Uniformity of 1560, and with a more unambiguously Calvinist theology than the Church of England after the passage of the Twelve Articles in 1567, the established church remained a thin Protestant shell around a thick Catholic core. There were few places where Protestant theology was effectively preached never mind fully implemented. Irish Catholic priests and laity remained within the Church without too much trouble until the pope excommunicated Queen Elizabeth in 1570. Thereafter, Irish elites sustained the "Old Religion" by sending relatives abroad to become priests, then giving them space to practice and shielding them from prosecution when they returned.[16]

Deprived of indigenous support, the Church of Ireland was institutionally weak. Only the arrival of thousands of New English immigrants to Munster in the 1580s finally gave it a substantial number of committed Protestants. However, those immigrants also reinforced the colonial character of the Church, whose preaching clergy and lay membership remained overwhelmingly immigrant until well into the seventeenth century. For many of these immigrants, the fact that the Church of Ireland was less tainted by popery than the Church of England was a real attraction. Even after Ireland finally got its own university in 1591, Trinity College was as likely to attract English puritans like John Winthrop Jr. as Irish-born individuals.[17]

This colonial church became the leading voice of radical anti-Catholicism by the 1580s, a stance that occasionally pitted the clergy against the secular rulers of the island, who could not afford to be so intransigent. In 1586, for example, a bishop denounced a government proposal for the "use of toleration in matter of oath and religion." His sermon "flatly" rejected that "the magistrate may tolerate with papists" and criticized the lord deputy for trusting such "idolators, papists and infidels." Instead they should "root them out." The Irish were no longer "to be counted children but to be dealt withal sharply and punished severely" for their failure to conform. "If yee profess the truth of Godds religion, the sinceritie of his word," intoned another churchman, "let it appeare, halte no more with idolators: they doe not halte with you, neither in their profession, neither yet in the effectes thereof."[18]

The Church's anti-popish ethos made a strong impression on its handful of native converts, most importantly James Ussher. This internationally famous scholar and churchman regularly identified the papacy with Antichrist—in his writings for non-Irish audiences. At home, however, Ussher was more tactful. He insisted that Saint Patrick was a Protestant and that "the Celtic church [was] free from all popish corruptions," but, in hopes of converting his Old English neighbors in the Pale, he toned down the anti-Catholic rhetoric. He and his colleagues instead favored gentler forms of religious controversy like staged confrontations, public disputes, printed polemics, and visible religious performance. Ultimately, "attacking Catholicism without attacking Catholics" demanded a rare degree of circumspection, skill, and sensitivity. It also persuaded few Irish to convert. Meanwhile, important conformists like the bishop of Limerick were lost to Roman Catholicism, as was Richard Stanihurst, a leading humanist from one of Dublin's magisterial families and a relative of Ussher's.[19]

It was not long before New English immigrants began to criticize the Church for its failure to convert the Irish. In a 1589 tract promoting colonization around Limerick, Robert Payne admitted that "a great part of the Irish . . . are greatly inclined to papistrie." However, he did not fault the Irish. Instead, he blamed the "want of good preaching & discipline." Insisting the Irish were fundamentally loyal, he divided them into three sorts. The "better sort" were "very civill and honestly given," mostly "inclined to husbandrie" and hospitable to visitors. The "Kernes" were "warlike men," but mostly "slayne in the late warres." The rest were "very idle people, not unlike our English beggers, yet for the moste part, of pure complexion and good constitution of body." Certainly, some feared "the Spaniards will enter the land, & that the Irish wil releeve them," but "the greater number, and the better sort" of Irish had a "deadly hate" for the Spanish. After all, they had killed off many of the survivors of the Great Armada of 1588 when they landed in Ireland, "notwithstanding they brought the popes holy candles & pardons." Payne believed they had lost affection for "Spanish government" after reading the book of Bartolomé de Las Casas describing "their murderous cruelties in ye West Indias, where they most tiranously have murthered many millions more of those simple creatures then now liveth in Ireland." What Irishman would be "so foolish" as "to entertain such proud guests knowing their tyrannie" even though the Spanish were "the popes champions"? And how could the Spanish be "so unwise to trust those irish, who so lately imbrued their hands in their bloud, slaying them as doggs in such plentifull maner"? Of course, there were "some Traytors in Ireland," but there were traitors in England too: "our [English] Catholickes" were guilty of "all the Traiterous practices against" Queen Elizabeth. Payne recommended they too read Las Casas's book.[20]

New English colonists who aspired to govern Ireland, like Payne, the poet Edmund Spenser, and the courtier, translator, poet, and veteran of the Nine Years'

War Sir John Harington, generally favored a condescending style of anti-popery that aspired to win the Irish over through persuasion. Edmund Spenser broke down the "evils" of Irish society in the 1590s into three categories: laws, customs, and religion. While arguing that both Irish Brehon law, which was "in many things repugning quite both to Gods Law, and mans," and some Irish customs, which were "very strange and almost heathenish," needed to be anglicized, regarding religion, he felt the primary issue was ignorance. The Irish were "so blindly and brutishly informed, (for the most part) that not one amongst a hundred knoweth any ground of Religion, or any Article of his faith, but can perhaps say his *Pater noster* or his *Ave Maria,* without any knowledge or understanding what one word thereof meaneth." Harington, who aspired to the positions of both lord chancellor of Ireland and archbishop of Dublin, thought the Irish should be won over through "myld conferences" and presented his moderate anti-Catholicism as a model. When he "saw Crosses or Images remayinging in any of theyr Churches or howses," he told their owners, "ower Church did not condemne the use but the abuse of thease." Abuse was, for example, "when throwgh a neglygent and affected ygnorawnce the peeple creep to them and are prostrate afore them as to deytyes." Pointing out that the papacy's claim to "exoticall power . . . over all hath slender fowndacion in Scripture," Harington once gleefully "confuted" the earl of Tyrone's "preests in an argument before him, and made him say all was not so cleer as they made yt." Finally, he debunked miraculous sites like Saint Patrick's Purgatory by discovering their "naturall cawses." Alas, such aggressive deployments of reason proved a not especially effective method of proselytization.[21]

Fynes Moryson's famous travelogue illustrates this moderate Irish anti-popery in action in its account of Lord Mountjoy, the lord deputy who won the Nine Years' War and successfully oversaw the transition to King James's rule. When news of Queen Elizabeth's death reached Ireland, townspeople across Munster had set up "the publicke exercise of the Popish Religion, without publike authority." Their excuse was that James was "a Roman Catholike." Faced with this unexpected challenge, Mountjoy chose indulgence over aggression. Blaming the "lying Priests" who had taken advantage of the people's "simplicity" and "seduced" them into that error, he ordered the townsmen "to desist from the disordered course they had taken, in celebrating publikely the idolatrous Masse." Then he pardoned them. The so-called recusancy revolt fizzled.[22]

It is important to keep in mind this moderate strain of Irish anti-popery because other ambitious laymen were advocating more ferocious policies. The opening up of Ulster to colonization after its leading lords, dissatisfied with Mountjoy's peace, fled abroad in 1607 in a vain search for international support, gave their ideas an unprecedented opportunity. To begin with, the so-called "Flight of the Earls" confirmed the views of those who mistrusted Irish Catholic loyalty, most importantly

Arthur Chichester, a veteran of the Nine Years' War and lord deputy from 1605 to 1616. Chichester worked to suppress Irish Catholicism by enforcing conformity to the established church, employing the Oath of Supremacy to purge Catholics from the government, and encouraging Protestant immigration. By creating new, Protestant-dominated boroughs, he also allowed Protestants a greater voice in the Irish Parliament. His anti-Catholic campaign culminated in February 1612 with the public execution of two priests for treason. The two priests quickly became martyrs, but the decline in Irish Catholic power was clear. Ulster soon switched from being the least to the most Protestant of the four Irish provinces.[23]

Some Ulster planters, like the Welshman Sir John Davies, retained moderate views. As royal attorney, Davies still believed Irish Catholics could be persuaded to abandon their "Barbarisme" and loyalty to the pope. After all, in Henry VIII's day, "when the Irish had once resolved to obey the king, they made no scruple to renounce the Pope." Like Spencer, Davies emphasized the ability of English law and customs to assimilate the Irish. "The strings of this Irish Harpe, which the Civill Magistrate doth finger, are all in tune (for I omit to speak of the State Ecclesiasticall) and make a good Harmony in this Commonweale." In other words, the Irish were fundamentally loyal. Like Mountjoy, Davies preferred to blame Irish resistance on "the practises of Priests and Jesuites."[24]

Other planters favored more radical measures. One, inspired by the Old Testament story of "the planting of the Jews in the land Canaan," called the Irish Catholics no "better than Cananites," for they "contemne God and Religion observing neither the rites of Baptisme nor Matrimony." He proposed they "be translated out of Ireland" and sent to work as servants in England where, isolated from each other, the Irish would become tractable once their "malice can not profit them anye waye." Ireland, meanwhile, would be turned over to English and Dutch Protestant immigrants. Captain Thomas Lee, another veteran of the Irish wars, wanted to ensure that all Irish were educated as Protestants by severely punishing any and all proselytizing by Roman Catholic priests, Jesuits, or friars: first by branding them on the face, then by execution "as a rogue or idle vagrant." The "goods of those who harboured them" would "be confiscated for the 'physick and survery' of the sick and wounded soldiery." Matthew De Renzy, originally from Cologne, preferred a divide-and-conquer strategy. He would "intermix" the loyal Irish to "match the contrary part" and "prevent future dangers." Elites would be favored, educated, and converted while the untrustworthy "mere" (i.e., Gaelic) Irish, and especially women (bastions of Irish Catholicism) would be forced to conform and assimilate. Richard Boyle, a New English planter who made a fortune in Munster and became earl of Cork, also favored coercion, but only at the beginning of a three-stage process. After subjugating the Irish, "the promotion of manufacturing" could lure them "from their erstwhile idleness to an attachment of civil living." Finally, education would lead to conversion. By 1630 it seemed the Catholics were indeed learning industrious habits from their Protestant neighbors. Boyle believed they displayed a disposition for peace and "an honest and fair course of life" and were "well affected to the English monarchy."[25]

Meanwhile, the colonization of Ulster added a significant new wrinkle to Ireland's ethnic mix: Scots. By 1622, the approximately twelve thousand Scottish immigrants in Ulster slightly outnumbered their New English neighbors. Initially they conformed to the Church of Ireland, and some even became ministers and bishops in it. Graduates of Aberdeen University tended to be more comfortable in a church with bishops than those from Glasgow University. Ultimately, however, the Presbyterian influence of southwestern Scotland, where most of the immigrants came from, was too strong. These Scots brought imported anti-episcopal attitudes and customs that challenged the Church, like the large public communion festivals known as Holy Fairs, a precursor to early American camp meetings.[26]

Before long, what had been a unidirectional confrontation with popery was transformed into a three-front struggle. The Church of Ireland faced challenges from, on the one hand, Scottish Presbyterian dissidents and, on the other, an increasingly intrusive Church of England. The old campaign against the pope's "apish toys" persisted, exemplified by the preaching of men like the English minister George Andrews against the "drugs of Rome, dregs of superstition, counterfeit, relics, hallowed beads, consecrated grains," and other "false coins" that the "mint masters of Rome" sent over "to their hucksters here to delude the people of this land." However, Scottish Presbyterian criticisms of the Church of Ireland's "idolatry" led men like Henry Leslie, a Scottish graduate of Saint Andrews who became a bishop in Ulster, to plead for Protestant unity by pointing to the more important struggle against Roman Catholicism. Leslie objected that "contesting about trifles" only gave "occasions to the papists to insult over us." With Protestants "divided in sundry sects and opinions," the Catholics would smugly conclude "that we are not the true church." Finally, there were those like the Englishman Christopher Hampton, recently appointed archbishop of Armagh, who defended the Church's use of ceremonies as not "popish" but merely "exercises of piety" that produced "order and peace" in worship. Like some Laudians in England, Hampton had a rather favorable view of Catholicism, admitting he "could accept the Roman church as a church, but 'miserably deformed and infected with infinite errors.'"[27]

Initially, the Church responded by reinforcing its Calvinist character. In 1615 it adopted a thorough set of one hundred and four articles to avoid "diversities of opinions" and secure "the establishment of consent touching true religion." However, in 1634 Lord Deputy Thomas Wentworth called another convocation to alter those articles and encourage conformity to the Church of England. His scheme was interrupted by the upheaval of the 1640s and 1650s, but the aspiration for closer union with the Church of England did not fade. Finally, in 1665 a new Act of Uniformity for the Church of Ireland erased the differences in theology and liturgy between the two churches. Adopting the Church of England's Thirty-nine Articles, Protestants of the Irish establishment became Anglicans like their fellows in England.[28]

In the meantime, the Church of Ireland continued to oppose any toleration for Roman Catholicism. When, during the Anglo-Spanish War of 1625–30, King Charles I proposed to moderate official religious policy in exchange for regular subsidies from Ireland's Parliament, the archbishops and bishops denounced these so-called "Graces." Their petition claimed the concessions threatened "to set religion to sale" along with "the soules of the people." Tolerating Catholicism was a "grievous sinne" because Roman Catholic "faith and Doctrine" was "erroneous and Hereticall" and their church "Apostaticall." Toleration would make the Church of Ireland "accessarie, not onely to their Superstitions, Idolatries, Heresies, and in a word, abominations of Poperie, but also" as a consequence, "to the Perdition of the seduced people" who would perish in a false religion. In 1628, Lord Deputy Henry Cary, Viscount Falkland, added his voice to the protests even though (or because?) his wife, to his chagrin, had recently converted to Catholicism. The "universal toleration of religion" was "dangerous, and ought to be interrupted." Instead he favored a selective approach that would "banish some Papists and regulate others so that the loyal Papists may have full liberty, yet with absolute security and safety to the State."[29]

Charles did not heed the churchmen's pleas. He suspended the enforcement of laws against Catholicism, allowing the Catholic Church to recuperate its strength. Over the next decade it revived to different degrees from province to province and town to town, but the overall result was impressive. Places that had not had Catholic bishops since the 1580s saw the hierarchy of bishops reestablished. More priests (many of them members of religious orders) circulated through the country. With them came the Roman Catholicism of the Council of Trent, which now became the norm for all Catholics in Ireland—Gaelic, Old English, New English, and Scots. Theirs was no longer a hidden religion. Even in Leinster and the Pale Catholic Irish freely proclaimed their religious allegiance, wearing crosses and openly attending mass in private settings. Traveling through these regions in the mid-1630s, the future puritan revolutionary Sir William Brereton was stunned to see how Catholics were "not ashamed of their religion, nor desire to conceal themselves."[30]

By 1640, the Church of Ireland confronted a crisis of legitimacy. Then, the bishop of Waterford and Lismore, John Atherton, made everything worse by getting convicted of sodomy as well as various "acts of fornication and adultery." This recent English immigrant had few friends because he strongly supported Wentworth's efforts at Church reform. Worse, sodomy had just become a capital crime six years earlier, in the wake of a sex scandal (with anti-Catholic undertones) involving the second earl of Castlehaven. Atherton was executed in December 1640 and news of the "whorish incestuous Bishop" spread to England, where Wentworth faced charges of misgovernment (including that he had raised an army full of Irish "Papists" who were "readie to march"—presumably upon England) for which he would be executed in May 1641. A few weeks before then, an "anonymous pamphlet on the state of Ireland" used the Atherton incident to indict Irish episcopacy. The conviction of "a bishop . . . for the sin of sodomy," demonstrated that "it is time for the church to look into and suppress" bishops "with their increasing superstition, idolatry and shameful iniquity."[31]

The daunting task of reducing the damage Atherton had done to the Church's reputation while also turning Atherton's fate to evangelical benefit was taken up in his funeral sermon, preached by Nicholas Bernard. The sermon, published in Dublin in the spring of 1641 with a dedication to Archbishop Ussher, mixed anti-popery with anti-anti-popery to hold Protestant dissidents at bay while wooing Catholics. His sermon commanded Protestant critics not to "be such hatefull birds, as to defile their own nests by imputing" Atherton "as an aspersion to the whole profession." Insisting that a "Church ought not to be judged by the lives of a few Professors, but by the doctrine professed," he then defused potential criticisms from Catholics by holding anti-popery in tactical reserve. "Papists" should not "object this scandal to our Church, least we returne them such foule stories from that Holy Sea [*sic*], which we have no mind to raise." Bernard then emphasized how un-anti-Catholic the whole incident had been. Atherton had gone out of his way to absolve Catholics of blame for his trouble in his final speech, claiming none of his Waterford neighbors "of the Romish Church, though differing from me in points of Religion, had a hand in this complaint against me." Instead, Atherton "judged and condemned himself, and . . . cryed to Heaven for pardon," hoping his deep contrition might inspire Catholics to convert. Bernard claimed "the very Papists, and some Priests I saw" at the execution "kneeled downe and wept." After Atherton's confession, they began "begging of mercy, that his soule might be bathed in the bloud of Christ." One of those "Papists" was so "affected" that he "was converted" and began attending Protestant services. But this effort to sustain the Church's hegemony would soon be forgotten after chaos broke out in October 1641.[32]

Ireland's Catholics rose in a revolt that would last for a decade. Before it ended, the civil war led to the deaths of some 400,000 people, most of them Catholics, representing almost 20 percent of the country's roughly 1.5 million inhabitants. Initially intended as a limited strike against certain plantations, the uprising inadvertently tapped into a deep vein of Catholic resentment and produced a wave of violence that, by the spring of 1642, killed as many as 5,000 Protestants. Captured Protestants were urged to convert. Some did. Many others chose to suffer for their faith. Despoiled of their property and driven them from their homes,

Irish Protestant refugees and rumors spread word of their suffering to Britain, unleashing a hostile flood of propaganda that exaggerated the crisis by drastically inflating the number of victims to 150,000 or even 300,000—far more than Ireland's actual Protestant population (about 100,000, mostly in Ulster [roughly 80,000] and Munster [about 20,000]). Some even claimed the Catholics wanted to massacre all the Protestants.[33]

England's initial reaction to the news was divided into moderate and radical responses mirroring its stark political divide. Parliamentarians adopted the language of John Foxe's *Acts and Monuments* to paint a picture of anti-Christian Irish persecuting godly Protestants with savage cruelty. Worse, the king's failure to protect Irish Protestants suggested he was involved in a larger popish plot against his true Protestant subjects. Royalists, on the other hand, claimed the rebellion represented less an attack on true religion than a loss of respect for the established social order. Refusing to exaggerate the level of atrocities, they held out hope that order could be restored and the rebels returned to their proper loyalty and obedience.[34]

Scotland shared the Parliamentarians' interpretation. The Irish rebels had "taken up arms to destroy the Protestant Religion, and set up Popery, to rend away one of His majesties Kingdoms and deliver it up into the hands of strangers." This was a war against "execrable antichristian rebels, who have made a covenant with Hell, to destroy the Gospel of Christ" and needed to be put down. There was no time for "any agreement of Peace" or "respite from Hostility." Irish Catholics were dangerous "Creatures" like "Wolves or Tygers, or ravenous Beasts, destroyers of Mankind." The Scots sent an army to protect their countrymen. Once in Ulster, the Scots set up a Presbyterian church in the territory they controlled, giving the split within Irish Protestantism permanent institutional form.[35]

Irish Protestants largely agreed with the Scots and English Parliamentarians in attributing the revolt to a mix of popish conspiracy and cultural barbarity. Indeed, they had first promoted the idea. In March of 1642, Dr. Henry Jones, Protestant dean of Kilmore, presented the case to the English Parliament. Having served on the committee that collected testimony from over 600 victims of the uprising, Jones selectively used that information to represent Ireland's Protestants as deserving English charity and support—something the New English of Munster had failed to accomplish in the 1590s. Jones also claimed there was "a most bloody and antichristian combination and plot hatched by well-nigh the whole Romish sect . . . against this our church and state." Other tracts reiterated these arguments, most importantly, Sir John Temple's substantially researched history *The Irish Rebellion*. This New English lawyer and Trinity College graduate filled his account with victims' eyewitness testimony to argue that "any reasonable man will conclude with me, that the very first principles of this inhumane Conspiracy, were roughly drawn and hammered out at the Romish Forge" and "fomented by the treachery and virulent animosities of some of the chief Irish natives." Unable to say whether it was first hatched "at Rome" or "in Ireland, or in any other place," Temple blamed the priests and friars. These "most vigilant and industrious Emissaries" wanted "to make way for the re-establishment of the Romish Religion in all parts where it hath been suppressed." Their "venimous infusions" took "deep roots in the minds of a blind, ignorant, superstitious people," inspiring "the great ones mischievously to plot and contrive," and "the inferiour sort tumultuously to rise up and execute whatsoever they should command." Initially written in 1646 to prevent the conclusion of peace with the rebels, Temple's book succeeded far beyond that. Regularly reprinted into the nineteenth century, it decisively shaped Protestant attitudes toward Irish Catholics around the British-American world.[36]

This anti-Irish rhetoric encouraged the parliamentary army that arrived in 1649 to treat the rebels with exemplary cruelty. Denouncing the Catholic bishops' covenant with "death and hell," their general, Oliver Cromwell, targeted priests for execution or banishment and rejected all requests for "a liberty to exercise the

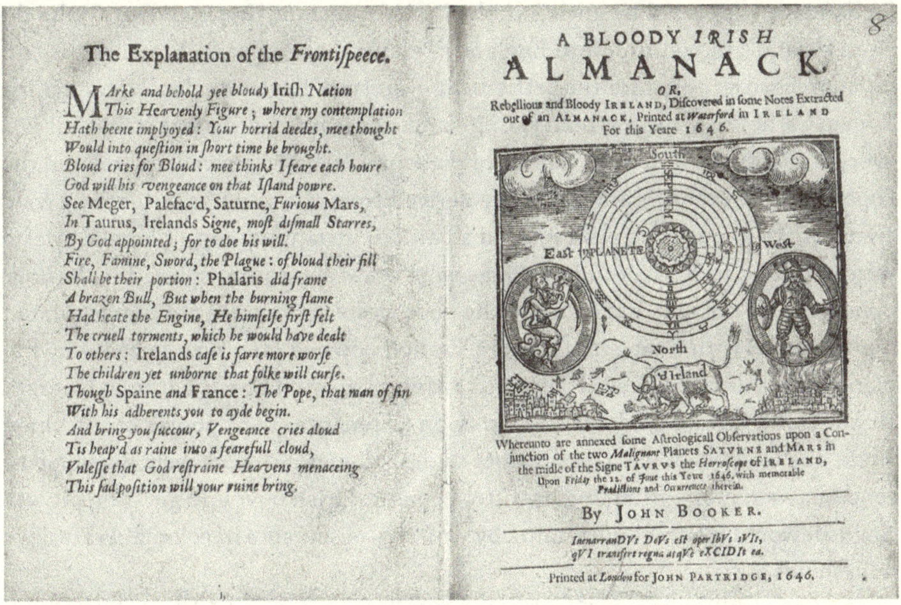

The Explanation of the *Frontiſpeece.*

Marke and behold yee bloudy Iriſh *Nation*
This Heavenly Figure ; where my contemplation
Hath beene implyoyed : Your horrid deedes, mee thought
Would into queſtion in ſhort time be brought.
Bloud cries for Bloud : mee thinks I feare each houre
God will his vengeance on that Iſland powre.
See Meger, Paleface'd, Saturne, *Furious* Mars,
In Taurus, Irelands *Signe, moſt diſmall Starres,*
By God appointed ; for to doe his will.
Fire, Famine, Sword, the Plague : of bloud their fill
Shall be their portion : Phalaris *did frame*
A brazen Bull, But when the burning flame
Had heate the Engine, He himſelfe firſt felt
The cruell torments, which he would have dealt
To others : Irelands *caſe is farre more worſe*
The children yet unborne that folke will curſe.
Though Spaine *and* France *: The Pope, that man of ſin*
With his adherents you to ayde begin.
And bring you ſuccour, Vengeance cries aloud
Tis heap'd as raine into a fearefull cloud,
Vnleſſe that God reſtraine Heavens menaceing
This ſad poſition will your ruine bring.

A BLOODY *IRISH*
ALMANACK.
OR,
Rebellious and Bloody IRELAND, Diſcovered in ſome Notes Extracted out of an ALMANACK, Printed at *Waterford* in IRELAND For this Yeare 1646.

Whereunto are annexed ſome Aſtrologicall Obſervations upon a Conjunction of the two *Malignant* Planets SATVRNE and MARS in the midle of the Signe TAVRVS the *Horroſcope* of IRELAND, Upon *Friday* the 12. of *June* this Yeare 1646. with memorable *Predictions* and *Occurrences* therein.

By JOHN BOOKER.

InenarranDVs DeVs eſt operIbVs sVIs,
qVI tranſfert regna atqVe eXCIDIt ea.

Printed at *London* for JOHN PARTRIDGE, 1646.

John Booker, *A Bloody Irish Almanack; or, Rebellious and Bloody Ireland, Discovered in some Notes Extracted out of an Almanack, Printed at Waterford in Ireland for this Yeare 1646*, 1646. (Courtesy of the Folger Shakespeare Library)

Booker republished this Irish almanac because its astrological predictions indicated God will pour "his vengeance on that Island" through "Fire, Famine, Sword, the Plague." He warned the "bloudy Irish Nation" that neither Spain, France, nor the pope could prevent the ruin caused by "Your horrid deedes."

mass." Most notoriously, he allowed his army to kill several thousand civilians at Drogheda and Wexford. However, Cromwell claimed he had no intention of massacring all the "Catholique Inhabitants," as some priests claimed. He merely wanted to separate the laity from the influence of their clergy. Only the "Papists" caught "seducing" the people and violating the laws would be punished. Those who kept "matters of Religion in their owne breasts" would be left alone "if they walke honestly and peaceably." This strategy was made public in the 1650 Declaration against "the Popish Prelates and Clergy." The Declaration blamed the clergy for the "unprovoked . . . most unheard of & most barbarous massacre." Labeling them "a part of Antichrist, whose Kingdome the Scripture so expressly speakes should be layed in blood, yea in the blood of the Saints," it accused them of shedding "great store of it already." Threatening the Irish with "misery and desolation, blood and ruine" if they resisted, Cromwell claimed to want peace. Nevertheless, his army would "rejoice to exercise utmost severity against" those who "shall headily run on after the Councells of their Prelates and Clergy and other Leaders."[37]

By 1652, the English army had thoroughly defeated the rebellion. For the first time in history, the English had complete control over the whole island. England's Parliament, supported by anti-Catholic Irish Protestant "Independents" who desired Ireland's integration into England's "empire," then decided to annex it and its Church with the Act for the Settlement of Ireland. England's penal laws against Roman Catholicism were extended to Ireland. The leaders of the revolt and "all and every Jesuit priest, and other person or persons who have received orders from the Pope or See of Rome or any authority derived from the same," a potentially wide swath of the population, were refused a pardon. In January 1653, Catholic priests were banished from the country. Plans were drawn up to transplant the Catholic population of the east and south to the poor western province of Connaught and replace them with Protestants. More Catholic-owned land was seized, but the plan was never completed. Protestant planters wanted cheap Catholic laborers. They allowed former landowners to stay on as tenants. Their poorer countrymen worked as laborers or went as servants to the colonies. Schemes were drawn up to send out even more, including over two thousand Irish boys and girls who, it was claimed, would become Protestants by working as servants in colonial Protestant households.[38]

The Cromwellian occupation fundamentally transformed Irish society in several ways, not least of which was to make it more religiously diverse than ever. The Presbyterian Church gained a permanent foothold in Ulster. Communities of Baptists, Congregationalists, and Quakers sprouted in the major ports and garrison towns. Additionally, scientists became involved in Irish policy, serving explicitly anti–Irish Catholic ends with the support of Samuel Hartlib's circle of ecumenically minded Protestant intellectuals. Land surveys, works of natural history and geography, even land law strove to undo Irish Catholicism. Hartlib helped publish Gerard Boate's *Natural History of Ireland,* which the Dutch-born physician wrote before he moved to the island. Boate drew on a variety of sources including Irish Protestant refugees in London and information from his brother Arnold, who had spent a decade working in Ireland as a physician to the Protestant elite. Gerard Boate's descriptions of Irish geography and natural resources are sprinkled with references to the "horrible Rebellion of the bloody Irish," those "Barbarians," a "wild Nation," and "one of the most barbarous Nations of the whole earth." He even devoted a whole section to debunking the pilgrimage site of "St. Patriks Purgatory." He called it "but a little cell" wherein some friars would lock up pilgrims after making them "watch and fast excessively: whereby, and through the recounting of strange and horrible apparitions and fantasmes, which he would meet withall in that subterranean pilgrimage," they would emerge telling "wonderfull stories." To "prevent this delusion in future times," the English drove away the friars then broke open "the hole or cell" to deprive it of its powers.[39]

Another figure associated with the Hartlib circle, William Petty, made his fortune surveying Irish lands to facilitate their redistribution to Protestants. He believed popery was not just delusional but also unhealthy and bad for the economy. The pope's "Power of forbidding meats" gave "him power over the Lives and Healths of all the People." He could also "empoverish the People to what Degree hee pleases" by forbidding them to "Labour as many dayes as hee pleases." Nevertheless, Petty thought repression was not the solution. Instead, he favored diluting Ireland's Catholics within Britain's Protestant population. After the Restoration of the monarchy he ran through a series of calculations and arguments to develop a "Remedy to the fears & Jealousys, w[hi]ch the King of Englands Non:papist subjects, may conceive concerning their being forc't from their Religion." It included an elaborate scheme to distribute thousands of Irishmen as soldiers throughout Scotland and England while British Protestant soldiers colonized Ireland.[40]

In the event, Catholicism survived and the Restoration of 1660 revived hopes for toleration. Even during the rebellion, Old English elites had sought to secure their position by emphasizing their political allegiance to their monarch over their religious allegiance to the pope. When the papacy's Italian representatives had taken an uncompromising stance against heretical monarchs, including the Stuarts, they responded by disclaiming the political pretensions of the pope. In 1661 the Old English revived this stance with a public declaration of loyalty that claimed their connection to Rome was purely spiritual and did not encroach on their loyalty to the king. They highlighted Catholicism's "tenents . . . in point of loyaltie and submission" and affirmed "that all absolute Princes and Supreme Governors, of what Religion soever they be, are Gods Lieutenants on Earth and that obedience is due them, according to the Law of each Common wealth respectively, in all civil and temporall affairs." Singling out the Protestant regicide of Charles I, they argued it was "impious, and against the Word of God, to maintain that any private Subject may kill or murther the anointed of God, his Prince, though of a different belief and Religion from his." Some Irish Catholics supported this proclamation with anti-papal Gallican arguments. Many others rejected it, defending the political and religious prerogatives of the pope.[41]

Irish anti-popery now expanded to account for the island's growing religious diversity. The once proud Cromwellian conquerors, reduced to the status of a dissenting minority, relied on anti-popery to bolster themselves against both Protestant bishops and the Roman Catholic majority. Already in September 1660, the Congregational minister of Dublin, Samuel Mather, a graduate of Harvard and older brother of the famous New England minister Increase Mather, was preaching sermons "Against Idolatry and Superstition" that criticized episcopacy. He called on King Charles II to reform the Church, as Hezekiah had done, by purging it of ceremonies and other anti-Christian inventions. Exhorting "the Episcopal Party, not to revive the Superstitions and Idolatries of former times, or at least not to impose them," Mather warned that "if once you super-adde the sin of Persecution to the sin of Superstition, you will be quickly ripe for final ruine, and for the vengeance of eternal fire." The government responded by forbidding Mather to preach in public. Continuing to minister to Dublin's Independents, Samuel Mather managed to send his sermon notes to Massachusetts, where Increase had them published with a preface explaining that the Church of England's "Ceremonies are Monuments of Popery, the Trophies of Antichrist, and the Reliques of Romes Whorish Bravery." Retaining them gave "Scandal to many Protestants" and "to Papists, who are thereby hardened in their Idolatries." In 1670 Samuel was selected to pen *A Defence of the Protestant Christian Religion against Popery* in response to criticisms of Protestantism by "one of their Learned men in Holy Orders." Before dying in 1671 he also composed a plan for ecumenical cooperation among Presbyterians, Independents, and Baptists. After all, despite their differences they had much in common against both the "Prelates" of the restored Church, who were in "Compliance with Rome" and violent "against us for the Truth," and the "Papists," against whom "the Saints and Martyrs" as well as "all our Protestant Divines" bore witness. His brother Nathanael, who replaced him in the pulpit, also took advantage of Increase to publish a sermon he had preached in Dublin. Speaking on the duty "of Believers in Christ, to Live in the Constant Exercise of Grace," he began by refuting the "Corrupt and destructive Doctrine" that believers could be justified "by observing the Ceremonial Law."[42]

Anthony Sharp, a prominent Quaker and successful Dublin businessman, preferred a more individualistic approach. He directly confronted Roman Catholic priests in debates about religious authority, the nature of the true church, the kingdom of Antichrist, and the burning of reputed heretics, asking "How many

Murthers, treacheries and Vile actions hath some popish committed"? With John Foxe's *Acts and Monuments* in mind, he urged one Catholic priest to "put away that Egyptian, Babylonish, prejudiciall Spirit of Enmity against the truth." As for the Church of Ireland, Sharp accused it of retaining "various Catholic 'reliques'" and espousing "popish Inventions" rather than "the Seal of the New Covenant."[43]

The Church of Ireland, having adopted the doctrine and liturgy of the Church of England, was now vulnerable to the same criticisms of popery. An Irish Franciscan friar who converted in the early 1670s acknowledged this problem in his conversion sermon. Preaching in London, Anthony Egan admitted that some would think he had "gone from Popery to Popery, that is, unto the same Church, though of another Denomination, it being objected, that the Constitutions of this Church are framed out of Popery, and the Common Prayer Book compiled out of the Mass Book." However, "all is not Popery that is in the Mass-book," Egan insisted. He blamed the machinations of the devil "and the Papists" for the anti-popish criticisms of his new Church. They wanted "to distract Protestants" and "make us worry one another . . . to break our Communion." He went on to confirm a number of Anglican anti-popish views. He insisted his conversion rested on intellectual and moral principles and purgatory was simply the "fire which makes the Popes Pot boyl." He criticized the use of Latin in religious services. It prevented the laity from knowing "the reason and meaning of that Service we perform to God," while "grand impostures" were used to "delude the people to fix them in their gross Errors and Superstitions." He traced the "Cruelties" of the Irish to the "ridiculous . . . Doctrine of Infallibility," remembering "with horror . . . those barbarous Massacres which were committed in my own Country, as if Papists had guts, but no bowels" (i.e., empathy). When he had been a Catholic, "I am sure I ever thought it a meritorious action to murther either Prince, or any Protestant Subject, provided I was commissionated so to do by the Pope." Now, however, he could not see "how to serve two Masters . . . the Pope and the King." He was also sure that more Irish would convert if Catholicism were not preached "with fire and faggot." The Irish were only held "to their Superstition" by the "fear of losing their Lives by the fury and rage of the Papists there." He himself had been forced "for safeguard of my Life, to come for England" after his countrymen "persecuted and assaulted" him.[44]

Other members of the Church of Ireland also adopted the conservative strain of anti-popery that claimed the Dissenters were "the Spawn of the jesuits" and thus the divisions among Protestants were really the fault of popery not Protestantism. This "bewitching and blasphemous, erroneous people" encouraged religious pluralism to undermine the Church, as Robert Ware, son of the Trinity College graduate James Ware, claimed. His father had collected and published historical documents, including Edmund Spenser's "View of the State of Ireland." Robert assembled his own collection of sources, *The Hunting of the Romish Fox*, to present a history of the Reformation in England and Ireland, Roman Catholic resistance to it, and Dissenting Protestant criticisms of it. He argued that "all our Divisions have sprung from Rome" and the "sectarian fire-brands" were "a specimen of popery & separation." Both Wares were ardent royalists who enjoyed a close relationship with the lord deputy, James Butler, duke of Ormond. Robert dedicated *The Hunting of the Romish Fox* to him, describing Ormond, an Irish Catholic convert to the Church, as the target of both the "Romish as well as the Reformed Fanaticks" and praising him for having "bravely defended the Royal cause and (as inseparable from it) our holy Mother the British Church, with a pious Constancy" when commanding Ireland's royalist forces in the 1640s. The book accuses Cromwell of being "a Succourer of Romish Clergymen," and recounts the allegation of a Dublin merchant that Cromwell brought with him a "Romish Priest, supposed to be a Jesuit." For proof, the book presented the "Confession of a Jesuit" who claimed Jesuits "headed the Presbyterians, and all Sectaries," including Separatists and Quakers, using them to "cry down the Pope and his Religion, with all the Church of England that are called Protestants; and to give Toleration to all other Sectaries whatsoever" and so "lessen the Interest of the Church of England." Drawn away from the Church, Ireland's bewildered Protestants would "lay hold of any new Opinion" and eventually fall "back again to the See of Rome."[45]

This royalist Anglican mistrust of Dissenters helps explain why Ireland was not actively involved in the paranoia that gripped England during the Popish Plot panic of 1678–81. Instead, one of Ormond's correspondents fretted that the words "French and Papists, two terms of art in every malicious mouth," could be used to take "revenge on whomsoever either can be pinned." Such anti-popish "jealousy" threatened to "leave us no Protestants" as Dissenters disparaged "the decency of our disciplines" with the "nickname superstition" and called "all who do conform, Papists." No doubt, were "Our Saviour himself on earth again there would be those who would brand even him with that fashionable calumny of Papist, and if Papist Frenchman too." In fact, however, the "Papists have of late so interwoven themselves with all sorts of Dissenters" that refusing to conform to the Church "gives supposition *ipso facto* of conformity to that of Rome."[46]

Only the next civil war, unleashed by the Glorious Revolution, returned Anglican attention the primacy of the Catholic threat. With Irish Jacobite forces laying siege to Londonderry in 1688–89, George Walker, a Church of Ireland clergyman and one of the city's governors, rallied his countrymen by arguing that "a Papist is a Papist still, where even the Principle of Religion instills a kind of Fierceness and Barbarity into their Nature." Walker was the son of a New English family that had been refugees in 1641. After Londonderry's liberation by Williamite forces, he gave a sermon that painted a picture of civilizational and confessional conflict. Now was the time "for Protestants to become Valiant for the Truth," and to be "bold as Lyons, not only for their Religion, but temporal Interest, the preservation of their Wives and Children, from Murthers, Rapes, and Deflowerings, and all manner of Violence and Wickednes." Reminding Ireland's Protestants of the need to "stand as Bulwarks against the Rapid Innundation of Antichristian Tyranny," he concluded with "A Protestant Prayer for our Deliverance from Popish Enemies": may God "Defeat their Plots, and Confound their Devices" and "Defend us from the Clouds and Mists of Popery and Error." This brief sermon was printed in London and Edinburgh, both cities that Walker visited on a celebrated tour to deliver a loyal address from the people of Londonderry to King William.[47]

During the war, Richard Cox, another Anglican son of a New English family that had been in Ireland for generations, insisted, "we know no difference of Nation but what is expressed by Papist and Protestant." To explain Ireland's many "Fewds, Wars and Rebellions," he published a history, *Hibernia Anglicana,* and dedicated it to William and Mary in hopes they would inspire "Reformation and Religion" in "that degenerate Nation." *Hibernia Anglicana* traced the current conflict back to "those great Antipathies which were created by Difference in Nation, Interest or Religion." The "Difference of Nation" boiled down to "Irish on one side, and the British on the other." Interest, on the other hand, pitted "the Irish and the Old English" against "the New English," who had robbed them of their lands. This conflict pointed to the most significant division: religion, the "great concern" that had "silenced all the rest." Since religion now mattered more than ethnicity, a Gael who became Protestant would count as an "English-Man; and if a Cockny be a Papist, he is reckoned, in Ireland, as much an Irish-man as if he was born on Slevelogher."[48]

The defeat of the Irish Jacobites, marked by the 1691 Treaty of Limerick, proved a major turning point in Protestant-Catholic relations. Initially, there was some promise for toleration. The treaty allowed about fourteen thousand Jacobite soldiers to sail off to France and fight for King James II, but, hoping to secure the loyalty and cooperation of those who chose to stay, King William allowed them to retain their property and even their arms if they swore allegiance to him. In 1693, desperate for new troops, William wanted to recruit them into his armies. However, the New English controlling Ireland's Parliament rejected the idea. As lord lieutenant Henry Sidney (a descendant of the Elizabethan lord deputy) explained, the "mere Irish" could not be trusted. They had been "brought up in the customs, manners, and religion of their ancestors" and had "a natural aversion to the laws, government and religion of the English." Only "known protestants" should be recruited.[49]

The New English went on to overrule or severely restrict the promises of Limerick while embarking on a new wave of land confiscations that brought all but 5 percent of the country's land under Protestant ownership. They then passed a series of strict penal laws between 1695 and 1728. Catholics were banned from holding public offices, serving in Parliament or the military, or exercising virtually any profession save medicine. With the exception of the fortunate few who already had licenses, they could not own guns or horses suitable for military service. They could not send their children abroad to Catholic Europe for education, become teachers, intermarry with Protestants, inherit property from Protestants, or gain custody of orphans. They were prevented from consolidating family property through primogeniture. Instead, they had to follow the traditional Gaelic custom of *gavelkind*, or partible inheritance, and divide the property equally among all the children. However, if one of the children converted to Protestantism, the convert automatically inherited all the property. Conversion from Protestantism to Catholicism was made illegal. Catholic worship, when it was tolerated at all, was severely restricted. Finally, a disfranchising act prevented Catholics from exercising even the most limited of voting rights.[50]

To bolster the legitimacy of this Protestant Ascendancy, a ritual calendar was developed to commemorate the challenges Catholics had posed to Protestant dominance. The notorious marching tradition that remains a focus of anti-Catholic conflict in Northern Ireland today developed alongside the "loyal healths, bonfires, illuminations and all other demonstrations of joy" of these commemorations. They included England's Gunpowder Plot (November 5), but mostly celebrated specifically Irish events: July 1, the anniversary of King William's defeat of the Jacobite army at the Battle of the Boyne; October 23, the anniversary of the outbreak of the 1641 rebellion; November 4, King William's birthday; and local anniversaries, like the siege of Londonderry. The celebrations linked this past to ongoing struggles. In 1745, the town of Youghal commemorated October 23 ("ever memorable to the Protestants of this kingdom") by burning an effigy of "the Pretender's eldest son" that "was drest in a Highland plaid, with a halter and brick about his neck, a wooden sword on his right side, a blue bonnet on his head, with a white cockade on one side, and a white rose on the other." To these anti-Scottish and Jacobite symbols were added "a bundle of Rosarys . . . hung on his nose, to shew his obedience to the Pope."[51]

With the Irish firmly subjugated, the focus of anti-Catholic fears switched to foreign policy. The French, who threatened to invade at several points between 1665 and 1811, became the primary target of these fears. William King, the son of Presbyterian Scottish immigrants who had converted to the established church while a student at Trinity College, managed to rise to archbishop of Dublin by articulating the new Francophobia in defense of the Glorious Revolution. In an influential sermon on "Europe's Deliverance from France and Slavery" preached in November 1690, King defended the Williamite cause as God's providential delivery of Ireland from an international, "deeply laid . . . Contrivance and Design" involving the "Power and Money of France, the Cunning and Craft of the Jesuits," and "the numerous and bigotted Roman Clergy." He accused Catholic priests of not only targeting all "Princes in Europe, especially such as profess the Reformed

Religion" but also exploiting "the Indigent and desperate Papists of Ireland" and making King James II a tool of "French interests." Francophobia mattered more to William King than anti-popery. He proudly pointed out that the French were so "intolerable" that even "the Pope himself" found it necessary to unite with the international "Confederacy" of Roman Catholic and Protestant princes against their "Encroachments."[52]

William King mastered the art of pamphlet debate in Ireland's newly expanded print culture to defend the Ascendancy and its patron, King William. He even wrote an extensive history of Irish Protestant suffering to demonstrate that the "Protestants of Ireland" had been forced to rebel against King James II to avoid "slavery and destruction." Clearly, he had aspired "to destroy and utterly ruin the Protestant Religion, the Liberty and Property of the Subjects in general, the English Interest in Ireland in particular, and alter the very Frame and Constitution of the Government." If a prince used his subjects "cruelly, or endeavours to enslave or destroy them," did they not have the right to seek the protection of a foreign prince?[53]

When he published *Hibernia Anglicana* in 1689, William King's colleague Richard Cox had insisted that Irish Protestants took "very little notice of" the "Difference in Religion between the Episcoparians [*sic*] and the Dissenters," but the unity in the "common Interest of opposing Popery" did not last long, as Cox's own career demonstrates. Having fled Ireland in 1687, Cox returned with the victorious Williamite forces in 1690 to take a role in the new government. After supporting the ruthless suppression of Jacobite irregulars, he then made a point of keeping Protestant Dissenters out of power. Most importantly, he successfully opposed a 1695 toleration bill that would have granted Dissenters an equal standing with Anglicans. By then, Cox had come to regard the Irish Catholic majority as "poor insignificant slaves, fit for nothing but to hew wood and draw water." Dissenters were the real threat, "because assuredly if they were in, they would put us out." After 1691, William King also devoted most of his energy to defending Anglican prerogatives against the Dissenters. With their help, the Ascendancy remained firmly Anglican until it its dissolution in 1800.[54]

The Anglican hostility to Dissenters contributed to the decline of Dissenting religion almost everywhere outside of Dublin and Ulster. Huguenots assimilated into the established church. English Presbyterians and Baptists were reduced to insignificance through intermarriage, conversion to the Church, or emigration to America. In 1700, James Wansborough, a Baptist in Westmeath, had joyfully announced to his relatives in West Jersey "our deliverance" from "popery." Twenty-eight years later, he was contemplating joining them in "your Contrey" to escape high land rents. The Quaker community persisted, but remained small.[55]

The great exception was Ulster Presbyterianism. Strengthened by a new wave of immigrants from Scotland, it acquired local majorities in several areas, including

Belfast and Londonderry. To defend their hegemony, Anglicans shifted the old anti-Irish tropes onto the Scots. During the Glorious Revolution the merchant Francis Brewster had professed that "all Protestants ought to be united against the Common Enemy," but when Scotland's national church became a firmly Presbyterian church, he denounced the Presbyterians' "Cruelties and Barbarities." Was their intolerance of the Episcopalians not hypocritical? Presbyterians once had "been the great Champions of Liberty of Conscience, and Declaimers against Persecution." Would Ulster Presbyterians attempt a similar ecclesiastical coup in Ireland? Brewster certainly believed they shared the "furious Zeal, and Spirit of Persecution" of their brethren in Scotland. He claimed to have overhead some "of the vulgar Scotch of Ireland, belonging to the Army" say that after they conquered the "Papists" they hoped to fight "the Bishops (meaning the Episcopal Party)."[56]

Instead, Ulster Presbyterians, resenting discrimination as well as rapidly rising land rents, began moving to America. One of the first migrants, the Reverend James MacGregor (a veteran of the siege of Londonderry), gave a sermon in 1718 justifying emigration on four anti-popish grounds: "1. To avoid oppression and cruel bondage. 2. To shun persecution and designed ruin. 3. To withdraw from the communion of idolaters. 4. To have an opportunity of worshipping God, according to the dictates of conscience and the rules of his inspired Word." He then led a group of Ulster Scots (many of them also veterans of the siege) to establish Londonderry, New Hampshire. In 1736, a Scottish Presbyterian in Donegal complained that churchmen treated his fellows like "Bound Slevs" with "theire hurrying yus into Bis[h]ops Corts if we doe not met ther time and Leseur." He threatened to join "my friends" in "ye Deserts of America," where "we might be freed from thos Burdings that we ar Labring yunder."[57]

Old English elites continued to insist on their respectability by drawing a line between their religious and political allegiances. They demonstrated that loyalty by refusing to rise in support of the Scottish-led Jacobite cause in 1715 or 1745.[58] Meanwhile, the bulk of the Catholic population, too poor to emigrate and escape their repression, became objects of charity. Their extreme poverty could perturb Protestant observers, especially during times of suffering like the horrible famine of 1740–41. However, Protestants generally blamed the Irish Catholics' misery on their religion. After all, Catholicism encouraged idleness, not least through an excessive number of religious holidays. Still, the Ascendancy hoped to convert them and developed schemes linking conversion to social and economic improvement. In 1733, in response to reports demonstrating that the Roman Catholic community was actually growing, the Incorporated Society in Dublin for Promoting English Protestant Schools in Ireland was founded. It established schools across the country to educate poor Catholic children into industriousness and true religion. One way or another, several thousand Catholics converted, or at least conformed, across the eighteenth century. However, once the reform acts of 1778 and 1782 relieved Catholics from much of the pressure of the penal laws, conversions almost completely ceased.[59]

The Ascendancy's many schemes for improvement in agriculture, husbandry, gardening, and manufactures were inseparable from its dream of converting Ireland and the Irish into a profitable, Protestant, territory. George Berkeley, churchman, philosopher, and former fellow at Trinity College, extended that dream to America in the 1720s with his plan to establish an American university to educate both colonists and Indigenous inhabitants before the Spanish and French could "spread the religion of Rome, and with it the usual hatred to protestants, throughout all the savage nations of America." His project failed for lack of funds. Returning to serve as bishop of Cloyne in southwest Munster, Berkeley then devoted himself to impressing the culture of improvement on the poor local Catholics. In 1749 he addressed a pamphlet, *A Word to the Wise,* to the Roman Catholic clergy of Ireland because they "are known to have great Influence on the Minds of your People." Explaining that he was "no Enemy to your Persons, whatever I may think of your Tenets," but a "sincere Well-Wisher," Berkeley asked them to "be so good as to use this Influence for their Benefit" by persuading them to "shake off the Shackles of Sloth" and take up "an honest Industry." That included working to "be clean." Admitting that many "suspect your Religion to be the Cause of that notorious Idleness," he pointed out that Roman Catholics in Flanders, France, and northern Italy exhibited "an honest Diligence." Why, "even the POPE himself, is at this Day endeavouring to put new Life into the Trade and Manufacture of his Country."[60]

Berkeley's *Word to the Wise,* reprinted in Boston in 1750, was one of the few books about Ireland published by colonial American presses. Another was Sir John Temple's *Irish Rebellion,* excerpts from which were published anonymously in Boston in 1753. The subtitle of *Popish Cruelty Displayed* demonstrated how closely colonial Americans echoed Irish Protestant propaganda. It summarized the book as "a full and true account of the bloody and hellish massacre in Ireland, perpetrated by the instigation of the Jesuits, priests and fryars, who were the chief promoters of those horrible murthers, unheard of cruelties, barbarous villanies, and inhuman practices, executed by the Irish Papists upon the English Protestants, in the year 1641." The book advertised itself as "Very proper to be in the hands of every honest Protestant, of what country soever he may be." It was dedicated "To all haters of Popery, by what Names or Titles soever dignified or distinguished."[61]

Into the nineteenth century, Anglo-Americans' understanding of Ireland was filtered almost exclusively through this Protestant experience, in part because Irish Catholics did not begin to migrate in significant numbers until after 1798. Irish Protestants migration to America reached a peak between 1760 and 1775, when some "55,000 Irish Protestants, or 2.3 per cent of the total Irish population," arrived. By 1790, Ulster Scots alone made up a little over 10 percent of the population of the United States. Some of each sort of Irish could be found in virtually all the colonies, but most favored provinces sympathetic to their religion. Catholics preferred Maryland, Quakers Pennsylvania. The Ulster Scots (or Scotch-Irish as they became known in America) favored Pennsylvania, Delaware, and the western frontier. Anglicans preferred places like New York City where the Church of England was established. Overall, Protestants were much more likely to have some property or professional skills than Catholics. The few Old Irish who came over were mostly found at the lower end of the social scale as artisans, servants, laborers, and sometimes soldiers.[62]

The lowly social position of Irish Catholics figured in conspiracy theories that linked them with Native Americans, African slaves, and the Catholic empires of France and Spain. In 1758, for example, the Prussian-born Moravian Frederick Post, acting as a frontier agent for Pennsylvania, dismissed rumors that "the French and English intend to kill all the Indians, and then divide the land among themselves" by blaming the Irish. Post told a Delaware sachem, "you must know, that there are a great many Papists in the country, in the French interest, who appear like gentlemen, and have sent many runaway Irish papist servants among you, who have put bad notions in your heads, and strengthened you against your brothers the English." Post urged the man to "not hearken to what lying and foolish people say."[63]

Sometimes, the American context reconfigured Irish anti-popery. John Moore, a recent Presbyterian immigrant from Ulster, was troubled by the murderous hatred soldiers and colonists expressed toward Native Americans ("kill them, kill them, they are vile barbarious savage brutes"). He worried they had "got too much of the Spanish spirit towards the Indians."[64] Most Irish immigrants had no such qualms, however. On the contrary, a shared hostility to the French empire as well as Pennsylvania Quakers' policies of peace with Native Americans led Thomas Barton, an Anglican minister from Ulster, to express common cause with the Scots-Irish. When the Seven Years' War broke out, Barton became something of a frontier hero by publishing a call for "Unanimity and Public Spirit." The sermon turned out to be rather guilelessly plagiarized from a 1745 anti-Catholic and anti-Jacobite sermon. When his patron pointed this out, Barton simply responded it is "no *Crime,* in a Protestant Country, to stand up in Defence of a Protestant Cause." He then became a volunteer chaplain to Pennsylvania's Anglican soldiers—a minority among forces dominated by the Scots-Irish. When, after the war's end, Scots-Irish colonists murdered a hapless group of Native Americans under Quaker protection, Barton defended them in an anonymously penned tract dated March 17th, "A day dedicated to LIBERTY and ST. PATRICK." Mocking the Quakers for "embracing Barbarians" and "cruel Monsters" and even defying their professed beliefs to take up arms to defend the "treacherous Savages," he supported the right of the Scots-Irish, those "unhappy people," and "free born Subjects of Britain," to obtain their "REVENGE."[65]

Opponents of the Scots-Irish, meanwhile, discredited them by combining anti-Presbyterian stereotypes with the tropes of Irish barbarism. In Philadelphia, a short "farce" claiming to be "Translated from the original French, by a native of Donegall" included a Presbyterian character who announces that, "agreeable to my Forefathers Oliverian Spirit, I would freely Sacrifice my Life and Fortune for this Cause, rather than those Miscreants of the Establish'd Church of England, or those R——ls [Rascals] the Q——s [Quakers], should continue longer at the head of Government" and protect "those heathen Enemies." A Quaker character denounces the Presbyterian's "Barbarity," claiming he has "the Mark of the Beast." In the Carolina backcountry, Charles Woodmason, an Anglican minister from England, complained of the thousands of "Ignorant, mean, worthless, beggarly Irish Presbyterians, the Scum of the Earth and Refuse of Mankind" who resisted his efforts to promote Anglican worship. They tore down part of a pulpit in one chapel, prevented the building of another, threatened a minister with whips, and in one incident left "their Excrements on the Communion Table." Echoing longstanding anti-Irish tropes, Woodmason blamed their "roving Teachers" for stirring "up the Minds of the People against the Establish'd Church, and her Ministers." He also suggested there were "many concealed Papists" among them "in the Shape of New Light Preachers."[66]

Irish Protestant habits, people, and history became ever more evident in British America as the Imperial Crisis reached its peak. Thomas Leland's *History of Ireland from the Invasion of Henry II* was published in Philadelphia in 1774, only a year after it first appeared in his native Ireland. Leland, a Church of Ireland clergyman who had taught at Trinity College, described his book as a "connected history" of "the progress of English power in Ireland" from the Anglo-Norman invasion to the Treaty of Limerick. For all that had been written, no single work of Irish history had yet addressed the process through which Ireland became "a respectable member of the British empire." Where previous histories were "dictated by pride, by resentment, by the virulence of faction" or "particular interests and competitions," Leland hoped that the "increasing liberality of sentiment, may have sheathed the acrimony of contending parties" and allow historians to study the past with "indifference" to its "contentions" and avoid "misrepresentation." Unfortunately, he did not succeed as well as he hoped. Irish Catholic intellectuals criticized his history for repeating old claims about their disloyalty and their religious doctrine's influence on the 1641 rebellion. To set the record straight, they began to write histories of their own, a revisionist movement that reached America after the young Roman Catholic printer Matthew Carey, having protested against Ireland's penal laws, found sanctuary in Philadelphia in 1784.[67]

On the eve of the Revolution, Ireland's Ascendancy recognized its special affinity with British America. Both shared a resentment of the British Parliament. It had dominated Irish affairs since it passed a Declaratory Act in 1720, leading Henry Flood to claim in 1770 that the British ministry was using "a mercenary majority in the British parliament and under cover of this battery of corruption, to sap the very foundation of our constitution." For proof, he pointed to its "cruel treatment of the Americans." Having poisoned "the fountain of legislature," Britain's chief minister could easily "vote the Irish, American, East India Company etc to be horses, asses, and slaves at his pleasure." Irish patriots shared the Americans' outrage over the Quebec Act of 1774. Members of Dublin's Society of Free Citizens raised a toast for "a repeal to the unconstitutional Quebec bill, which establishes popery," while the *Hibernian Magazine* reported on the "universal indignation, which seems to prevail through these kingdoms, at the sanction given to popery."[68]

Sadly, the fellowship was soon broken. In July 1775, two months after fighting broke out at Lexington and Concord, the Continental Congress, which contained several descendants of Irish immigrants, felt compelled to explain its side of the story "to the People of Ireland." Using anti-popish terms they knew the Irish would understand, they accused Britain's Ministry of spending the previous ten years trying "by fraud and violence to deprive them" of their "rights." It was "a black and horrid design . . . to convert us from freemen into slaves, from subjects into vassals, and from friends into enemies." Intent "on pulling down the pillars of the constitution," the Ministry clearly wanted "to erect the standard of despotism in America." If it were "successful, Britain and Ireland may shudder at the consequences!" Congress extended its "most grateful acknowledgements for the friendly disposition you have always shewn towards us—We know that *you* are not without your grievances." With hopes that "the iniquitous schemes of extirpating liberty from the British empire may be soon defeated," they defended their resort to violence as necessary and worthy of "that ancestry from which we derive our descent." They could not simply "submit with folded arms to military butchery and depredation, to gratify the lordly ambition, or sate the avarice of a British Ministry." Still, they held out the hope that their friends "beyond the Atlantic" might still restore peace—should, even, if they did not want to be the "last devoured." Meanwhile in Ireland, "a very numerous and respectable body of Roman Catholic gentlemen of property, eminent merchants, and other his majesty's loyal, faithful and affectionate subjects of that religion . . . took the oaths of allegiance" that had recently been passed into law.[69]

Irish anti-popery was an important strand of the anti-popish ideology of the first British Empire, forging a powerful bond between Protestants within Ireland and those without it. The lessons of Irish barbarity and priestly treachery taught in the various accounts of Irish history and politics published between the sixteenth and eighteenth centuries lingered in American's consciousness well into the nineteenth century. It affected their perception of Irish immigrants whether they were Catholic or Protestant, but especially if they were Catholic, and especially in the 1830s–1850s. The Irish did not rebel in America as they once had in Ireland, but that history was easily attached to any rowdy behavior by working-class Irishmen, as a poem printed in the February 1855 edition of the nativist newspaper *American Patriot* demonstrates:

Who is it that disturbs our peaceful slumbers,
By "rows" and quarrels without numbers?
The Irish.
Who is it we have some cause to fear,
And all their tales with jealous ear to hear?
The Irish.

. . .

Who stand among us as a deadly bane,
Ready to bind upon us superstition's chain?
The Irish.
Who must we aim to rule, lest they rule us,
And learn to know their place, and not to fuss?
The Irish.[70]

The American category "Irish" simplified and ignored the complexity of Irish history, where people of many ethnicities—Old Irish, Old English, New English, and Scots—and various religious and political interests jostled for power in an uneven and unsteady coexistence. This simplified anti-Irish anti-Catholicism was the fruit of centuries of (mis)representations by British and Anglo-Irish observers, none of whom had much of an interest in conveying the complexity and diversity of Irish society.

Within Ireland, however, Irish anti-popery evolved in response to that diversity in a variety of ways. Beyond the radical anti-Catholic bias advocated by certain individuals, especially the Church of Ireland and the Ulster Scots, there was a more moderate version favored by those who realized some sort of coexistence with Irish Catholics was necessary. In addition, different attitudes toward the power and influence of the pope figured in disputes between Irish Catholics, especially between the Gaelic Old Irish and the Old English. Protestants were also not immune to anti-popery's ability to explain or aggravate intra-Protestant disputes. In these cases, Irish anti-popery had much in common with its British cousins elsewhere. What set it apart was the ethno-national dimension that transformed ancient, papal prejudices against Gaelic Irish Catholics into a clear hostility to their efforts to retain some power and authority over the world in which they were forced to live—be it in Ireland or overseas. In the Age of Revolutions those prejudices would be temporarily transformed by the nationalist dream of the United Irish, who allied Irish Catholics, Ulster Scots, and Anglo-Irish with French revolutionaries against British rule. Their failed bid for independence prompted Britain to annex Ireland into the United Kingdom, mixing the dilemmas of Irish anti-popery more tightly than ever with its British cousins.

Notes

1. Jerome S. Handler and Matthew C. Reilly, "Father Antoine Biet's Account Revisited: Perspectives on Irish Catholics in Mid-Seventeenth Century Barbados," in *Caribbean Irish Connections: Interdisciplinary Perspectives,* ed. Alison Donnell, Maria McGarrity, and Evelyn O'Callaghan (Kingston: University of the West Indies Press, 2015), 39–41, quote on 40; *A Brief and True Remonstrance of the Illegal Proceedings of Roger Osburn (an Irish Man Born) Governor of Mount:Serrat . . .* (London, 1654); Serena R. Zabin, ed., *The New York Conspiracy Trials of 1741: Daniel Horsmanden's Journal of the Proceedings with Related Documents* (Boston: Bedford/St. Martin's, 2004), 121, 135, 149–50; Stephen Williams, "At Lm Febry 26, 1758," f. 17, folder February 26, 1758, Box Stephen Williams, Sermons, 1727–1803, Massachusetts Historical Society; Devereaux Jarrat, *The Life of the Reverend Devereux Jarratt,* ed. John Coleman (New York: Arno Press, 1969), 60.
2. John Gibney, *Ireland and the Popish Plot* (New York: Palgrave Macmillan, 2009), 12–13; Toby Barnard, "The Uses of the 23rd of October 1641 and Irish Protestant Celebrations," in his *Irish Protestant Ascents and Descents, 1641–1770* (Dublin: Four Courts Press, 2004), 142.
3. Gerald of Wales, *The History and Topography of Ireland,* trans. and ed. John O'Meara (New York: Penguin, 1982), 102–3; James Muldoon, *Identity on the Medieval Irish Frontier: Desperate Englishmen, Wild Irishmen, Middle Nations* (Gainesville: University Press of Florida, 2003), quote on 73; John Gillingham, "The English Invasion of Ireland," in *Representing Ireland: Literature and the Origins of Conflict, 1534–1660,* ed. Brendan Bradshaw, Andrew Hadfield, and Willy Maley (Cambridge: Cambridge University Press, 1993), 24–42.
4. Ian R. McBride, "'When Ulster Joined Ireland': Anti-Popery, Presbyterian Radicalism, and Irish Republicanism in the 1790s," *Past and Present* 157, no. 1 (November 1997): 63–93, quotes on 93–94. See also Edward D. Snyder, "The Wild Irish: A Study of Some English Satires against the Irish, Scots, and Welsh," *Modern Philology* 17, no. 12 (1920): 687–725; David Hayton, "From Barbarian to Burlesque: English Images of the Irish, c. 1660–1750," *Irish Economic and Social History* 15 (1988): 5–31; Jacqueline R. Hill, "Popery and Protestantism, Civil and Religious Liberty: The Disputed Lessons of Irish History, 1690–1812," *Past and Present* 118, no. 1 (1988): 96–129; Benjamin Bankhurst, "Early Irish America and Its Enemies: Ethnic Identity Formation in the Era of the Revolution, 1760–1820," *Journal of Irish and Scottish Studies* 5, no. 2 (Spring 2012): 17–38.
5. A.T.Q. Stewart, *The Narrow Ground: Aspects of Ulster, 1609–1969* (London: Faber and Faber, 1977); Aidan Clarke, "The 1641 Rebellion and Anti-Popery in Ireland," in *Ulster 1641: Aspects of the Rising,* ed. Brian Mac Cuarta, S.J. (Belfast: Queen's University Institute of Irish Studies, 1993), 139–58; John Brewer and Gareth Higgins, *Anti-Catholicism in Northern Ireland, 1600–1988: The Mote and the Beam* (New York: St. Martin's Press, 1998).
6. Tim Harris, "Politics, Religion, and Community in Later Stuart Ireland," in *Community in Early Modern Ireland,* ed. Robert Armstrong and Tadhg Ó hAnnaracháin (Dublin: Four

Courts Press, 2006), 51–68, quote on 63. Kathleen M. Noonan, "'The Cruell Pressure of an Enraged, Barbarous People': Irish and English Identity in Seventeenth-Century Policy and Propaganda," *Historical Journal* 41, no. 1 (1998): 151–77, argues that Sir John Temple's history of the 1641 uprising is more anti-Irish than anti-Catholic. Norah Carlin likewise claims the Cromwellian invaders were more anti-Irish barbarity than anti-Catholic: "Extreme or Mainstream?: The English Independents and the Cromwellian Reconquest of Ireland, 1649–1651," in *Representing Ireland*, ed. Bradshaw, Hadfield, and Maley, 209–26.

7. Jane H. Ohlmeyer, "'Civilizinge of Those Rude Partes': Colonization within Britain and Ireland, 1580s–1640s," in *The Oxford History of the British Empire*, Vol. 1: *The Origins of Empire: British Overseas Enterprise to the Close of the Seventeenth Century*, ed. Nicholas Canny (Oxford: Oxford University Press, 1998), 124–47; Martin MacGregor, "Civilizing Gaelic Scotland: The Scottish Isles and the Stewart Empire," in *The Plantation of Ulster: Ideology and Practice*, ed. Éamonn Ó Ciardha and Micheál Ó Siochrú (Manchester: Manchester University Press, 2012), 33–54; R. Scott Spurlock, "Confessionalization and Clan Cohesion: Ireland's Contribution to Scottish Catholic Renewal in the Seventeenth Century," in *The Scots in Early Stuart Ireland: Union and Separation in Two Kingdoms*, ed. David Edwards with Simon Eagan (Manchester: Manchester University Press, 2015), 169–202. Saint David represented an ancient Irish-Welsh connection that was extended after the Norman Conquest, then modified with the arrival of Protestant Welsh: see Bernadette Cunningham and Raymond Gillespie, "The Cult of St. David in Ireland before 1700," in *Contrasts and Comparisons: Studies in Irish and Welsh Church History*, ed. John R. Guy and W. G. Neely (Powys: Welsh Religious History Society, 1999), 27–42, esp. 40.

8. Steve Bruce, Tony Glendinning, Iain Paterson, and Michael Rosie, *Sectarianism in Scotland* (Edinburgh: Edinburgh University Press, 2004); *New Perspectives on the Irish in Scotland*, ed. Martin J. Mitchel (Edinburgh: John Donald, 2008). The debate on modern Welsh anti-Catholicism is instructive: Trystan Owain Hughes, "Anti-Catholicism in Wales, 1900–1960," *Journal of Ecclesiastical History* 53, no. 2 (2002): 312–25; Paul O'Leary, "When Was Anti-Catholicism?: The Case of Nineteenth- and Twentieth-Century Wales," *Journal of Ecclesiastical History* 56, no. 2 (2005): 308–25; and Trystan Owain Hughes, "When Was Anti-Catholicism? A Response," *Journal of Ecclesiastical History* 56, no. 2 (2005): 326–33.

9. Steven Ellis, "An English Gentleman and His Community: Sir William Darcy of Platten," in *Taking Sides? Colonial and Confessional Mentalités in Early Modern Ireland*, ed. Vincent P. Carey and Ute Lotz-Heuman (Dublin: Four Courts Press, 2003), 19–41, quote on 33–34; Hans Claude Hamilton, ed., *Calendar of State Papers, Ireland, 1509–1573* (London, 1860), 135. On the *Laudabiliter* mentality, see Alan Ford, *James Ussher: Theology, History, and Politics in Early-Modern Ireland and England* (Oxford: Oxford University Press, 2007), 20; and James Murray, *Enforcing the English Reformation in Ireland: Clerical Resistance and Political Conflict in the Diocese of Dublin, 1534–1590* (Cambridge: Cambridge University Press, 2009), 128, 210.

10. Brendan Bradshaw, "Cromwellian Reform and the Origins of the Kildare Rebellion, 1533–34," *Transactions of the Royal Historical Society* 27 (1977): 69–93; Brendan Bradshaw, *The Dissolution of the Religious Orders in Ireland under Henry VIII* (Cambridge: Cambridge University Press, 1974); Mary Ann Lyons, *Church and Society in County Kildare, c. 1470–1547* (Dublin: Four Courts Press, 2000); Nicholas P. Canny, *From Reformation to Restoration: Ireland 1534–1660* (Dublin: Helicon, 1987), chaps. 1–4; Colm Lennon, *Sixteenth-Century Ireland: The Incomplete Conquest* (Dublin: Gill and Macmillan, 1994), chaps. 6–10.

11. Toby Barnard, *A New Anatomy of Ireland: The Irish Protestants, 1649–1770* (New Haven, CT: Yale University Press, 2003); C.E.J. Caldicott, H. Gough, and J.-P. Pittion, eds., *The Huguenots and Ireland: Anatomy of an Emigration* (Dun Laoghaire: Glendale Press, 1987); Kathleen

Chater, "The Huguenots in Ireland," *Irish Roots* 93, no. 1 (2015): 24–25; D. L. Edwards, "A Haven of Popery: English Catholic Migration to Ireland in the Age of Plantations," in *The Origins of Sectarianism in Early Modern Ireland,* ed. Alan Ford and John McCafferty (Cambridge: Cambridge University Press, 2005), 95–126.

12. John Bale, *The Vocacyon of Johan Bale to the bishoprick of Ossorie in Ireland, his persecutions in ye same and final delyveraunce* (Wesel, 1553), fols. 17v, 20v, 27–28r, 44r; Katherine Walsh, "Deliberate Provocation or Reforming Zeal? John Bale as the First Church of Ireland Bishop of Ossory (1552/53–1563)," in *Taking Sides?,* ed. Carey and Lotz-Heumann, 42–60; Andrew Hadfield, "Translating the Reformation: John Bale's Irish *Vocacyon,*" in *Representing Ireland,* ed. Bradshaw, Hadfield, and Maley, 43–59; Richard Bauckham, *Tudor Apocalypse: Sixteenth-Century Apocalypticism, Millenarianism, and the English Reformation, from John Bale to John Foxe and Thomas Brightman* (Abingdon: Sutton Courtenay Press, 1978).

13. John Derricke, *The Image of Irelande* (London, 1581) [42], [54], [56–57], [67]; James A. Knapp, "'That most barbarous Nacion': John Derricke's *Image of Ireland* and the 'delight of the well disposed reader,'" *Criticism* 42, no. 4 (2000): 415–50; Maryclaire Moroney, "Apocalypse, Ethnography, and Empire in John Derricke's 'Image of Irelande' (1581) and Spenser's 'View of the Present State of Ireland' (1596)," *English Literary Renaissance* 29, no. 3 (1999): 355–74; Vincent Carey, "Icons of Atrocity: John Derricke's *Image of Irelande* (1581)," in *World Building and the Early Modern Imagination,* ed. Allison B. Kavey (New York: Palgrave Macmillan, 2010), 233–54.

14. Sir Philip Sidney, "A Discourse on Irish Affairs," in *The Prose Works of Sir Philip Sidney,* ed. Albert Feuillerat, 4 vols. (Cambridge: Cambridge University Press, 1968), 3:46–50, quote on 50; Ciaran Brady, ed., *A Viceroy's Vindication? Sir Henry Sidney's Memorial of Service in Ireland, 1556–1578* (Cork: Cork University Press, 2002), esp. 12–19; Ciaran Brady and James Murray, "Sir Henry Sidney and the Reformation in Ireland," in *Enforcing Reformation in Ireland and Scotland, 1550–1700,* ed. Elizabethanne Boran and Crawford Gribben (Aldershot: Ashgate, 2006), 14–39.

15. Alan Ford, "'Firm Catholics' or 'Loyal Subjects'? Religious and Political Allegiance in Early Seventeenth-Century Ireland," in *Political Discourse in Seventeenth- and Eighteenth-Century Ireland,* ed. D. G. Boyce, Robert Eccleshall, and Vincent Geoghegan (London: Palgrave Macmillan, 2001), 1–31; Michael A. Mullet, *Catholics in Britain and Ireland, 1558–1829* (London: Macmillan, 1998), 57; Micheál Ó Siochrú, *Confederate Ireland, 1642–1649: A Constitutional and Political Analysis* (Portland, OR: Four Courts Press, 1999); Jerrold Casway, "Gaelic Maccabeanism: The Politics of Reconciliation," in *Political Thought in Seventeenth-Century Ireland: Kingdom or Colony,* ed. Jane Ohlmeyer (Cambridge: Cambridge University Press, 2000), 176–88; Ian W. S. Campbell, "John Punch, Scotist Holy War, and the Irish Catholic Revolutionary Tradition in the Seventeenth Century," *Journal of the History of Ideas* 77, no. 3 (2016): 401–21. Lennon, *Sixteenth-Century Ireland,* chaps. 5 and 11, reviews Irish religious life before and after the Protestant reforms.

16. Aidan Clarke, "Varieties of Uniformity: The First Century of the Church of Ireland," in *The Churches, Ireland, and the Irish,* ed. W. J. Sheils and Diana Wood (Oxford: Blackwell, 1989), 105–18; Murray, *Enforcing the English Reformation in Ireland;* Henry A. Jeffries, *The Irish Church and the Tudor Reformations* (Dublin: Four Courts Press, 2010). Surveying recent scholarship, Henry A. Jeffries, "Why the Reformation Failed in Ireland," *Irish Historical Studies* 40, no. 158 (2016): 151–70, concludes it had failed by the 1580s.

17. Richard S. Dunn, James Savage, and Laetitia Yeandle, eds., *The Journal of John Winthrop, 1630–1649* (Cambridge, MA: Harvard University Press, 1996), 159–60; Nicholas Canny, *Making Ireland British, 1580–1650* (Oxford: Oxford University Press, 2001), 121–64; Crawford

Gribben, "Puritanism in Ireland and Wales," in *The Cambridge Companion to Puritanism,* ed. John Coffey and Paul C. H. Lim (Cambridge: Cambridge University Press, 2008), 159–73; Alan Ford, *The Protestant Reformation in Ireland, 1590–1641,* 2nd ed. (Dublin: Four Courts Press, 1997); Alan Ford, "The Church of Ireland, 1558–1634: A Puritan Church?" in *As by Law Established: The Church of Ireland since the Reformation,* ed. Alan Ford, James McGuire, and Kenneth Milne (Dublin: Lilliput Press, 1995), 52–68. On the colonial character of the church, see Alan Ford, "Dependent or Independent: The Church of Ireland and Its Colonial Contexts, 1536–1647," *Seventeenth Century* 10 (1995): 163–87.

18. Quotes in Ford, *James Ussher,* 28–30.
19. Declan Gaffney, "The Practice of Religious Controversy in Dublin, 1600–1641," in *Churches, Ireland, and the Irish,* ed. Sheils and Wood, 145–58, quote on 158; Michael MacCarthy-Morrogh, *The Munster Plantation: English Migration to Southern Ireland, 1583–1641* (Oxford: Clarendon Press, 1986), 92. See also Brian Jackson, "The Construction of Argument: Henry Fitzsimon, John Rider, and Religious Controversy in Dublin, 1599–1614," in *British Interventions in Early Modern Ireland,* ed. Ciaran Brady and Jane Ohlmeyer (Cambridge: Cambridge University Press, 2005), 97–115.
20. Robert Payne, *A Briefe Description of Ireland* (London, 1589), 2–4, 6–8. For similar texts, see Lisa Jardine, "Encountering Ireland: Gabriel Harvey, Edmund Spencer, and the English Colonial Ventures," and Sheila T. Cavanagh, "'The fatal destiny of that land': Elizabethan Views of Ireland," in *Representing Ireland,* ed. Bradshaw, Hadfield, and Maley, 60–75; 116–31; Joan Fitzpatrick, *Irish Demons: English Writings on Ireland, the Irish, and Gender by Spenser and His Contemporaries* (Lanham, MD: University Press of America, 2000); Oona Frawley, "Edmund Spenser and Transhistorical Memory in Ireland," *Irish University Review,* 47, no. 1 (2017): 32–47.
21. Edmund Spenser, "A View of the State of Ireland," in *The Historie of Ireland, Collected by Three Learned Authors, viz. Meredith Hanmer, Edmund Campion, and Edmund Spenser,* ed. James Ware (Dublin, 1633), 2, 4, 34, 35, 59, 60, 113; Sir John Harington, *A Short View of the State of Ireland, Composed in 1605,* ed. W. Dunn Macray (Oxford, 1879), 5, 14–19, 22. Few of the works on Spenser discuss his anti-Catholicism, which indeed seems moderate compared to that of other Protestants in Ireland at the time, but see Andrew Hadfield, "Spencer's Description of the Execution of Murrogh O'Brien: An Anti-Catholic Polemic," *British and Irish Literature* 46, no. 244 (1999): 195–96. For other Protestant efforts to reason away Catholic beliefs, see Raymond Gillespie, *Devoted People: Belief and Religion in Early Modern Ireland* (Manchester: Manchester University Press, 1997), 117–19.
22. Fynes Moryson, *An Itinerary Written by Fynes Moryson, Gent.* (London, 1617), Part II, Book 1, 3, 11, 13; Moryson, *Itinerary,* Part II, Book 3, 286–87, 289, 290–91; Anthony Sheehan, "The Recusancy Revolt of 1603: A Reinterpretation," *Archivum Hibernicum* 38 (1983): 3–13.
23. John McCavitt, *Sir Arthur Chichester: Lord Deputy of Ireland, 1605–16* (Belfast: Institute of Irish Studies, Queen's University, 1998); Alan Ford, "'Force and Fear of Punishment': Protestants and Religious Coercion in Ireland, 1603–33," in *Enforcing Reformation in Ireland and Scotland, 1550–1700,* ed. Boran and Gribben, 91–130.
24. Sir John Davies, *A Discoverie of the True Causes why Ireland was never entirely Subdued . . .* (London, 1612), 4, 11, 82, 95, 97, 241–42, 284, 287; Sean Kelsey, "Davies, Sir John (*bap.* 1569, *d.* 1626)," *Oxford Dictionary of National Biography* (Oxford: Oxford University Press, 2004); online ed., 2008–19 [hereafter *ODNB*].
25. David B. Quinn, ed. "'A Discourse of Ireland' (circa 1599): A Sidelight on English Colonial Policy," *Proceedings of the Royal Irish Academy, Section C: Archaeology, Celtic Studies, History, Linguistics, Literature* 47 (1941–42): 164–65; John McGurk, "A Soldier's Prescription for the

Governance of Ireland, 1599–1601: Captain Thomas Lee and His Tracts," and Brian Mac Cuarta, "'Sword' and 'Word' in the 1610s: Matthew De Renzy and Irish Reform," in *Reshaping Ireland, 1550–1700: Colonization and its Consequences,* ed. Brian Mac Cuarta (Dublin: Four Courts Press, 2011), 43–60, quotes on 58; 101–30; Brian Mac Cuarta, ed., "Matthew de Renzy's Letters on Irish Affairs, 1613–1620," *Analecta Hibernica* 34 (1987): 107–82, quotes on 112, 120; Nicholas Canny, *The Upstart Earl: A Study of the Social and Mental World of Richard Boyle, First Earl of Cork, 1566–1643* (Cambridge: Cambridge University Press, 1982), quotes on 130–31. For other seventeenth-century writings on Ireland, see Deana Rankin, *Between Spenser and Swift: English Writing in Seventeenth-Century Ireland* (Cambridge: Cambridge University Press, 2005).

26. Canny, *Making Ireland British,* 165–242; Raymond Gillespie, "Scotland and Ulster: A Presbyterian Perspective, 1603–1700," in *Scotland and the Ulster Plantations: Explorations in the British Settlements of Stuart Ireland,* ed. William P. Kelly, and J. R. Young (Dublin: Four Courts Press, 2009), 84–107; Phil Kilroy, "Protestantism in Ulster, 1610–1641," in *Ulster 1641,* ed. Mac Cuarta, 25–36; Clarke, "Varieties of Uniformity," and Raymond Gillespie, "The Presbyterian Revolution in Ulster, 1600–1690," in *Churches, Ireland, and the Irish,* ed. Sheils and Wood, 107–20, 159–62; Leigh Eric Schmidt, *Holy Fairs: Scottish Communions and American Revivals in the Early Modern Period* (Princeton, NJ: Princeton University Press, 1989).
27. Phil Kilroy, "Sermon and Pamphlet Literature in the Irish Reformed Church, 1613–1634," *Archivium Hibernicum* 33 (1975): 110–21, quotes on 111, 112, 113, 114, 115; Alan Ford, "Criticising the Godly Prince: Malcolm Hamilton's *Passages and Consultations,*" in *Taking Sides?,* ed. Carey and Lotz-Heumann, 116–37; Alan Ford, "Hampton, Christopher (*c.* 1551–1625)," Ciaran Diamond, "Leslie, Henry (1580–1661)," and John McCafferty, "Andrews, George (*d.* 1648)," *ODNB.*
28. *Articles of religion agreed upon by the archbishops and bishops, and the rest of the clergie of Ireland . . .* (Dublin, 1615); Ford, *James Ussher,* chaps. 4–8; Alan Ford, "'That Bugbear Arminianism': Archbishop Laud and Trinity College, Dublin," in *British Interventions,* ed. Brady and Ohlmeyer, 135–60.
29. Anon., *The Protestation of the Archbishops and Bishops of Ireland, against the Toleration of Poperie* (London, 1641), sig. A2; Cary to King, January 14, 1628, in *Calendar of the State Papers Relation to Ireland of the Reign of Charles I, 1625–1632,* ed. Robert Pentland Mahaffy (London: Eyre and Spotiswood, 1900), 304, #902; Sean Kelsey, "Cary, Henry, First Viscount Falkland (*c.* 1575–1633)," *ODNB.*
30. Sir William Brereton, *Travels in Holland, the United Provinces, England, Scotland, and Ireland, 1634–1635,* ed. Edward Hawkins ([London?], 1844), 141, 156. On the range of local diversity, compare Jason McHugh, "'For our owne defence': Catholic Insurrection in Wexford, 1641–2," in *Reshaping Ireland,* ed. Mac Cuarta, 214–40; Brian Mac Cuarta, S.J., "The Catholic Church in Ulster under the Plantation, 1609–42," in *Plantation of Ulster,* ed. Ó Ciardha and Ó Siochrú, 119–42. For the big picture, see John Bossy, "The Counter-Reformation and the People of Catholic Ireland, 1596–1641," *Historical Studies* 8 (1971): 155–69.
31. Aidan Clarke, "A Woeful Sinner: John Atherton," in *Taking Sides?,* ed. Carey and Lotz-Heumann, 138–249, quotes 126–29; Wallace Notestein, ed., *Journal of Sir Simonds D'Ewes: From the Beginning of the Long Parliament to the Opening of the Trial of the Earl of Strafford* (New Haven, CT: Yale University Press, 1923), 13–14. On the Castlehaven affair's anti-Catholic and anti-Irish dimensions, see Cynthia Herrup, *A House in Gross Disorder: Sex, Law and the 2nd Earl of Castlehaven* (Oxford: Oxford University Press, 1999), 15–16, 33–37.
32. Nicholas Bernard, *The Penitent Death of a Woefull Sinner* (Dublin, 1641), n.p., 1, 29, 32; Clarke, "A Woeful Sinner," 147–49.

33. Canny, *Making Ireland British*, 461–550; Michael Perceval-Maxwell, "Ulster 1641 in the Context of Political Developments in the Three Kingdoms," Raymond Gillespie, "Destabilizing Ulster, 1641–2," and Hilary Simms, "Violence in County Armagh, 1641," in *Ulster 1641*, ed. Mac Cuarta, 93–106; 107–22; 123–38; McHugh, "'For our owne defence,'" 214–40. On the role of survivors' testimony in shaping the published accounts, see David Frederic Greder, "Providence and the 1641 Irish Rebellion" (PhD. diss., University of Iowa, 2015).
34. Canny, *Making Ireland British*, 243–300; Ethan Howard Shagan, "Constructing Discord: Ideology, Propaganda, and English Responses to the Irish Rebellion of 1641," *Journal of British Studies* 36, no. 1 (1997): 4–34.
35. Robert Armstrong, *Protestant War: The "British" of Ireland the Wars of the Three Kingdoms* (Manchester: Manchester University Press, 2005), quotes on 134; Micheál Ó Siochrú, *Confederate Ireland, 1642–1649: A Constitutional and Political Analysis* (Dublin: Four Courts Press, 1999); Jane Ohlmeyer, "The Civil Wars in Ireland," in *The Civil Wars: A Military History of England, Scotland, and Ireland, 1638–1660*, ed. John Kenyon, Jane Ohlmeyer, and John Morrill (Oxford: Oxford University Press, 1998), 73–102; Jane Ohlmeyer, ed., *Ireland from Independence to Occupation, 1641–1660* (Cambridge: Cambridge University Press, 1995).
36. Joseph Cope, "Fashioning Victims: Dr. Henry Jones and the Plight of Irish Protestants," *Historical Research* 74, no. 186 (2001): 370–91, quote on 370; Sir John Temple, *The Irish Rebellion . . . with the Barbarous Cruelties and Bloody Massacres Which Ensued Threupon* (London, 1646), 66; Clarke, "1641 Rebellion"; Raymond Gillespie, "Temple's Fate: Reading *The Irish Rebellion* in Late Seventeenth-Century Ireland," in *British Interventions*, ed. Brady and Ohlmeyer, 315–33; Robert Dunlop, "Temple, Sir John (1600–1677)," rev. Sean Kelsey, *ODNB*. Joan Redmond, "Memories of Violence and New English Identities in Early Modern Ireland," *Historical Research* 89, no. 246 (November 2016): 708–29, contrasts the successful propaganda campaign of the 1640s with the failed pleas in support of the Munster planters in the 1590s.
37. Micheál Ó Siochrú, *God's Executioner: Oliver Cromwell and the Conquest of Ireland* (London: Faber and Faber, 2008), quotes on 100 and 117; *A Declaration of the Lord Lieutenant of Ireland for the undeceiving of deluded and seduced people* . . . (Cork and London, 1650), [3], [6], [9–11], [15]. On the role of violent incidents in creating perceptions of persecution and martyrdom, Catholic and Protestant, see Clodagh Tait, "Persecution and Toleration in Early Modern Ireland," in *Voices for Tolerance in an Age of Persecution*, ed. Vincent P. Carey (Seattle: University of Washington Press for the Folger Shakespeare Library, 2004), 131–44.
38. Samuel Rawson Gardiner, ed., *The Constitutional Documents of the Puritan Revolution, 1625–1660* (Oxford: Clarendon Press, 1968), 395, 399; W. Noel Sainsbury et al., eds., *Calendar of State Papers: Colonial Series, America and West Indies*, 37 vols. (London: Longman, 1860–), vol. 1, *1574–1660*, 429–30, 450, 453; Patrick Little, "The Irish 'Independents' and Viscount Lisle's Lieutenancy of Ireland," *Historical Journal* 44, no. 4 (2001): 941–61; Karl S. Bottigheimer, *English Money and Irish Land: The 'Adventurers' in the Cromwellian Settlement of Ireland* (Oxford: Clarendon Press, 1971); John Cunningham, *Conquest and Land in Ireland: The Transplantation into Connacht, 1649–1680* (Woodbridge: Boydell, 2011). Sarah Barber, "Settlement, Transplantation, and Expulsion: A Comparative Study of the Placement of Peoples," compares the expulsion of the Irish case with the Spanish expulsion of the Moriscos while Toby Barnard, "Interests in Ireland: the 'Fanatic Zeal and Irregular Ambition' of Richard Lawrence," examines the career of the most fervent advocate of expulsion and dispossession (a radically anti-popish Baptist) in *British Interventions*, ed. Brady and Ohlmeyer, 280–98; 299–314.

39. Gerard Boate, *Ireland's Natural History: Being a True and Accurate Description . . .* (London, 1652), 72, 75, 76–78 [76–77 mis-paginated as 74–75], 89, 124; Elizabeth Baigent, "Boate, Gerard (1604–1650)," and Elizabethanne Boran, "Boate, Arnold (1606–1653)," *ODNB*. For the broader picture, see Alexandra Walsham, *The Reformation of the Landscape: Religion, Identity, and Memory in Early Modern Britain and Ireland* (Oxford: Oxford University Press, 2011).
40. British Library, Add. MS 72888, "Material relating to William Pettty's thoughts on the Catholic religion and ancillary issues," f. 92r and passim; Ted McCormick, *William Petty and the Ambitions of Political Arithmetic* (Oxford: Oxford University Press, 2009), 241–48, quotes on 246.
41. Anon. *The Declaration and Remonstrance, of the . . . gentlemen of the Roman Catholic Religion in the Kingdom of Ireland . . .* (London, 1662), 3, 6; Anne Creighton, "The Remonstrance of December 1661 and Catholic Politics in Restoration Ireland," *Irish Historical Studies* 34, no. 133 (2004): 16–41; Anthony Joseph Brown, "Anglo-Irish Gallicanism, c. 1635–c. 1685," (PhD diss., University of Cambridge, 2004); Bernadette Cunningham, "Representations of King, Parliament, and the Irish People in Geoffrey Keatin's *Foras Feasa* and John Lynch's *Cambrensis Eversus* (1662)," and Tadhg Ó Hannracháin, "'Though Heretics and Politicians Should Misinterpret Their Good Zeale': Political Ideology and Catholicism in Early Modern Ireland," in *Kingdom or Colony*, ed. Ohlmeyer, 131–54; 155–75.
42. Samuel Mather, *A Testimony from the Scripture against Idolatry & Superstition* (Cambridge, MA, 1670), Sig A3[i], 73, 75; Samuel Mather, *A Defence of the Protestant Christian Religion against Popery: In Answer to a Discourse of a Roman Catholick* (Dublin, 1672), Sig. A2; Samuel Mather, *Irenicum; or, An Essay for Union* (London, 1680), 6, 13; Nathanael Mather, *A Sermon . . . to Live in the Constant Exercise of Grace* (Boston, 1684), 1; Richard L. Greaves, *God's Other Children: Protestant Nonconformists and the Emergence of Denominational Churches in Ireland, 1660–1700* (Stanford, CA: Stanford University Press, 1997), 55–56, 249–60.
43. Richard L. Greaves, *Dublin's Merchant-Quaker: Anthony Sharp and the Community of Friends, 1643–1707* (Stanford, CA: Stanford University Press, 1998), chap. 10, quotes on 229, 231, 238, 243.
44. Anthony Egan, *The Franciscan Convert; or, A Recantation-Sermon . . .* (London, 1673), 7, 9, 10–12, 13, 14, 15, 19, 28. See also Michael Brown, Charles Ivar McGrath, and Thomas P. Power, eds., *Converts and Conversion in Ireland, 1650–1850* (Dublin: Four Courts Press, 2005).
45. Greaves, *Dublin's Merchant-Quaker*, 232; *The Hunting of the Romish Fox, and the quenching of the sectarian fire-brands being a specimen of popery & separation*, ed. Robert Ware (Dublin, 1683), A1–A2, 236–41; Alfred Webb, "Ware, Sir James," in *A Compendium of Irish Biography* (Dublin, 1878), 547–49. On the English parallels of this conservative anti-popery, see Ian Y. Thackray, "Zion Undermined: The Protestant Belief in a Popish Plot during the English Interregnum," *History Workshop* 18 (Autumn 1984): 28–52; and Stephen A. Kent, "The 'Papist' Charges against the Interregnum Quakers," *Journal of Religious History* 12, no. 2 (December 1982): 180–90.
46. Colonel Edward Cooke to Ormond, March 29, 1679, in Caesar Litton Falkiner, ed., *Calendar of the Manuscripts of the Marquess of Ormonde, K.P., preserved at Kilkenny Castle*, New Series 5, *Miscellaneous Correspondence, 1679–1681*, Historical Manuscripts Commission (London: Anthony Brothers, 1908), 7–8; Gibney, *Ireland and the Popish Plot*.
47. George Walker, *A Sermon being an Incouragement for Protestants . . .* (London, 1689), 6–7, 11; Piers Wauchope, "Walker, George (1645/6–1690)," *ODNB*.
48. Richard Cox, *Hibernia Anglicana; or, The History of Ireland from the Conquest thereof by the English, to this Present Time*, 2 vols. (London, 1689), 1: Sigs. A1v, B2v, C1v, C2r.
49. Charles Ivar McGrath, "Securing the Protestant Interest: The Origins and Purpose of the Penal Laws of 1695," *Irish Historical Studies* 30, no. 117 (1996): 25–46, quotes on 30–31.

50. McGrath, "Securing the Protestant Interest," insists on the harshness of the laws. Earlier interpretations claimed the influence of "Lockean theory" and the "near absence of sanguinary punishments" rendered them mild. See Robert E. Burns, "The Irish Popery Laws: A Study of Eighteenth-Century Legislation and Behavior," *Review of Politics* 24, no. 4 (1962): 485–508, quotes on 485, 491. See also Maureen Wall, *The Penal Laws, 1691–1760* (Dublin: Dublin Historical Association, 1961); Colum Kenny, "The Exclusion of Catholics from the Legal Profession in Ireland, 1537–1829," *Irish Historical Studies* 24, no. 100 (1987): 337–57; S. J. Connolly, *Religion, Law, and Power: The Making of Protestant Ireland, 1660–1760* (Oxford: Oxford University Press, 1992), chap. 7; Thomas Bartlett, *The Fall and Rise of the Irish Nation: The Catholic Question, 1690–1830* (Savage, MD: Barnes & Noble Books, 1992), chap. 2; John Gerald Simms, *The Williamite Confiscation in Ireland, 1690–1713* (Westport, CT: Greenwood Press, 1976). Stephen Duane Jr., "Firearms, Legitimacy, and Power in Eighteenth-Century Ireland" (PhD. diss., King's College, London, 2016), demonstrates the penal laws' remarkable effectiveness in keeping guns out of Catholic hands.

51. John Brady, *Catholics and Catholicism in the Eighteenth-Century Press* (Maynooth: Catholic Record Society, 1965), 72–73; James McConnel, "Remembering the 1605 Gunpowder Plot in Ireland, 1605–1920," *Journal of British Studies* 50, no. 4 (2011): 863–91; Toby Barnard, "Athlone, 1685; Limerick, 1710: Religious Riots or Charivaris?" *Studia Hibernica* (1993): 61–75; Barnard, "Uses of the 23rd of October 1641," 111–42; James Kelly, "The Emergence of Political Parading, 1660–1800," in *The Irish Parading Tradition: Following the Drum*, ed. T. G. Fraser (New York: St. Martin's Press, 2000), 9–26; John Gibney, *The Shadow of a Year: The 1641 Rebellion in Irish History and Memory* (Madison: University of Wisconsin Press, 2013); Micheál Ó Siochrú and Jane Ohlmeyer, eds., *Ireland: 1641, Contexts and Reactions* (Manchester: Manchester University Press, 2013); Ian McBride, *The Siege of Derry in Ulster Protestant Mythology* (Dublin: Four Courts Press, 1997); William Kelly, ed., *The Sieges of Derry* (Dublin: Four Courts Press, 2001).

52. William King, *Europe's Deliverance from France and Slavery* (Dublin, 1691), 2–3; William King, *The State of the Protestants of Ireland under the Late King James's Government* (London, 1691), 7; James Kelly, "'Disappointing the Boundless Ambition of France': Irish Protestants and the Fear of Invasion, 1661–1815," *Studia Hibernica* 37 (2011): 27–105; Philip O'Regan, *Archbishop William King of Dublin (1650–1729) and the Constitution in Church and State* (Dublin: Four Courts Press, 2000).

53. King, *The State of the Protestants of Ireland*, 5–6; Raymond Gillespie, "Irish Print and Protestant Identity: William King's Pamphlet Wars, 1687–1697," in *Taking Sides?*, ed. Carey and Lotz-Heumann, 231–50.

54. Cox, *Hibernia Anglicana*, 1: Sig. C2v; S. J. Connolly, "Cox, Sir Richard, first baronet (1650–1733)," and S. J. Connolly, "King, William (1650–1729)," *ODNB;* Phil Kilroy, *Protestant Dissent and Controversy in Ireland, 1660–1714* (Cork: Cork University Press, 1994), 171–87.

55. Kerby A. Miller, Arnold Schrier, Bruce D. Boling, and David N. Doyle, *Irish Immigrants in the Land of Canaan: Letters and Memoirs from Colonial and Revolutionary America, 1675–1815* (Oxford: Oxford University Press, 2003), 15–16, 21–22.

56. Sir Francis Brewster, *A Discourse Concerning Ireland and the Different Interests Thereof* (London, 1698), 15–34, quotes on 15, 28, 31.

57. Edward L. Parker, *The History of Londonderry, Comprising the Towns of Derry and Londonderry, N.H.* (Boston, 1851), 34, 35; Ian McBride, *The Siege of Derry in Ulster Protestant Mythology* (Dublin: Four Courts Press, 1997), 24–25; Miller et al., eds., *Irish Immigrants in the Land of Canaan*, 26; Warren R. Hofstra, ed., *Ulster to America: The Scots-Irish Migration Experience, 1680–1830* (Knoxville: University of Tennessee Press, 2012).

58. Jacqueline Hill, "Loyalty and Monarchy in Ireland, c. 1660–c. 1840," in *Loyalism and the Formation of the British World, 1775–1914*, ed. Allan Blackstock and Frank O'Gorman (Rochester, NY: Boydell Press, 2014), 81–102; Maureen Wall, "Catholic Loyalty to King and Pope in Eighteenth-Century Ireland," in *Catholic Ireland in the Eighteenth Century: Collected Essays of Maureen Wall*, ed. Gerard O'Brien (Dublin: Geography Publications, 1989), 107–14.
59. Kenneth Milne, *The Irish Charter Schools, 1730–1830* (Dublin: Four Courts Press, 1997). Thomas P. Power, "Converts," in *Endurance and Emergence: Catholics in Ireland in the Eighteenth Century*, ed. Thomas P. Power and Kevin Whelan (Dublin: Irish Academic Press, 1990), 101–28, finds about 5,800 total official converts, but argues many of them were nominal; converts served more as mediators between the religious groups than as controversial symbols of division. Monica Brennan, "Taking Sides: Conformity in Early Modern Kilkenny," in *Taking Sides?*, ed. Carey and Lotz-Heumann, 251–65, finds hundreds of Catholics of varying social degrees conforming for a variety of reasons, from the personal to the political.
60. George Berkeley, *A Word to the Wise; or, The Bishop of Cloyne's Exhortation to the Roman Catholick Clergy* (Boston, 1750), 3, 5, 6, 10, 14, 15, 16; Edwin S. Gaustad, *George Berkeley in America* (New Haven, CT: Yale University Press, 1979), 31–34, 95–96, 175–176; Gordon Rees, "'The most miserable scene of universal distress': Irish Pamphleteers and the Subsistence Crisis of the Early 1740s," *Studia Hibernica* 41 (2015): 87–108; Toby Barnard, "Gardening, Diet, and Improvement in Later Seventeenth-Century Ireland," in his *Irish Protestant Ascents and Descents*, 208–34.
61. [Sir John Temple], *Popish Cruelty Displayed . . .* (Boston, 1753), 3.
62. Benjamin Bankhurst, *Ulster Presbyterians and the Scots Irish Diaspora, 1750–1764* (New York: Palgrave Macmillan, 2013), 1, 4; Joyce D. Goodfriend, "'Upon a Bunch of Straw': The Irish in Colonial New York City," in *The New York Irish*, ed. Ronald H. Bayor and Timothy J. Meagher (Baltimore: Johns Hopkins University Press, 1996), 35–47; Patrick Griffin, *The People with No Name: Ireland's Ulster Scots, America's Scots Irish, and the Creation of a British Atlantic World* (Princeton, NJ: Princeton University Press, 2001).
63. Charles Frederick Post, "Two Journals of Western Tours," in *Early Western Journals, 1748–1765*, ed. Reuben Gold Thwaites (Cleveland, 1904), 216–17; Thomas Hughes, "An Alleged Popish Plot in Pennsylvania: 1756–7," *Records of the Catholic Historical Society* 10, no. 2 (1899): 208–21.
64. Bankhurst, *Ulster Presbyterians*, 135.
65. *The Conduct of the Paxton Men, Impartially Represented* (Philadelphia, 1764), 22, 24, 29–30, 33, 34; James P. Myers Jr., "Thomas Barton's 'Unanimity and Public Spirit' (1755): Controversy and Plagiarism on the Pennsylvania Frontier," *Pennsylvania Magazine of History and Biography* 119, no. 3 (1995): 225–48, quote on 242; Miller et al., eds., *Irish Immigrants in the Land of Canaan*, 487–99; James P. Myers Jr., "The Rev. Thomas Barton's Authorship of *The Conduct of the Paxton Men, Impartially Represented* (1764)," *Pennsylvania History: A Journal of Mid-Atlantic Studies* 61, no. 2 (1994): 155–84.
66. *The Paxton Boys, a farce* (Philadelphia, 1764), 7, 12; Richard J. Hooker, ed., *The Carolina Backcountry on the Eve of the Revolution: The Journal and Other Writings of Charles Woodmason, Anglican Itinerant* (Chapel Hill: University of North Carolina Press for the OIEAHC, 1953), 11, 42, 46–47n, 60–61; Benjamin Bankhurst, "A Looking-Glass for Presbyterians: Recasting a Prejudice in Late Colonial Pennsylvania," *Pennsylvania Magazine of History and Biography* 133, no. 4 (2009): 317–48.
67. Thomas Leland, *The History of Ireland from the Invasion of Henry II* (Philadelphia, 1774), i–iii; Jacqueline R. Hill, "Popery and Protestantism, Civil and Religious Liberty: The Disputed Lessons of Irish History, 1690–1812," *Past and Present* 118, no. 1 (1988): 96–129; John

Gibney, "'Facts newly *stated*': John Curry, the 1641 Rebellion, and Catholic Revisionism in Eighteenth-Century Ireland, 1747–80," *Eire-Ireland* 44, nos. 3–4 (2009): 248–77; Padhraig Higgins, "Matthew Carey, Catholic Identity, and the Penal Laws," *Éire-Ireland* 49, nos. 3–4 (2014): 176–200; Martin J. Burke, "The Politics and Poetics of Nationalist Historiography: Mathew Carey and the *Vindiciae Hibernicae*," in *Forging in the Smithy: National Identity and Representation in Anglo-Irish Literary History*, ed. Joep Leerssen, A. H. van der Weel, and Bart Westerweel (Amsterdam: Rodopi, 1995), 183–94.

68. James Kelly, *Henry Flood: Patriots and Politics in Eighteenth-Century Ireland* (Notre Dame, IN: University of Notre Dame Press, 1998), 144; Vincent Morley, *Irish Opinion and the American Revolution, 1760–1783* (Cambridge: Cambridge University Press, 2002), 86–87.

69. *An Address of the Twelve United Colonies of North-America by Their Representatives in Congress, to the People of Ireland* (Philadelphia, 1775), 2–3, 7, 9–10; Brady, *Catholicism in the Eighteenth-Century Press*, 173.

70. "The Irish, by George A. M," *American Patriot* 4, no. 1, February 24, 1855, American Antiquarian Society.

PART II

Hegemony

Shuffling Tyranny

POPISH PLOTS, PLAYING CARDS, AND POLITICAL THEORY

Andrew R. Murphy, Gregory Smulewicz-Zucker, and Susan P. Liebell

IN RECENT YEARS, POLITICAL theorists have increasingly raised questions about traditional understandings of the texts they study, and consequently about conventional understandings of political theory as a mode of discourse communicated (exclusively or primarily) through philosophical treatises. No one disputes that such treatises are essential to the enterprise of political theory; it is difficult to imagine, for example, the emergence of the liberal tradition without such works as Thomas Hobbes's *Leviathan,* John Locke's *Two Treatises,* and John Stuart Mill's *On Liberty.* Nevertheless, to confine one's view of political theory to such authors and the treatises they produced results in an impoverished understanding of political thinking and the many ways in which the political, however defined, has been communicated over time. Such a constrained understanding of political theory fails to recognize the essential political work done by texts appearing in such divergent media as popular song, doggerel verse, broadsheets, pamphlets, trial transcripts, and visual images.[1]

This focus on treatises as the normative model for political theorizing has had several consequences for the study of political thought. It has led to a neglect of the important ways in which a wide range of genres helped disseminate competing social visions and facilitated political debate and mobilization. It has also ignored the ways in which such variegated texts illuminate the social locations in which political organizing, arguing, and mobilizing have historically taken place, and the diverse publics (including semi- and nonliterate publics) that have occupied those spaces. Finally, it has overlooked the role played by such productions in forming the broader cultural context within which works of canonical political theory so often emerge, the intellectual and rhetorical backgrounds against which they are most profitably understood and interpreted.

This essay examines one such political text: a deck of playing cards produced in 1679, at the height of the political, social, and constitutional ordeals known as the Popish Plot and Exclusion Crisis. The playing cards represent, in an important sense, both *texts* (in that they articulate salient political dangers and thus present a vision of the political good under threat) and important *contexts* for understanding other, more widely known political works. This deck not only presents scenes of purported historical events, but also implicitly offers a substantive political theory of anti-popery by depicting Catholics as working diligently to undermine the English system of balanced government. The cards enabled (or, perhaps, required) their "readers" to attend to issues of political power, imperiled liberties, the relationship between religion and politics, and the looming threat of tyranny.

Insofar as this deck of cards constitutes a political text, it is a text that interacts with its reader or audience in a particular way: not only by placing its component parts directly into the hands of the public, but by packaging itself in a particular popular format ("gaming"). As players held and rearranged the deck's fifty-two cards—either in the games popular at the time or by simply viewing the various scenes depicted on the cards, alone or in conversation with others—they facilitated plural interpretations and public discussion of events rumored to be under way at the time. As they circulated around coffeehouses, pubs, and other public spaces, the cards' visual imagery and broad accessibility created a form of public intellectual exchange that is easily overlooked when political theory is understood as primarily principled and philosophical.

After briefly laying out the chronology of events between 1678 and 1681, when rumors of Catholic intrigue at the highest levels of government and society roiled the political waters across England, Scotland, and Ireland, this essay moves to a close reading of the cards themselves and the ways in which they communicate a political theory of anti-Catholic "English liberty." It closes with some general remarks about the visual communication of political ideas and the enduring importance of anti-popery in early modern political thought and the emergence of the liberal tradition. In doing so, we shed light not only on the complex legacy of liberal theory and practice, but also on the enterprise of political theorizing more generally.

The Cards, and the Plot

"There is newly published the late horrid Popish Plot, lively represented in a pack of cards . . . wherein is represented the several consults for killing His Majesty, and extirpating the Protestant religion." So announced an advertisement in the October 21, 1679, *Domestick Intelligence*, which went on to inform readers of the price (one shilling, sixpence) and locations (King's Arms in the Poultry, and the Peacock in Saint Paul's Church-Yard) at which interested parties could obtain their own pack.[2] The

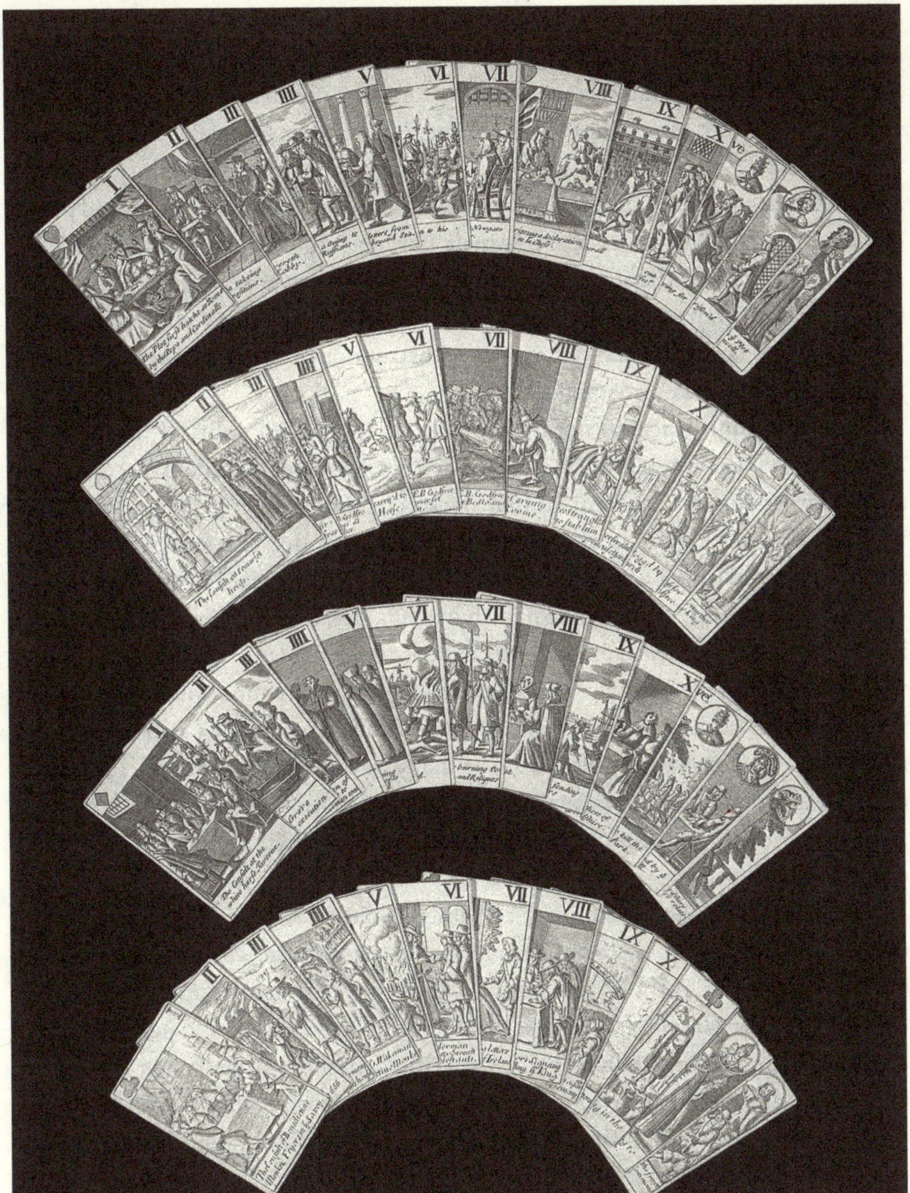

Pack of Popish Plot playing cards, engraving, c. 1679. (© Victoria and Albert Museum, London)

Note how each suit contains a different series of episodes associated with the Popish Plot.

advertisement was apparently quite effective, and the deck was "enormously successful, and . . . widely pirated."[3] The cards, which measure roughly 2 by 3.5 inches, are backed with a common geometrical pattern and numbered 1 to 10, along with face cards (knave/queen/king) in each of the four familiar suits.[4] Each card features an illustrated scene related to the Popish Plot accompanied by a descriptive caption about the alleged incident or incidents. The (unknown) engraver reproduced pencil drawings by noted English artist Francis Barlow (1626–1704), who has been described as "the first identifiable English artist of any distinction to have dealt with contemporary affairs." Barlow apparently wrote the captions as well, and the cards thus include both visual and descriptive "illustrations of scenes, whether actual or fabricated, that Barlow imagined."[5]

Given the conspiratorial nature of much early modern political rhetoric—to say nothing of the intense anti-Catholicism that permeated English discourse—it is not surprising that several similar decks circulated during these years. Two months after the notice in the *Domestick Intelligence,* for example, an advertisement for another deck appeared in *Mercurius Domesticus.* This deck featured not one but four "popish" plots (the Spanish Armada, Dr. Parry's plot, the Gunpowder Plot, and the Popish Plot); or, as it was described for readers, "all the popish plots that have been in England . . . excellently engraven on copper plates, with very large descriptions under each card."[6] The Rye House Plot of 1683 also received its own deck. In all, there may have been as many as five different Popish Plot decks circulating around London in late 1679 and 1680. We attend solely to the 1679 deck in this chapter, though our comments and analysis arguably apply to other similar decks of the period.[7]

That the Popish Plot was almost certainly a wild fabrication should not lessen our appreciation of the power of the images on these cards, which intersperse fanciful allegations of Catholic treachery with images of actual happenings such as testimony to Parliament and the execution of convicted plotters. A purported conspiracy to murder King Charles II and install his Catholic brother James, then Duke of York, on the throne, the plot came to light in August 1678 when Israel Tonge, an Anglican clergyman with a fanatical anti-Catholic streak, and Titus Oates, a disgraced former Anglican priest recently arrived in London from France, reported it to authorities.[8] Over the course of fall 1678, Oates implicated a number of high-ranking Catholic officials, including Sir George Wakeman, the queen's physician, in a series of explosive allegations that confirmed longstanding English suspicion about Catholic subversion and revived the rhetoric of "popery and arbitrary government" that had long defined English political discourse.[9] The disappearance of staunch Protestant Justice of the Peace Sir Edmund Berry Godfrey, who turned up dead in mid-October 1678 just weeks after taking Oates's depositions, further inflamed tensions and gave credence to the plot's allegations. Over the next several years, in addition to the popular outcry and paranoia, a concerted (ultimately unsuccessful) political effort sought to exclude James from the succession. Hence, the two terms—Popish Plot and Exclusion Crisis—often appear in tandem to refer to the tumultuous time between summer 1678 and spring 1681.

These contentious developments were rooted in the politics of religion in Restoration England and, more generally, in the longstanding anti-Catholicism that shaped early modern English political and religious life. Religious politics had fired the disputes that led to the Civil Wars of the 1640s, and Charles II was restored to the throne in 1660 professing a desire to relieve peaceful Dissenters, as well as Roman Catholics, from civil penalties for religious exercise.[10] Charles had a number of reasons to look favorably on Catholics. Many had loyally supported the crown during the difficult years of civil war and Interregnum; his mother and wife were Catholics; and his younger brother James (the supposed beneficiary of the plot, who later ruled as King James II) would follow his own wife, Anne Hyde, into the Roman Catholic fold by the end of the decade. Moreover, after a brief Anglo-French War in 1666–67, Charles maintained an alliance with France for much of his reign, twice taking England into war against the Protestant Dutch. Louis XIV's financial support aided Charles in his efforts to assert his independence from Parliament.

Throughout the Restoration, Charles's aggressively Anglican Parliament, jealous of its own prerogatives and eager to reassert its role in the realm's governance, took issue with the king's attempt to implement toleration by royal decree, especially when it included Catholics, and forced him to withdraw Declarations of Indulgence in 1663 and 1672.[11] In the view of many parliamentarians, accepting the king's toleration on the king's terms raised procedural and substantive concerns, legitimating both rule by decree and religious activity outside the established church. Anglican parliamentarians early in the Restoration worried deeply about sectarian Protestants, who (in their view, at least) had spurred on the Civil Wars of the 1640s and brought Oliver Cromwell to power; after 1670 concern about Catholic influences predominated, given the king's increasingly close relationship with France and an increasingly bold Catholic presence, centered around the queen, at court. Several of the cards depict such purported influences: On the 1 of spades, plotters meet at Somerset House, the queen's official residence; the 6 of spades shows Godfrey's murdered body being spirited out of Somerset House. (See page 135.)

One consequence of this growing suspicion was the 1673 Test Act, which aimed to purge Catholics from public office by requiring all officeholders to swear the Oaths of Allegiance and Supremacy, disavow Catholic doctrine, and receive the Anglican sacraments.[12] Charles grudgingly acceded to this legislation, which reflected longstanding concerns about Catholics' political loyalty, stoked the ever-present fires of religious and political division, and reinforced the growing mistrust between Parliament and the king. His brother, long suspected of Catholic sympathies, promptly confirmed those suspicions by resigning his naval commission. James's actions were especially troubling since, as Charles had no legitimate male heir, his brother was next in the line of succession.

For the rest of the decade, suspicions about Catholic and absolutist influence in high places grew more powerful. Lord Shaftesbury's 1675 *Letter from a Person of Quality* discerned a plot, dating back to the early years of the Restoration, to "declare the government absolute and arbitrary, and allow monarchy as well as episcopacy to be Iure Divino, and not to be bounded, or limited by humane laws."[13] Two years after Shaftesbury's *Letter*—and just a year before the rumors of murderous papists would race through London—Andrew Marvell's *Account of the Growth of Popery and Arbitrary Government* made similar arguments as it carried the narrative up through 1677. "There has now for diverse years, a design been carried on, to change the lawful government of England into an absolute tyranny, and to convert the established Protestant religion into down-right popery . . . [N]othing can be more destructive or contrary to the interest and happiness, to the constitution and being of the King and Kingdom."[14] Marvell understood Charles's 1672 Declaration of Indulgence as designed to advance popery ("that it might thence forward pass like current money over the nation, and no man dare to refuse it") and setting "a precedent to suspend . . . other laws that respect the subject's [property] . . . till there should be no further use for the consent of the people in Parliament."[15] The prospect of a Catholic successor horrified many in Parliament and the established church, as it "assaulted two hallmarks of Englishness: Protestantism and parliamentary liberty."[16] Because Catholicism and tyranny went hand in hand in the English popular imagination, robust defenses of Protestantism proliferated during these years, which saw an "explosion of illustrated Protestant primers" that could be employed by individuals with varying literacy levels. When the Popish Plot playing cards finally appeared in 1679, then, they formed "part of a growing emphasis on visual material within the wider context of a Protestant education," an education at once both theological and political.[17]

Shaftesbury and Marvell each used the language of subterfuge and conspiracy, promoting a view of the English king as increasingly in the thrall of Catholic France and as either the active instigator or the naïve abettor of a plan to bring absolute government into the Three Kingdoms. Scenes on a number of the cards show purported examples of Catholic subversion of the English monarchy. On the 8 of hearts Edward Coleman, a Catholic courtier at the English court, writes to Pere La Chaise, Louis XIV's confessor; the 9 of diamonds depicts English youth being sent from Dover to the Jesuit college at Saint Omer's, France.

Allegations of Catholic intrigue and conspiracy landed in the midst of this preexisting climate of suspicion and mistrust in late summer 1678. The king and his advisors received the early reports of Jesuit plotters with a great deal of skepticism:

documents had clearly been forged, Oates's own background was shadowy, and witnesses proved unreliable, contradictory, or both. Yet the accusations confirmed what many English Protestants had long suspected: that Catholics wanted nothing more than to overthrow the rightful monarch, and that they would stop at nothing in order to do so. Oates claimed to have been present at a secret meeting held in London's White Horse tavern (shown on the 1 of hearts), where the plot was discussed by several conspirators, although originally it was hatched in Rome (shown on the 1 of diamonds). The 3 of diamonds depicts Jesuit provincial Thomas Whitbread authorizing Jesuits to pay Wakeman 10,000 pounds to poison the king, while the knave of diamonds shows a purported attempt on the king's life while His Majesty walked in Saint James' Park.

Influential figures in Parliament saw an opportunity to capitalize on these allegations politically and weaken Catholics and their sympathizers at the royal court. They seized on reports of the plot as further evidence of the existential threat that Catholics posed to the realm. On November 1, the Commons declared, "This House is of opinion that there hath been and still is a damnable and hellish plot contrived and carried out by the popish recusants for assigning and murdering the King."[18] Protestant Dissenters attempted to use the plot rumors to push for their own toleration, as part of a unified front against Catholic (and French) subversion.

Oates's charges represented the opening salvo in what became not only a protracted political struggle between king and Parliament, but also a widespread and divisive social conflict in the streets of London and across the nation. Mark Knights views the plot years as bringing into focus "a debate about the relationship between King and Parliament, and between Anglican and Dissenter, that had been rumbling, and at times raging, since 1660"; J. P. Kenyon writes that "London was gripped by the kind of panic not seen since 1666."[19] The year 1666 referred, of course, to the Great Fire of London, which many conspiracy-minded observers also blamed on Catholic influence and which was represented on the 2 of clubs in the Popish Plot deck. Events moved quickly during subsequent months: five Catholic members of the House of Lords were imprisoned based on Oates's testimony in October 1678; the king banished all Catholics from London the same month; and a second Test Act was passed at year's end, extending the act's jurisdiction to the Parliament itself.

These rumors, half-truths, and innuendoes—originating in Oates's charges, but seized on by self-interested political actors with scores to settle and their own agendas to pursue—emboldened the effort to pass legislation excluding James from the succession. The ensuing Exclusion Crisis dominated English politics during the next several years.[20] If the king's brother was not part of the plot—and not even Oates claimed that he was—James nonetheless stood to benefit from it, and Catholics would surely profit from James's accession to the throne. Shaftesbury introduced exclusion bills in each of three successive Parliaments between 1679 and 1681, and a flood of political agitation ensued. Finally, facing a deadlock over finances—Commons would not grant funds unless the king assented to an exclusion bill and Charles would betray neither his brother nor his prerogative—the king dissolved Parliament in January 1679. Preparations began for the first general election in eighteen years. The plot allegations intertwined with the issue of exclusion and called forth the formidable political skills of a range of performers, engravers, journalists, and artists like Francis Barlow, whose scenes adorn the cards.

Oates, joined now by additional witnesses, continued to testify before Parliament and at the trials of suspected Catholics, and the first published accounts of the plot began to make details known to broader publics.[21] During summer 1679, English Catholics faced arrests, trials, and death, as anti-Catholic hysteria ran rampant in what Mark Goldie has called "Plot fever" and Kenyon has characterized as "the great holocaust of the plot": "Between June 20th and August 27th, 1679, and including those tried in London, fourteen Catholics were executed . . . To Catholics it must have seemed that the reign of terror would henceforth mount in intensity, engulfing at least those priests still in prison."[22] The scenes on the deck's cards—Catholics engaged in plotting the king's assassination, murdering a well-known justice of the peace (4–10 of spades), and suborning treason and destruction of property (3 of clubs)—testify to the enormous fear that Catholics engendered for a wide swath of the political nation. Scenes depicting the capture and execution of conspirators, on the other hand (9 of hearts, 5 of clubs), offered hope to beleaguered defenders of English liberties and the nation's Protestant identity, that popular vigilance could contain or overcome these threats.

As summer turned to fall, unrest in the streets continued. The pope was burned in effigy at anti-Catholic processions, including one in November that apparently attracted 200,000 spectators (see page 147).[23] And of course the politics of Catholicism in England only exacerbated the political environment in Ireland. Protestant-Catholic tensions there ran deep and reflected the long legacy of English colonization and appropriation of Catholic land.[24] Catholic priests were expelled and the Catholic archbishops of Dublin and Armagh imprisoned.

In short, the years 1678–81 saw a frenzy of political expression in a variety of genres, contributing not simply to a political crisis, but to a broader social upheaval in which countless thousands took part. Some accounts appeared in the form of narratives, like *The Discovery of the Popish Plot,* which elaborated eighty-one particular allegations sworn by Oates before Godfrey in September 1678; Godfrey's disappearance, shortly after taking Oates's deposition, and the discovery of his corpse in late October threw further fuel on the fire. *The Discovery* implicated ninety-one individuals by name, and provided an account of Oates's testimony before Parliament. A broad and contentious public debate took place in newspapers, broadsides, prints, satirical verse, and massive public processions. Popular ballads were (retro)fitted with plot-related lyrics.[25] Ultimately, Peter Hinds argues, the Popish Plot years represent "a fascinating, yet an ultimately tragic, lesson in the historical importance not of what happened, but of what people believed to have happened."[26] And in the midst of it all appeared our deck of cards.

Cards and Contexts

Before moving to the "work" done by the cards in communicating and reinforcing the centrality of anti-popery to early modern English political theorizing, several further remarks about the cards themselves are in order. Each card presents one alleged episode, and these individual elements are "divorc[ed from] their original contexts (as part of subjective/contested witness reports) and inject[ed] into another (as part of a seemingly objective illustrated record of 'the Plot')."[27] Although the cards do not lay out these purported events in any kind of chronological order, several features of the deck suggest that its producers attended to the arrangement of images and, by building on broader popular familiarity with cards as instructional devices, sought to maximize their political impact.[28]

Each suit's "1" card presents a secret gathering of Catholics intent on subverting the British monarchy. The plot's ultimate origins lay in Rome with "the pope and the cardinals" (hearts), but its success depended on meetings of "Benedictine monks and friars" at the Benedictine college in London (clubs), or a Jesuit gathering at the White Horse tavern in London (diamonds), or—most provocative of all—at Somerset House, the official residence of the queen, who was herself Catholic (spades). The use of the early modern noun "consult"–with its implications of "sedition or intrigue, a cabal"—on three of the four suggests a sort of primacy to these particular cards in each suit.[29] In other words, Catholics work in secret—in Rome, in London, in taverns, even within the royal family—to accomplish their seditious purposes.

Viewing the deck by suit provides additional insights into the political thrust of its imagery. The deck's spades all pertain to the death of Godfrey. Removing the 1 and king cards and arranging the spades in descending order, the suit lays out the saga of Godfrey's murder: plans laid in a pub (queen); the murder itself (knave, 10, 9); the movement of the body to its eventual dumping ground (8, 7, 6, 5); and the murderers celebrating after the deed is done (4). The remaining cards in the suit show Godfrey's funeral and the execution of those convicted of his murder. The diamonds focus their attention on Jesuit perfidy. Several feature Thomas Whitbread, the Jesuit who became provincial of England in 1678 (depicted on the 4) and who allegedly offered the queen's physician 10,000 pounds to poison the king (3). Jesuits are also depicted receiving orders to incite rebellion in Scotland (5), while Jesuit priest John Fenwick is shown sending English students across the Channel to the Jesuit college at Saint Omer's (9).[30] Two other cards depict John Gavan, a Staffordshire Jesuit, and Stephen Dugdale, one of the chief propagandists of the plot (10, king). The 2 shows Jesuits William Ireland and John Grove being driven to their execution in January 1679; the 8, a consult at Grove's residence, Wild House.[31] The deck's hearts lean heavily on images of Oates and Coleman. On the 2, Oates gives his deposition to Godfrey, on the 5 he receives letters from "the fathers" to deliver overseas, and on the king Oates informs the king and Council of the plot. Coleman, executed in December 1678, is shown giving money to encourage "Irish Ruffians" (4), with his legs chained while under examination in Newgate Prison (7), and reading his Bible on the way to his execution (6). The letters that got Coleman in such political trouble, his correspondence with Pere François de la Chaise (confessor to King Louis XIV of France), also decorate one card (8).

Understanding the cards' political salience and the political work they do entails taking into consideration the multiple contexts within which they made their appearance. At the most immediate level, the deck represents one particularly evocative aspect of the political campaign to exclude James from the throne and to target Catholics as threats to the security of the realm, "a central part of the propaganda war to secure the support of public opinion."[32] As Mark Knights has observed: "Playing cards depicting non-political scenes became available early in the restoration, for there were a number of packs carrying engraved images available in the 1660s and 1670s, such as those with county maps that were published in about 1675. But . . . it was the Popish Plot of 1678 that seems to have fostered the innovation of topical and polemical cards, a development that continued into the eighteenth century."[33] The artists, engravers, and printers responsible for these cards, and the sellers who distributed them, sought to further this political objective by vivifying, in image and text, the ongoing threat Catholics posed to the civil and religious liberties of English subjects. In other words, they sought to "use the formal, organizational, and cultural tropes of the playing-card to their full potential in conveying the Whig message to its best possible effect," presenting a skeptical public with visual evidence to bolster the rumors circulating around London.[34] The cards function, then, as political and polemical corollaries to newspapers and other printed material. The cards not only "visualized polemical concepts and debates," but also uniquely combined text, image, and format to create "an independent form of discourse in its own right."[35] That more than three-quarters of the scenes on the cards represent specific scenes from this particular religio-political crisis gives further credence to this interpretive approach, one that ties the cards to the most immediate circumstances of their production.

Moving to a slightly broader context, we might view the cards, and the images that appear on them, as pictorial or visual analogs to longstanding English anti-Catholic tropes: Catholics were politically unreliable at best and positively treacherous at worst, given their dangerous political allegiance to a foreign prince and their fondness for absolute government. Such arguments had circulated widely in English culture and political debate for more than a century, and would appear a decade later, most famously, in Locke's *Letter Concerning Toleration.*[36] Such a framework includes, but transcends, the narrower anti-Catholic and exclusion goals mentioned above. As such, the pictorial representations on the cards recounted a series of micro-episodes that reinforced widespread English views about Catholics and the threat they had posed to civil and religious liberties for decades. "By creating a series of distinct visual symbols, which both drew upon and fed into an existing body of anti-Catholic motifs," Naomi Lebens has written, "the Popish Plot cards were able to use the 'narrative' of the Plot to extend the significance of the episodes beyond the single 'moments' they represented."[37] Laying out the cards outside of game play, an active and engaged "reader" of the cards could assemble a tableau of scenes from 1666, 1678, and 1679, across the three kingdoms, into a self-created narrative consisting of numerous allegations against Catholic plotters. A reader in possession of the deck depicting four separate Catholic plots could construct a century-long tableau of Catholic perfidy stretching back to the Spanish Armada of 1588.

The various contexts sketched above surely represent valid and fruitful ones within which to locate the significance of these cards. Then again, these fifty-two images of Catholic treachery and endangered English liberty did not appear haphazardly, but in four suits of thirteen cards each, in an arrangement designed for a particular set of purposes. They are *playing cards.* According to Cyril Hartmann, "At no time probably in the history of England has the passion for gambling reached a greater height or spread over a larger section of society than it did during the latter half of the seventeenth and the opening years of the eighteenth centuries."[38] Catherine Perry Hargrave argues that, after a lull during the Cromwellian years, "With the accession of Charles II, cards were again in favor."[39] One estimate suggests that cards specifically—as opposed to, say, dice games—enjoyed an enormous surge of popularity during these years, with English card makers producing in the neighborhood of one million packs per year during the 1680s.[40]

Gaming took place not only at Whitehall, where it was considered the price of admission to courtly circles, but also at countless taverns and coffeehouses in the capital and across the realm. (The practice of gaming in private homes, with its suggestion of middle-class sociability, would not emerge until the eighteenth century.) Emphasizing the gaming context in which the cards appeared raises the intriguing possibility that a hand assembled in the course of playing one of the popular games of the period, such as picket, ruff and honours, ombre, cribbage, or gleek, might form a politically powerful visual narrative. (Then again, not all seventeenth-century card games depended on the skillful assembly of winning hands. Games like faro operated almost entirely on chance draws.) Even in the absence of firm knowledge about the likelihood of any such outcome, however, players would encounter images of Catholic plotting repeatedly in the course of any game, and a range of potential groupings could highlight different aspects of English anti-Catholicism.[41]

Playing Cards as Political Theory

Looking closely at this deck of playing cards contributes to a broader understanding of the enduring legacy of English anti-popery in at least three ways. First, the cards played an important role in the spatial diffusion of politics, bringing political content to diverse social locations through their use of visual imagery and their circulation in coffeehouses and taverns.[42] The blend of imagery and text also facilitated political discourse among a variety of publics, politicized the social locations in which they were viewed, and incorporated individuals who might not otherwise have had the opportunity to participate in politics. As Adam Morton has recently argued, cultural products like the playing cards in question constitute part of a larger universe of visual imagery, one of several "genres with a wide social readership—pamphlets, ballads, newssheets," whose authors "expected a well-informed audience conversant in day-to-day politics," politically literate if not part of the social elite.[43] Falling prices due to competition among card makers, to say nothing of the sharing of packs by individuals or alehouse keepers, made the cards widely available. What Margaret J. M. Ezell has written about illustrated broadsheets holds true as well for ephemera like this deck: they appealed to "a variety of types of readers who existed within complex and different literacies, creating multiple reading cultures."[44] Hence, the sites in which individuals engaged with the cards became places where the transmission of political information and propaganda as well as political education took place, and presumed a politically aware and informed audience of "active readers hungry to grapple with texts."[45]

Recent scholarship has elaborated the ways in which the English coffeehouse came into its own as a locus of political debate and a nexus for the circulation of news and gossip during these years. One defender of the monarchy recommended their closure, referring to them as "nurseries of sedition and rebellion"; royal censor Roger L'Estrange lamented in his satirical *Citt and Bumpkin* that his contemporaries "make every coffee-house tale an article of faith."[46] Beyond the coffeehouses, political argument and invective also went hand-in-hand with a broader, politicized culture of drinking and revelry: As Vicki Hsueh has put it, "Alehouses, taverns, and inns were . . . spaces of political association reflective of broader national political dynamics."[47] By bringing nightmarish scenarios to the attention of patrons of coffeehouses and taverns, the cards brought the debate over the threat to British liberty out of courtrooms and Parliament, placing it squarely into the emerging public sphere and the "people out of doors."[48] They function like broadsides, ballads, newspapers, and other forms of visual and print culture that circulated beyond the reach of the royal censor and among the institutions of an emerging civil society.

Second, by virtue of their participatory nature, the cards provide a unique vehicle for political theorizing, not reducible simply to "picturing" political philosophy but rather a multimedia form of communicating the political that enlisted the active agency of the reader. Through the deck's virtually infinite permutations of cards, the audience members (players) become co-creators of their own text.[49] Regardless of how the cards were employed, the term player seems more appropriate than reader or viewer to describe those who used them. The cards provide the opportunity for players' active engagement (with other players, with bystanders and onlookers in public places), facilitating political conversations and making possible the creation of an almost infinite number of narratives. Separately from the rules of games like cribbage, players could arrange different combinations of cards to construct a narrative that would make sense of the crisis for themselves and for others. Furthermore, such engagements would have taken place through face-to-face encounters between individuals within those institutions mentioned above (alehouses, taverns, coffeehouses), and were heavily intertwined with an expanding news media and its attendant discourses, as well as the newly established Penny Post in London, which made possible inexpensive and anonymous circulation of materials around the capital.[50]

The difference between the cards and a standard political treatise seems clear enough. But it is helpful to distinguish the cards from other forms of visual polemic as well. Consider, in addition, *The Solemn Mock Procession* of 1679, a broadside also attributed (at least in part) to Barlow. Unlike the card decks, *The Procession* offers a fixed image with accompanying explanatory text. It depicts a single event, in this case a procession with a beginning, middle, and end.[51] Or consider the "storyboard print" like *A Representation of the Popish Plot in Twenty-nine Figures,* some of whose images appear on the cards themselves. Productions like *A Representation* "attempted to fix a narrative of the plot out of the nebula of conflicting information/misinformation which the trials and other commentaries spewed into the public sphere."[52] The cards, in a sense, encourage another approach. Given their representation of multiple scenes occurring over the course of years, and the nearly innumerable possible combinations that the card format made possible, employing (and enjoying) them required users' active engagement. In doing so, such users make themselves into active agents in the construction of visual political narratives. This protean nature differentiates the cards from other sorts of texts and media

A Representation of the Popish Plot in Twenty-nine Figures, as ye manner of killing Sr Edmond-bury Godfrey, & their horid designes to kill the King, and the manner of the Plotters Execution, playing cards, c. 1678. (© The Trustees of the British Museum; all rights reserved)

Vignettes illustrate specific episodes, real and imagined, from the time the pope and cardinals hatched the plot in Rome to the execution of alleged conspirators.

The Solemn Mock Procession of the Pope, Cardinalls, Jesuits, Fryers, etc., engraving, 1680. (© The Trustees of the British Museum; all rights reserved)

Describing a 1679 parade that expressed the "Detestation and Hatred of the English Nation against the Tyranny and Superstition of the Popish Religion" and "their Abhorrence" of the Popish Plot, this broadside concludes with a song praising "Queen Bess, Who sav'd your Souls from Popish Thrall."

that attempted to reach similar publics; the cards are distinctive not only because of the locations or publics they reached, but also because of the way they allowed members of these publics to actively construct their own political narratives.[53]

Third, in addition to the fact that the cards took political debate to new publics and institutional locations, and provided a unique vehicle for communicating the political, they also conveyed a particular mode of rhetoric, one that we might broadly call dystopian. As noted, the cards illustrate a number of scenarios in which political and religious liberty is threatened or under attack at a particular moment in the history of a particular society (or, rather, three societies). Given the dystopian vision that the cards depicted (and that the plot rumors sought to stoke), the cards provide a way for the user to imagine, construct, develop, and communicate an explanatory framework for directing blame and apportioning or justifying punishment.

The dystopian nature of the political vision is nearly impossible to overemphasize: each scene on the cards aims to drive home to its audience the horrors of papal tyranny. Dystopianism is by no means devoid of constructive political principles, and while the cards present a variety of barbaric and horrific images, they simultaneously provide a vision of the political order they seek to defend.[54] Even if the cards offered their users visions of that which they opposed and feared (Catholic subversion, impending tyranny, regicide), they still presume some positive vision of a just society. For example, cards depicting Godfrey's murder, or showing testimony before Parliament, emphasize the importance of vigilant representative political institutions in the capital. Other cards show foreign threats, like Irish ruffians, French Jesuits, or the pope himself, and the ways in which each one threatened English liberties. The intertwining of harms to be avoided and substantive goals to be pursued is part and parcel of all political rhetoric, of course, and utopianism and dystopianism might more profitably be theorized as poles of a continuum rather than a dichotomous choice. The preponderance of stark visual warnings about Catholic threats to liberty places these cards firmly in the dystopian corner, yet since they draw on longstanding tropes about Catholics and their tyrannical tendencies, they also contributed to understanding what it meant to be a free Englishman.

For early modern Protestants, denunciations of "popery" brought together critiques of Catholicism as a set of doctrinal claims (transubstantiation, prayer to saints, papal infallibility) and as a structure of ecclesiastical offices (bishops, archbishops, cardinals, popes); both of which departed from scripture, set up human traditions as articles of faith, and preyed on people's credulity and ignorance. But popery was never merely a religious term, and one contemporary account viewed religion as "but the mantle which covers the design of the popishly affected party and their leaders, to keep off the sitting of Parliaments."[55] Charges of popery always appeared in the heat of political and religious contestation, and were always self-serving, allowing "true Protestants" to associate themselves with rationality, enlightenment, and knowledge, while branding their opponents as embracing a "ritual-based vision of ignorance, superstition, and unthinking tradition."[56] Those who favored the toleration of Dissenters often attacked persecuting Anglicans for behaving in much the same way as the Catholics they so vigorously denounced: William Penn warned, "Let us also have a care of popery in Protestant guise. . . . For in vain do we hope to be delivered from papists, till we deliver ourselves from popery." "You are afraid of popery," he wrote in the midst of the plot turmoil, "and yet many of you practice it; For why do you fear it, but for it's compulsion and persecution? And will you compel or persecute . . . ? If you will, pray let me say, You hate the papists, but not popery."[57]

Antipopery is best understood, then, as a polemical weapon, evoking a far more expansive set of fears than one would find by considering Roman Catholicism merely as a set of doctrines and offices.[58] It is an intensely political term not strictly limited to criticisms of Catholicism, despite the obvious affinity of its nomenclature and the routine trotting-out of Catholics as politically dangerous foreign agents bent on the subordination of England to papal control. For staunch Protestants such as those who vigorously pursued the plot allegations, the continuing presence of Catholicism in seventeenth-century England represented a fatal weakness at the heart of society, a potential fifth column just waiting to be activated by Jesuits sent from Rome or Saint Omer.

Yet while the cards sought to heighten the idea of Catholics as nefarious influences, other actors attempted to normalize them and to emphasize the shared civil interest of all of England's religious communities. Some years later, when Penn was working in support of James II's program to bring toleration to English Dissenters—both Protestants and Catholics—he sought to downplay the threat posed by English Catholics. Hysteria over Catholics "hav[ing] a few offices with us" was, in his view, wildly overblown, since the two communities had been living, working, and loving side-by-side for years (in his words, "hunting, hawking, gaming, and marrying").[59] Penn's (and James's) was a decidedly uphill, and ultimately unsuccessful, battle; the spectacular collapse of James's tolerationist program in 1688 was due largely to his public embrace of Catholicism, and illustrates the persistence of anti-popery as a potent political force in English public life.[60]

Conclusion

This remarkable deck of cards presented its seventeenth-century audience, and continues to present twenty-first-century scholars, with a plethora of multidimensional political material. What we have here is one text (the deck itself), four texts (the deck divided by suit), fifty-two texts (the cards considered individually), and an almost limitless number of texts (hands). Each one emphasizes a particular element or elements of the Popish Plot as an episode in the religio-political life of early modern Britain. Nor did this deck stand alone: as noted earlier, a contemporaneous deck combined selected images from the Popish Plot with three other instances of Catholic aggression nearly a century earlier, casting the Catholic threat on an even grander historical stage. To make things more complex, twenty-nine of the engravings that decorate these cards also appeared on one sheet, presumably to hang in homes or to pass around to politically like-minded family members, friends, or neighbors; others adorned ceramic tiles. Using the same images in various media resulted in "a *brand* of Exclusion . . . iconographically consistent across print, the pope-burning processions, playing cards, and ceramics."[61] And of course the brand of exclusion was coterminous with a politically aggressive Protestantism shot through with anti-popery. Placing the images individually onto playing cards allowed them to escape detection and gain entrée into another set of social locations (coffeehouses, pubs, or other public spaces, as opposed to hanging on the walls of private residences). It also dictated a different relationship with audiences, changing readers or viewers into active participants or players.

Most of our discussion of these cards has treated them as texts. But viewed from another perspective, they represent part of a larger context, since the political campaign to exclude James produced some of the central works of seventeenth-century English political theory: in the words of Peter Laslett, "*Two Treatises* is an Exclusion Tract, not a Revolution Pamphlet."[62] Much the same could be said for Algernon Sidney's *Discourses Concerning Government*, which like Locke's *Treatises* was occasioned by the republication of Robert Filmer's *Patriarcha* in 1679 and 1680. Taken for granted by almost all early modern English Protestants was the assumption that no Roman Catholic would countenance liberty of conscience for his Protestant subjects, to say nothing of political liberty more generally. Protestations to the contrary were generally viewed as a subterfuge, a Trojan horse, by which liberty for Catholics would be introduced, the easier to later impose Catholicism on the nation and finish the work of extirpating English Protestantism.

Considering these various genres alongside each other in the temporal context of the Popish Plot years fruitfully blurs lines between "political theory" and other forms of political speech and action. Considering the cards as unique vehicles of political communication promises a broad and deep engagement with the conditions under which political theorizing in all its guises takes place, and relates political theory to political practice in concrete ways. Nor were the ramifications of these events limited to England. The conclusion of the Exclusion Crisis coincided with William Penn's receipt of a charter for his colony of Pennsylvania. A number of scholars have suggested that getting troublesome religious Dissenters out of the realm in the wake of such a divisive crisis formed part of the impetus for the king's approval of Penn's grant. Once again, we are led to the importance of this three-year episode in English history as generative not only for classics of political theory (Locke, Sidney, James Tyrrell, Filmer), but for the theory-practice nexus in the broader Anglo-American tradition.[63]

The anonymous and uncountable individuals who employed these cards were engaged in the systematic and evocative communication of political content, the articulation of good government and a just social order that lies at the heart of all political theorizing. That they did so visually and in a dystopian way—by arranging images from a nightmare scenario, not by defending explicit principles and propositions—should not blind us to the significant political work that the originators and distributors of these cards set out to accomplish. If communicating political ideas and offering a vision of good governance, legitimate authority, and popular liberty in the midst of conflict are some of the hallmarks of political theorizing, then this deck of cards—visually arresting, small enough to fit into a pocket, engraved from prints drawn by a famed political cartoonist, and available at a reasonable cost—represents a gold mine of early modern political speech and rhetoric. At the broadest level of analysis, these cards, when viewed alongside contemporary narratives, ballads, engravings, and so on, bring viewers (and scholars) into a full-fledged, multidimensional political alarm about impending tyranny.

Attempting to understand the power of such an unconventional political text introduces a host of intriguing interpretive questions. Since the 1960s, historians of political thought have adopted a number of innovative approaches for dealing with the interpretation of political texts and concepts. Yet such work has focused almost exclusively on political texts and concepts proper. Consequently, much attention has been given to authorial intentionality, as in Quentin Skinner's appropriation of J. L. Austin and J. R. Searle's speech act theory, or the transformation of concepts in different political contexts as examined by J.G.A. Pocock.[64] But given the ways in which these cards invite, almost require, their own arrangement and rearrangement, it may make little sense to speak of an "author" other than the individuals holding the cards in their own hands. Those individuals who made use of the cards essentially created new variations on the plot narrative through the arrangement and rearrangement of the cards, and did so far from the gaze of state power.

On a concluding note, it is also worth pointing out that politically themed (and politically charged) decks of playing cards are hardly unique to the seventeenth century. They appear throughout history in a range of cultures. Political decks of cards and have continued to serve as conduits for political commentary to our own day. Many Americans surely remember the "Iraqi Most Wanted" deck, produced by the Defense Intelligence Agency and U.S. Central Command in Iraq in April 2003. Compared to the Popish Plot deck, the Iraqi deck comes across as fairly weak tea. Most of the cards feature simply a photograph of one of fifty-two Iraqi government officials then wanted by coalition forces, shown from the shoulders up, along with the individual's name and official position. Still, as in the case of seventeenth-century playing cards, the "Iraqi Most Wanted" deck served as an ever-present reminder of the enemy. In that deck, of course, Saddam Hussein adorns the ace of spades.

Notes

We thank Eric Macgilvray, Keith Topper, and the Penn Political Theory Workshop.

1. Patricia Fumerton, ed., *Ballads and Broadsides in Britain, 1500–1800* (Surrey: Ashgate, 2009); Andrew Murphy, "Trial Transcript as Political Theory: Principles and Performance in the Penn-Mead Case," *Political Theory* 41, no. 6 (2013): 775–808; Elizabeth Wingrove, "Sovereign Address," *Political Theory* 40, no. 2 (2012): 135–64; Michael Hunter, ed., *Printed Images in Early Modern Britain* (Farnham: Ashgate, 2010); and Quentin Skinner on the frontispiece to *Leviathan* in *Hobbes and Republican Liberty* (Cambridge: Cambridge University Press, 2008), 186–96.
2. *Domestick Intelligence; or, News from Both City and Country* (London: Benjamin Harris), no. 31, October 21, 1679.
3. Anthony Griffiths, *The Print in Stuart Britain, 1603–1689* (London: British Museum, 1988), 283.
4. Although the cards are numbered with Roman numerals, we use standard Arabic numbers in this essay for ease of reference. Decks are held by several historical libraries and museums such as the British Museum and the Victoria and Albert (with minor differences unrelated to the imagery); for high-quality digital images, see, e.g., http://collections.vam.ac.uk/item/O77469/the-popish-plot-pack-of-playing-barlow-francis/.
5. Edward Hodnett, *Francis Barlow: The First Master of English Book Illustration* (Berkeley: University of California Press, 1978), 26. See also Nathan Flis and Michael Hunter, *Francis Barlow: Painter of Birds and Beasts* (London: Robert Boyle Project, 2011).
6. *Mercurius Domesticus,* December 19, 1679, 2. On the deck with four "popish plots," see William Andrew Chatto, *Facts and Speculations on the Origin and History of Playing Cards* (London, 1848), 153–54; S. Taylor, ed., *The History of Playing Cards,* rev. ed. (London, 1865), 168–69; and Griffiths, *The Print in Stuart Britain,* 284. This deck is British Museum 1896,0501.913.1–52; for images see http://www.britishmuseum.org/research/collection_online/collection_object_details.aspx?assetId=517371001&objectId=3120261&partId=1.
7. The figure of five related decks is suggested by Mark Knights, "Possessing the Visual: The Materiality of Visual Print Culture in Later Stuart Britain," in *Material Readings of Early Modern Culture: Texts and Social Practices, 1580–1730,* ed. James Daybell and Peter Hinds (New York: Palgrave Macmillan, 2010), 97.
8. For more detailed historical information, see J. P. Kenyon, *The Popish Plot* (London: Heinemann, 1972); and Peter Hinds, *"The Horrid Popish Plot": Roger L'Estrange and the Circulation of Political Discourse in Late Seventeenth-Century London* (Oxford: British Academy/Oxford University Press, 2010), 71–81.
9. Jonathan Scott, "England's Troubles," in *The Politics of Religion in Restoration England,* ed. Tim Harris, Paul Seaward, and Mark Goldie (Oxford: Basil Blackwell, 1990), 108; see also Mark Knights, *Politics and Opinion in Crisis* (Cambridge: Cambridge University Press, 2006), 29–31. The phrase "second Stuart crisis of popery and arbitrary government" forms the leitmotif of Scott's *Algernon Sidney and the Restoration Crisis, 1677–1683* (Cambridge: Cambridge University Press, 1991). The first such crisis took place in the 1630s and 1640s, leading up to the outbreak of the Civil Wars: see Caroline M. Hibbard, *Charles I and the Popish Plot* (Chapel Hill: University of North Carolina Press, 1983).
10. Declaration of Breda, April 4, 1660.

11. Jacqueline Rose, *Godly Kingship in Restoration England: The Politics of the Royal Supremacy, 1660–1688* (Cambridge: Cambridge University Press, 2014), 93–97.
12. 25 Car. II. c. 2.
13. Lord Shaftesbury, *A Letter from a Person of Quality to His Friend in the Country* (London, 1675), 1.
14. [Andrew Marvell], *An Account of the Growth of Popery and Arbitrary Government in England* (Amsterdam, 1677), 3.
15. [Marvell], *Account*, 35.
16. Adam Morton, "Popery, Politics, and Play: Visual Culture in Succession Crisis England," *Seventeenth Century* 31 (2016): 415.
17. Naomi Lebens, "Playing with Politics: The Portrayal of the Popish Plot on Playing-Cards in Late Seventeenth-Century London" (MA thesis, Courtauld Institute of Art, 2012), 14.
18. *Commons Journal*, November 1, 1681.
19. Knights, *Politics and Opinion in Crisis*, 17; Kenyon, *The Popish Plot*, 78.
20. Mark Knights dubs it, more accurately, a "succession crisis"; *Politics and Opinion in Crisis*, 29, and chap. 2; see also O. W. Furley, "The Whig Exclusionists: Pamphlet Literature in the Exclusion Campaign, 1679–81," *Cambridge Historical Journal* 13 (1957): esp. 21–22.
21. Titus Oates, *A true narrative and discovery of . . . the horrid popish plot . . .* (London, 1679); William Bedloe, *A narrative and impartial discovery of the horrid Popish plot* (London, 1679).
22. Mark Goldie, "Roger L'Estrange's *Observator* and the Exorcism of the Plot," in *Roger L'Estrange and the Making of Restoration Culture*, ed. Anne Dunan-Page and Beth Lynch (Aldershot: Ashgate, 2008), 76; Kenyon, *The Popish Plot*, 180.
23. A remarkable visual representation of the procession, with accompanying text, was published as *The Solemn Mock Procession . . . through the City of London, November the 17th, 1679* [see page 147]. See also Sheila Williams, "The Pope-Burning Processions of 1679, 1680, and 1681," *Journal of the Warburg and Courtald Institutes* 21 (1958): 104–18.
24. See Nicholas Canny, *Making Ireland British 1580–1650* (Oxford: Oxford University Press, 2001).
25. Harris, *London Crowds*, chaps. 5–6. See Mark Knights, "London's 'Monster' Petition of 1680," *Historical Journal* 36 (1993): 39–67.
26. Hinds, *Horrid Popish Plot*, 12.
27. Morton, "Popery, Politics, and Play," 416–17.
28. See David Kunzle, *The Early Comic Strip* (Berkeley: University of California Press, 1973), 136. On instructional cards and the broader educational context of the time, see Lebens, *Playing with Politics*, 7–9.
29. *OED*, s.v. "consult," definition 2 (seventeenth century). The 8 of diamonds also uses the term: "Consult at Wild House." See also Lebens, *Playing with Politics*, 31–32.
30. This John Fenwick should not be confused with his contemporary, the Quaker founder of West Jersey, of the same name, although anti-Quaker polemicists would surely have enjoyed the overlap.
31. One non-Jesuit Catholic does figure prominently: Thomas Pickering, a Benedictine lay brother, appears on the knave, attempting to shoot the king while the monarch walks through Saint James' Park; the 6 shows Pickering's execution.
32. Griffiths, *Print in Stuart Britain*, 280.
33. Knights, "Possessing the Visual," 96.
34. Lebens, "Playing with Politics," 5.

35. Knights, "Possessing the Visual," 85; Morton, "Popery, Politics, and Play," 412. This notion of visualizing concepts as a form of discourse suggests links to Gilles Deleuze's idea of dramatization; see Deleuze, "The Method of Dramatization," in *Desert Islands and Other Texts, 1953–1974* (Los Angeles: Semiotexte, 2004); and Andrew R. Murphy, "Trial Transcript as Political Theory: Principles and Performance in the *Penn-Mead* Case," *Political Theory* 41, no. 6 (2013): 775–808.
36. See, e.g., John Miller, *Popery and Politics in England, 1660–1688* (Cambridge: Cambridge University Press, 1973).
37. Lebens, "Playing with Politics," 27.
38. Cyril Hughes Hartmann, "Introduction," in *Games and Gamesters of the Restoration* (London: Routledge, 1930), ix.
39. Catherine Perry Hargrave, *A History of Playing Cards and a Bibliography of Cards and Gaming* (New York: Houghton Mifflin, 1930), 205, 173. Naomi Lebens suggests that this deck may represent the "first time that playing-cards were used to disseminate current political polemics" (*Playing with Politics*, 37).
40. Nicholas Tosney, "The Playing Card Trade in Early Modern England," *Historical Research* 84 (2011): 637–38. In the words of Anthony Griffiths, "Sets of playing cards with pictorial subjects enjoyed an enormous vogue in the last quarter of the seventeenth century" (*Print in Stuart Britain*, 284). See also Stephanie Koscak, "Gaming Restoration Politics: Playing Cards, the Penny Post, and Conspiratorial Thinking," *Restoration: Studies in English Literary Culture, 1660–1700* 42 (2018): 95–133.
41. See Tosney, "The Playing Card Trade," 653; for details on these games see Charles Cotton, *The Compleat Gamester* (London, 1674); also Lebens, "Playing with Politics," 23, 31–36. Knights, "Possessing the Visual," also emphasizes how little we know about how the cards were actually used.
42. Brian Cowan, *The Social Life of Coffee: The Emergence of the British Coffeehouse* (New Haven: Yale University Press, 2005); Steve Pincus, "'Coffee Politicians Does Create': Coffeehouses and Restoration Political Culture," *Journal of Modern History* 67 (1995): 807–34.
43. Morton, "Popery, Politics, and Play," 413–14.
44. Margaret J. M. Ezell, "Multimodal Literacies, Late Seventeenth-Century English Illustrated Broadsheets, and Graphic Narratives," *Eighteenth-Century Studies* 51 (Spring 2018): 371. See also Robert A. Houston, *Literacy in Early Modern Europe: Culture and Education 1500–1800* (London: Longman, 1988). On falling prices, see Knights, "Possessing the Visual," 114.
45. Morton, "Popery, Politics, and Play," 412. Chatto distinguishes French from English card production, claiming that the latter addressed a broader audience and a more diverse range of topics, including politics (*Facts and Speculations*, 149–50).
46. F. K., *The present great interest both of King and people* (London, 1679), 4; Roger L'Estrange, *Citt and Bumpkin* (London, 1680). Peter Hinds notes that although L'Estrange criticized coffeehouses, he regularly patronized "Sam's" in Ludgate (*Horrid Popish Plot*, 318). See also *Crackfart & Tony; or, knave and fool* (London, 1680); *The Coffee-house dialogue examined and refuted* (London, 1680).
47. Vicki Hsueh, "Intoxicated Reasons, Rational Feelings: Rethinking the Early Modern English Public Sphere," *Review of Politics* 78 (2016): 29.
48. Jürgen Habermas has advanced the notion that coffeehouses played a seminal role in the development of the modern public sphere in *The Structural Transformation of the Public Sphere: An Inquiry into a Category of Bourgeois Society*, trans. Peter Berger (Cambridge, MA: MIT Press, 1989). For an alternative to Habermas's account, see Peter Lake and Steve Pincus, "Rethinking the Public Sphere in Early Modern England," *Journal of British Studies* 45 (2006): 270–92.

49. "Virtually infinite" here means 52 factorial, something like 8 followed by 67 zeros. On the participatory nature of the cards see Lebens, "Playing with Politics," 18; and on the interplay between discrete scenes and the larger narrative of the Popish Plot, Lebens, "Playing with Politics," 23.
50. On the Penny Post, see Koscak, "Playing Cards and Political Legerdemain."
51. On Barlow's role in the procession—both the actual event in London and the print illustrating it—see Joseph Monteyne, *The Printed Image in Early Modern London: Urban Space, Visual Representation, and Social Exchange* (Aldershot: Ashgate, 2007), 160.
52. Morton, "Popery, Politics, and Play," 416.
53. In this respect, consider the study of satirical or pornographic popular literature in the French context, e.g., Lynn Hunt, ed., *The Invention of Pornography: Obscenity and the Origins of Modernity* (Cambridge, MA: MIT Press, 1993), or Jeffrey Merrick's study of the mazarinades, in which Cardinal Mazarin is often depicted as seducing Queen Anne to exert influence over the French crown. For Merrick on the mazarinades, see "The Cardinal and the Queen: Sexual and Political Disorders in the Mazarinades," *French Historical Studies* 18 (1994): 287–307. This point might also speak to broader questions concerning the way different segments of society became politicized, which has been an ongoing concern of social historians at least since E. P. Thompson, *The Making of the English Working Class* (London: V. Gollancz, 1963).
54. On dystopianism in political theory, see Gregory Claeys, *Dystopia: A Natural History* (Oxford: Oxford University Press, 2017); and Michael A. Richards, "Dystopophobia: Aversion to the Worst in the Philosophy of Thomas Hobbes, Edmund Burke, and Karl Popper" (PhD diss., Rutgers University, 2019), chap. 1.
55. Jean-Paul Cerdan, *Europe a Slave, unless England break her chains* (London, 1681), 64.
56. Peter Lake, "Anti-Popery: The Structure of a Prejudice," in *Conflict in Early Stuart England: Studies in Religion and Politics, 1603–1642,* ed. Richard Cust and Ann Hughes (London: Longman, 1989), 77.
57. William Penn, *An address to Protestants upon the present conjuncture* (London, 1679), 143, 225; Penn, *Englands great interest* (London, 1679), 4.
58. See Scott Sowerby, "Opposition to Anti-Popery in Restoration England," *Journal of British Studies* 51 (2012): 28–30.
59. Penn, *A Second Letter to a Gentleman in the country* (London, 1687), 16.
60. See Scott Sowerby, *Making Toleration: The Repealers and the Glorious Revolution* (Cambridge, MA: Harvard University Press, 2013); Murphy, *Liberty, Conscience, and Toleration: The Political Thought of William Penn* (New York: Oxford University Press, 2016), chap. 6; and Andrew R. Murphy and Sarah Morgan Smith, "Law and Civil Interest: William Penn's Toleration," in *Religious Tolerance in the Atlantic World: Early Modern and Contemporary Perspectives,* ed. Eliane Glaser (Basingstoke: Palgrave Macmillan, 2013), 111–33.
61. Morton, "Popery, Politics, and Play," 416, emphasis in original.
62. Peter Laslett, "Introduction," in John Locke, *Two Treatises of Government,* ed. Peter Laslett (Cambridge: Cambridge University Press, 1960), 61.
63. See Andrew R. Murphy, "The Limits and Promise of Political Theorizing: William Penn and the Founding of Pennsylvania," *History of Political Thought* 34 (2013): 639–68; and *Liberty, Conscience, and Toleration,* chap. 5.
64. Quentin Skinner, *Visions of Politics,* Volume 1: *Regarding Method* (Cambridge: Cambridge University Press, 2002); J.G.A. Pocock, *Politics, Language, and Time: Essays on Political Thought and History* (Chicago: University of Chicago Press, 1989).

The Virgin Mary and Violated Mothers in British Anti-Catholicism

Laura M. Stevens

THIS ESSAY EXAMINES THE seventeenth- and eighteenth-century Anglophone genealogy of one of anti-popery's most obvious features: condemnation of Roman Catholics for their devotion to the Virgin Mary. On its face this element of anti-Catholicism can be explained as Protestants' view of Mariolatry as an egregious form of idolatry. Clearly, however, Protestant horror at what they called the worship of Mary also expressed discomfort with the power Catholicism apparently granted to a woman. Walter J. Ong went so far as to theorize that a suppression of femininity in the divine was "the obsession which has constituted separatism," while Patricia Crawford asserted that reactions against Mary's exaltation led Protestants to "devalue maternity."[1] The notion that the Reformation's turn away from Mary narrowed the horizon of spiritual expression available to Protestant women has undergone revision in the work of Christine Peters, but the centrality of misogyny to English anti-Catholic writings is clear.[2] Frances Dolan has shown how seventeenth-century anti-Marian commentary drew upon longstanding misogynist conceits while articulating newer concerns about the roles played by women in preserving English Catholicism.[3] Much of this commentary focused on the power that Catholics believed Mary possessed through her embodiment as mother. "With their emphasis on breast milk, virginity, original sin, and bodily decay, debates over Mary drew on and fueled a visceral, corporal misogyny that recoiled from yet was fascinated by porous, leaking female bodies."[4] Anti-Catholic rhetoric thus found traction on the well-trodden territory of gender.

Anglophone Protestant attitudes toward Mary, however, were not static. A survey of references to this figure reveals a shift toward more nuanced and complex depictions, as the seventeenth century transitioned to the eighteenth and especially as anti-Catholic feeling ebbed somewhat from the intensity of the 1680s, the decade that began with the Popish Plot hysteria, saw the accession of an openly Roman Catholic monarch who actively sought concessions for fellow Catholics, and ended with ousting of that king in the Revolution of 1689.[5] These later writings contain surprises, such as a 1697 Presbyterian funeral sermon's description of Mary as "*like the* Ark, *overlaid with* Gold, *and* glorious within,"[6] or Cotton Mather's recommendation in 1710 that women emulate Mary's acceptance of God's will while preparing for childbirth.[7] Others distinguish between Mary and Mariolatry, as did William Reading, keeper of the library at Sion College, in 1717: "The excesses of that Devotion, which has been paid to the Blessed Virgin, and the Legendary Tales and lying Visions of Monks, cannot in reason blemish her real Excellencies."[8] Still, there are texts that hearken back to earlier attacks. A print attributed to William Hogarth, "Transubstantiation Satirized" (1735), in which Mary drops a cherubic Jesus into a windmill from which emerge communion wafers, shows how Marian images still could be deployed in the service of anti-Catholicism.[9]

A contrast in the density of literary studies of Anglophone anti-Catholicism parallels this shift, beginning approximately in the last decade of the seventeenth century, toward more finely calibrated and complex interpretations of Mary. There is an abundance of literary scholarship on anti-Catholicism from the beginnings of the Protestant Reformation through the Glorious Revolution, including the work of Arthur Marotti, Alison Shell, and Frances Dolan, as well as a multitude of close readings of anti-Catholic aspects of specific texts or genres, especially pamphlets and theatrical writings.[10] The scene of anti-Catholicism in the succeeding century, from 1690 to the Gordon Riots or even to Catholic emancipation in 1830, is decidedly sparser in spite of exciting developments over the past twenty years. As Karen Gevirtz has observed of English Catholic studies more generally, the long eighteenth century is "a relatively new arrival to the narrative of English Catholicism," even as the years between the dissolution of the monasteries and the Glorious Revolution have constituted "a lively field for decades."[11] Work on both English Catholicism and anti-Catholicism in the eighteenth century is now flourishing, thanks partly to the approaches enabled by New Historicism and gender studies, and it has extended beyond England proper to include the North American colonies.[12]

Much of this work is inherently interdisciplinary and attentive to several forms of evidence, including literature, material culture, and the arts, while scholarship on the discourses of anti-Catholicism and anti-popery has unfolded in complex counterpoint to studies of Catholic communities and individuals, including authors such as John Dryden, Jane Barker, Elizabeth Inchbald, and Alexander Pope.[13] Publications on Jacobitism simultaneously have contained and obscured some attention to anti-Catholicism, especially when specifically religious beliefs and prejudices are elided by politics.[14] Gothic literature constitutes a vibrant subfield of Catholic and anti-Catholic studies, offering a kind of relief map of popular tropes of anti-Catholic feeling in the late eighteenth and early nineteenth centuries.[15] Amid these various developments, two aspects of recent or forthcoming literary

William Hogarth, "Transubstantiation Satirized," engraving, 1735. (© The Trustees of the British Museum; all rights reserved)

The Virgin Mary is shown to be complicit in the ritual cannibalization of the baby Jesus by Roman Catholics thanks to their priests' ability to turn his body and blood into communion wafers, here presented as an industrial milling process.

work on anti-Catholicism in the long eighteenth century are particularly salient: first, the inclination to consider this prejudice as it contributes to the formation of British Protestant identity; second, the tracing of anti-Catholic feeling as it is expressed through writings about women.[16] Both inclinations are seen in, for example, Alison Conway's examination, in *The Protestant Whore,* of how Protestant identity developed through stories about the Stuart kings' royal mistresses.[17] This essay's project is in keeping with the recent prominence of women—both actual and depicted—in eighteenth-century studies of anti-Catholicism, but rather than whores, it focuses on images of Mary and other mothers.

Considering motherhood, especially the bodies of mothers, is crucial to understanding the complexities of English anti-Catholic rhetoric as it relates to the British Protestant engagement with the Virgin Mary. The references to Mary cited above, with her marked both as papist anathema and as exemplar of virtuous female conduct, appear confusing until we take into account that they share an effort to separate her inner spiritual substance from her external body. When viewed as maternal body, Mary evokes Catholic idolatry and monstrous femininity. When she is lifted out of her body to be regarded as montage of godly attributes, she can be reclaimed as Protestant exemplar.

I will examine this shift, which took place gradually in the decades surrounding the Glorious Revolution of 1689, by presenting it alongside a seventeenth-century tradition of anti-Catholic writing that gained its impetus from a focus on the female body. This was the effort to depict popery's agents as the propagators of gratuitous violence toward innocents, especially babies growing within wombs or nursing at their mothers' breasts. There is ancient as well as medieval precedent for condemnations of such excessive forms of cruelty that were absorbed into political propaganda,[18] but one early modern point of origin for this particular cluster of images seems to be Bartholomé de Las Casas, whose efforts to reform Spanish policies toward Indigenous Americans were appropriated by the English as evidence to support what has come to be called the Black Legend. As Las Casas wrote of the Spanish in Hispaniola, "They forced their way into native settlements, slaughtering everyone they found. . . . They hacked them to pieces, slicing open their bellies with their swords. . . . They grabbed suckling infants from their mothers' breasts, dashed them headlong against the rocks."[19] The events described by Las Casas are almost indistinguishable from those depicted in the Baptist Benjamin Keach's description of the Irish rebellion in *Zion in Distress; or, The Groans of the Protestant Church* (1670):[20]

> The youngest on the Mothers breast did stick,
> Cries, *Mammy, Mammy,* yet is buried quick.
> Some hack to pieces, travailing Women strip'd,
> And half born Infants from their bellies rip'd![21]

Such images provide a broader context for the trope of outraged maternity that several scholars have examined in Indian captivity narratives, suggesting a fully articulated English vision of the Atlantic basin as a theater of Catholic cruelty.[22]

A duality that verges on contradiction governs this trope, for the early modern Anglophone canon of writings from or about the Americas appropriated Las Casas's vignettes of outraged maternity to mark Indigenous women and infants as popery's innocent victims. At the same time, though, early American Anglophone writings, especially captivity narratives, held up the Native peoples of regions where the English had settled as specters of popish savagery toward the most vulnerable. This rhetorical trend applies even for Native captors who were not Catholic, because the superstition and idolatry that colonists associated with Indians easily fit within an ideology of anti-popery that, as Peter Lake has observed, defined Catholicism as "an anti-religion, a perfectly symmetrical negative image of true Christianity."[23] Mary Rowlandson's widely read narrative of her captivity during King Philip's War (1675–77) opened by describing an attack on the settlement of Lancaster, Massachusetts, in which amid gunfire and burning houses, "There were five persons taken in one house, the Father, and the Mother and a sucking Child, they knockt on the head." The attack locks Rowlandson and her young daughter in the grisly intimacy of simultaneous wounds, for "one [bullet] went through my side, and same (as would seem) through the bowels and hand of dear Child in my arms." Much of what makes Rowlandson's account so powerful is its focus on mothers and children as their bodies are alternately torn from each other and brought together in violent death. She describes "the Infidels haling Mothers one way, and Children another" as they organize the captives for their removal. At the same moment, Rowlandson's older sister, hearing that her son is dead and her younger sister wounded, prays aloud, "Lord, let me dy with them; which was no sooner said, but she was struck with a Bullet, and fell down dead." Rowlandson herself does survive, but she describes in harrowing detail the protracted and painful ordeal of holding her daughter while she slowly dies from her wound. "Thus nine days I sat upon my knees, with my Babe in my lap, till my flesh was raw again; my Child being even ready to depart this sorrowfull world." The Indigenous are designated in this text as "merciless Heathen," but the theological distinctions between Catholics and heathens matter far less than the tacit grouping of those inclined to unrestrained and compassionless butchery with the opponents of the civilized and the godly.[24]

Based on real events we all would rather not visualize, these scenes of infants torn from mothers' bodies are stylized and formulaic by the late seventeenth century. Indeed, it is in this stylization that this cluster of images stands out from the many accusations of atrocities focused on maternal bodies that fill accounts of war throughout human history. Gestured to in countless anti-Catholic writings, these vignettes allude to Herod's slaughter of the innocents (Matthew 2:16–18) and pharaoh's killing of newborn Hebrew males (Exodus 1:22), with all the attendant connotations of martyrdom.[25] In their focus on torn bodies and rampant slaughter they resemble Hosea's prophecy, "Samaria shall become desolate; for she hath rebelled against her God: they shall fall by the sword: their infants shall be dashed in pieces, and their women with child shall be ripped up" (13:16). There is also an echo of the apocryphal song of Judith, which notes that Assur, head of Holofernes's army, "bragged that he would burn up my borders, and kill my young men with the sword, and dash the sucking children against the ground" (Judith 16:5). These last two references depart from the language of martyrdom in marking gruesome suffering as punishment for the victims' disloyalty or as threat demanding a bold demonstration of faith.

Like the scriptural verses they echo, these early modern anti-Catholic writings epitomize the enemies of God's innocent and faithful through images of mass slaughter.[26] They also seek to elicit aesthetic disgust at the excess quantity as well as gruesome quality of carnage, which in turn heightens moral revulsion at the basic fact of murdering innocents. At the core of what is delivered as a plenitude of carnage is the grotesque parody of birth, the pregnant belly torn open to expose the baby within.[27] Almost pornographic in their excited rendering of physical detail, these accounts describe a baroque excess to which is opposed, implicitly, the aesthetic and appetitive restraint of Protestantism. Focused as they are on the emptying out of the female body, with bellies torn open, arms grasping for a missing baby, these descriptions present the Madonna-with-child as popery's victim rather than its idol. Protestantism thus configures itself as a force striving to keep intact the vulnerable bodies that Roman Catholicism tears apart.

It is important to note that these two types of English writing did not directly influence each other. In fact, these traditions seem to have developed in almost exactly parallel and inverse proportion to each other, with the political turmoil of 1689 providing the fulcrum to these shifts in patterns of maternal representation. During the seventeenth century, the violated womb and slaughtered infant came to constitute the most horrifying example of popery's rapaciousness. Just as these images began to appear with less frequency, with the exile of England and Scotland's openly Catholic king and the securing of a Protestant succession, the Virgin Mary emerged within devotional and didactic writings as Protestant exemplar. She was rescued, in a sense, from the clutches of Catholicism through an abstraction of her self from her womb, just after this womb had become fixed within the ideology of anti-popery as vulnerable container of Protestant life. Ultimately, the maternal body came to exhibit rather than oppose a Protestant understanding of godliness as the prizing of well-regulated spiritual substance over physical shell. These trends gesture to a broader process of redefining the maternal body, in keeping with broader cultural shifts in depictions of women over the course of the eighteenth century, as an object crucial to the self-image of British Protestantism.

On October 23, 1698, the fifty-seventh anniversary of the Irish Rebellion, John Travers, minister of Saint Andrew's Church in Dublin, asserted, "No Rebellion in the World ever . . . was more Barbarous. . . . Sucking Children were pluck't from their Mothers Breasts, & their Brains dash'd out before their faces; Women with Child ript up, and their untimely Fruit thrown to the Swine."[28] Commemorating this event in 1692, Edward Wettenhall, bishop of Cork and Ross, compared the violence Protestants had suffered to the fears Jacob had voiced about his brother Esau: "Their Design, Attempt, and diligent Endeavour was, to have cut off Root and Branch, *the Mother with the Child.*"[29] That both preachers would summarize the rebellion through references to slaughtered mothers and babes is less striking than that they could do so by shorthand, deploying these images as synecdoche for a brutalized people.

Such rhetorical economy was possible because by the 1690s the ravaged bodies of mothers, along with the offspring they enclosed or held, had been propagated in the English imagination as signifiers of Catholic rapaciousness. This spectacle, often juxtaposed to the voracious femininity of the Whore of Babylon, had been part of anti-popish discourse at least since the reign of Mary I. George Fox and Ellis Hookes's *The Arraignment of Popery,* which saw eight editions in the seventeenth century and another in 1792, punctuated omnibus lists of atrocities with vignettes of violence toward maternal bodies: "The Mother whipt, and her Dugs pull'd off," "Womens Bellies ript open, and Barly put into them, and so devoured by Swine," and "Some had their infants cut out of their Wombs, and thrown to Dogs."[30] In George Walker's *The Protestant's Crums of Comfort,* which invoked the Irish Rebellion as the ousted James II was summoning Irish support, women victimize women, heightening popery's savagery: "A Protestant Woman being delivered in the Fields, they gave the new born Infant to the Dogs to be devoured. The *Irish* Women followed the Camp, and stirred up the Men to Cruelty, crying, *Kill them all; spare neither Man, Woman, or Child.*"[31] Childbirth becomes a grotesque parody of itself, so that newborns are fed to animals or "have been found sucking the Breasts of their dead Mother."[32] Women epitomize the inverted worlds of popery and Protestantism, providing cause and effect of popish rapaciousness, which produces horror through its conflation of morbidity and birth.

Such compilations resemble Protestant martyrologies like John Foxe's *Acts and Monuments,* which featured violated motherhood in the story of Perotine Massey, a woman of the Channel Islands who was burnt at the stake along with her mother and sister for their Protestant beliefs during Queen Mary I's persecutions. Perotine was in advanced pregnancy, and as Foxe narrates, "the wombe of the sayd Paratine being burned, there dydde issue from her a goodly man chylde, which by the officers was taken vp and . . . throwne into the fyre, and there also with the sely mother moste cruelly burnt."[33] This gruesome execution, which was rather vividly illustrated in a woodcut of 1563, featured Roman Catholic authorities as gratuitously merciless, going so far as to throw a newborn back into a fire for what they perceived to be the transgressions of his mother. But while there is overlap between these genres in a focus on the murdered mother and child, the descriptions I am studying differ from Foxe's text in the style and origin of the violence they record. As Raymond Tumbleson has noted of such texts, "[W]hereas the burnings in [*Acts and Monuments*] are legalistic inflictions by a tyrannizing hierarchy . . . the crimes Temple and Fox see are . . . the barbaric acts of primitives who ought to be more strictly controlled rather than less."[34] To Tumbleson's point I would that add such accounts gain dramatic traction through a clash between the events presented and the manner of presenting them. That is, the atrocities are uncontrolled, but the texts describing them strive to contain them. This is not to say that the relations of atrocity eschew emotion, for they clearly seek tears and outrage. Through catalogs, depositions, and compact verse forms, however, they construct a stiff textual frame around the image of a body spilling grotesquely beyond its natural bounds. The result is the modeling of a highly controlled Protestant response to a Catholicism aligned with rapaciousness and lack of self-command.

Temple's *Irish Rebellion* provides one example of this tension between content and form. Temple, who had taken up his appointment as master of the rolls of Ireland before the rebellion broke out and thus could claim eyewitness status, delivered an exaggerated account that incorporated depositions of the rebellion's survivors by the Commission for the Despoiled Subject.[35] In his text the mere fact of murdered noncombatants is overshadowed by episode after episode of bodies stabbed, burned, hanged on hooks, or eviscerated. He devotes particular attention to ruptured bodies, especially the spectacle of intestines spilling out: "Some had their Bellies ript up, and so left with their guts running about their heels. But this horrid kinde of cruelty was principally reserved by these inhumane Monsters for Women, whose sexe they neither pitied nor spared, hanging up severall Women, many of them great with childe, whose bellies they ripped up as they hung, and so let the little Infants fall out. . . . And sometimes they gave their Children to Swine; Some the Dogges eat; and some taken alive out of their Mothers bellies, they cast into ditches."[36] This inventory of atrocities depicts popery as negative reflection of the natural, orderly, and good. Animals eat humans, bodies are turned inside out, and birth collapses into death. Papists are murderous, but more importantly, in the messiness of their overkill they appear as an animalistic horde who "could contain themselves no longer, but . . . furiously broke out . . . with most abominable cruelty."[37]

Temple meets such horrors with investigative exactitude, contrasting his methodology with the chaos of the rebellion. He conveys the scale of the carnage by tallying the dead, as when he mentions "one thousand men, women and Children carried out . . . , and all unmercifully drowned at the Bridge of *Portnedowne*."[38] The text sorts the various types of documentation visually, with Temple's account running down a centered column, and the italicized depositions, including provenance and annotation, enclosed in rectangles on either side. Those depositions are eye-searing records of trauma. One, which seems to inspire the lines by Keach quoted earlier, culminates in the murder of a young child:

> William Parkinson *of* Castle Cumber *in the County of* Kilkenny Gent. *deposeth, That by the credible report both of* English *and some* Irish, *who affirmed they were eye-witnesses of a bloody murder committed neer* Kilfeale *in the* Queens County, *upon an* English man, *his wife, four or five children, and a maid. All which were hanged by the command of Sir* Morgan Cavanah, *and* Robert Harpoole, *and afterwards put all in one hole, the youngest child being not fully dead, put out the hand and crying mammy, mammy, when without mercy they buried him alive,* Jurat. Feb. 11. 1642.

In such accounts the fact of mass murder is overshadowed by the poignancy of a smothered child crying for his dead mother. The specifics of name, date, and place draw a line of verification around events that would seem, in their repulsiveness, to spill beyond any rhetorical frame. Throughout Temple presents himself as government-commissioned documentarian, affected by the horrors he has recorded but still demonstrating, in his painstaking sorting of data, what distinguishes him from the aggressors he describes. In his attentiveness to gory details, and in the horror he elicits over violations of women and children, he constructs Protestantism as a force that strives to keep bodies intact.

Benjamin Keach's *Sion in Distress* is markedly different from Temple's account, written in heroic couplets and forgoing documentary detail in favor of millenarian allegory. Like Temple, however, Keach frames gruesomely violated bodies within testimony, placing the Whore of Babylon on trial for her brutality. Images of pregnancy drive much of the trial's dialogue, with slaughtered fetuses rebutting the Whore's claim to be "*guiltless as the Child unborn*."[39] Christ, acting as judge, proclaims to the Whore, "*[T]hou hast not spared delicate Women, and sucking Children. . . . Thou hast ripped up Women with Child*."[40] The summary of her crimes exhibits tension between uncontrolled violence and the spare, measured description of it. Literary form is a crucial aspect of Keach's argument, for the match of iambics to atrocity is jarring, showing overpowering savagery reduced to refrains. The "*Waldenses, Albigenses,* Protestants of *Piedmont, Savoy,* &c." describe "Our Children rent to pieces, thrown to Dogs" during a massacre in which "thirty thousand Souls she did destroy," while France reports "Rap't Maidens stab'd, poor infants yet unborn, / From Mothers wombs by *bloody hands were torn!*"[41] Portraits of carnage are reduced to nuggets of evidence, made pithy to the point of trivialization by clichéd rhyme and choppy rhythm. Consider the description of slaughter in England: "Some thou didst cut to pieces very small, / And Infants Brains didst dash against the wall."[42] Were the actual content of this couplet ignored, it would fit nicely within a Dr. Seuss book.

To some degree this is just mediocre poetry, exhibiting a mismatch of content to form used deliberately by contemporaries like John Dryden in the service of satire. It also indicates some exhaustion of the rhetoric of popish atrocity, with a diminished capacity to shock. But even in its staleness the poem exemplifies an effort to enclose Catholic chaos within Protestant order. The references to shredded bellies are woven into a highly scripted indictment of the Whore, and the trial, in its concession to procedure and law, exhibits restraint. This is true even of a trial that merely nods to the conventions of the form, for its preordained outcome conveys the ultimate vindication Protestants will receive at the Final Judgment.

Embodying this opposition are contrasts between good and bad females in the Whore of Babylon and Sion. The Whore is a woman described almost entirely through her womb and her mouth. Burlesquing standard associations of motherhood with tenderheartedness, she is a violent creature driven by pregnancy cravings to feed the "*Bastard*" within:

> Fearing *Miscarriage,* when her Spirits faint,
> She drinks *the hearts-blood of some Martyr'd* Saint.
> Than *Horse-leech* more insatiable, she cries,
> *Give, give me that, or nothing will suffice*
> My Craving Paunch.[43]

No ice cream with pickles will satisfy this mom-to-be. This vivid rendering of Revelation 17:6 presents the pregnant Whore, through the metaphor of horseleech, as bloated with blood and ravenous, thus impelled to order violence against other women's wombs. Her minions, she threatens, are "*Try'd Villians! that will never start / From* Mothers Womb *to tear the heart / Of* Unborn Infants."[44] As in *The Protestant's Crums of Comfort,* producers of life are transformed into objects of violent consumption. The trial unfolds in response to this monstrous femininity, described with intimations of gang rape as Sion's sons call out, "*Her Crimes lay open, and her Facts declare, / Turn up her Skirts and let her Faults appear.*"[45] The Whore's punishment is that reserved for an adulterous or traitorous woman: she is to "be utterly burnt with *Fire.*"[46] This patriarchal correction of unruly femininity purges the savage desecration of mothers and children with violence that is equally thorough but far more controlled.

It is striking that the only woman to survive the poem, Sion, is embodied only as much as is required for her to perform her core capacities of emoting and praying. Although pregnant, this allegory of the true Church is metaphorically so, "with Complaint."[47] Elsewhere Christ promises that the child she carries will be birthed by others.[48] While the Whore is a "hateful *Carcass,*"[49] Sion's body appears as a canvas of pain, whether involving the goring of her sides by a dragon, or the anguish expressed through eyes that stream "Rivulets" and arms with which she *"implore*[s] *the skies.*"[50] If the Whore's central organ is her womb, Sion's is her heart, which is torn into pieces, or her breast, which Grief "rends."[51] As a mother, she resembles no one so much as the Virgin Mary. She intercedes for her sons with Christ; she declares, "I am *Christ*'s Spouse, his undefiled One"; and in echo of the *Magnificat* she proclaims, *"My Ravisht Spirit must exalt the high.*"[52] The goring of her side evokes Simeon's prophecy to Mary, "a sword shall pierce through thy own soul also" (Luke 2:35). Christ even promises that with an iron hoof she will "tread down the Serpents."[53] This line combines Micah's exhortation to the daughter of Zion (4:13) with an allusion to God's prophecy (Genesis 3:15) that a woman, usually read as Mary, will crush the serpent's head.

What does it mean that such a virulently anti-Catholic poem, one that musters monstrous femininity in service of its attacks, can appropriate Marian terminology to describe the true Church? When read alongside other accounts of popish atrocity, Keach's poem suggests how a focus on the grotesquely violated female victim makes possible a new sorting out of Protestantism and popery in relation to femininity. The gruesome female bodies that have informed anti-Catholic writings, focused on the figuring of Mary as disturbingly powerful nursing mother alongside the blood-drunken spectacle of the Babylonian Whore, are matched by other images of monstrous maternity that exhibit the savaging of godly mothers and offspring. This transference of maternal grotesquerie, informed subtly by Protestant withdrawal from the baroque excess of popery into aesthetic simplicity and self-control, leaves room for a new acceptance of an increasingly disembodied Mary toward the end of the seventeenth century.

In 1677 Simon Patrick, later bishop of Ely, located Catholic adoration of the Virgin Mary in the insidious influence of a mother's breast: "If you receive him for the *King of Heaven,* upon the same account that she is set up for the *Queen* (because it is the common opinion, which you have suckt in with your Mothers milk, *&c.*) your love to him is just like their love to her: nothing Divine or Heavenly, but a natural passion."[54] Intertwining anti-popery with misogyny, a gesture with lengthy precedent, Patrick aligned Catholicism with the female realm of the body, to which he opposed the masculine arena of the mind. True religion, he suggested, has its source in reason, while Catholicism is a passion imbibed without conscious thought.

Of course, the Mariolotry that Patrick attacked was to some degree a caricature of Catholicism. The Protestant disinclination to focus on Jesus's mother was a magnification and trigger of a similar transition from medieval to early modern Catholicism. Donna Spivey Ellington has noted that the increasingly sacramental and affective aspects of piety in the twelfth through fourteenth centuries enhanced a focus on Mary's "bodily relationship to Christ."[55] In this era Franciscans led a movement to recognize the feast of the Immaculate Conception, Dominicans promoted the cult of the Virgin's milk, and preachers made allegorical use of the Song of Songs to feature Mary's womb as an "'enclosed garden of delights.'"[56] In reaction to the Reformation, but also in response to the growth of literacy and modern subjectivity, Catholic depictions of Mary changed, so that "her virtues of humility, absolute obedience, and even her 'spiritual' motherhood of Christ began to assume at least an equal importance with her bodily maternity."[57] Christine Peters has observed similar shifts in late medieval England, such as "a re-evaluation of the role of Mary: she became primarily a witness who was intimately involved with the sufferings of Christ."[58] Pre- and Counter-Reformation interpretations of Mary thus were not as far from Protestant ones as the rhetoric of anti-popery would suggest.

Still, that Catholics focused on Mary's motherhood was not just an invention of anti-popery. Catholic publications like *The Instruction of Youth in Christian Piety* (*Instruction de la jeunesse en la piété chrétienne*) by Charles Gobinet, a principal of the College of Plessis-Sorbonne, demonstrate as much. Gobinet's "*Prayer to the Blessed Virgin before Communion*" encourages Catholics to imaginatively reenact the physical intermingling of mother and child: "O Blessed Virgin . . . behold me upon the point of receiving the same person, whom thou didst conceive in thy chaste bowels."[59] Mary's physical role as mother is the basis for her spiritual role as intercessor; her womb provides the entry-point for understanding the mystery of transubstantiation as a reworking of the Incarnation. There can be little wonder, upon reading such texts, that Protestants reacted against the Catholic treatment of Mary. Her body is the hinge upon which pivots almost every doctrine anathema to most Protestants—from Immaculate Conception through intercession to transubstantiation.

It is therefore not surprising that some seventeenth- and eighteenth-century Protestant publications generated anti-popish condemnation from a focus on the power Mary was seen to have through her motherhood of Jesus. Increase Mather sought to rebut the Catholic figuration of Mary through ridicule that exposed her human weakness: "As for the *Papists,* there are Thousands, it may be Millions of them, praying at once to the *Virgin Mary;* its [*sic*] impossible that she being a Creature only should hear all those prayers at once."[60] Thomas Lewis, known for his writings against Dissenters and Catholics, insisted that to elevate Mary beyond the status of ordinary human was "to exempt her from the natural Infirmities of her Sex." If only not to undermine "a Fundamental Article of our Faith, that a *Woman* was the Mother of *Christ*," Mary must be represented with the weaknesses all women have.[61]

Such direct disputations of Mary's perfection often found scriptural authorization in Jesus's rebuke of her at the wedding in Cana: "Woman, what have I to do with thee?" (John 2:4). Henry Killigrew, master of the Savoy, preached that these words "utterly o'erthrow all the vain and false Glories, which the Church of *Rome* Superstitiously, Idolatrously, and injuriously, rather than Devoutly, heap upon our Lady." Jesus's response to his mother, he argued, demonstrated his "impartial Deportment," so that "The very Womb that bare him, in an Unadvis'd Action, shall not go away without a Rebuke."[62] Killigrew's focus on the insignificance of Mary's womb pertains to another approach to Mary, which was to downplay her status as Jesus's mother while elevating her spiritual worth. In doing so Protestants were hardly inventing new doctrine, but rather following theologians like Augustine, who had written of Mary, "She kept truth safe in her mind even better than she kept flesh safe in her womb."[63] In *Looking unto Jesus* (1658), Isaac Ambrose, who became a nonconformist after 1662, also conceded that Mary was "blessed" for serving as the "material temple" of God, but cautioned it was as "spiritual temple" that Mary enjoyed benefits to her soul. She thus held no status not available to all believers, because "if we believe in Christ, and if we obey the word of Christ, we are the mothers of Christ."[64] Ambrose's conceit has surprising overlap with Gobinet's prayer after receiving communion but without the accompanying rhapsodies on her womb. The space between Catholic and Protestant lies in the relative emphasis or deemphasis on her body.

The scripture most often cited in support of this approach was Luke 11:27–28: "[A] certain woman of the company lifted up her voice, and said unto him, Blessed is the womb that bare thee, and the paps which thou hast sucked. But he said, Yea rather, blessed are they that hear the word of God, and keep it." The dialogue fit seamlessly within a Protestant elevation of interior piety over external observance. In *The Life of Jesus Christ Consider'd, as Our Example*, John Tillotson, archbishop of Canterbury, cited Luke 11:27 as proof against the exceptionality Catholics grant to Mary.[65] Nathaniel Marshall, an Anglican authority on the ancient church, cited the same exchange while observing, "The Honours paid to the Person thus qualified, have been, 'tis confessed, extravagant; so that we are almost afraid to call her Blessed."[66] Such readings were not unique to Anglicans. The Quaker Thomas Ellwood wrote, "it is more blessed to bear him in the heart, by believing in him, and obeying his commandments, than to bear him in the womb only."[67] Philip Doddridge exhorted, "Let us not only hear, but keep the word of Christ; and we shall thus be happy in a neerer union with him, than ever could arise from any natural relation to him."[68] John Wesley dismissed the woman's blessing with gendered condescension:

"How natural was the Thought for a Woman! And how gently does our Lord reprove her?"[69] Still, his reading concurred with the Protestant elevation of Mary's spiritual grace over physical closeness to her son. Nehemiah Walter, minister of Roxbury, Massachusetts, stands out among Protestants for his favorable treatment of Mary as mother, writing, "There Scarce ever was a more *wonderful sight* than that of the Son of God's *Sucking* and *Living upon* the Breasts of a Woman." Even this reading, however, served to prove the humiliation Christ underwent through the Incarnation, for "He that *as God* upheld all in Life, was yet *as Man* upheld in Life by his Mothers Milk."[70] For Protestants across many denominations, then, the role of mother was emptied of physical meaning to become a metaphor for commitment to Christ.

The elevation of Mary's spiritual kinship with Christ was part of an effort to encourage emulation of her non-physical qualities. This approach certainly appears in the seventeenth century, as in *Mary's Choice,* a funeral sermon of 1674 by "P. W., Rector of Edlington." The sermon focused on Mary the sister of Martha, but it described "*Mary* the Mother of our Lord, saluted by the Angel, the favorite of Heaven, and blessed among Women; of the Blood Royal, of the house of *David;* admirably devout; a great hoarder of heavenly treasure; she abode by the Lord at his Death, and with his Church after his Ascension; was much vers'd in Affliction, &c. as was foretold by holy *Simeon.*"[71] Such depictions were more common toward and in the eighteenth century, however, in the writings of both Anglicans and Dissenters.[72] Mary received particular notice for the *Magnificat,* her song of praise to God, versions of which were included in collections of sacred songs from Isaac Watts onward.[73]

One outcome of this focus on Mary's comportment was the increased citing of her as proof of women's potential for virtue. William Reading noted that Mary "observed the extraordinary Things which were said of her Son with silence, and *pondered them in her Heart.*" Her contemplative silence was "A rare Instance of Modesty and Humility, and a Demonstration that Talkativeness is no inseparable Infirmity of the Female Sex, but rather the Fault of ill Custom and Education."[74] Backhanded as Reading's comment on female prattle is, it is distinct from many other writings on women from the early eighteenth century in that it asserts the natural worth of women while arguing for their education. This was certainly a concept that figures such as Mary Astell would forward, but it was hardly received opinion. In this way Mary became a wedge to split nurture from nature in assessments of female potential. More typical was the argument, going back at least to Cornelius Agrippa, that Mary undid Eve's sins and thus proved the worth of women. As Thomas Foxcroft, pastor of Boston's First Church, observed in a funeral sermon, "We may justly esteem it a superior Glory to the female Sex, that *GOD sent forth his Son, made of a Woman,* . . . by which means He has in a great measure wiped off theReproach, [*sic*] that was fallen upon that Sex, upon account of the Woman's being first in the Transgression."[75] The contrast with the seventeenth-century anti-Catholic commentary voiced by figures such as Patrick is striking. Rather than suggesting the monstrous inversions and idolatries that distinguish Roman Catholicism from so-called "true" religion, the Mary of Foxcroft's sermon serves as the key example for a Puritan audience of the spiritual and moral worth of women.

The late medieval period saw an elevation of the Virgin Mary within popular devotional practice and eventually within church theology by virtue of her status as God's mother, an elevation that was at the core of the Protestant critique of the Roman Catholic Church beginning with Martin Luther. English ministerial and theological writings from several confessions in the seventeenth and eighteenth centuries reveal another transformation in the interpretation of this figure. Mary migrated from the front lines of anti-popish and anti-Catholic critique to the quieter arenas of Protestant scriptural commentary, homiletics, and even conduct literature. No longer signaling the errors of popery, especially idolatry, she transformed in Protestant eyes from a despised object of popish devotion to a model of spiritual emulation. This alteration did not occur, however, until another female symbol of anti-popery, that of the maternal body torn apart by Catholic aggressors, had waned from widespread circulation with the forced exile in 1689 of England's openly Roman Catholic king.

Very few elements of Marian commentary in the eighteenth century are absent in the seventeenth. It is not as though Mary undergoes a Protestant parthenogenesis, springing from the wreck of her condemned image to become an exemplar of virtue. The change in her depiction lies in shifts of emphasis and tone. Some of this adjustment signals the abatement of the Catholic threat in England with the Revolution of 1689 and the accession of a reliably Protestant monarch (or monarchs). It is hard to imagine that ten years earlier Timothy Rogers could have cited what "a devout *Popish* Writer says of the *Blessed Virgin,* on her Reading attended Meditation; on her Meditation Prayer; on her Prayer Action," as he did in 1697.[76] What such alterations also show is a growing sentiment that Mary should not be a Catholic possession, even if her statues are. Underlining this more positive understanding of Mary was an obscuring of her physical body. Her womb in particular transformed from reproductive organ into metaphor for the Christian's soul. Mary's body thus became a sign for precisely what is not the body.

It is at the level of metaphor and symbol that depictions of Mary and images of popish massacre are mutually most resonant. What renders the accounts of popish atrocity so horrifying, after all, is that they open to the viewer's gaze what should be unseen. Guts are torn out of bellies; wombs are ripped open to expose still germinating infants within. Catholicism is identified with the incapacity to regulate actions or maintain boundaries between inside and outside, body and soul, metaphor and material fact. Protestant horror is directed at monstrous inversion and conflation—birth mixed with death, guts with skin—as much as at the snuffing out of innocent or fruitful life. In these later readings of Mary, the womb is, in a sense, returned to its appropriate place in the arena of the unseen. Her womb rendered metaphorical, Mary becomes a beloved possession of Protestants.

This shift away from the body of Mary, preceded as it was by a valuation of the maternal body as victim of violence, is an alteration in keeping with what has been established for a long time about the depiction of women in eighteenth-century Britain and the early United States. In 1976 Marlene Gates explored the political underpinnings of a shift from "the misogyny which had characterized traditional satire and philosophical thought from the ancient Greeks through the seventeenth century" to "the eighteenth-century version of the Cult of True Womanhood."[77] Two years later Ruth Bloch charted a striking neglect of motherhood in America until after the Revolution, when "large numbers of . . . works began to appear that stressed the unique value of the maternal role."[78] Much scholarship on the culture of sensibility has shown how an attentiveness to emotion and a moral code rooted in sympathy were propelled by and magnified an alteration in attitudes to women. Although the origins and permutations of this change have been subject to debate, there has been little dispute about the basic outlines of this shift in the appraisal of women, a shift that paralleled the marginalization of elite women from politics.[79] Over the same stretch of time, the woman's body has been explored as a canvas upon which both Britain and the United States depicted new political identities.[80]

While much of this work has referenced the role of religion, little of it has considered the relevance of the Protestant response to the Virgin Mary, the figure who stands at the center of the West's longstanding contemplation of womanhood through tropes of penetration, sanctity, and reproduction. Alterations in the treatment of Mary, when viewed alongside presentations of maternal bodies torn apart by popish hordes, remind us that the Protestant response to Catholicism expressed itself through a reimagining of gender. We might consider that quintessentially female space, the womb, to be one of the "'Lost' Spaces of Catholicism" that Frances Dolan has shown were carved out after the English Reformation, positioning Catholicism in the household, in the court chapels maintained for Henrietta Maria and Catherine of Braganza, or in the conscience—a "terrain . . . transcending space"—of the privately observant Catholic.[81] During the century following the Revolution of 1689 the Protestant residents of the British Isles and their American colonies reclaimed this space as one standing for a Protestant form of virtue that was brave in the face of violation from Catholics. They accomplished this process by abstracting it from its manifestly physical status and repositioning it as metaphor. It is possible that the reign of Queen Anne, whose rhetorical positioning as "nursing mother" to Britain was painfully belied by her multiple miscarriages, dead children, and ensuing anxiety over the end of the Protestant Stuart line—exacerbated by conspiracy theories over Mary of Modena's birthing of James III—clinched the centrality of the vulnerable mother to the Protestant refutation of Catholicism as both theology and global political force, even as it facilitated the abstraction of the female body, whether Mary or Britannia, into allegory.[82] Certainly the maternal body, abstracted in one collection of writings, violated in the other, played a crucial role in the self-definition of Protestant Britain and its colonies. Just as anti-popery generated much of its energy from the monstrously feminized figures of the pope and the Babylonian Whore, British Protestantism distinguished itself from Catholicism by exhibiting shock at the ravaged bellies of popery's victims and reconfiguring the Virgin's womb as blessed soul. Mary became Protestant, and Britain manifested itself, on a certain level, in the image of a woman.

Notes

1. Walter J. Ong, *In the Human Grain: Further Explorations of Contemporary Culture* (New York: Macmillan, 1967), 193. Quoted in Ivy Schweitzer, *The Work of Self-Representation: Lyric Poetry in Colonial New England* (Chapel Hill: University of North Carolina Press, 1991), 3; Patricia Crawford, *Women and Religion in England, 1500–1720* (New York: Routledge, 1993), 47.
2. Christine Peters, *Patterns of Piety: Women, Gender, and Religion in Late Medieval and Reformation England* (Cambridge: Cambridge University Press, 2003).
3. Frances E. Dolan, *Whores of Babylon: Catholicism, Gender, and Seventeenth-Century Print Culture* (Ithaca, NY: Cornell University Press, 1999).
4. Dolan, *Whores of Babylon*, 106.
5. Of the intensity of anti-Catholicism in the 1680s, especially after the accession of the openly Catholic King James II in 1685, Brent Sirota has noted, "Just two years into the reign of James II, the churchmen [of London] had produced roughly seventy volumes against popery. The number of such works would pass two hundred before the end of the reign," *The Christian Monitors: The Church of England and the Age of Benevolence* (New Haven, CT: Yale University Press, 2014), 52.
6. Timothy Rogers, *The Character of a Good Woman, Both in a Single and Marry'd State, in a Funeral Discourse on Prov. 31.10. Who can find a vertuous Woman? for her Price is far above Rubies. Occasion'd by the Decease of Mrs. Elizabeth Dunton, Who Died May 28. 1697* (London, 1697), preface. Emphasis always in original unless otherwise noted.
7. Cotton Mather, *Elizabeth in Her Holy Retirement. An Essay to Prepare a Pious Woman for her Lying In* (Boston, 1710), 28.
8. William Reading, *Life of the Blessed Virgin Mary*, preface to *The History of Our Lord and Saviour Jesus Christ* (London, 1717), 8.
9. William Hogarth, "Transubstantiation Satirized" (1735), in Samuel Ireland, *Graphic Illustrations of Hogarth*, 2 vols. (London, 1799), 1:123, reprinted in *Religion in the Popular Prints, 1600–1832*, by John Millar (Cambridge: Chadwyck-Healey, 1986), 215. Original in British Museum, BMC 2156 from *Catalogue of Political and Personal Satires* by F. G. Stephens and M. D. George.

10. Arthur F. Marotti, *Religious Ideology and Cultural Fantasy: Catholic and Anti-Catholic Discourses in Early Modern England* (Notre Dame, IN: University of Notre Dame Press, 2005); Arthur F. Marotti, ed., *Catholicism and Anti-Catholicism in Early Modern English Texts* (Houndmills, Hampshire: Macmillan, 1999); Dolan, *Whores of Babylon;* Alison Shell, *Catholicism, Controversy, and the English Literary Imagination, 1588–1640* (Cambridge: Cambridge University Press, 2006). Studies focused on single texts or genres are too numerous to list here, but a few examples include: Alison Brunning, "Jonson's Romish Fox: Anti-Catholic Discourse in *Volpone,*" *Early Modern Literary Studies: A Journal of Sixteenth- and Seventeenth-Century English Literature* 6, no. 2 (2000): (electronic resource); Demetriou Eroulla, "Fiercer than the Pope's Bulls: Jesuits in Early 17th Century Anti-Catholic, Anti-Spanish English Pamphlets," *Grove: Working Papers on English Studies* 13 (2006): 73–91; Andrew Hadfield, "Spenser's Description of the Execution of Murrogh O'Brien: An Anti-Catholic Polemic," *Notes and Queries* 46 (1999): 195–97; Lee Oser, "Shakespeare and the Catholic Spectrum," *Religion and the Arts* 16 (2012): 381–90.
11. Karen Gevirtz, "Recent Studies in 17th and 18th-Century English Catholic Studies," *Literature Compass* 12, no. 2 (2015): 53.
12. In the 1990s two wide-ranging explorations of eighteenth-century anti-Catholicism were published: a historical survey, Colin Haydon, *Anti-Catholicism in Eighteenth-Century England, c. 1714–80: A Political and Social Study* (New York: St. Martin's Press, 1993); and a literary one: Raymond Tumbleson, *Catholicism in the English Protestant Imagination: Nationalism, Religion, and Literature, 1660–1745* (New York: Cambridge University Press, 1998). Historians are ahead of literary scholars in studies of British America, with work including Jason K. Duncan, *Citizens or Papists? The Politics of Anti-Catholicism in New York, 1685–1821* (New York: Fordham University Press, 2005); and Michael S. Carter, "A 'Traiterous Religion': Indulgences and the Anti-Catholic Imagination in Eighteenth-Century New England," *Catholic Historical Review* 99, no. 1 (2013): 52–77.
13. Studies of the religious aspects of Roman Catholic authors include G. Douglas Atkins, *Alexander Pope's Catholic Vision: 'Slave to no sect'* (New York: Palgrave Macmillan, 2013); Anna Battigelli, "John Dryden's Trojan Horse: *Religio Laici,*" in *Approaches to Teaching the Works of John Dryden,* ed. Jayne Lewis and Lisa Zunshine (New York: MLA, 2013), 30–36; Annibel Jenkins, *I'll Tell You What: The Life of Elizabeth Inchbald* (Lexington: University Press of Kentucky, 2003); Bridget Keegan, "'Bred a Jesuit': *A Simple Story* and Late Eighteenth-Century English Catholic Culture," *Huntington Library Quarterly* 71, no. 4 (December 2008): 687–706; Kathryn R. King and Jane Barker, *Exile: A Literary Career, 1675–1725* (Oxford: Clarendon Press, 2010); Niall MacKenzie, "Jane Barker, Louise Hollandine of the Palatinate, and 'Solomons Wise Daughter,'" *Review of English Studies* 58, no. 233 (February 2007): 64–72. Anna Battigelli is writing a book on Catholicism and John Dryden, and Coby Dowdell is at work on a project on depictions of nuns in texts such as Pope's *Eloisa and Abelard.*
14. Paul Kleber Monod, *Jacobitism and the English People, 1688–1745* (Cambridge: Cambridge University Press, 1993); Murray G. H. Pittock, *Poetry and Jacobite Politics in Eighteenth-Century Britain and Ireland* (Cambridge: Cambridge University Press, 1994). Monod approaches this topic as a historian and Pittock as a literary scholar, but both projects are closely attuned to the literature of Jacobitism and opposition to it.
15. See, for example, Maria Purves, *The Gothic and Catholicism: Religion, Cultural Exchange, and the Popular Novel, 1785–1829* (Cardiff: University of Wales Press, 2009); Diane Long Hoeveler, "Regina Maria Roche's *The Children of the Abbey:* Contesting the Catholic Presence in Female Gothic Fiction," *Tulsa Studies in Women's Literature* 31, nos. 1–2 (Spring–Fall 2012): 137–58;

Diane Long Hoeveler, *The Gothic Ideology: Religious Hysteria and Anti-Catholicism in British Popular Fiction* (Cardiff: University of Wales Press, 2014).

16. See, for example, the special topics double issue of *Tulsa Studies in Women's Literature*, "Eighteenth-Century Women and English Catholicism," coedited by Anna Battigelli and Laura M. Stevens, 31, nos. 1–2 (2012).
17. Alison Conway, *The Protestant Whore: Courtesan Narrative and Religious Controversy in England, 1680–1750* (Toronto: University of Toronto Press, 2010).
18. See Daniel Baraz, *Medieval Cruelty: Changing Perceptions, Late Antiquity to the Early Modern Period* (Ithaca, NY: Cornell University Press, 2003). My thanks to Philippe Rosenberg for recommending this text.
19. Bartolomé de Las Casas, *A Short Account of the Destruction of the Indies*, ed. and trans. Nigel Griffin (New York: Penguin, 1992), 15.
20. Quotations are from the third edition, the title of which is spelled slightly differently than that of the first, and the content of which includes additions made in reference to the Popish Plot. Benjamin Keach, *Sion in Distress; or, The Groans of the Protestant Church* (Boston, 1683), preface.
21. Keach, *Sion*, 97.
22. See, e.g., Laurel Thatcher Ulrich, *Good Wives: Image and Reality in the Lives of Women in Northern New England, 1650–1750* (New York: Vintage, 1980); Teresa Toulouse, "'My Own Credit': Strategies of (E)Valuation in Mary Rowlandson's Captivity Narrative," *American Literature* 64 (1992): 660; Julie Ellison, "Race and Sensibility in Early America: Ann Eliza Bleecker and Sarah Wentworth Morton," *American Literature* 65 (1993): 445–74; Teresa Toulouse, "Hannah Duston's Bodies," in *A Centre of Wonders: The Body in Early America*, ed. Janet Moore Lindman and Michele Lisa Tartar (Ithaca, NY: Cornell University Press, 2001), 196.
23. Peter Lake, "Anti-Popery: The Structure of a Prejudice," in *Conflict in Early Stuart England: Studies in Religion and Politics, 1603–1642*, ed. Richard Cust and Ann Hughes (New York: Longman, 1989), 73.
24. Mary Rowlandson, *A Narrative of the Captivity and Restauration of Mrs. Mary Rowlandson*, in *The Heath Anthology of American Literature*, Vol. A, ed. Paul Lauter et al. (Boston: Wadsworth, 2014), 486, 487, 491.
25. All biblical references are to the Authorized King James Version (New York: Family Library, 1973).
26. A crucial starting point for an analysis of anti-Catholic writings of this era is Marotti, *Religious Ideology and Cultural Fantasy*.
27. My analysis of the slaughtered maternal body draws upon Elaine Scarry's interpretation of the injured bodies of war. As Scarry writes, "wounding . . . provides, by its massive opening of human bodies, a way of reconnecting the rerealized and disembodied beliefs with the force and power of the material world," *The Body in Pain: The Making and Unmaking of the World* (New York: Oxford University Press, 1985), 128, 77.
28. John Travers, *A Sermon Preached in St. Andrew's Church, Dublin. Before the Honourable the House of Commons the Twenty-Third of October, 1698. Being the Anniversary Thanksgiving for the Deliverance from the Irish Rebellion of 1641* (Dublin, 1698), 7.
29. Edward Wettenhall, *A Sermon Setting Forth the Duties of Irish Protestants, Arising from the Irish Rebellion, 1641, and the Irish Tyranny, 1688* (Dublin, 1692), 14, citing Genesis 23:11.
30. G[eorge] F[ox] and E[llis] H[ooke], *The Arraignment of Popery* (London, 1667), 128, 129, 131.
31. George Walker, *The Protestant's Crums of Comfort* (London, 1690), 97.
32. Walker, *Protestant's Crums*, 99.

33. John Foxe, *Acts and Monuments of Martyrs* (1563 edition), Book 5, 1614 https://www.dhi.ac.uk/foxe/index.php. Accessed: July 18, 2020.
34. Raymond D. Tumbleson, *Catholicism in the English Protestant Imagination: Nationalism, Religion, and Literature, 1660–1745* (New York: Cambridge University Press, 1998), 88–89.
35. John Temple, *The Irish Rebellion; or, An History of the Beginnings and First Progress of the General Rebellion Raised within the Kingdom of Ireland, upon the Three and Twentieth Day of October, in the Year 1641* (London, 1646). A digital edition of the 1641 depositions, along with an explanation of their origin, is at http://1641.tcd.ie/index.php. For a description of the partisan intentions informing what he calls Temple's "deliberate exaggeration of the bloodletting," see Robert Dunlap, "Sir John Temple," *ODNB*. On the importance of Temple's text to depictions of the Irish see Kathleen Noonan, "'The Cruell Pressure of an Enraged, Barbarous People': Irish and English Identity in Seventeenth-Century Policy and Propaganda," *Historical Journal* 41, no. 1 (1998): 151–77.
36. Temple, *Irish Rebellion*, 96–97.
37. Temple, *Irish Rebellion*, 90. Drawing upon Kendall Thomas's analysis of "overkill, . . . the pattern of stabbing and mutilating bodies even after the victim is fatally shot," Nancy Isenberg uses this term to analyze William Cobbett's sensationalistic depictions of carnage of the French Revolution in *The Bloody Buoy* (1796 and 1797), "Death and Satire: Dismembering the Body Politic," in *Mortal Remains: Death in Early America*, ed. Andrew Burstein and Nancy Isenberg (Philadelphia: University of Pennsylvania Press, 2003), 85, 221n45, quoting Thomas, "Beyond the Privacy Principle," *Columbia Law Review* 92 (1992): 1466.
38. Temple, *Irish Rebellion*, 92, 95.
39. Keach, *Sion*, 88.
40. Keach, *Sion*, 114.
41. Keach, *Sion*, 92–93, 94.
42. Keach, *Sion*, 102.
43. Keach, *Sion*, 7.
44. Keach, *Sion*, 85.
45. Keach, *Sion*, 88.
46. Keach, *Sion*, 115.
47. Keach, *Sion*, 2.
48. Keach, *Sion*, 76.
49. Keach, *Sion*, 40.
50. Keach, *Sion*, 4.
51. Keach, *Sion*, 8, 23.
52. Keach, *Sion*, 74, 81.
53. Keach, *Sion*, 79.
54. Symon [*sic*] Patrick, *Jesus and the Resurrection Justified by Witnesses in Heaven and Earth* (London, 1677), 550.
55. Donna Spivey Ellington, *From Sacred Body to Angelic Soul: Understanding Mary in Late Medieval and Early Modern Europe* (Washington, DC: Catholic University of America Press, 2001), 33.
56. Ellington, *From Sacred Body*, 52–57, 58, 62. See also Caroline Walker Bynum, *Jesus as Mother: Studies in the Spirituality of the High Middle Ages* (Berkeley: University of California Press, 1984).
57. Ellington, *From Sacred Body*, 155.
58. Peters, *Patterns*, 74.

59. Charles Gobinet, *The Instruction of Youth in Christian Piety*, 3rd ed., 2 vols. (London, 1741), 2:341.
60. Increase Mather, *The Mystery of Christ Opened and Applyed* (Boston, 1686), 143. Evans Catalogue, accessed January 4, 2008.
61. Thomas Lewis, *An Inquiry into the Shape, the Beauty, and Stature of the Person of Christ, and of the Virgin Mary* (London, 1753), 17.
62. Henry Killigrew, *Sermons Preached Partly Before His Majesty at White-Hall. And Partly Before Anne Dutchess of York, at the Chappel at St. James* (London, 1685), 48–49.
63. Augustine of Hippo, Sermo 72/A, 7. Translation on website of the Holy See, http://www.vatican.va/spirit/documents/spirit_20001208_agostino_en.html, accessed April 9, 2020. The original Latin is: "[E]t ideo plus est Mariae discipulam fuisse Christi, quam matrem fuisse Christi: plus est, felicius est discipulum fuisse Christi, quam, matrem fuisse Christi." https://www.augustinus.it/latino/discorsi/discorso_094_testo.htm, accessed April 9, 2020.
64. Isaac Ambrose, *Looking unto Jesus*, in *The Compleat Works of that Eminent Minister of God's Word Mr. Isaac Ambrose* (Dundee, Scotland, 1759), 477.
65. John Tillotson, *The Life of Jesus Christ Consider'd, as Our Example*, in *The Works of the Most Reverend Dr. John Tillotson*, 2nd ed., 3 vols. (London, 1717) 2:240.
66. Nathaniel Marshall, *Sermon V. Preach'd on the Annunciation of the Blessed Virgin*, in *Sermons on Several Occasions*, 3 vols. (London, 1731), 3:124.
67. Thomas Ellwood, *Sacred History: or the Historical Part of the Holy Scriptures of the Old and New Testaments*, 3 vols., 4th ed. (London, 1778), 3:132.
68. P[hilip] Doddridge, *The Family Expositor; or, A Paraphrase and Version of the New Testament; with Critical Notes and Practical Improvements of Each Section* (London, 1773), 1:324–325.
69. John Wesley, *Explanatory Notes upon the New Testament* (London, 1755), 177.
70. Nehemiah Walter, *A Discourse Concerning the Wonderfulness of Christ. Delivered in Several Sermons* (Boston, 1713), 80.
71. P. W., *Mary's Choice Declared in a Sermon Preached at the Funeral of the Right Honourable Lady Mary Wharton, Late Wife of the Honourable Sir Thomas Wharton, Knight of the Bath* (London, 1674), 9.
72. See, for example, D[euel] Pead, *A Practical Discourse upon the Death of our Late Gracious Queen. Being a Sermon Preach'd the 10th of March, 1694/5 at St. James Clarkenwell* (London, 1695), 1; Cotton Mather, *A Companion for Communicants. Discourses upon the Nature, the Design, and the Subject of the Lords Supper* (Boston, 1690).
73. On the *Magnificat* see Laura M. Stevens, "Mary's *Magnificat* in Eighteenth-Century Britain," *Journal of Religious History, Literature, and Culture* 3, no. 2 (2017): 91–107.
74. Reading, *History*, viii.
75. Thomas Foxcroft, *The Character of Anna, the Prophetess, Consider'd and Apply'd. In a Sermon Preach'd after the Funeral of that Honourable and Devout Gentlewoman, Dame Bridget Usher* (Boston, 1723), 2. Rick Kennedy, "Thomas Foxcroft," 1999, *American National Biography Online*, https://www.anb.org/.
76. Rogers, *Character*, 39.
77. Marlene LeGates, "The Cult of Womanhood in Eighteenth-Century Thought," *Eighteenth-Century Studies* 10 (1976): 21–39, quote on 21.
78. Ruth H. Bloch, "American Feminine Ideals in Transition: The Rise of the Moral Mother, 1785–1815," in Bloch, *Gender and Morality in Anglo-American Culture, 1650–1800* (Berkeley: University of California Press, 2003), 57–77.
79. On this marginalizing of elite women see Mary Beth Norton, *Separated by Their Sex: Women in Public and Private in the Colonial Atlantic World* (Ithaca, NY: Cornell University Press, 2011).

80. See, e.g., Nancy Armstrong and Leonard Tennenhouse, "The American Origins of the English Novel," *American Literary History* 4 (1992): 386–410; Nancy Armstrong, *Desire and Domestic Fiction: A Political History of the Novel* (New York: Oxford University Press, 1987); Nancy Isenberg, "Death and Satire: Dismembering the Body Politic," in *Mortal Remains: Death in Early America*, ed. Burstein and Isenberg, 71–90; Shirley Samuels, *Romances of the Republic: Women, the Family, and Violence in the Literature of the Early American Nation* (New York: Oxford University Press, 1996), 3–22; Leonard Tennenhouse, "The Americanization of Clarissa," *Yale Journal of Criticism* 11 (1998): 177–96.
81. Frances E. Dolan, "Gender and the 'Lost' Spaces of Catholicism," *Journal of Interdisciplinary History* 32, no. 4 (Spring 2002): 641–65, quote on 663.
82. John Spurr notes that Queen Anne chose Isaiah 49:23, "And kings shall be thy nursing fathers, and their queens thy nursing mothers," as the text for her coronation sermon, *The Post-Reformation: Religion, Politics, and Society in Britain, 1603–1714* (London: Pearson Longman, 2006), 212. See, e.g., Elkanah Settle's dedication of *A Pindaric Poem on the Propagation of the Gospel* (London, 1711) to Queen Anne: "we see the Royal Piety laying those yet greater Plans of Glory, resolv'd to make her Britannia, with such expanded Arms and flowing Breasts, a more Universal Nursing Mother in so extensive a Filial Adoption" (v). On Mary of Modena see Rachel Weil, *Political Passions: Gender, the Family, and Political Argument in England, 1680–1714* (Manchester: Manchester University Press, 2010).

Challenging Catholicism

ANGLO-AMERICAN RESPONSES TO THE AUTHORITY OF ROMAN CATHOLIC ART, 1760–1820

Clare Haynes

THE SWEEPING AWAY OF art from churches is perhaps the most familiar feature of the Reformation. What is much less well known is that, beyond the church, Roman Catholic visual culture retained a position of immense, even unassailable, dominance throughout the post-Reformation period. This meant that artists and collectors continued to engage with Catholic culture in formative and emulative ways. The artistic canon—established and reinforced in the academies, art markets, and elite collections of Europe—consisted largely of the Renaissance and baroque art of Catholic Italy and France: the paintings of Raphael, Michelangelo, Domenichino, Guercino, and Poussin, for example. Although not all the works of these artists were popish in content, of course, many did present Catholic ideas that were alien, blasphemous, or even idolatrous to the Protestant spectator. Nevertheless, Protestants admired, collected, and reproduced them just as eagerly and frequently as they did secular subjects. Their acceptance of popish art did not result from a form of relativism, in which content was ignored. Rather, it was the product of a complexly dualistic approach that acknowledged artistic value while simultaneously denying a work's ultimate truth.[1]

In Protestant spectatorship, then, truth and beauty were ambivalently related. The situation exemplifies the essential and much more general characteristic of early modern anti-Catholicism: prejudice, intolerance, and principle were bound together. Rejection was never complete and principle was rarely absent. After all, the continuous observation and maintenance of difference from Catholicism was fundamental to the existence, identity, and evolution of Protestantism. Even for those who saw their Church as developing from, not reacting to, the Church of Rome, opposition had to be actively maintained to explain the separation and superiority of Protestantism.

Consequently, observing how Protestants chose to face the aesthetic, moral, and intellectual challenges of Catholic art presents an opportunity to enrich our understanding of anti-Catholicism more generally. The life and work of the transatlantic artist Benjamin West (1738–1820) provides an excellent case for examining this process at work in the Anglo-American context. West's own religiosity is unclear. Born into a Quaker family, he was buried in Saint Paul's Cathedral. In a long career, he produced both a considerable amount of work for the Anglican Church, as well as a range of religious works that seem more aligned with radical nonconformity in their treatment of, for example, the Book of Revelations. Despite this ambiguity, West's value as a case study is that, while he was unusual in the range of his experience—as an Anglo-American, a portraitist, a major history painter, a writer, a client of King George III, and the president of the Royal Academy—his approach to Catholic culture was quite conventional. Therefore, his career can reveal the full extent of the enmeshment of anti-Catholicism in the production and reception of art in the Anglo-American world.

Benjamin West is certainly the most studied Anglo-American artist of the long eighteenth century, the focus of a great deal of scholarly endeavor on both sides of the Atlantic.[2] While much of this work is not of immediate relevance to the matters under discussion here, the work of a handful of scholars must be mentioned. In the 1970s J. D. Meyer broke ground in a series of articles that drew attention to West's religious paintings, demonstrating how ambitious and largely unprecedented they were as Protestant art.[3] At that time the importance of anti-Catholicism to Anglo-American identity had yet to be seriously considered. Certainly its significance to the reception of art had not been explored.[4] Gradually, however, the religious context for his artistic practice has developed into a prominent theme. Most recently, Nicholas Grindle and William Pressly have considered West's religious paintings afresh, shedding new light on West's position as an American in Britain, his ambiguous politics, his artistic ambition, and the implications of all this for his practice as an artist.[5] Nevertheless, the formative and structural role of anti-Catholicism in West's artistic practice and theory has yet to be recognized.[6]

West's first encounter with the manner and meaning of Catholic art may well have taken place in the course of making a portrait of his early patron, the Reverend William Smith (1727–1803), the first provost of the College of Philadelphia (later the University of Pennsylvania). West based his depiction of Smith on a portrait of Saint Ignatius Loyola (1491–1556) that was owned by the governor of Pennsylvania, James Hamilton (c. 1710–1783). Hamilton's painting was said to have been the work of a member of the school of the Spanish painter Murillo (1617–1682) but, unfortunately, it cannot be traced and is otherwise unknown. West's portrait of Smith, which survives in a very poor state, does in fact bear a resemblance to the portrait of Loyola made by Peter Paul Rubens (1577–1640) of which copies and engravings circulated widely in the seventeenth and eighteenth centuries. Uncertainty over precisely which painting West based his portrait on need not detain us. What is

John Sartain after Benjamin West, *William Smith, D.D.*, engraving, n.d. (Courtesy of the Pennsylvania Academy of the Fine Arts, Philadelphia; bequest of Dr. Paul J. Sartain)

Peter Paul Rubens, *Saint Ignatius Loyola,* c. 1620–22. (Courtesy of the Norton Simon Art Foundation)

more important here is to come to an understanding of West's use and transformation of an image of the founder of the Jesuit order into that of the Anglican William Smith.[7]

Firstly, we must consider the presence and authority of a portrait of Saint Ignatius in Philadelphia. It was not unusual for portraits of leading Catholic figures—popes, priests, and even saints regarded as false—to be found in Protestant collections such as Governor Hamilton's. Such ownership was certainly not a sign of Catholic leanings but a matter of cultural prestige. The artist's name and his position in the canonical hierarchy superseded any other concerns. While the portrait would have been understood to communicate valuable information about the character and reputation, within Roman Catholicism, of Saint Ignatius, its meanings went far beyond those matters. As Iain Pears has shown, the collection and knowledge of canonical art had a privileged role in the attainment and demonstration of the political and social identity of British elites: "possession of taste not only indicated education and hence virtue but also implied and signified the fitness of its possessors to rule."[8] Taste was valued as a way of displaying and deploying good judgment, the essential qualification for citizenship. The benefits of knowing about and owning this pan-European art were clear. The power of these works of art, and the literature, associations, and practices that surrounded them, was such that Protestants could not turn from them. There was simply nothing with enough tradition or prestige that could function as a substitute within the Protestant sphere.

The superiority of Catholic culture was frequently discussed. For example, the Scottish philosopher George Turnbull laid out what was a common explanation in his *Treatise on Ancient Painting* (1740). Turnbull argued that the works of Raphael and Michelangelo were unequivocally the greatest the world had known since those of Apelles, for "the analogy between the two ages of painting in many circumstances is indeed surprising; but is well vouched and not imagined."[9] Despite the great differences between the cultures of ancient Greece and the early modern papacy, Turnbull suggested that each provided a rich soil of love of learning and great and generous patrons. This model of the rise of the arts was used frequently to encourage Britain's elite to commission new works of art. As no nation had ever been great without producing great art, only through the encouragement of artists could a school of art be created that could enable a modern nation to rival the historic supremacy of ancient Greece and *cinquecento* Rome. In the absence of the homegrown talent that could rival them, the works of Raphael and Michelangelo and their followers remained canonical in Protestant Europe. No alternative aesthetic was found or even looked for.[10] Thus it was a complicated mixture of flattery, expectation, and hope that provoked some to call West the "American Raphael" and William Hogarth, Sir Thomas Lawrence, and others the "English Raphael."

In terms of early-modern art theory, which emerged in the academies of Catholic France and Italy, this situation was paradoxical. Central to the claims of art to be a liberal practice was the genre of history painting, the large-scale narrative painting of the kind Raphael and Michelangelo were most famous for. History painting was understood to be the summit of artistic achievement (above portraiture) in which the artist integrated excellent skills, intellectual prowess, and important ideas. It was the genre reserved for the narration of stories from the Bible, classical literature, and other authoritative sources, which demonstrated great, universal, moral and religious truths. Yet, when faced with history paintings depicting Catholic doctrine, Protestants could not assent to their truth as the discourses of art demanded.

If art was false, the edifice of the canon should have come tumbling down. It did not. Instead, struggles with the problems of content and the persistent suspicion of idolatry became a uniquely prominent feature of British art theory. For example, Jonathan Richardson (1667–1745), a painter and prominent art theorist, defended his project to encourage greater appreciation and patronage of painting in England in this way: "I plead for the art, not its abuses . . . if when I see a Madonna though painted by Raphael, I be enticed and drawn away to idolatry; or if the subject of a picture, though painted by Caracci pollutes my mind with impure images, and transforms me into a brute . . . may my tongue cleave to the roof of my mouth, and my right hand forget its cunning if I am its advocate as it is instrumental to such detested purposes."[11] Richardson's use of Psalm 137 is more than a rhetorical flourish. It demonstrates how charged, in religious terms, encounters with even the greatest art were. In a hugely influential essay on connoisseurship, which West and Smith both knew, Richardson adapted conventional European art theory for a Protestant milieu. Dispensing with its tacit understanding of the shared beliefs of artist and spectator, he offered Protestants not simply a secure means of approaching Catholic art but a justification for a wholehearted engagement with it:

> It is the glory of the Protestant church, and especially of the church of England, the best national church in the world. I say it is the glory of the reformation, that thereby men are set at liberty to judge for themselves. We are thus a body of free men; not the major part in subjection to the rest. Here we are all connoisseurs as we are Protestants; though (as it must needs happen) some are abler connoisseurs than others. And we have abundantly experienced the advantages of this, since we have thus resumed our natural rights as rational creatures.
>
> A man that thinks boldly, freely, and thoroughly; that stands upon his own legs, and sees with his own eyes, has a firmness, and serenity of mind, which he that is dependent upon others has not, or cannot reasonably have.[12]

Richardson reorientated the discourses of art and taste to fit British circumstances by first asserting that Protestantism was the only true motor of fine judgment, then making the exercise and improvement of that judgment the major benefit of a committed engagement with painting. Furthermore, Richardson aligned his ideas about art with John Locke's emphasis on discernment, and integrated painting into the sciences of human understanding.[13]

Thus, in Richardson's hands, Catholic art provided a test for Protestant judgment and a field for practicing discrimination. Through the resulting development of their reason and the influence of their religion, the British would inevitably be led to rival and surpass Italian and French achievements in the arts. Richardson's remodeling of European art theory thus offered the British viewer a means of approach to a work of Catholic art that did not involve the occlusion of popish content. On the contrary, it involved the explicit recognition of it, albeit from a standpoint of Protestant superiority.

If we return to West's portrait of Smith, we can see it as embodying this outlook. In this period, the copying and reusing of motifs from old masters was recognized as an essential part of an artist's formation as well as a means of bringing esteem to both the sitter and the owner of the painting reproduced. Ideally this would not be a servile procedure but a means by which the authority and allure of the original was transferred to the new work.[14] It also admitted of the possibility of improving on the original. In the case of this early portrait, West was still very young and his painting lacked the fluidity it would quickly develop on his arrival in Europe. Nevertheless, Smith saw great promise in the young man and his commission provided the artist with the opportunity to learn, by copying, from one of the best paintings in his locality.[15] Such juvenile dependence might appear at first glance to be a rather insubstantial and uninteresting form of appropriation, but there is more to it than that. Following Jonathan Richardson, Provost Smith and the young Benjamin West would have understood such copying to be an act of discernment, in which the artist demonstrated by his choice of model that he recognized art that was skillful in its execution and truthful in its content.[16] Unfortunately no records survive of what exactly Hamilton, Smith, or West thought of Loyola, nor of his portrayal. We can only speculate about the degree to which West's remaking of the portrait of Saint Ignatius for one of the leading Anglicans of his generation was imagined by the artist and the sitter to have been an act of meaningful transposition, in which, perhaps, the original was improved by its new content.

Some clue to Smith's outlook may be recognized in an address that he gave as part of the campaign to gather forces and money for the assault on Fort Duquesne in late 1758. After listing the many advantages that they lived under as Britons, Smith described the disadvantages that the French people had to cope with and which might be imposed on Pennsylvanians if the French were not driven off. Not only were the French subject to arbitrary government; they were deprived of the freedom of their minds:

> instead of being permitted to pour forth the genuine worship of the heart, according to the dictates of their own conscience, before the great creator of heaven and earth, they are obliged to pay a mock adoration to those who are no "gods"! Instead of putting their trust in his mercies through the only Mediator Jesus Christ, they are taught to put a vain confidence in relicks, and departed spirits, and those who can afford no help. Instead of following the plain dictates of common sense and the light of their own understandings, they must submit to be hood-winked, and to have their consciences ridden, by a set of priests and Jesuits and monks and inquisitors, swarming in every corner![17]

Such commonplace expressions of anti-Catholicism support the tantalizing notion that West, Smith, and Hamilton were engaging in an act of subtle but meaningful re-formation in this portrait. The echoes of Richardson's expressions reinforce the impression of appropriation. We will perhaps never know how explicit an operation it was. Nonetheless, this early episode in West's career exemplifies rather poignantly the dependence upon, and negotiation with, Catholic culture that were both fundamental to the making and reception of art in Protestant Europe and America.

For any ambitious artist, a visit to Italy, and to Rome in particular, was considered indispensable. Benjamin West, declaring the nature of his artistic aspirations, set his heart on visiting Italy and in 1760 he took passage on a merchant ship bound for Livorno, a voyage that had been arranged for him by Provost Smith.[18] He remained in Italy until 1763. The artist's journey was akin to the grand tour that was considered such an important element of elite education, through which the young man gained social polish from mixing in a different social milieu and an extended knowledge of the world that would fit him for governing.[19] Along with making observations of political economy, elite travelers aimed to develop skills such as fencing and dancing, to cultivate diverse and useful friendships, and to experience European culture first hand, both ancient and modern. Tourists sought out the experiences of walking on the same ground as Cato or Cicero, of seeing the *Apollo Belvedere,* the *Laocoön* as well as the *Venus de Medici* and the major works of Raphael, Michelangelo, and so on. Artists undertook the journey to Rome with similar social and educational aims. They too stocked their minds with knowledge and experience, met fellow artists, and, in the more informal society of the expatriate continental community, potential patrons.

Our understanding of West's encounters with Catholic Italy depends on the account provided by the Scottish novelist and biographer John Galt (1779–1839) in the "memoirs" of the artist that he wrote with and for West some fifty years later.[20] Although Galt's narration of West's life is unreliable in parts, it is perhaps all the more useful for that because it demonstrates the customary expectations for a British artist's encounter with Catholic Italy. The attitudes it reveals are complicated and conflicted: both admiring and disdainful, reverent and appalled.[21]

Galt's description of West's arrival at the outskirts of Rome exemplifies this ambivalence very well. It begins in a way that resembles the arrivals recorded in countless other grand tour journals and paintings:

> It was a beautiful morning; the air was perfectly placid, not a speck of vapour in the sky, and a profound tranquillity seemed almost sensibly diffused over the landscape. The appearance of Nature was calculated to lighten and elevate the spirits; but the general silence and nakedness of the scene touched the feelings with solemnity approaching to awe. Filled with the idea of the metropolitan city, the Artist hastened forward till he reached an elevated part of the high road,

> which afforded him a view of a spacious champaign country, bounded by hills, and in the midst of it the sublime dome of St. Peter's.

Galt might have been describing a painting by Richard Wilson, rather than recording West's experience.[22] It is a sublime *veduta* constituted of a high viewpoint over the city, which generated the complex mixture of admiration and fear that constitutes awe. The distance that West looked over was not just spatial but temporal too, as it prompted him to make a series of reflections on the contrast between Rome's present, a city in decay, and the bright future of America that it prophesied to the young artist.[23] As such thoughts of the cyclical nature of history on first seeing Rome were quite conventional, Galt is showing that even with so little experience of the world, and a less than thorough education, West was already displaying the enlarged historical imagination essential for a history painter and gentlemanly grand tourist.

This panoramic viewpoint was, in fact, one that tourists rarely discarded. As they entered the city, they often maintained a position of studied distance from contemporary Rome. Thus (according to Galt), West acknowledged that Pope Clement XIII exercised a positive influence on Roman society, which had, under his direction "attained a pitch of elegance and a liberality of sentiment superior to that of any other

Richard Wilson, *Rome: St. Peter's from the Janiculum*, c. 1753. (Tate London; photo © Tate)

city of Christendom." He acknowledged too that while many arrived in Rome confident that they would be "disgusted with the degenerated Romans," they often left with quite contrary memories of their "urbanity and accomplishments." However, the visitor could only experience "the most various and delightful exercises of the faculties of memory, taste, and judgment" that life in Rome consisted of, if he forgot "that the name of Christianity was employed in supporting a baneful administration to the vices, or could withdraw his thoughts from the penury and suffering that such an administration necessarily entailed on the people."[24] Most commonly, this act of forgetting was successfully achieved in two ways. First, while tourists mixed with Romans, they found that "it was the foreigners that constituted the chief attraction of Rome." Second, they maintained that the main purpose of traveling to Rome was a historical one: it was "a pilgrimage to the shrine of antiquity."[25] Thus, in the company of strangers in pursuit of the past, not present, glories of Rome, the Protestant visitor to Rome could negotiate his way through what was alien territory: "every thing in Italy was in a state of disease," Galt recorded. Thus "every recreation of the stranger in Rome was an effort of memory, of abstraction, and of fancy."[26]

This imaginative and intellectual distance could be challenged by the approach or encroachment of contemporary Catholicism. Galt records the "universal tacit resolution" adopted by visitors that "national and personal peculiarities and prejudices were forgotten, and that all strangers simultaneously turned their attention to the transactions and affairs of former ages, and of statesmen and authors no more."[27] However, while days might be filled with visiting the remains of ancient Rome and evenings with discussions of their merits, visits to see works of religious art prompted a different series of reflections. These were works "by which the fraudulent disposition of the priesthood had, in the decay of its power, rendered itself venerable to the most enlightened minds," leading visitors to speculate on how genius developed and the "events which tend to stifle and overwhelm its powers."[28] Again, we can observe how the distancing of abstraction, through a focus on historical lessons from the ancient and modern history of the city, was the first priority for the tourist.

We might ask what were the detailed procedures of reception that West, and others like him, performed when looking at works of Catholic religious art that allowed them to venerate the "priesthood . . . in the decay of its power." A partial answer may be found in another biographical account of West, published a few years earlier by Alexander Stephens in *Public Characters*. There, the author explains how in Rome West developed a strong sense of the serious moral and philosophical capacity of art. Paradoxically, West understood these powers to be best used in the service of religion, in ways described in a passage worth quoting at length.

> [West] . . . observed that the early efforts of painting in the eleventh and twelfth centuries were directed to the same pious and beneficent ends as poetry, that they were employed to instruct men in their duty towards God, by delineating passages from scriptural events, as transmitted by the prophets and apostles. . . . He likewise observed, that in the fifteenth and sixteenth centuries its powers were cherished by a proud patronage and a princely liberality, to call forth what would most dignify religion, philosophy, and morality, and that it did by these exertions raise itself to such excellence and glory, that whole state, communities, and individuals, were proud of their illustrious men in the art. . . . The munificent patronage of the house of Medici, at Florence, and its influence under Leo X in the pontifical seat at Rome, advanced those efforts which had been making in the arts for the three preceding centuries, to the highest perfection, in the works of Michael Angelo and Raphael. The wars and intestine [*sic*] commotions with which Italy was soon after distracted, together with the imbecility in the minds of those who succeeded in the following centuries, caused that proud patronage to decline, and with it the art of painting. . . . Mr West observing the degraded state of painting in Italy and France, and its employment to inflame bigotry, darken superstition, and stimulate the baser passions of our nature, resolved to struggle for a recovery of its dignity.[29]

This history is remarkably selective, rather inaccurate, and somewhat tenuous, not least in its isolation of superstitious practices to the period after Raphael and Michelangelo were active. Note for example the description of medieval painters as depicters only of "scriptural events, *as transmitted by the apostles and prophets*" [my emphasis]. The fact that medieval artists depicted nonscriptural events from the lives of the saints (such as those gathered in *The Golden Legend*) and used images in what Protestants saw as superstitious ways is overlooked. Instead these medieval artists are depicted as virtuous proto-Protestants depicting only what scripture authorized. The corruption of religion and the misuse of art is actually ascribed to the period of the Reformation and after, not that which led up to it. The fact that both Raphael and Michelangelo depicted biblical events in idolatrous ways is forgotten.

Thus, in establishing a historical continuity and foundation for his longed-for rise of Anglo-American art, West seems to have misplaced the Reformation or forgotten some of the reasons for it. In this he was not alone. Similarly elliptical versions of the history of the rise and fall of art (based largely on a reading of Vasari) were commonly offered to British readers; inaccurate but apparently plausible, they could be addressed to the British elite as exemplary and worthy of emulation.[30] It was a history that was designed to open up the possibility for art to flourish in Britain, in which readers could find echoes of their own patriotic view of the present promise of British culture, if the same conditions of patronage could only be matched.

This history, offered in the context of West's biography, also suggested a flattering context for the trajectory that West's career had, to an extent, taken by this time. West's ambition for himself, and for Anglo-American art, was enormous. In his lectures to the Royal Academy delivered in the 1790s, he said more than once that British art had since the mid-eighteenth century made such enormous strides that its progress was faster than that of any other nation.[31] He did not address directly the question of whether it yet rivaled the production of Italy or Greece at their height. However, Galt was not alone in describing West as having attained some parity with Raphael and Michelangelo. These judgments, which seem unrealistic, can only be understood by considering the strongly patriotic agenda that attended artistic production in Britain's long eighteenth century. When Galt implied that West's presence had been instrumental in the great progress that had been made, it is possible that this reflected West's view of his own career.[32] Crucial to justifying this appraisal of West was the remarkably large number of history paintings, and in particular, ecclesiastical commissions that he had received, certainly more than any other painter working in Britain in the eighteenth century. The patronage of the church was understood to be essential if Anglo-American art was to flourish for two distinct reasons. Firstly, for art to be great, it had to be of the most ambitious kind, serving public worship, as it had done in ancient Greece and Rome and Christian Italy and France. Secondly, religious patronage would bring art to more public notice, stimulating artists to produce their best work. The market for art would then expand as art became more and more desirable to private patrons.

West's religious art thus took on a significance for him, and others, that may, at first glance, seem unwarranted if considered only in the context of the larger history of European art where, in Catholic countries, ecclesiastical painting had always played a major part. If, however, we consider it in the context of post-Reformation Anglo-American art, these works appear unprecedented, revolutionary, and hugely ambitious. This is not to make a new claim for West; it was first advanced by J. D. Meyer in the 1970s and has been explored by others subsequently.[33] The point here is to indicate how Catholic culture and anti-Catholicism dictated the forms and meanings of Protestant art and its reception.

The presence of art in church was still, in the mid eighteenth century, strongly associated with popery in Protestant minds. Consequently, any work of art placed in an Anglican church in this period had to adhere to a very strict set of principles of what we might call pictorial decorum.[34] Before West began to receive ecclesiastical commissions in the 1770s, art in cathedrals and parish churches was, with only a few exceptions, of a very narrow repertoire: portraits of Moses and Aaron with the texts of the Lord's Prayer, Ten Commandments, and Creed predominated, while occasionally the Last Supper and Christ's Nativity were represented above the communion table. These subjects were considered safe enough to withstand the charge of idolatry and forestall the idolatrous gaze. However, the legitimacy of having art, at all, in church was still questioned. One seminal incident for eighteenth-century British art illustrates this neatly.

In 1773, Benjamin West, with Joshua Reynolds and four other members of the Royal Academy, proposed to the dean and chapter of Saint Paul's Cathedral, London, that they should each give a painting to the cathedral, which would hang in places apparently intended for paintings by the building's architect, Sir Christopher Wren. The plan was abandoned even though it apparently had the support of the dean and chapter, the archbishop of Canterbury, and the king. Although there appears to have been a breakdown of communication between the parties that may have left the bishop of London, Richard Terrick (1710–1777), feeling aggrieved, ultimately his reason for not allowing the scheme to proceed was that it might be viewed as the "introduction of popery." Nothing in the proposed subjects was extra-biblical, and the approval and early involvement of the dean suggests that there was probably little in the manner of the proposed paintings to prompt this response. What Terrick was almost certainly expressing was the commonly held view that art in church would *always* lead to idolatry, especially among the uneducated. This fear was the restraint that prevented art from being used widely in the Church.

Nevertheless, there were others in the Anglican Church who were confident that the Reformation had in fact been more successful than Terrick believed. West had been offered his first ecclesiastical commission, an altarpiece for Rochester Cathedral, in 1772, shortly before Terrick quashed the scheme for Saint Paul's. His patron was Joseph Wilcocks (1724–1791), whom West had known in Rome and whose father had been bishop of Rochester. A letter from Wilcock to West, discussing the content of the painting, provides a rare written record of the boundaries of Protestant picture-making being recognized and established. In commenting on a sketch for the work West had provided him, Wilcocks wrote

> You have very pleasingly designed I think the attitude of the two Angels, & the Glory opening over them.—May the Spectators of your picture whether English or foreign . . . long retain the good Ideas which the sight of this piece by your hand must raise in their minds. But tho' these two Angels are selected from the rest of the heavenly host as two peculiarly bright Examples of Devotion and Charity . . . ; yet extreme attention is to be given also to the other parts of the picture that nothing in it may appear unsuitable or contradictory to the history as in the Gospel of St. Luke or other parts of Scripture.

Wilcocks proceeded to direct West to the appropriate verses of Luke 2 and discuss how other elements of the painting should be portrayed. He wanted to prevent West from portraying the angels, as he had apparently suggested, "scattering flowers or other doings; tho' that Idea is very pleasing: I cou'd wish it might be justified: but fear it too like the descriptions of the Zephyrs by Heathen Poets or Sculptors."[35]

Wilcocks's overriding concern is for the painting to be an accurate representation of the facts and the spirit of the biblical narrative. Nothing was to be added, contradictory, or unsuitable to it. The painting that West produced for the cathedral, which hung above the altar only from 1788 to 1826 and unfortunately has since the 1920s been missing, was given further authority by the inclusion of the words of Luke 2:14 on the scrolls held by the angels. There is nothing explicitly anti-Catholic in this position. However, Wilcocks's careful attention to the content of the painting was designed to ensure that it was free of those liberties with the text (or "licenses," to use the eighteenth-century term) that were identified as popish. Painting and its traditions of iconography had to be policed. This is a point to which we will return.

Despite the failure of the Saint Paul's proposal, West received a number of other major commissions for altarpieces in the next few years.[36] Beyond these in scale by a huge margin was the request West received from George III that he should decorate a chapel at Windsor Castle that became known as the Chapel of Revealed Religion. This was what West referred to later as "the great work of my life."[37] The idea emerged, Galt reported, from conversations that the king and West had about the development of the fine arts, which probably took place while West was working on one of the many portraits of the royal family that the artist was commissioned to make in the 1770s.[38] What the two men envisaged was the largest scale scheme of ecclesiastical decoration in Britain since the Reformation.

The king requested West draw up a list of subjects that "Christians, of all denominations, might contemplate without offence to their tenets."[39] The king then sought the opinion of several clergymen attached to the court, who included Richard Hurd (1720–1808), John Douglas (1721–1807), and almost certainly Anselm Bayly (1718/19–1794), as to the propriety of the scheme. According to Galt, the king said,

> When I reflect how the ornaments of art in churches were condemned at the Reformation, and still more recently in the unhappy times of Charles the First, I am anxious to govern my own wishes not only by what is right, but by what is prudent, in this matter. If it is conceived that I am tacitly bound, as Head of the Church of England, to prevent any such ornaments from being introduced into places of worship; or if it be considered as at all savouring in any degree of a popish practice, however decidedly I may myself think it innocent, I will proceed no farther in the business.[40]

At a subsequent meeting the clergymen expressed the view that the scheme, which was outlined in West's list of subjects, would "in no respect whatever, violate the laws or usages of the Church of England."[41] Galt's reporting of the incident,

William Sharp after Benjamin West, *The Angels Appearing to the Shepherds*, print, 1779.

especially the words of the king, is almost certainly close to fictional but it expressed in brief the conventional caution with which art in church was approached. It also suggests the historic importance that the scheme would take on, at least for the artist.[42]

West worked on the chapel for thirty years. He produced over two dozen paintings, changing and refining the details of the scheme from time to time. In the end it was not completed. The project was finally halted in circa 1810 for reasons that cannot be definitely ascertained. The king's health, West's other commitments, what appears to have been a degree of procrastination on his part, as well as professional rivalries all seem to have played a part.[43] Nevertheless, from the plans, the works that West did complete, and his response to the scheme's ultimate cancellation, we can learn a great deal about the intentions of the participants.

The choices of subjects that West made from the Bible, numbering at different times between thirty-two and perhaps thirty-eight, were almost certainly guided by Richard Hurd and Anselm Bayly. West arranged them into four groups, each representing one of the four dispensations of God's revelation: antediluvian and patriarchal; Mosaic; Gospel and Revelations. Beginning with the expulsion of Adam and Eve from Paradise and ending with scenes from Revelations including *The Destruction of the Beast and False Prophet,* the paintings were designed to relate in appropriately diverse manners the facts, drama, and sublimity of the biblical events. Arranged around the large rectangular interior of the planned chapel, the main focus would have been on the huge *Moses Receiving the Law,* which had been West's planned subject for Saint Paul's, above a substantial depiction of the *Last Supper,* which would have hung above the communion table.[44] However, with another thirty very substantial paintings, including dramatic depictions of the Flood, Moses showing the Brazen Serpent to the Israelites, and scenes from Christ's childhood and so on, the chapel would have been a visually complex space, quite unlike any other British or American church interior.

As Meyer noted, West may well have turned to the Sistine Chapel as a model for the arrangement of so many subjects. There, in paintings and tapestries by fifteenth- and sixteenth-century artists, biblical history from the Creation to the Last Judgment was narrated in an arrangement consisting of four slightly different groups: pre-Mosaic, the history of the Hebrews under the Law, scenes from Christ's life, and the Last Judgment.[45] However, Meyer also noted that West did not depend on the chapel in any other way, either in his choice of subjects or in the design of particular works.[46] This assessment of the extent of West's reference to the Sistine Chapel is correct but it overlooks his main purpose. The Sistine Chapel had a very prominent place in eighteenth-century histories of art, one that in fact had been growing in new ways as the taste for the more sublime works of Michelangelo began to develop in the later eighteenth century. It was, together with the Raphael

Benjamin West, *Moses Receiving the Laws on Mount Sinai,* 1784. (© Parliamentary Art Collection, WOA 5215)

Benjamin West, *Design for a Wall of the Chapel of Revealed Religion*, c. 1780. (Courtesy of the Yale Center for British Art)

Stanze, the *locus classicus* of high art and, furthermore, in the minds of Protestants, a place that most clearly demonstrated the indebtedness art had to popery. Those elements of similarity between West's scheme and the Sistine Chapel betray the stakes that West was aiming for: he was planning an interior that would rival, or indeed, in certain ways, surpass the Sistine Chapel.

West's breathtaking ambition can be glimpsed in a letter he wrote to the king when the scheme was first halted in 1801: "Your Majesty's known zeal for promoting religion, and the elegant arts, had enrolled your virtues with all the civilized world; and your gracious protection of my pencil had given to it a celebrity throughout Europe, and spread a knowledge of the great work on Revealed Religion, which my pencil was engaged on, under Your Majesty's patronage: it is that work which all Christendom looks with a complacency for its completion."[47] While he did not explicitly justify and urge the scheme on the basis of the quality of his own work, West reminded the king that the narration of the progress of Revealed Religion was designed and arranged with such "circumspection . . . that the most scrupulous amongst the various religious sects in this country, about admitting pictures into churches, must acknowledge them as truths, or the Scriptures fabulous."[48]

West's aim, then, was a work of Protestant art that would rival Catholic productions. It would be thoroughly biblical and could serve Protestantism as artists had served Catholicism. Indeed, its scrupulous narration of the Bible meant it could be accepted by Catholics too. In a letter written some time later to a friend, West expanded on his view of the chapel's significance: "Had the great work of my life on Revealed Religion for his Majesty's Chapel not been checked some years past . . . it would have marked itself as worthy of His Majesty's protection as a Christian, and a Patriot King, and all Christendom would have received it with affection and piety."[49]

West's ambition was nothing less than to wrest art from the grip of popery. The failure of the Windsor scheme was thus much more than a personal blow for West: it was a collective loss for Anglo-American art. Indeed, the inability of Protestant artists to compete with the great achievements of Raphael, Michelangelo, and the other great *cinquecento* artists because of the lack of ecclesiastical patronage continued to exercise artists and critics for decades. It was still an issue for John Ruskin and his contemporaries in the 1850s.[50]

West thus understood his role and ambition as an artist as one of both religious identity and artistic merit. In different situations as young artist, grand tourist, and venerable president of the Royal Academy in London, West repeatedly had to negotiate with Catholic culture in his bid for artistic excellence in the promotion of British and American art. Although he was an exceptional man in many respects, not least in his spectacular rise to prominence, in respect of the issues under consideration here he was not. Certainly, as we have seen, his perspective on them was not unique. The account of him given here is intended to be read as exemplary: the diversity and extent of West's production over a long career providing good examples of the many ways in which art's associations with Catholicism were encountered and managed by artists and collectors over the long eighteenth century. It shows that anti-Catholicism was, in the field of visual culture, an antagonism of a subtle kind. Being coupled frequently with admiration, it was often tacit and hardly aggressive. Nevertheless, it constituted a powerful antipathy, formative in its influence on both artistic production and reception. It demonstrates that long after the Reformation might be thought to have been settled, Roman Catholicism continued to present cultural, philosophical, and religious challenges that had to be met, negotiated, and overcome.

Notes

1. Clare Haynes, *Pictures and Popery: Art and Religion in England, 1660–1760* (Aldershot: Ashgate, 2006).
2. The standard and indispensable monograph on West's oeuvre is Helmut von Errfa and Allen Staley, *The Paintings of Benjamin West* (New Haven, CT: Yale University Press, 1986).
3. J. D. Meyer, "Benjamin West's Chapel of Revealed Religion: A Study in Eighteenth-Century Protestant Religious Art," *Art Bulletin* 57, no. 2 (1975): 247–65; J. D. Meyer, "Benjamin West's

St. Stephen's Altar-Piece: A Study in Late Eighteenth-Century Protestant Church Patronage," *Burlington Magazine* 118, no. 882 (1976): 634–42; and J. D. Meyer, "Benjamin West's Window Designs for St. George's Chapel, Windsor," *American Art Journal* 11, no. 3 (1979): 53–65.

4. Meyer did refer briefly to the relevance of anti-Catholicism for one of West's later commissions, the Chapel of Revealed Religion, in an exchange with K. Porter Aichele in "Letters to the Editor," *Art Bulletin* 58, no. 3 (1976): 474–77. I will discuss this further later in the essay.
5. Nicholas Grindle, "Sublime and Fall: Benjamin West and the Politics of the Sublime in Early Nineteenth-Century Marylebone"; and William Pressly, "Benjamin West's Royal Chapel at Windsor: Who's in Charge, the Patron or the Painter" in *Transatlantic Romanticism: British and American Art and Literature, 1790–1860*, ed. Andrew Hemingway and Alan Wallach (Amherst: University of Massachusetts Press, 2015), 83–101, 102–21. For a quite different and insightful approach to West's political position see Sarah Monks, "The Wolfe Man: Benjamin West's Anglo-American Accent," *Art History* 34, no. 4 (2011): 652–73.
6. For a brief discussion of West's theoretical writings see Clare Haynes, "In the Shadow of the Idol: Religion in British Art Theory 1600–1800," *Art History* 35, no. 1 (2012): 62–85.
7. It does prevent us from pressing too hard on the differences between the portraits, most significantly the quite different gazes: Saint Ignatius looks upward toward the streaming light from heaven while gesturing toward the viewer, which is in striking contrast to Smith's mundane but more direct address of an imagined earthbound public. For the history of the portrait, of which two versions once existed, see von Erffa and Staley, *The Paintings of Benjamin West*, 554–55.
8. I. Pears, *The Discovery of Painting: The Growth of Interest in the Arts in England, 1680–1768* (New Haven, CT: Yale University Press, 1988), 36.
9. George Turnbull, *A Treatise on Ancient Painting*, ed. V. M. Bevilacqua (Munich: Wilhelm Fink, 1971), xxii. For Turnbull in relation to the Scottish Enlightenment see A. Broadie, *The Scottish Enlightenment* (Edinburgh: Birlinn, 2007); and for the *Treatise* also see C. Gibson-Wood, "Painting as Philosophy . . . ," in *Aberdeen and the Enlightenment*, ed. J. J. Carter and M. H. Pittock (Aberdeen: Aberdeen University Press, 1987), 187–98.
10. One exception to this was William Hogarth, who in his writings and works of "modern" morality was seeking an alternative aesthetic. This theme has been explored in some respects by Ronald Paulson in a series of works on Hogarth. For Hogarth's views in the context of the religious foundations of art see Haynes, "In the Shadow of the Idol," 62–85.
11. J. Richardson, *Two Discourses* (London, 1719), 39–40.
12. Richardson, *Two Discourses*, 230–32.
13. Carol Gibson-Wood, *Jonathan Richardson: Art Theorist of the English Enlightenment* (New Haven, CT: Yale University Press, 2006), esp. 179–208.
14. This procedure received its most thorough treatment in the writings of Sir Joshua Reynolds, particularly in his *3rd Discourse to the Royal Academy*. See P. Rogers, ed., *Sir Joshua Reynolds, Discourses* (Harmondsworth: Penguin, 1992), 102–15.
15. For West's copy of the painting of Saint Ignatius see von Erffa and Staley, *The Paintings of Benjamin West*, 446.
16. Von Erffa and Staley, *The Paintings of Benjamin West*, 2. For Richardson as an Enlightenment figure see Gibson-Wood, *Jonathan Richardson;* and Clare Haynes, "'To Put the Soul in Motion': Connoisseurship as a Religious Discourse in the Writings of Jonathan Richardson," *Religion in the Age of Enlightenment* 5 (2015): 1–24.

17. "An Earnest Address to the Colonies, particularly those of the Southern District . . . ," in *The Works of William Smith, D.D., Late Provost of the College and Academy of Philadelphia*, 2 vols. (Philadelphia, 1803), 2:20–21.
18. Von Erffa and Staley, *The Paintings of Benjamin West*, 13.
19. In the period under discussion the grand tour was almost completely a male preserve, although married women might travel with their husbands. Single women travelers to the continent were rare until well into the nineteenth century.
20. For the nature of this biography and West and Galt's ambitions to cement West's standing as an American artist, see Susan Rather, "Benjamin West, John Galt, and the Biography of 1816," *Art Bulletin* 86, no. 2 (2004): 324–45.
21. For a discussion of grand-tour reception of Catholic art see Haynes, *Pictures and Popery*, 14–45.
22. Benjamin West arrived in England armed with a number of letters of recommendation to Richard Wilson and the two artists became friends. J. Galt, *The Life, Studies, and Works of Benjamin West*, 2 vols. (London, 1820), 2:5.
23. Galt, *Benjamin West*, 1:91–94.
24. Galt, *Benjamin West*, 1:95–96.
25. Galt, *Benjamin West*, 1:97.
26. Galt, *Benjamin West*, 1:97–98.
27. Galt, *Benjamin West*, 1:98.
28. Galt, *Benjamin West*, 1:98–99.
29. [Alexander Stephens], *Public Characters of 1805* (London, 1805), 536–37.
30. Haynes, "Shadow of the Idol," 64–78.
31. Galt, *Benjamin West*, 2:83 and 140.
32. For a very useful discussion of West's career-making see Susan Rather, "Benjamin West's Professional Endgame and the Historical Conundrum of William Williams," *William and Mary Quarterly*, 3rd ser. 59, no. 4 (2002): 821–64.
33. Haynes, "Shadow of the Idol," 74–78.
34. See notes 3–5 above and in addition, Nancy L. Pressly, *Revealed Religion: Benjamin West's Commissions for Windsor Castle and Fonthill Abbey* (San Antonio: San Antonio Museum of Art, 1983).
35. Quoted in Von Erffa and Staley, *The Paintings of Benjamin West*, 328.
36. Among the first of which were Saint Stephen Walbrook, a church half a mile to the east from Saint Paul's, in the City of London, Winchester Cathedral, and Trinity College, Cambridge.
37. Pressly, "Revealed Religion," 15.
38. Over the same period, West also completed a number of historical subjects for the king and had from 1772 been titled "Historical Painter to the King."
39. Galt, *Benjamin West*, 1:53.
40. Galt, *Benjamin West*, 1:54.
41. Galt, *Benjamin West*, 1:55.
42. See references by others to the aborted scheme in Aichele, "Letters to the Editor," 475–76.
43. Meyer, "Chapel of Revealed Religion," 261–63; and Pressly, "West's Royal Chapel," 102–21.
44. The paintings are now, respectively, in the Palace of Westminster and Tate Britain.
45. It is in relation to the paintings narrating episodes from Revelations that Meyer acknowledges a possible anti-Catholic significance, discussing Richard Hurd's work on prophecy and the papacy as the "seat of the Antichrist." Meyer, "Letters to the Editor," 477.
46. Meyer, "Chapel of Revealed Religion," 254.

47. Galt, *Benjamin West,* 1:195.
48. Galt, *Benjamin West,* 1:194.
49. Quoted in Pressly, *Revealed Religion,* 23.
50. See Andrew Tate, "'Archangel' Veronese: Ruskin as Protestant Spectator," in *Ruskin's Artists: Studies in the Victorian Visual Economy,* ed. Robert Hewison (Aldershot: Ashgate, 2000), 131–45.

PART III

Transformations

Protestant Empire?

ANTI-POPERY AND BRITISH-AMERICAN PATRIOTISM, 1558–1776

Evan Haefeli

GOD PRESERVE ME FROM . . . slavery & popish Inquisition & give me wisdome in all my affayrs," prayed Thomas Gorges, deputy governor of Maine, in 1643 before embarking on a voyage back to England that would pass through a Spanish port.[1] This incidental remark suggests just how commonplace was anti-Catholicism (in the sense of animus to Roman Catholic religion and those who upheld it) in England's American colonies. Permeating colonial culture, it had been part of how colonists imagined their place in the empire—and the world since the 1580s, when Roanoke's first commander, Ralph Lane, described the colony as part of a global struggle for "ye Churche of Chryste thoroughe Chrystendom," that would "by ye mercy of God in shorte tyme finde a relyfe and freedom from ye servytude, and tyrannye" of "Spayne (beynge ye swoorde of ye Antychryste of Rome and hys secte)."[2] At a time when neither naked power nor bureaucratic efficiency could compel colonial loyalty, anti-Catholicism instilled in their widely scattered societies a sense of a shared cause. A variety of media, including sermons, songs, oral traditions, images, rumors, speeches, published histories, and material culture, regularly reminded colonists of the popish threat to their existence, feeding their patriotism for the Protestant empire even as they built it.

With the empires of Spain and France looming just over their horizon, colonists' fears of these foreign Catholic (potential) enemies is understandable.[3] Yet Gorges's real enemy was not Spain but his Protestant king. Like hundreds of other New Englanders, he was returning to fight for Parliament and to defend "civil and religious liberty."[4] Anti-popery, the close cousin of anti-Catholicism that opposed the corruption and tyranny associated with the papacy, taught that popery was an internal as well as a foreign threat. Even Protestants like King Charles I could be suspected of it. Popery was the political as well as religious antitype to Protestant ideas of civil and religious liberty. Anti-popery kept colonists invested in the fate of a country that, after about 1650, many had never seen, teaching them vital lessons about power and corruption. By the 1760s they had learned those lessons so well that John Adams boasted that "the people in America" had "the most accurate judgment about the real [British] constitution." Their "whole behavior" was predicated on the idea that "liberty is its end, its use, its designation, drift, and scope."[5]

Local context shaped when, how, and why anti-popery and anti-Catholicism manifested in the colonies. While the phenomenon has been well studied in New England, that region had no monopoly on anti-popery and anti-Catholicism.[6] It can be found everywhere from Newfoundland to Bombay. Deeply English in style and content, anti-popery and anti-Catholicism forged a powerful affinity between colonists and the metropole through laws, political culture, religion, history, and more. Yet ultimately these ideas disrupted the empire, in large part because it was never completely Protestant. In Britain and overseas, Roman Catholics were a constant presence.[7] English, Irish, and even Scottish Catholics played a role in some early colonial enterprises (most importantly Maryland). Irish Catholics provided an important source of labor while expansion and conquest brought thousands of Spanish, French, and Portuguese Catholics into the empire. As their numbers grew, the challenge of incorporating Catholics into the empire compelled various individuals, particularly those at the center, to rethink imperial policies toward Catholics. However, when the empire began to move away from its anti-Catholic roots, anti-popery compelled the colonists to abandon the empire.

Most colonists agreed with the many English who believed the Protestant Reformation had rescued their liberty as well as their true religion from a long night of papal oppression. Unfortunately, the history of the Reformation also taught them that both could be lost again. After all, between 1553 and 1558 Queen Mary I not only undid the Protestant reforms of Kings Henry VIII and Edward VI by restoring Roman Catholicism: she married a Spanish prince and brought in the Inquisition, the epitome of spiritual tyranny. Colonists were familiar with John Foxe's *Book of Martyrs,* whose chronicle of the deaths of devout Protestants at the hands of Mary's Inquisition perpetuated both their memory and an abiding hostility to Catholic rule. Only Mary's sudden death in 1558 allowed Elizabeth Tudor to secure England for Protestantism. As Elizabeth later described it to Parliament, God had made her "an instrument to deliver you from dishonor, from shame, from infamy, from out of servitude and slavery under our enemies, to keep you from cruel tyranny and vile oppression intended against us." Colonists took this religious and political vision to heart.[8]

Since the kingdoms of Spain and Portugal made it around the world first, they served as both rivals and countermodels for the first English colonists. This Iberian threat allowed the English to imagine their early expansion as both generous and defensive.[9] In 1585, Richard Hakluyt urged the English to start colonizing and draw overseas peoples "by all courtesie into loue with our nation" and not become "hatefull vnto them, as the Spaniard is in Italie and in the West Indies, and elsewhere" because of their "crueltie and tyrannie." The Virginia Company described its colony "as a Bulwarke of defence" in 1610. In 1612, East India Company agents claimed that the "Lord did merciefullie defend us" in a successful battle with the Portuguese, their victory being evidence that "yt was the Lords glorie in preserveinge of us for His Gosepells sake and His truthes sake." John Winthrop, in his 1629 list of justifications for "the Intended Plantation in New England," said it would be "a service to the Church of great consequence to carry the Gospell into those p[ar]ts. Of the world, to help on the cominge in of fulnesse of the Gentiles and to rayse a Bulworke against the kingdome of Antichrist, w[hi]ch. the Jesuites labour to rear up in those parts."[10]

The defensive mentality was not entirely inappropriate. Sometimes the Protestants lost. The Spanish destroyed a French outpost in Florida in 1565 and killed the Huguenots they found there. They then built the fortress town of St. Augustine, which defended the Spanish Catholic presence in eastern North America until 1763. During Elizabeth's long war against Spain (1585–1604), Roanoke failed, as did a 1597 effort to establish a colony in the Gulf of Saint Lawrence. In 1641, the Caribbean colony of Providence Island was lost to a Spanish attack. Memories of these and other failures were folded into the broader narrative of Protestant suffering at Catholic hands. They also became an argument against tolerating Catholics in the colonies. The Scottish courtier Sir William Alexander blamed the failure of French Brazil on "the difference of Religion" between its Catholic and Protestant colonists. Anti-Catholicism offered no guarantee of colonial success, but it seemed a more reliable formula than toleration.[11]

Roman Catholics' omnipresence overseas also made them a convenient scapegoat for English failures to establish good relations with overseas peoples. Confronted with difficulties in his negotiations for a trade deal with India's Mughal rulers, William Hawkins blamed "the Jesuits and Portugalls [who] slept not, but by all means sought my overthrow." He was sure that they even neglected "their masses and church matters for studying how to overthrow my affaires." Edward Terry, one of the first East India Company chaplains, claimed the Jesuit mission to India produced only superficial converts driven by material desires, "poore men, who for want of meanes, which they give them, are content to weare crucifixes, but for want of instruction are only in name Christians." English Protestant missionaries could do better (although, much to the scandal of the East India Company's directors, they did not). Cotton Mather made similar accusations in Massachusetts during the 1690s to explain why New England missionary efforts had been so meagre compared to the "Missionaries of the Pope." Mather accused the Catholics of aiming at

“Tears of ye Indians or Inquisition for Bloud,” frontispiece to Bartolomé de Las Casas, *The Tears of the Indians: Being an Historical and True Account of the Cruel Massacres and Slaughters of above Twenty Millions of Innocent People; Committed by the Spaniards in the Islands of Hispaniola, Cuba, Jamaica, etc. As also, in the Continent of Mexico, Peru, & Other Places of the West-Indies, to the Total Destruction of Those Countries*, 1656. (© The Trustees of the British Museum; all rights reserved)

This 1656 translation of Bartolomé de Las Casas’s *Destruction of the Indies* by John Milton’s nephew John Phillips was dedicated to Oliver Cromwell. Urging him to take “revenge” against the “Bloudy and Popish Nation of the Spaniards,” whose aim was to conquer and “enslave the People of this Nation,” Phillips claimed the “blood of Ireland” was “spilt by the same faction.”

"the riches of the Savages" teaching only "a part of the Christian faith, disguised and corrupted by the abominations of popery, which is at bottom nothing but a true copy of Paganism." Nevertheless, he hoped that "these Papal missions have prepared the way for something more sincere and salutary" by bringing "the Proselytes to the door . . . to receive and embrace a greater Light when it will please God to send it to them."[12]

New Englanders were still blaming the French for their poor relations with their Indigenous neighbors on the eve of the American Revolution. In Braintree, Massachusetts, the octogenarian minister, Harvard graduate, and sometime-slaveholder Samuel Niles drafted a "Summary Historical Narrative of the Wars in New England with the French and Indians" as the Seven Years' War drew to a close. As Niles explained to his young neighbor, John Adams, he was chronicling "all the slaughter and bloodshed committed by [the French and Indians] that I could find, from the beginning [the Pequot War of 1636–38] to this day" (Niles stopped writing in 1761 and died in 1762). Niles blamed the French for encouraging Native Americans "to root out and destroy the English settlements," supplying them with arms and ammunition, using Jesuits to instigate them, and even teaching Native Americans the art of scalping. He hoped his history might "be made, through grace, effectual to awaken, reform, and quicken us to our duty, civil and religious." Recalling the conversation many years later, after serving as president of the United States, Adams believed the still unpublished manuscript "might be of great value to this country."[13]

To combat the pernicious influence of Catholics, colonists formally excluded them by requiring new arrivals to swear oaths of loyalty and supremacy that (as in Britain and Ireland) denied the pope's authority over the Church and his power to dispense with a person's obedience to his monarch. As Virginia's 1609 charter proclaimed, the oaths helped "guard against the superstitions of the church of Rome." In 1629, Virginians insisting they preserved the "freedome of our Religion wch wee have enioyed" even demanded the former secretary of state of England and future proprietor of Maryland, George Calvert, Lord Baltimore, swear them. Calvert, a well-known convert to Roman Catholicism, refused and was expelled. As Virginia's governor and council explained, "noe papists have beene suffered to settle their aboad amongst us." With occasional exceptions like Maryland (which initially did not enforce them), such oaths frequently kept Catholics marginalized if not completely excluded. After the Glorious Revolution of 1688–89, the oaths were introduced in all of the colonies including Maryland and were not abandoned until the revolutionary changes of 1776.[14]

Anti-Catholic oaths were not enough to keep the colonies free of Catholics, however. Catholics could circumvent the Protestant system of oaths by avoiding having to take them or adopting the European custom of occasional conformity. Such tactics sustained an Anglo-Irish Catholic community in the Caribbean, especially on the island of Montserrat, where Irish Catholics formed a majority of the free European population into the eighteenth century. Then, occasionally, the monarchy supported Catholic access to colonial power. Several received permission to establish colonies overseas in the 1630s, the years of Charles I's "Personal Rule." Maryland was the most notable product of this era. Despite many challenges over the ensuing century and a half, its Catholic community survived to become the center for Roman Catholicism in North America and the early United States. Other Catholic-led colonies, like Sir Edmund Plowden's colony of New Albion in the mid-Atlantic, fared less well.[15]

The revolutionary upheaval of the 1640s and 1650s ended Catholic-led colonization, but it also drastically increased the religious diversity of the English world. Initially, anti-popery gave the new sects a common reference point. It even opened a door for Jews. In Springfield, Massachusetts, William Pynchon, worried that contemporary Jews had adopted "popish" rites and ideas about clerical authority, but he held up the ancient Jewish synagogues as a model for church government. In England, Manuel Martinez Dormido, "of the Hebrew nation," petitioned Oliver Cromwell for permission to settle in England by emphasizing Jewish suffering at the hands of "the violent court of ye Inquisition." Its "cruelties" forced Jews to flee Spain and Portugal for safety in "other Republics & Lordships." Such arguments appealed to influential men like the Scottish minister John Dury, whose irenic and philo-semitic views of the colonies rested on an anti-Catholic foundation: Jews, like Native Americans and Protestants, were victims of Roman Catholic cruelty. However, neither men like Dury, nor the evangelical Protestants who dominated Cromwell's church and government, nor their fellows in New England, wanted to establish a permanent Jewish community on English soil: they hoped to convert them along with the Native Americans. The idea that Native Americans were descended from the Lost Tribes of Israel grew out of this era's apocalyptic excitement that the Jews and Native Americans were about to convert.[16]

Meanwhile, a series of conquests added more Catholics to the English world. Cromwellian forces conquered Ireland and Scotland, seized Acadia from the French, and took Jamaica and Dunkirk from the Spanish. Expelling priests and discouraging religious gatherings, they proved remarkably effective at suppressing the practice of Catholicism everywhere but Dunkirk, where a mix of international and local considerations forced the English to tolerate Roman Catholic worship. Under the watchful and resentful eyes of the garrison, Catholic priests operated with a freedom that, in the English world, was rivaled only by Madras. There, despite occasional protests by zealous agents and directors, local circumstances compelled the East India Company to tolerate the Roman Catholicism of their Indian soldiers and workers virtually from the time the outpost was established in 1640.[17]

* * *

With the Restoration of the monarchy in 1660, England's empire became less anti-Catholic, at least officially. The pre-Commonwealth Church of England was reestablished in England as well as in Virginia and the Caribbean. New Englanders were reduced to the unwelcome position of Dissenters as the monarchy once again entrusted Catholics with positions of power. The Catholic Calverts regained control of Maryland. A Scottish Catholic served as the last governor of Dunkirk and the first of Tangiers, recently brought into the budding empire along with Bombay as part of the dowry of King Charles II's Portuguese Catholic wife. In both places Roman Catholic worship was tolerated. The Irish Catholic Thomas Dongan served as lieutenant governor of Tangiers and governor of New York, where he not only employed several Catholics as officers but also welcomed English Jesuit missionaries, hoping they could replace the French Jesuits working among the colony's Iroquois allies. Most of the Catholic colonies—Dunkirk, Acadia, and Tangiers—were soon lost. Bombay, however, remained. With Catholics now a tolerated part of the empire, Roger Williams worried from Rhode Island that "Pralacie and Papacie" would dominate "this wilderness" and "God-land will be (as now it is) as great a God with us English as God Gould was with the Spaniards."[18]

Colonial Protestants responded by developing a profound attachment to England's anti-Catholic political culture. The celebration of November 5th, called "Pope's Day" in North America, became the cornerstone of imperial patriotic rituals. It is not clear exactly when it started, but by 1661, "commemorating the Gunpowder Treason by pistol firing" had become customary on Barbados. Scattered evidence suggests it was being celebrated in most other colonies as well. New Englanders initially resisted such ungodly celebrations, but listened approvingly when sailors brought stories from London about anti-papal processions. One in the winter of 1674 told of thousands of apprentices who made effigies of "the Pope and his Cardinals . . . dance on the ropes," before carrying them to Smithfield to be burnt "with great shouts, saying were the Pope there they would serve him so." By the eighteenth century, New Englanders had become the most enthusiastic celebrants of Pope's Day.[19]

New immigrants kept alive colonists' apprehension of the popish threat. Huguenots and other Protestant refugees from the continent were one obvious source, but migrants from England as well kept the fears of domestic popery alive. Shortly before heading to America, Edward Taylor, who became a minister and poet in western Massachusetts, penned an anti-popish ditty in response to a Roman Catholic rhyme claiming the Great Fire of 1666 was God's punishment of England's "Hereticks." The Catholic poem had urged the English to convert before it was too late. Wrong, Taylor retorted. The true heretics were the Catholics. With their

"Holy-water" coming "out of the Stygian Lake" and their "Pope Jone," the papal Church was no more than the fruit of the ongoing union of the Whore of Babylon and the "Devill." Protestants like Taylor hoped "To make a Bonefire of your Pope." They also worried that Anglican clergymen had popish inclinations: "Our Cler(g)y dip (as you do wishe) / Their spoon for broth within your dish."[20]

Like many in Britain, colonists feared Roman Catholic influence over the monarchy. When England's Popish Plot and Exclusion Crisis broke, they partook in the greater drama. In 1679, a leading New Hampshire colonist read out "a paper . . . in derision of the Government of England." Turning to one of his companions, he then said there "was no more a king in England than thou." In March 1680, the governor of Barbados, Sir Jonathan Atkins, reported a widespread rumor that "the Island was to be sold to the French." The alarm was triggered by the fact that Atkins had received a letter from England "when the French were cruising in these parts." As Atkins explained, "because I spoke French, I was put down as Frenchified and the fitest man to deliver [Barbados] up" to them. The colony's assembly responded by passing a special Oath of Allegiance. Atkins supported it, saying that, "the heat here was such that if I had not passed the law, I should myself have passed for as arrant a Papist as ever was hanged at Tyburn." Alas, he lamented, it "is easy to deceive these people, but very hard to rectify it."[21]

In certain colonies, the presence of Catholics aggravated these conspiracy fears. Maryland was especially rife with rumors of an alliance between Catholics (French, Irish, and English) and Native Americans against the Protestants. Antoinette Sutto calls it a "particularly American version of familiar confessional politics." In just one small example, a couple of men hunting in March 1681 debated whether forty families of Irish immigrants that had recently arrived "will prove in the End to be ffourty thousand to cutt the Protestants throats." Meanwhile, in March 1682 readers of the London newssheet *Smith's Protestant Intelligence* saw an account from Boston about a man believed to be from "New York, where there are many Papists," who had tried to burn down "one of our Churches or Meeting houses." Here the colonies were incorporated into a portrait of an empire-wide popish conspiracy that included reports of suspicious acts in Bristol, London, and Leicestershire.[22]

In India, Madras's governors continued to tolerate the Roman Catholicism of its "Portuguese" garrison, but Bombay's anti-Catholicism was palpable. There, both the Catholic community and the English presence were larger, but the English relied on Muslims and Hindus instead of Catholics for soldiers, servants, laborers, and business partners. Bombay's Roman Catholics were rich and propertied. In one incident from 1689, rumors circulated that Bombay's senior Jesuit had invited a Muslim Mughal commander "to exterminate all the Protestants" in the colony if the Mughals would then restore to the Portuguese the property and churches that had been seized by the English. The Mughals attacked but failed to drive away the English, who pointed to "these and such other perfidious Actions" to justify their subsequent seizure of Portuguese "Lands and Estates," especially those of the Jesuits.[23]

Nevertheless, some colonists felt obliged to indulge Roman Catholics, especially after the Catholic Duke of York became King James II in the winter of 1685. In Pennsylvania, the Quaker William Penn, willing to distinguish between the errors and abominations of popery and the character of individual Roman Catholics, eschewed the anti-Catholic oaths that discriminated against Catholics in other colonies. A few individuals went even further, especially after James's Declaration of Indulgence in the spring of 1687 suspended the penal laws against Catholics. Writing from Nevis in March 1688, the new governor of the Leeward Islands reported how, "Soon after my arrival I was petitioned by the Roman Catholics for the free exercise of their religion, which was granted." Moreover, he "exempted them from contributing towards the support of Protestant ministers," noting that, "the expense of building and decorating chapels, which they have already begun in Montserrat and St. Christopher's, will be very heavy on them."[24]

The majority of colonists, however, resented having a Roman Catholic king. On Bermuda, the governor complained that colonists wanted him "to subscribe to their orders" because they claimed "that I have no power to govern but through the Duke of York, a Papist." Around the same time, a group of Bahamian colonists who had fled to Jamaica to escape a Spanish attack set up a community that excluded "all Jews, Quakers, and Roman Catholics." The consistory of a Dutch Reformed Church in New York complained in 1685 that the "adherents of popery (our Noble Lord Governor [Thomas Dongan] being a papist) utilize all means for the advancement of the same." In New England, the once separate colonies were unwillingly united into the Dominion of New England. As its government had no representative assembly, some worried it would "abridge them of their liberty as Englishmen."[25]

News of the Glorious Revolution broke the tension. In what Owen Stanwood calls "the Protestant Moment," colonists demonstrated their enthusiasm for Protestant supremacy as soon as they learned that the Dutch Protestant Prince William of Orange had invaded England. The lieutenant governor of Barbados spoke for many when he claimed Divine Providence was working through William and Mary, "who God was pleased to Raise up to be a Protector & preserver of his pure & protestant religion & to Save us from popery, arbitrary power & Slavery." In most colonies, events proceeded peacefully. In Virginia, for example, when a rumor spread of a "conspiracy of Papist and Indian against ye Protestants," level heads prevailed. An investigation found it was just a few Virginians who had spread the rumor because they wanted to "plunder and rob." Under questioning, their Native American source admitted "they writt much more then he told them."[26]

Elsewhere, however, the revolution produced confusion and violence. Maryland's inadvertent failure to immediately proclaim William and Mary caused an "apprehension of feares" among Protestant colonists who then overthrew the Calverts' government. In New England and New York, anti-popery pitted Protestants against each other. The vast majority of New Englanders had rallied to overthrow the Dominion of New England and its Anglican governor, Edmund Andros. However, Gershom Bulkeley, a sometime Presbyterian minister living in Connecticut, wondered whether the revolt was the inspiration of "some Jesuit" who realized it was "the most probable way to ruin us at this time: for it is the old trade of that Diabolical sort of men by their plausible crafty Counsells, to make protestants destroy themselves, by stiring up, and fomenting divisions among them."[27]

In New York, which also had been incorporated into the Dominion of New England, the wealthy merchant and militia captain Jacob Leisler led the resistance against Andros's lieutenant governor, the outspokenly Anglican Francis Nicholson. Nicholson had employed the Roman Catholic Matthew Plowman (a relative of the would-be lord of New Albion) as a customs collector. When news of the events in England arrived, Leisler, "with his sword by his side & cane in his hand," defied an agent of Plowman's who wanted to seize some wine Leisler had landed without paying customs. Shaking his cane, Leisler yelled, "You rougue to serve under a papish let that papish rouge goe to Roome and serve there." A few days later, Nicholson fled. A Committee of Safety took over. After five weeks, it appointed Leisler commander in chief of the colony. He immediately poured his energies into mobilizing New York and its neighbors for an invasion of New France. When the expedition fell apart, Leisler blamed a conspiracy. Imprisoning his perceived enemies, he claimed to be defending New York for King William and Queen Mary "against all Rebels, Papists, and disaffected persons." His victims complained of being "opprest" under a "burthen of Slavery and Arbitrary Power." Not only were their "Liberties" being "taken away," but their "Religion" was "in great danger." When English troops and a new governor arrived in 1691, Leisler's victims successfully pressed for his execution.[28]

As war broke out on the northern frontier, French and Amerindian raids captured colonists, forcing these captives to confront a new popish threat. One of the first captives was the young John Gyles. He encountered his first Jesuit when his Indigenous captor brought him back to his village in what is now Maine. Still only a boy, Gyles "dare not eat" a biscuit the Jesuit gave him, even though he was hungry. Gyles "fear[ed] that he had put something in it to make me love him." As Gyles later explained, "I was very young and had heard much of the Papists torturing the Protestants, etc., so that I hated the sight of a Jesuit." One can sympathize with him after seeing the reaction of his mother to "talk of my being sold to a Jesuit." "Oh my dear child!" she exclaimed. Held captive in the same Abenaki village, she told the poor boy, "If it were god's will, I had rather follow you to your grave, or never see you more in this world than you should be sold to a Jesuit, for a Jesuit will ruin you, body and soul." When captives like Gyles returned, they circulated narratives of their captivity, orally, in manuscript, and in print, keeping alive the memory of the Catholic threat along the frontier. Young and old, male and female, most captives followed Gyles's example and resisted the blandishments of popish priests and warriors. A minority, however, succumbed and converted.[29]

The Glorious Revolution rooted anti-popery and Protestant ascendancy firmly in the empire's constitution. In line with the 1701 Act of Settlement excluding Roman Catholics from inheriting the monarchy, local acts across the colonies barred Catholics from holding office. When Queen Anne was proclaimed in 1702, British Americans responded with patriotic enthusiasm. In Boston, the entire provincial government, "Council, Representatives, Ministers, Justices," raised a toast while an infantry regiment fired volleys. Despite his irritation with these unaccustomed new ceremonies, the puritan diarist Samuel Sewall assured the royal governor "of our inward Grief for the Departure of K. William" and gratitude to the "Goodness of God, who has at this time peacably [*sic*] placed Queen Anne upon the Throne." Later, in 1750, that governor's son would endow an annual lecture against popery at Harvard University that still exists (although its tone became more liberal over time). The 1707 Union with Scotland was also a welcome development. By making the Presbyterian Church of Scotland the second official church of the empire, it gave the many reformed Protestants in the colonies a respectability that previously had been denied them as mere Dissenters from the Church of England.[30]

Anti-Catholicism's role further cemented colonial patriotism for the empire during the long series of wars against France and Spain that followed the Glorious Revolution (five wars in the seven decades between 1689 and 1763). The conflicts nicely coincided with colonists' increasingly ambitious aims for territorial expansion. During King William's War they tried but failed to capture New France. In Queen Anne's War, South Carolinians attacked Spanish Florida. They failed to capture St. Augustine's fort, but destroyed the town as well as a number of surrounding Apalachee mission villages. Burning churches and homes to the ground, they killed or enslaved more than a thousand of the Indigenous Catholic allies of the Spanish. To the north, New Englanders captured Acadia.[31]

Imperial conflict, land hunger, and anti-Catholic patriotism complimented one another. The colony of Georgia, established as a bulwark against Spanish Florida in the 1730s, offered "a Free Exercise of their Religion" to all inhabitants "Except Papists." It prohibited Catholics from owning land, and required local ministers to report on the number of Catholics in their district (the most was four in Savannah). When its garrison of soldiers mutinied, they were suspected of being in Spanish pay. A former Italian monk who had converted and become an Anglican priest was denied permission to serve in Savannah. Still, there were limits to its anti-Catholic discrimination. In 1741, the governing trustees in England told the colonists not "to make 'any Inquisition on the private Opinions of anyone.'"[32]

Anti-Catholicism therefore facilitated mutual toleration among the proliferating Protestant denominations accompanying the growing number of European Protestants immigrants. Everywhere from Georgia to Nova Scotia, the backcountry attracted a mix of Scots, Germans, Scots-Irish, Huguenots, and others. Some of these immigrants, like the Salzburgers, were directly fleeing persecution by Catholics. Although they were not English, being Protestant gave them more rights than English-born Catholics. As a German Jesuit missionary working in Pennsylvania moaned, its Protestants were "divided into more than 50 sects" that "never agree in what they teach," but were "united in one thing—hatred of our holy Catholic religion."[33]

At the same time, anti-popery figured in a variety of local conflicts between Protestants, especially over questions of liberty of conscience and religious practice. Baptists in Massachusetts criticized the Congregational establishment for forcing them to contribute to the colony's church establishment. In Pennsylvania, those who resented Quakers' hegemony, Anglicans especially, criticized them for behaving like "the Pope of Rome" by denying them religious liberty. Anglicans made similar accusations elsewhere as they expanded and strengthened their church. An Anglican minister in Rhode Island complained about the "Bigottry" of his Dissenter neighbors who had such a "Love of Slavery" that they would not even read a book if the author was deemed to belong to the opposing "Party."[34]

Notwithstanding these differences, Jacobite conspiracy had little to no purchase. Colonists did not care very much that their monarchs after Anne's death in 1714 were neither English nor immediate descendants of the Stuart line. As long as they were good Protestants, colonists enthusiastically supported the Hanoverian kings, who were consistently portrayed on both sides of the Atlantic as, in the words of one historian, "active defenders of Protestantism." Bostonians were among the first people in the empire to add an effigy of the Stuart Pretender to their Pope's Day cart. They greeted news of the suppression of the 1745 Jacobite rebellion with delight. Even colonial Quakers offered thanks that divine Providence had protected their king and Great Britain from "the tyranny of a Popish Pretender" and "the superstition and idolatry of the Church of Rome."[35]

The major religious revivals of the 1730s and 1740s known as the "Great Awakening" took place against a background of anti-Jacobitism and wars against the Catholic empires of Spain (the War of Jenkins' Ear, 1739–48) and France (the War of the Austrian Succession, 1744–48), and concerns about the expanding Anglican Church. In February 1737, Stephen Williams, who had been taken captive by Catholic Abenaki allies of the French in 1704–5, preached a sermon to his

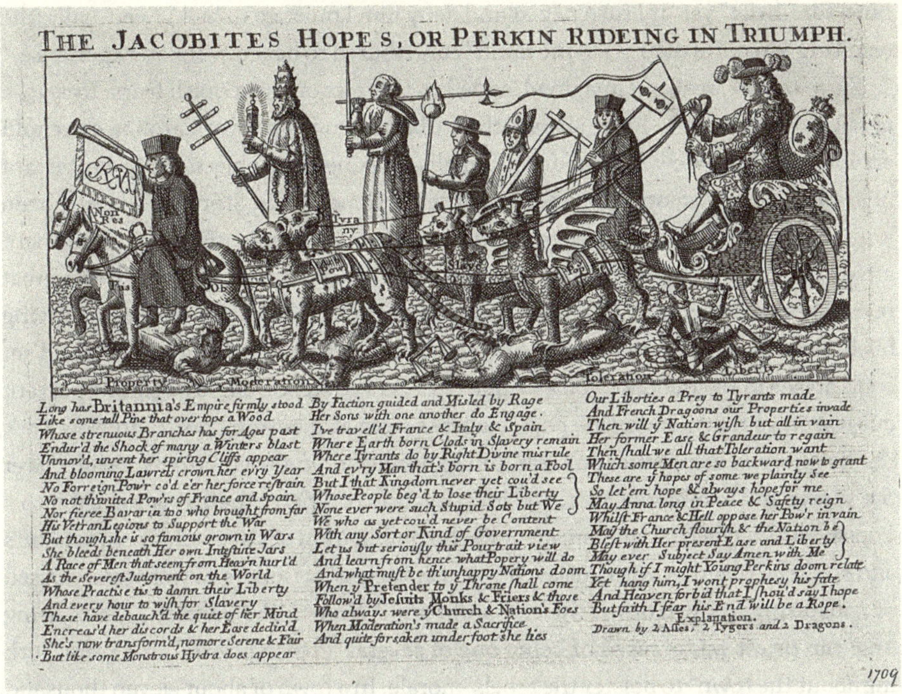

The Jacobites Hopes, or Perkin Rideing in Triumph, engraving, 1711. (© The Trustees of the British Museum; all rights reserved)

This Whiggish anti-Jacobite broadside likens the Stuart Pretender to Perkin Warbeck, a royal imposter executed in the 1490s, and Tories to Jacobites. The High Church Anglican priest Henry Sacheverell, dressed as a Jesuit, accompanies Catholic churchmen, the Pretender, and beasts labeled passive obedience, tyranny, arbitrary power, and slavery, who trample over "Property," "Moderation," "Toleration," and "Liberty."

Western Massachusetts congregation based on 2 Thessalonians, "yt ye pope or ye Bishop of rome is ye antichrist" who, together with "his followers," upheld "corrupt doctrines," such as teaching "men to pray to ye saints & Angells." He repeated it in the winter of 1738, shortly after his neighbor Jonathan Edwards published *A Faithful Narrative of the Surprising Work of God* describing the first religious revival in nearby Northampton in 1733–35. In July 1741, Williams offered special prayers to God, reflecting that "things look dark upon us—our fleet and Army in ye West Indies very much wastd by Sickness, and returnd (tis s[ai]d) without takeing Carthegine [Cartagena]." Five days later a major religious revival broke out in a neighboring town. In Southampton, New York, young Hannah Heaton began her spiritual journey after overhearing "talk of war with the papis nations." When her "father said if they overcame us we must expect fire and faggots except we turned papists," Heaton felt "great gilt." She worried that she was too scared to "burn for Christ" yet "if I turn papist and deny him I must go to hell." Eventually, the resulting "dreadful distress in my mind" contributed to her conversion experience.[36]

Slave revolts, real and imagined, added to this mix of anti-popish fears. In 1739, a revolt along the Stono River just south of Charleston frightened Carolina slaveholders into passing a new slave code and finally relaxing their objections to Protestant missionary work among their slaves. At least some of the Stono rebels had been Roman Catholics, and they were trying to escape to Spanish Florida. Soon thereafter, anxiety about papists and slave revolts traveled north along with the great revival preacher George Whitefield, a mighty anti-Catholic in his own right. Leaving his base in Georgia on the first of his many famous preaching tours, Whitefield set souls ablaze in the middle colonies while Georgia's governor, James Oglethorpe, sent out warnings that clandestine popish agents were also heading north. In New York, the heightened atmosphere of fear and expectation produced horrific results over the spring and summer of 1741. The investigation of a petty theft ring turned into a "Popish Plot"–style trial wherein an unlikely combination of slaves and Irish, servants and soldiers, together with enslaved Spanish "negro" prisoners of war were accused of conspiring to burn down the city and turn it over to the Spanish. A nonjuring Anglican priest was accused of being one of several "Popish priests" that were "lurking about the town" to bolster the rebels' morale. In a town of about eleven thousand, almost two hundred people were arrested and interrogated. The poor nonjuror, John Ury, was executed along with three other Europeans and thirty enslaved people.[37]

Anti-Catholic fervor filled the ranks of the hundreds of New England militiamen in 1745, when, with some help from the British Navy, they captured the mighty French fortress of Louisbourg on Cape Breton Island. Stephen Williams and his cousin Elisha Williams, former rector of Yale College, served as regimental chaplains for the expedition. Watching Elisha preach in the citadel's church, a soldier from Stephen's home county of Hampshire enthused, "Hardly any Can tell what Joy it was—to See God worshipped according to His own appointment where Anti Christ had Had His." A few days later, stopping by the "Hospital to See the French People Say Mass," the soldier shook his head upon seeing "Gentlemen who were men of Learning (I Supposs'd, and Doubtless of good Natural parts also)" and "many of all Ranks" be "So Led Aside as to worship Images, to Bow Down to A Cross of wood." Stephen, hoping the French fortress island would be transformed into a Protestant colony, was pleased to hear from the British naval commander, Admiral Peter Warren, that "he desird presbiterianism might be Established here." That evening, watching the "Great fireing of Small arms, and illuminations" of houses and "rockets" fired off in honor of King George II's coronation, Stephen mused, "the Lord Give us truly thankfull hearts for our civill and religious privileges."[38]

The assertion of Protestant dominance at Louisbourg resembled British policy in other recent conquests. The 1713 Treaty of Utrecht had banished the French from Newfoundland while adding Nova Scotia, Gibraltar, and Minorca to the empire. Diplomatic considerations required the British to extend a degree of religious toleration to their new French, Spanish, and Genoese Catholic subjects, but that did not prevent most of their British governors from trying to squeeze them into a Protestant mold. Their maneuvers included interfering with the work of priests, striving to transfer the Catholic parishes into a new episcopal jurisdiction dependent on British authority, and endorsing schemes to convert their Catholic charges.[39]

The potent colonial blend of anti-Catholicism and aggressive Francophobia contributed to the outbreak of the Seven Years' War (1755–63). In May 1754, some provincial troops commanded by George Washington fired on a French patrol along the Pennsylvania frontier. He later expressed his fear that the French intended "to give a final stab to liberty and property." That September an anonymous contributor to the *Pennsylvania Gazette* warned that if the French won, Pennsylvanians' children would be subject to "the mercy of 'bigoted Priests' who would banish or execute those 'such as they call Hereticks.'" Georgia's governor roused his assembly to action with the cry, "Your Religion! Your Liberty! Your All! Is at Stake."[40]

With war still not officially declared, British colonists turned on their Roman Catholic neighbors. In 1755, Massachusetts soldiers expelled the French Catholics living in Nova Scotia. Seven thousand Acadians were forced into a poorly organized odyssey across the British colonies during which several thousand died before the survivors found new homes. At the other end of the empire similar wartime expulsions took place, in Madras in 1747 and Calcutta in 1756. In Maryland, the Assembly imposed a double tax on its Catholic inhabitants (a number of whom were wealthy slaveowners) and proposed other measures, including disarming all Catholics in the colony (the measure failed by only one vote). In 1756, the governor of Pennsylvania expressed his conviction that "the Roman Catholicks who are allowed in this & the neighbouring Province of Maryland" were informing the French about the British war effort. The governor of New York agreed: "Treasonable correspondence must have been carried on by some Roman Catholics; I have heard you have an ingenious Jesuit in Philadelphia." Nevertheless, apart from a small wooden Catholic chapel burned down in Lancaster in 1760, violent anti-Catholic aggression was fairly limited in the middle colonies.[41]

The "Diplomatic Revolution" of 1756, which ranged the Catholic powers of France and Austria against the Protestant kingdoms of Prussia and Britain, aligned European geopolitics with confessional hostilities for the first time since the sixteenth century and convinced many colonists' that they were fighting a war for religion. Jonathan Edwards saw it as an important step in the inevitable decline of the papacy. Colonial ministers mobilized their congregations for war with accounts of the long history of Protestant sufferings under Roman Catholic persecution.

On the Virginia frontier, Samuel Davies reminded his listeners that, "in France . . . the Protestants are still plundered, chained to the gallies, broken upon the torturing wheel." In Massachusetts, Stephen Williams dusted off his twenty-year-old sermon on the pope as Antichrist and preached it twice in the winter of 1756. He then preached a new sermon on "Popish principles" four times. Warning that "ye worship of ye ch[urc]h of Rome is idolatrous & therefore sh[oul]d be carefully avoid'd by us," Williams traced its history of persecution from the Albigensians and Waldensians through the Hussites to the Saint Bartholomew's Day massacre, when Huguenots' "dead bodies . . . were thrown into the river Seine all now red wth blood" while "there was a great rejoicing at Rome." Another sermon on the sacrament of the Lord's Supper repeated his denunciations of "ye doctrines of Substantiation (or ye breadd & wine being turn'd into ye very body & blood of [Christ] upon consecration) and their communion in one kind only." Shall a "papist deprive us of our part of ye Sacrament"? Every believer had "an undenyable right" to communion in both kinds. Two years later, Stephen rounded out this series on anti-Catholic history with an extended account of "ye horrid massacre of Ireland, set on foot by ye pope & his clergy & cared on in a most inhumane & barbarous" manner. In England, the clergyman Thomas Secker, shortly before he became archbishop of Canterbury in 1758, agreed with these sentiments, expressing the hope that the Irish Catholics would soon be converted, for then "the inhabitants of the British Isles and Colonies will all have the same Friends and Foes."[42]

The message sank in, and not just with the soldiers. Sarah Osborn, a struggling schoolteacher in Newport, Rhode Island, recalled the suffering of the Marian martyrs and "swore that she would suffer anything—'Prisons, dungeons, racks and tortures, fire and faggots'—rather than forsake her faith." When the French had the upper hand in 1757, Osborn worried "that an angry God might have forsaken his 'British Israel.'" Convinced that the French and their Indigenous allies were in league with Satan, she prayed, "Make the antichrist and the Heathen know that Zion's God has not forsaken her though he has scourged Her." France's ultimate defeat inspired in her a "Hope the Glory of the Latter days is beginning to dawn." While British and colonial soldiers strode the streets of Quebec City, gazing with prurient fascination at the convents and experiencing the titillation that Protestants on both sides of the Atlantic associated with these hidden communities of women, Sarah Osborn began holding religious gatherings at her home. Eventually those gatherings sparked an evangelical revival that included a significant number of the town's inhabitants.[43]

The 1763 Peace of Paris marked the high point of British-American enthusiasm for the empire. Exuberant celebrations greeted the British victory, but this patriotism flourished just as the empire acquired more Roman Catholic territory than ever before: Florida; Quebec; the "Ceded" Caribbean Islands of Grenada,

Protestantism & Liberty, or the Overthrow of Popery & Tyranny, Dedicated to all true Protestants and Lovers of Liberty, engraving, 1757. (© The Trustees of the British Museum; all rights reserved)

Suggesting the Seven Years' War's religious dimension, figures representing Protestant Faith, Hope, Charity, and Liberty are pitted against the Devil, the Pope, Superstition, Tyranny, and the institution of the Inquisition. In the center, the Bible outweighs popish bulls, indulgences, pardons, etc. in the balance of Justice.

St. Vincent, Dominica, and Tobago; Senegal in West Africa. Their conquerors generally felt some toleration of their Roman Catholicism was needed. The British commander who conquered Cuba in 1762 was especially generous, agreeing to preserve the island's entire ecclesiastical and educational establishment as he found it "without any impediment to the public exercise of this religion," its holy festivals, or its property rights.[44] Cuba was returned to Spain in exchange for Florida in the 1763 peace treaty that, in Articles IV and XX, promised "the liberty of the Catholick religion" to the French and Spanish inhabitants in the territories acquired by the British. They would be allowed to "profess the worship of their religion according to the rites of the Romish church, as far as the laws of Great Britain permit."[45] When one adds Ireland's growing (and increasingly prosperous) Catholic population, other Catholic territories like Malta, and the acquisition of Bengal, it is clear that the empire was becoming drastically less Protestant.

Still, many on both sides of the Atlantic assumed that French Canada would, like the older colonies, be "settled either by foreign Protestants or the King's natural born Subjects who are intitled to British Liberty." A forgotten purpose of the notorious Proclamation of 1763 that forbade colonists to move west of the Appalachian Mountains was to encourage them to move north. In Quebec they could take up the roles of judges and legislators that the Catholic majority could not under British law. Surely the toleration of French Catholic priests was only to be temporary? Once they died off, imperial authorities could grant any Canadians who "may still adhere to Popery, the same Indulgences as is allowed his Majesty's Roman Catholick Subjects in Ireland," without allowing them new priests.[46]

Few British Protestant civilians, however, moved to Quebec beyond a small but determined group of anti-Catholic merchants. With a French Catholic population too numerous to be banished or deported like those of Louisbourg or Acadia, James Murray, the Scottish officer who took command of Quebec in 1760, decided toleration was necessary to keep the colony functioning. He not only allowed Frenchmen to serve on juries; he used their priests, friars, and nuns to help govern the province. When the Catholic bishop died, he even appointed a replacement rather than let the Roman Catholic hierarchy wither and die. Complaints by the Protestant merchants forced his return to London in 1766, but Murray's administration began an ominous new trend.[47]

Some governors continued to uphold Protestant supremacy even after the Treaty of Paris. On Grenada, a Scottish governor defended Protestants' "civil and religious rights" against those who wanted full political privileges for the "new Roman Catholick subjects." An "aggressively Protestant governor" strove to keep Irish Catholics out of Newfoundland. However, these efforts increasingly appeared to be rearguard actions of the old order. Back in Britain, opposition to such crass anti-Catholicism was growing. In 1770, a "man of sense," found it to be a "humiliating circumstance, for the glory of this kingdom . . . that most of the persecutions and embarrassments the new subjects [in Quebec and Grenada] have suffered, may be deduced from illiberal prejudices in point of religion." Claiming to live "at a time, and in an age, when the influence of speculative opinions in matters or government are thoroughly understood," he was outraged that "[m]axims of the meanest hypocrisy have been defended." Colonial Catholics should be allowed to prosper, "free from religious persecutions."[48]

British Americans disagreed.

As the imperial government made new demands on their trade and taxes, antipopery helped justify the colonists' resistance. The passage of the Stamp Act in 1765 prompted colonists to adapt the patriotic custom of Pope's Day processions to structure their street protests. John Adams, in his first critique of Parliament's taxation policies, insisted the colonists were inspired by "a love of *universal* liberty," and not "religion alone, as is commonly supposed." In truth, it was both. Colonists nourished "a hatred, a dread, an horror of the infernal confederacy" between "the Canon and Feudal Law" which sought to and hold "the common people" in "a state of ignorance of every thing divine and human" and "a state of servile dependence on their Lords."[49]

By 1772, anti-popish tensions were reaching a peak. In Rhode Island, a newspaper compared British revenue ships to the "Spaniards, taking your Whale-men in the West Indies." A week later, Rhode Islanders shot the commander of a royal schooner, the *Gaspée,* and burned his ship after it ran aground while trying to enforce the Navigation Acts against local smugglers. When the British threatened to extradite the culprits to Britain for trial, instead of trying them by a jury of their peers in Rhode Island (which likely would not convict them), the Newport *Mercury,* whose motto was "Undaunted by Tyrants—we'll DIE or be FREE," denounced the British Commission of Inquiry sent to investigate the affair as a "Star-Chamber" and "a court of inquisition, more horrid than that of Spain or Portugal." Death was "infinitely preferable to a miserable life of slavery, in chains, under a pack of worse than Egyptian tyrants." A subscription was then raised to publish a new edition of Henry Care's classic, *English Liberties; or, The Free-born Subject's Inheritance.* Available by August 1774, it had sold 642 copies by March 1775—the eve of the battle of Lexington and Concord. In the meantime, an obscure English Baptist minister by the name of John Allen, who had only recently arrived in Boston, preached a sermon in December 1772 entitled *An Oration on the Beauties of Liberty; or, The Essential Rights of the Americans* to an audience that apparently included more Sons of Liberty than Baptists. He denounced the appointment of the Commission of Inquiry as an "arbitrary dispotic power" that should "be feared, *abhorred,* detested and destroyed." Published in 1773, it went through two editions in Boston, a third in New London, and appeared in a Wilmington, Delaware, edition in 1775. Although leaders like John Adams did not think much of Allen's simple, direct prose, Adams had to admit it proved extremely popular among "large Circles of the common People."[50]

Ignoring the anti-popish ferment in the colonies, the Catholic-friendly trend at the heart of the empire continued. From an imperial perspective, Parliament's passage of the Quebec Act in the spring of 1774 was perfectly pragmatic. Building on the British experience of governing other distant Catholic territories, it tolerated Roman Catholic worship and French civil law but did not allow for an elected assembly. Instead, the government consisted of a royally appointed governor and council, all Protestants. That alone may not have been controversial if the act had not extended Quebec's borders south and west to include the Great Lakes region north of the Ohio River: the former borders of New France, which the colonists had just fought a long, bloody war to eliminate. In the debates over the act, Prime Minister Lord North expressed the view that it "would be a great hardship" to subject the Catholic majority "to an assembly composed of a few British subjects." Edmund Burke, the Anglo-Irish politician and colonial agent for New York, worried that the act seemed to establish "a despotic governor." Who could be sure that "this despotism is not meant to lead to universal despotism?"[51]

Most colonists agreed with Burke. The Quebec Act destroyed their faith in the empire. Had not King George III abandoned his constitutional responsibilities and broken his coronation oath by accepting the Act? George Washington lamented, "those from whom we have a right to seek protection are endeavouring by every piece of Art and despotism to fix the Shackles of Slavery upon us." He feared this "Invasion of our Rights and Priviledges by the Mother Country" would "make us as tame and abject slaves, as the blacks we rule over with such arbitrary sway." In New York, Alexander Hamilton argued the Quebec Act showed that Parliament was not "friends to the Protestant cause" and warned against trusting "men who are capable of such an action! They may as well establish Popery in New York, and the other colonies, as they did in Canada." In Connecticut, the Reverend Samuel Sherwood compared King George III unfavorably to the biblical King David, "who had, for many years, exercised an absolute sovereignty and dominion over the kingdom of Israel, [but] had no notion of aggrandizing himself, and his nobility, by enslaving his subjects, and striping them of their property, at his own arbitrary will and pleasure." His colleague Ebenezer Baldwin agreed that the Quebec Act exposed Parliament's "fix'd plan for inslaving the colonies, or bringing them under arbitrary government." Reminding his audience of their seventeenth-century origins, Baldwin insisted that once America lost its "civil liberty" an "ecclesiastical tyranny . . . will like a mighty torrent overspread our land." Baldwin then applied to British soldiers the anti-popish tropes that had long smeared the reputations of their Spanish and French counterparts: they stood ready "to execute every arbitrary mandate of their despotic masters. . . . Robberies, rapes, murders, etc. will be but the wanton sport of such wretches without restraint let loose upon us." Those who dared resist would be killed by "their murdering hands." If "taken captive," they would be dragged "to the place of execution."[52]

In 1775, the Continental Congress gathered in Philadelphia made a desperate final appeal to the "people of Great Britain" to preserve the empire. Proclaiming English rights to be "sacred," and boasting that the British nation had been led "to greatness by the hand of Liberty," Congress wondered why was it now "forging chains for her Friends and Children" by advocating "Slavery and Oppression"? Parliament's claim to "bind us in all cases without exception" was like "the interdicts of the Pope." It had no authorization "by the constitution to establish a

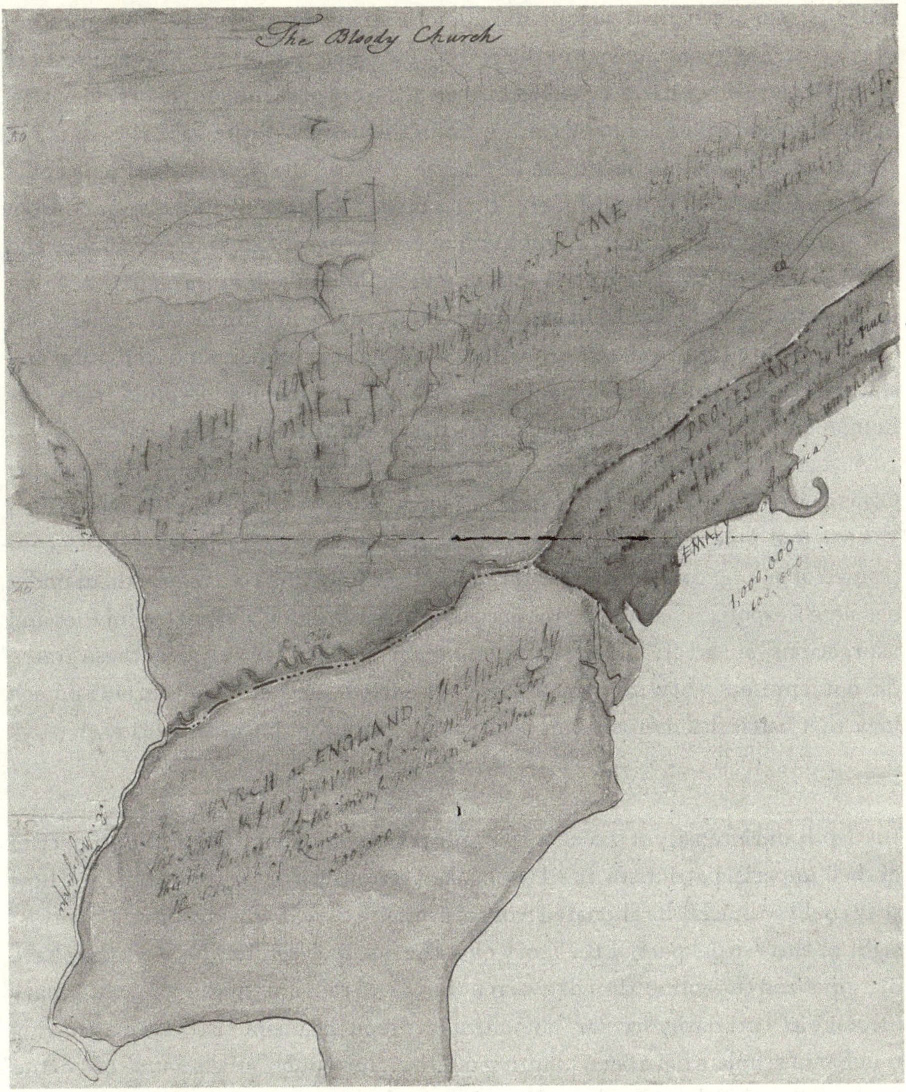

"The Bloody Church," map drawn by Ezra Stiles, August 1774. (Courtesy of the Beinecke Rare Book and Manuscript Library)

This map illustrates the effects of the Quebec Act in dramatic color. Quebec, where Parliament established "the Bloody Church," is red; the southern colonies, whose "Church of England" establishment sold Quebec "to Rome" are green; the northern colonies, full of the true "PROTESTANTS" the "Bishops" wanted "to restrain and suppress," are blue.

religion fraught with sanguinary and impious tenets, or to erect an arbitrary form of government in any quarter of the globe." The Quebec Act made "English settlers" within its jurisdiction live as "subjects of an arbitrary government, deprived of trial by jury, and when imprisoned cannot claim the benefit of the habeas corpus Act, that great bulwark and palladium of English liberty." The Americans simply could not "suppress" their "astonishment, that a British Parliament should ever consent to establish in that country a religion that has deluged your island in blood, and dispersed impiety, bigotry, persecution, murder and rebellion through every part of the world." Surely "the Ministry" intended to reduce the thirteen colonies to the condition of the Quebeckers? Brought down "to a state of perfect humiliation and slavery," British Americans would be taxed to pay for armies recruited from "the Roman Catholics of this vast continent" that would then "enslave you."[53]

A year later, with a British army disembarking in New York Harbor, the Continental Congress declared independence. In what has recently been called "the original American conspiracy theory," the Declaration of Independence complained of a "long train of abuses and usurpations" designed "to reduce them under absolute Despotism." However, the accusation that the king's "repeated injuries and usurpations" aimed at "the establishment of an absolute Tyranny over these States" did not represent a new conspiracy theory. It reflected the centuries-old anti-popish logic that had infused Anglo-American culture since the sixteenth century.[54]

The depth and intensity of the colonists' anti-popery, and the strong anti-Catholicism of their imperial patriotism, need to be taken seriously if we are to understand how they could so quickly be alienated from the empire they loved. Historians have lost sight of this crucial part of the story over the last half-century because they have marginalized the connection between politics and religion, treating revolutionary ideology as a primarily secular "liberalism" or "republicanism." However, a growing number of scholars have been pointing out that the republican discourse of "virtue" fits in well with Calvinist values. Situating revolutionary republicanism within the much longer tradition of anti-popery, it is clear that "classical republicanism" was perfectly compatible with the pervasive anti-Catholic animus of the British Empire. Protestant liberty had been opposed to slavery and Roman Catholicism since before the first permanent colonies took root and remained so through the American Revolution.[55]

Ironically, the anti-popish sentiments that inspired American independence soon contributed to the liberation of Roman Catholics. Having declared independence, one state constitution after another (with notable exceptions in South Carolina, New York, Connecticut, and Massachusetts) declared for religious freedom. Some historians see in these acts a turn away from anti-Catholicism: fighting the tyranny of Protestant Britain, the revolutionary states no longer saw a need to bolster their freedom with anti-Catholic legislation. Certainly, the new United States became a land of opportunity for Catholics. However, the American Revolution did not erase anti-popery. It just gave it a new dilemma: how to give Catholics their promised equality without abandoning Anglo-Protestant liberty?[56]

Notes

1. Robert E. Moody, ed., *The Letters of Thomas Gorges: Deputy Governor of the Province of Maine, 1640–1643* (Portland: Maine Historical Society, 1978), 135.
2. David B. Quinn, ed., *The Roanoke Voyages, 1584–1590: Documents to Illustrate the English Voyages to North America under the Patent Granted to Walter Raleigh*, 2 vols. (London: Hakluyt Society, 1955), 1:203.
3. Owen Stanwood surveys the battle between Protestant and Catholic forces for control of colonial North America in "Catholics, Protestants, and the Clash of Civilizations in Early America," in *The First Prejudice: Religious Tolerance and Intolerance in Early America*, ed. Chris Beneke and Christopher S. Grenda (Philadelphia: University of Pennsylvania Press, 2011), 218–40.
4. Some three thousand New England immigrants returned to England, a number of them to fight in the Civil War, see Susan Hardman Moore, *Pilgrims: New World Settlers and the Call of Home* (New Haven, CT: Yale University Press, 2007). Civil and religious liberty began as two distinct concepts. They were fused in the 1650s. See Michael P. Winship, "Freeborn (Puritan) Englishmen and Slavish Subjection: Popish Tyranny and Puritan Constitutionalism, c. 1570–1606," *English Historical Review* 124, no. 510 (October 2009): 1050–74; and Blair Worden, *God's Instruments: Political Conduct in the England of Oliver Cromwell* (Oxford: Oxford University Press, 2012) chap. 8. For colonial American awareness of this period as vital to their constitutional history, see Ronald Reid, "Puritan Rhetoric and America's Civil Religion: A Study of Three Special Occasion Sermons," in *Rhetoric, Religion, and the Roots of Identity in British Colonial America*, ed. James R. Andrews (East Lansing: Michigan State University Press, 2007), 65–120; and Michelle Orihel, "'All Those Truly Acquainted with the History of Those Times': John Adams and the Opposition Politics of Revolutionary England, ca. 1640–1641," *New England Quarterly* 86, no. 3 (September 2013): 433–66.
5. "John Adams on the British Constitution (1766)," in *Revolutionary America, 1750–1815: Sources and Interpretation*, ed. Cynthia A. Kierner (Upper Saddle River, NJ: Prentice-Hall, 2003), 24–25.
6. Arthur J. Riley, *Catholicism in New England to 1788*, Studies in American Catholicism, vol. 24 (Washington, DC: Catholic University of America Press, 1936); Nathan O. Hatch, *The Sacred Cause of Liberty: Republican Thought and the Millennium in Revolutionary New England* (New Haven, CT: Yale University Press, 1977); Gayle Kathleen Pluta Brown, "A Controversy Not Merely Religious: The Anti-Catholic Tradition in Colonial New England" (PhD diss., University of Iowa, 1990); Michael S. Carter, "A '*Traiterous Religion*': Indulgences and the Anti-Catholic Imagination in Eighteenth-Century New England," *Catholic Historical Review* 99, no. 1 (January 2013): 52–77.
7. There is still no general history of Catholics in the British-American world—a topic of more than parochial interest. For a start see Michael A. Mullet, *Catholics in Britain and Ireland,*

1558–1829 (London: Macmillan, 1998); and Robert Emmett Curran, *Papist Devils: Catholics in British America, 1574–1783* (Washington, DC: Catholic University of America Press, 2014). Nor is there a religious history of the first British Empire, but for a start see Carla Pestana, *Protestant Empire: Religion and the Making of the British Atlantic World* (Philadelphia: University of Pennsylvania Press, 2009).

8. "Elizabeth's Golden Speech (November 30, 1601)," in *Sources and Debates in English History, 1485–1714*, ed. Newton Key and Robert Bucholz (Oxford: Blackwell, 2004), 103. See also Susan Doran, "A 'Sharp Rod' of Chastisement: Mary I through Protestant Eyes during the Reign of Elizabeth I" and Thomas S. Freeman, "Inventing Bloody Mary: Perceptions of Mary Tudor from the Restoration to the Twentieth Century," in *Mary Tudor: Old and New Perspectives*, ed. Susan Doran and Thomas S. Freeman (New York: Palgrave Macmillan, 2011), 21–36, 78–100. On New Englanders' enthusiasm for Foxe, see Adrian Chastain Weimer, *Martyr's Mirror: Persecution and Holiness in Early New England* (New York: Oxford University Press, 2011).
9. In addition to the essay by Cynthia van Zandt in this volume, see David Harris Sacks, "Richard Hakluyt's Navigations in Time: History, Epic, and Empire," *Modern Language Quarterly* 67, no. 1 (March 2006): 31–62; David A. Borouchoff, "Piety, Patriotism, and Empire: Lessons for England, Spain, and the New World in the Works of Richard Hakluyt," *Renaissance Quarterly* 62, no. 3 (Fall 2009): 809–58; Douglas Bradburn, "The Eschatological Origins of the English Empire," in *Early Modern Virginia: Reconsidering the Old Dominion*, ed. Douglas Bradburn and John C. Coombs (Charlottesville: University of Virginia Press, 2011), 15–56; L. H. Roper, "Fear and the Genesis of the English Empire in America," in *Fear and the Shaping of Early American Societies*, ed. Louis H. Roper and Lauric Henneton (Leiden: Brill, 2016), 76–92.
10. Hakluyt's memorandum was reprinted in John Brereton, *A Briefe and True Relation of the Discoveries of the North Part of Virginia* (London, 1602), in *The English New England Voyages, 1602–1608*, ed. David B. Quinn and Alison M. Quinn (London: Hakluyt Society, 1983), ser. 2, no. 161, 188; "The Standish-Croft Journal," in *The Voyage of Thomas Best to the East Indies, 1612–14*, ed. William Foster (London: Hakluyt Society, 1934), ser. 2, vol. 75, 137; Lord De la Ware, Sir Thomas Smith, Sir Walter Cope, and Master Waterson, *A True and Sincere Declaration of the Purpose and Ends of the Plantation Begun in Virginia . . .* (London, 1610), 3; Peter C. Mancall, *Envisioning America: English Plans for the Colonization of North America, 1580–1640* (Boston: Bedford/St. Martin's, 1995), 134.
11. Sir William Alexander, *An Encouragement to Colonies* (London, 1624), 6, 13–14; Stanwood, "Clash of Civilizations," 221–22; Frank Lestringant, "Geneva and America in the Renaissance: The Dream of the Huguenot Refuge, 1555–1600," *Sixteenth Century Journal* 26, no. 2 (Summer 1995): 285–95; David Beers Quinn, "The First Pilgrims," in his *England and the Discovery of America, 1481–1620: From the Bristol Voyages of the Fifteenth Century to the Pilgrim Settlement at Plymouth: The Exploration, Exploitation, and Trial-and-Error Colonization of North America by the English* (London: George Allen & Unwin, 1974), 337–63; Karen Ordahl Kupperman, *Providence Island, 1630–1641: The Other Puritan Colony* (Cambridge: Cambridge University Press, 1995).
12. Sir William Foster, ed., *Early Travels in India, 1583–1619* (London: Oxford University Press, 1921), 89, 331; Evan Haefeli and Owen Stanwood, "Jesuits, Huguenots, and the Apocalypse: The Origins of America's First French Book," *Proceedings of the American Antiquarian Society* 116, pt. 1 (2006): 83–87, 109.
13. John Adams to William Tudor Sr., September 23, 1818, *Founders Online*, http://founders.archives.gov/documents/Adams/99-02-02-6993. Quotes from Niles's history in *Collections*

of the Massachusetts Historical Society, 3rd ser., 6 (1837): 154–55, 157; and *Collections of the Massachusetts Historical Society*, 4th ser., 5 (1861): 336, 387. For Niles's biography, see Clifford K. Shipton et al., eds., *Sibley's Harvard Graduates*, vol. 4, *Biographical Sketches of Those Who Attended Harvard College in the Classes 1690–1700* (Cambridge, MA: Harvard University Press, 1933), 485–91.

14. William Waller Hening, ed., *The Statutes at Large: Being a Collection of all the Laws of Virginia from the First Session of the Legislature in the Year 1619*, 13 vols. (Richmond, 1809–1823), 1:69, 73, 97–98; Governor John Pott et al. to Privy Council, November 30, 1629, National Archives of the UK [hereafter TNA] CO 1/5/101. The use of the oaths can be traced in Francis X. Curran, ed., *Catholics in Colonial Law* (Chicago: Loyola University Press, 1963). On their connection to early American citizenship, see James H. Kettner, *The Development of American Citizenship, 1608–1870* (Chapel Hill: University of North Carolina Press, 1978), esp. 113–14, who points out that exceptions were sometimes made, and that the oaths could be used against unconventional Protestants, like Quakers and Moravians.
15. John D. Krugler, *English and Catholic: The Lords Baltimore in the Seventeenth Century* (Baltimore: Johns Hopkins University Press, 2004); Louis H. Roper, "New Albion: Anatomy of an English Colonization Failure, 1632–1659," *Itinerario* 32, no. 1 (March 2008): 1–15; Donald Harman Akenson, *If the Irish Ran the World: Montserrat, 1630–1730* (Montreal: McGill-Queen's University Press, 1997); Shona Johnston, "Papists in a Protestant World: The Catholic Anglo-Atlantic in the Seventeenth Century" (PhD diss., Georgetown University, 2011).
16. TNA SP 84/160, fol. 92; Michael P. Winship, "William Pynchon's *The Jewes Synagogue*," *New England Quarterly* 71, no. 2 (June 1998): 290–97, quote on 291; Jeremy Fradkin, "Protestant Unity and Anti-Catholicism: The Irenicism and Philo-Semitism of John Dury in Context," *Journal of British Studies* 56, no. 2 (April 2017): 273–94; Richard W. Cogley, "The Ancestry of the American Indians: Thomas Thorowgood's *Iewes in America* (1650) and *Jews in America* (1660)," *English Literary Renaissance* 35, no. 2 (April 2005): 304–30.
17. Carla Gardina Pestana, "Cruelty and Religious Justifications for Conquest in the Mid-Seventeenth-Century English Atlantic," in *Empires of God: Religious Encounters in the Early Modern Atlantic*, ed. Linda Gregerson and Susan Juster (Philadelphia: University of Pennsylvania Press, 2011), 37–57; Clyde L. Grose, "England and Dunkirk," *American Historical Review* 39, no. 1 (October 1933): 5–17; Jangkhoman Guite, "The English Company and the Catholics of Madras, in the Age of Religious Conflicts in England, 1640–1750," *Studies in History* 28, no. 2 (2012): 179–201.
18. "Roger Williams to John Winthrop, Junior, May 28, 1664," in *The Correspondence of Roger Williams*, ed. Glenn W. LaFantasie et al., 2 vols. (Hanover, NH: University Press of New England, 1988), 2:528. On the religious changes in the empire more broadly, see Evan Haefeli, "How Special Was Rhode Island? The Global Context of the 1663 Charter," in *The Lively Experiment: Religious Toleration in America from Roger Williams to the Present*, ed. Chris Beneke and Chris Grenda (Lanham, MD: Rowman and Littlefield, 2015), 21–36; and Evan Haefeli, "Pennsylvania's Religious Freedom in Comparative Colonial Context," in *The Worlds of William Penn*, ed. Andrew Murphy and John Smolenski (New Brunswick, NJ: Rutgers University Press, 2019), 333–54.
19. W. Noel Sainsbury et al., eds., *Calendar of State Papers, Colonial Series, America and West Indies*, 44 vols. (London: H.M.S.O., 1860–1963) (hereafter *CSPC*), *1661–1668*, 105; "John Pynchon to John Winthrop Jr., April 24, 1674," in *The Pynchon Papers*, ed. Carl Bridenbaugh, 2 vols. (Boston: Colonial Society of Massachusetts, 1982), 1:126; Brendan McConville, *The King's Three Faces: The Rise and Fall of Royal America, 1688–1776* (Chapel Hill: University of North Carolina Press for the OIEAHC, 2006), chap. 2; Francis D. Cogliano, "Deliverance from Luxury: Pope's

Day, Conflict, and Consensus in Colonial Boston, 1745–1765," *Studies in Popular Culture* 15, no. 2 (1993): 15–28; Kevin Q. Doyle, "'A Rage and Fury Which Only Hell Could Inspire': The Rhetoric and Ritual of Gunpowder Treason in Early America" (PhD diss., Brandeis University, 2013).

20. David Sowd, "Edward Taylor's Answer to a 'Popish Pamphlet,'" *Early American Literature* 9, no. 3 (Winter 1975): 307–14, quotes on 307, 311, 312. The Pope Joan myth, used to criticize the papacy since the thirteenth century, became linked to the Whore of Babylon early in England's Reformation but faded out of use after 1689, Thomas S. Freeman, "Joan of Contention: The Myth of the Female Pope in Early Modern England," in *Religious Politics in Post-Reformation England: Essays in Honour of Nicholas Tyacke,* ed. Kenneth Fincham and Peter Lake (Rochester, NY: Boydell Press, 2006), 60–79.

21. TNA CO 1/46/320; *CSPC, 1677–1680*, 502–503.

22. Antoinette Sutto, *Loyal Protestants and Dangerous Papists: Maryland and the Politics of Religion in the English Atlantic, 1630–1690* (Charlottesville: University of Virginia Press, 2015), 9 and passim; Elodie Peyrol, "'Fforty thousand to cutt the Protestants Throats': The Irish Threat in the Chesapeake, 1620–1700," in *Fear,* ed. Roper and Henneton, 160–81; TNA CO 1/46/341.

23. J. Ovington, *A Voyage to Suratt in the Year 1689* (London, 1696), 148, 156–57; Glenn J. Ames, "The Role of Religion in the Transfer and Rise of Bombay, c. 1661–1687," *Historical Journal* 46, no. 2 (June 2003): 317–40.

24. *CSPC, 1685–1688,* 513. On Penn's anti-popery, see Andrew R. Murphy, *Liberty, Conscience, and Toleration: The Political Thought of William Penn* (New York: Oxford University Press, 2016), chaps. 4 and 6. Quakers' toleration of Catholics occasionally led them to be suspected of popery, Joseph J. Casino, "Anti-Popery in Colonial Pennsylvania," *Pennsylvania Magazine of History and Biography* 105, no. 3 (July 1981): 279–309.

25. *CSPC, 1685–1688,* 51 #210, 275; David William Voorhees, trans. and ed., *Records of the Reformed Protestant Dutch Church of Flatbush, Kings County, New York,* 2 vols. (New York: Holland Society of New York, 1998–2009), 1:169; Viola Barnes, *The Dominion of New England: A Study in British Colonial Policy* (New Haven, CT: Yale University Press, 1923), 87.

26. Owen Stanwood, "The Protestant Moment: Antipopery, the Revolution of 1688–89, and the Making of an Anglo-American Empire," *Journal of British Studies* 46, no. 3 (July 2007): 481–508; Edwyn Stede to Jacob Leisler, January 27, 1689/90, Massachusetts Secretary of State, Massachusetts Archives, Boston, 35:163–64; Nicholas Spencer to William Blathwayt, June 10, 1689, vol. 18, folder 3, William Blathwayt Papers, Rockefeller Library, Colonial Williamsburg (hereafter WBP); Rebecca Goetz, *The Baptism of Early Virginia: How Christianity Created Race* (Baltimore: Johns Hopkins University Press, 2012), 134–36; Richard S. Dunn, "Glorious Revolution and America," in *The Origins of Empire: British Overseas Enterprise to the Close of the Seventeenth Century,* ed. Nicholas Canny (Oxford: Oxford University Press, 1998), 445–66; Owen Stanwood, *The Empire Reformed: English America in the Age of the Glorious Revolution* (Philadelphia: University of Pennsylvania Press, 2013). See also James R. Hertzler, "Who Dubbed It 'The Glorious Revolution'?" *Albion: A Quarterly Journal Concerned with British Studies* 19, no. 4 (Winter 1987): 579–85.

27. Gershom Bulkeley, *The People's Right to Election; or, Alteration of Government, Argued* (Philadelphia, 1689), 11, 13.

28. Spencer to Blathwayt, June 10, 1689, vol. 18, folder 3, WBP; "Gustavus Kingsland Memorandum," New York Historical Society, BV New Netherland, f. 33; Edmund B. O'Callaghan and Berthold Fernow, eds., *Documents Relative to the Colonial History of the State of New York,* 15 vols. (Albany: Weed, Parson & Company, 1853–1887), 3:631; Peter Christoph, ed., *The Leisler*

Papers, 1689–1691 (Syracuse, NY: Syracuse University Press, 2002), 182–83; David William Voorhees, "The 'fervent Zeale' of Jacob Leisler," *William and Mary Quarterly* 3rd ser., 51, no. 3 (July 1994): 447–72; John M. Murrin, "The Menacing Shadow of Louis XIV and the Rage of Jacob Leisler: The Constitutional Ordeal of Seventeenth-Century New York," in *New York and the Union: Contributions to the American Constitutional Experience*, ed. Stephen L. Schechter and Richard B. Bernstein (Albany: New York State Commission on the Bicentennial of the Constitution, 1990), 29–71; David William Voorhees, "'Imprisoning persons at their pleasure': The Anti-Catholic Hysteria in the Middle Colonies," in *Fear*, ed. Roper and Henneton, 182–203; Jason K. Duncan, *Citizens or Papists? The Politics of Anti-Catholicism in New York, 1685–1821* (New York: Fordham University Press, 2005), chap. 1.

29. John Gyles, "Memoirs of Odd Adventures, Strange Deliverances, etc." in *Puritans among the Indians: Accounts of Captivity and Redemption, 1676–1724*, ed. Alden T. Vaughn and Edward W. Clark (Cambridge, MA: Belknap Press of Harvard University Press, 1981), 95, 99–100; J. M. Bumsted, "'Carried to Canada!': Perceptions of the French in British Colonial Captivity Narratives, 1690–1760," *American Review of Canadian Studies* 13, no. 1 (1983): 79–96; Evan Haefeli, "Making Papists of Puritans: Accounting for New English Conversions in New France," in *Varieties of Religious Conversion in the Early Modern Atlantic World*, ed. James Muldoon (Gainesville: University of Florida Press, 2004), 215–30; Evan Haefeli and Kevin Sweeney, *Captors and Captives: The 1704 French and Indian Raid on Deerfield* (Amherst: University of Massachusetts Press, 2003), 238–49; Evan Haefeli and Kevin Sweeney, "*The Redeemed Captive* as Recurrent Seller: Politics and Publication, 1707–1854," *New England Quarterly* 77, no. 3 (2004): 341–67; Evan Haefeli and Kevin Sweeney, eds., *Captive Histories: English, French, and Native Narratives of the 1704 Deerfield Raid* (Amherst: University of Massachusetts Press, 2006). For a New England girl who became a nun in New France, see Ann M. Little, *The Many Captivities of Esther Wheelwright* (New Haven, CT: Yale University Press, 2016).

30. M. Halsey Thomas, ed., *The Diary of Samuel Sewall, 1674–1729*, 2 vols. (New York: Farrar, Straus and Giroux, 1973), 2:468, 469, 470; McConville, *King's Three Faces*, chap. 2; Ned Landsman, "The Episcopate, the British Union, and the Failure of Religious Settlement in Colonial British America," in *First Prejudice*, ed. Beneke and Grenda, 75–97; Sister Mary Augustina Ray, *American Opinion of Roman Catholicism in the Eighteenth Century* (New York: Columbia University Press, 1936); Pauline Maier, "The Pope at Harvard: Dudleian Lectures, Anti-Catholicism, and the Politics of Protestantism," *Proceedings of the Massachusetts Historical Society* 97 (1985): 16–41; Douglas Stange, "The Third Lecture: One Hundred and Fifty Years of Anti-Popery at Harvard," *Harvard Library Bulletin* 16, no. 4 (2005): 354–69.

31. Mark A. Peterson, "The Selling of Joseph: Bostonians, Antislavery, and the Protestant International, 1689–1733," *Massachusetts Historical Review* 4 (2002): 1–22; Thomas S. Kidd, *The Protestant Interest: New England after Puritanism* (New Haven, CT: Yale University Press, 2004). Jon F. Sensbach, "Religion and the Early South in Age of Atlantic Empire," *Journal of Southern History* 73, no. 3 (August 2007): 631–32, sees these campaigns as a reminder of the need to incorporate "a strong sense of Protestant-Catholic antagonism into a general understanding of early southern religious history." For other anti-Catholic violence, see Susan Juster, "Iconoclasm without Icons? The Destruction of Sacred Objects in Colonial North America," in *Empires of God*, ed. Gregerson and Juster, 216–37. Linda Colley largely left colonial Americans out of her famous account of anti-Catholicism, war, and British nationalism, *Britons: Forging the Nation, 1707–1837* (New Haven, CT: Yale University Press, 2005), chap. 1 and 132–37; but Bob Harris, "'American Idols': Empire, War, and the Middling Ranks in Mid-Eighteenth Century Britain," *Past and Present* 150, no. 1 (February 1996):

111–41, sees British patriotic attachment to the American colonies as part of a broader transatlantic Protestant struggle against the French.

32. Reba Carolyn Strickland, *Religion and the State in Georgia in the Eighteenth Century* (New York: AMS Press, 1967), 79–82.

33. Albert B. Saye, ed., *Georgia's Charter of 1732* (Athens: University of Georgia Press, 1942), 49; Mark Häberlein, *The Practice of Pluralism: Congregational Life and Religious Diversity in Lancaster, Pennsylvania, 1730–1820* (University Park: Pennsylvania State University Press, 2009), 157; Stanwood, "Clash of Civilizations," 233–34; Verner W. Crane, "Dr. Bray and the Charitable Colony Project, 1730," *William and Mary Quarterly* 19, no. 1 (January 1962): 49–63; Harvey H. Jackson and Phinizy Spalding, eds., *Forty Years of Diversity: Essays on Colonial Georgia* (Athens: University of Georgia Press, 1984); Warren Hofstra, "'The Extension of His Majesties Dominions': The Virginia Backcountry and the Reconfiguring of the Imperial Frontiers," *Journal of American History* 84, no. 4 (March 1998): 1281–312; Karen Auman, "'English Liberties' and German Settlers in Colonial America: The Georgia Salzburgers' Conceptions of Community, 1730–1750," *Early American Studies* 11, no. 1 (Winter 2013): 37–54.

34. Samuel Chew, "Advertisement against the Quakers," (1742), Chew Family Papers, ser. 1: Samuel Chew (1693–1744), box 2, folder 13, f. 1v, Historical Society of Pennsylvania; [James Honeyman], *Faults on all sides: The case of religion consider'd* . . . (Newport, RI, 1728), preface; J. Logan Tomlin, "Papal Plots and Muslim Mischief: Religious Fear and Democratic Sensibilities in Early America" (PhD diss., University of Tennessee, 2018).

35. Hannah Smith, "The Idea of a Protestant Monarchy in Britain, 1714–1760," *Past and Present* 185 (November 2004): 91–118, quote on 94; Geoffrey Plank, *John Woolman's Path to the Peaceable Kingdom: A Quaker in the British Empire* (Philadelphia: University of Pennsylvania Press, 2012), 21–22. On anti-Jacobitism in the colonies, see Geoffrey Plank, *Rebellion and Savagery: The Jacobite Rising of 1745 and the British Empire* (Philadelphia: University of Pennsylvania Press, 2006). David Parrish, "'Now the mask is taken off': Jacobitism and Colonial New England, 1702–1727," *Historical Research* 88, no. 240 (May 2015): 249–71, argues that Jacobitism had more potential in the colonies than is commonly thought.

36. "Sermon preached at evening meeting February 20, 1737," f. 4, folder April 18, 1727, February 1737, box Stephen Williams, Sermons, 1727–1803, MHS; Stephen Williams Diary, July 2, 1741, microfilm edition of typescript transcription, 10 vols., 3:373, Storrs Library, Longmeadow, MA, available at http://www.longmeadowlibrary.org/stephen-williams-diary-available-online/; *The World of Hannah Heaton: The Diary of an Eighteenth-Century Farm Woman,* ed. Barbara E. Lacey (DeKalb: Northern Illinois Press, 2003), 3–4.

37. Mark M. Smith, ed., *Stono: Documenting and Interpreting a Southern Slave Revolt* (Columbia: University of South Carolina Press, 2005), esp. 13–14, 108–18; Darold D. Wax, "'The Great Risque We Run': The Aftermath of Slave Rebellion at Stono, South Carolina, 1739–1745," *Journal of Negro History* 67, no. 2 (Summer 1982): 136–47, esp. 142–43; Serena R. Zabin, ed., *The New York Conspiracy Trials of 1741: Daniel Horsmanden's 'Journal of the Proceedings' with Related Documents* (Boston: Bedford/St. Martin's Press, 2004), 121. On Whitefield's anti-Catholicism, see Thomas A. Kidd, *George Whitefield: America's Spiritual Founding Father* (New Haven, CT: Yale University Press, 2014), esp. 51–52, 195–97, 219–22.

38. Louis Effingham De Forest, ed., *Louisbourg Journals 1745* (New York: Society of the Colonial Wars, 1932), 33, 34, 152.

39. For examples of these anti-Catholic practices, see Geoffrey Plank, *An Unsettled Conquest: The British Campaign against the Peoples of Acadia* (Philadelphia: University of Pennsylvania Press, 2001), esp. 95, 115; George Hills, *Rock of Contention: A History of Gibraltar* (London: Robert Hale & Company, 1974), 175–77, 214–23, 231–34; 273, 291–93; Bruce Laurie, *The Life*

of Richard Kane: Britain's First Lieutenant-Governor of Minorca (Rutherford, NJ: Fairleigh Dickinson University Press, 1994), chap. 9. Geoffrey Plank, "Making Gibraltar British in the Eighteenth Century," *History* 98, no. 331 (July 2013): 346–69, examines Gibraltar's integration into British patriotic consciousness, while Hannah Weiss Muller, "The Garrison Revisited: Gibraltar in the Eighteenth Century," *Journal of Imperial and Commonwealth History* 41, no. 3 (2013): 353–76, emphasizes how ties with neighboring Catholic communities meant it was never a completely isolated Protestant garrison.

40. George Washington to Governor Robert Hunter Morris, April 9, 1756, in *George Washington: A Collection,* ed. W. B. Allen (Indianapolis: Liberty Fund, 1988), 21; Chris Beneke, *Beyond Toleration: The Religious Origins of American Pluralism* (New York: Oxford University Press, 2006), 111–12; Strickland, *Religion and the State in Georgia,* 120.

41. Samuel Hazard et al., eds., *Pennsylvania Archives,* 1st ser., 12 vols. (Philadelphia, 1852–1856), 2:691, 694; John Mack Faragher, *A Great and Noble Scheme: The Tragic Story of the Expulsion of the French Acadians from Their American Homeland* (New York: W. W. Norton, 2005); Penny, *Church in Madras,* 1:323–38; Stephen Neill, *A History of Christianity in India, 1707–1858* (Cambridge: Cambridge University Press, 1985), 106–12; J. William Black, *Maryland's Attitude in the Struggle for Canada* (Baltimore: Johns Hopkins University Press, 1892), 64–66; Timothy W. Bosworth, "Anti-Catholicism as a Political Tool in Mid-Eighteenth-Century Maryland," *Catholic Historical Review* 61, no. 4 (October 1975): 539–63; A. G. Roeber, *Palatines, Liberty, and Property: German Lutherans in Colonial British America* (Baltimore: Johns Hopkins University Press, 1998), 251; Thomas Hughes, "An Alleged Popish Plot in Pennsylvania: 1756–7," *Records of the Catholic Historical Society* 10, no. 2 (June 1899): 208–21; Häberlein, *Practice of Pluralism,* 159–60.

42. George E. Marsden, *Jonathan Edwards: A Life* (New Haven, CT: Yale University Press, 2003), 415–16; Samuel Davies, "The Mediatorial Kingdom and Glories of Jesus Christ (1756)," in *Political Sermons of the American Founding Era, 1730–1805,* ed. Ellis Sandoz (Indianapolis: Liberty Press, 1991), 198; Stephen Williams, "Sermon preached at evening meeting February 20, 1737," folder April 18, 1727, February 1737; "On ye Popish principles," f. 14 and "At LM before ye Sacrament March 4, 1756," f. 1, folder January 30, 1756, March 4, 1756; "At Lm Febry 26, 1758," f. 17, folder February 26, 1758, box Stephen Williams, Sermons, 1727–1803, MHS; Thomas Secker, *A Sermon Preached before the Society Corresponding with the Incorporated Society in Dublin, for Promoting English Protestant Working Schools in Ireland . . . on . . . April 12, 1757* (London, 1757), 26; Robert G. Ingram, ed., "'Popish Cut-Throats against Us': Papists, Protestants, and the Problem of Allegiance in Eighteenth-Century Ireland," in *From the Reformation to the Permissive Society: A Miscellany in Celebration of the 400th Anniversary of Lambeth Palace Library,* ed. Melanie Barber and Stephen Taylor with Gabriel Sewell (Woodbridge: Boydell Press for the Church of England Record Society, 2010), 151–209.

43. Catherine A. Brekus, *Sarah Osborn's World: The Rise of Evangelical Christianity in Early America* (New Haven, CT: Yale University Press, 2013), 192, 203, 232, 252; Ann M. Little, "Cloistered Bodies: Convents in the Anglo-American Imagination in the British Conquest of Canada," *Eighteenth Century Studies* 39, no. 2 (Winter 2006): 187–200. Ana M. Acosta, "Hotbeds of Popery: Convents in the English Literary Imagination," *Eighteenth-Century Fiction* 15, nos. 3–4 (April–July 2003): 615–42, notes a number of "Convent novels" written by English women in 1765–1800 included stories about Quebec.

44. Fernandeo Diaz-Plaja, ed., *La Historia de España en sus documentos: El Siglo XVIII* (Madrid: Instituto de Estudios Politicos, 1955), 245–46.

45. "Treaty of Paris, 1763," http://avalon.law.yale.edu/18th_century/paris763.asp.

46. Verner W. Crane, ed., "Hints Relative to the Division and Government of the Conquered and Newly Acquired Countries in America," *Mississippi Valley Historical Review* 8, no. 4 (March 1922): 367–73, quotes on 371, 372; R. A. Humphreys, "Lord Shelburne and the Proclamation of 1763," *English Historical Review* 49, no. 194 (April 1934): 241–64, esp. 256.
47. Lawrence A. Uzzell, "James Murray: A Forgotten Champion of Religious Freedom," *Catholic Historical Review* 104, no. 1 (Winter 2018): 57–91.
48. *A narrative of the proceedings upon the complaint against Governor Melvill* (London, 1770), vi, 47–51, 89–91; Peter E. Pope, *Fish into Wine: The Newfoundland Plantation in the Seventeenth Century* (Chapel Hill: University of North Carolina Press for the OIEAHC, 2004), 236.
49. John Adams, "A Dissertation on the Canon and Feudal Law," in Anon., *The True Sentiments of America, contained in a collection of letters sent from . . . Massachusetts* (London, 1768), 116–17; Peter C. Messer, "Stamps and Popes: Rethinking the Role of Violence in the Coming of the American Revolution," in *Between Sovereignty and Anarchy: The Politics of Violence in the Revolutionary Era,* ed. Patrick Griffin, Robert G. Ingram, Peter S. Onuf, and Brian Schoen (Charlottesville: University of Virginia Press, 2015), 114–38. Thomas S. Kidd, *God of Liberty: A Religious History of the American Revolution* (New York: Basic Books, 2010), 33, claims America embraced "a new kind of civil spirituality" after 1763, one that "put a heavy emphasis on political values," but this is more likely a symptom of anti-popery's return to its seventeenth-century roots.
50. William R. Leslie, "The Gaspee Affair: A Study of Its Constitutional Significance," *Mississippi Valley Historical Review,* 39, no. 2 (September 1952): 235, 244–45, 247–48, 250; John M. Bumsted and Charles E. Clark, "New England's Tom Paine: John Allen and the Spirit of Liberty," *William and Mary Quarterly* 21, no. 4 (October 1964): 564, 566, 570.
51. Quotes in Hilda Neatby, *The Quebec Act: Protest and Policy* (Toronto: Prentice-Hall, 1972), 38–40. On the act's religious effects, see Peter Doll, *Revolution, Religion, and National Identity: Imperial Anglicanism in British North America, 1745–1795* (Madison, NJ: Fairleigh Dickinson University Press, 2000).
52. *George Washington: A Collection,* ed. Allen, 31, 39; Richard B. Vernier, ed., *The Revolutionary Writings of Alexander Hamilton* (Indianapolis: Liberty Fund, 2008), 30; Samuel Sherwood, *A Sermon, containing Scriptural Instructions to civil rulers . . . Also, an appendix stating the heave grievances the colonies labour under . . . By Rev. Ebenezer Baldwin* (New Haven, 1774), 13, 67, 72, 74; Paul Langston, "'Tyrant and Oppressor!': Colonial Press Reaction to the Quebec Act," *Historical Journal of Massachusetts* 34, no. 1 (January 2006): 1–17; Matthew L. Rhoades, "Blood and Boundaries: Virginia Backcountry Violence and the Origins of the Quebec Act, 1758–1775," *West Virginia History* 3, no. 2 (2009): 1–22. See also Kidd, *God of Liberty,* 16–18, 66–73; Vernon P. Creviston, "'No King Unless It Be a Constitutional King': Rethinking the Place of the Quebec Act in the Coming of the American Revolution," *The Historian* 73, no. 3 (Fall 2011): 463–79. Stanwood argues that the act "allowed American revolutionaries to interpret their new contest as just a new chapter in the centuries-long Protestant struggle for America," in "Clash of Civilizations," 239. On the revolutionary transition in anti-popish thought, where sermons once directed at French and Spanish enemies proved equally useful against the British (with slight modifications), see Glenn A. Moots, "Samuel Cooper's Old Sermons and New Enemies: Popery and Protestant Constitutionalism," *American Political Thought* 5, no. 3 (Summer 2016): 391–419. Kidd, *God of Liberty,* 90–95, sees revolutionary Americans' making an alteration in "the identity of Antichrist" from "Catholicism and Islam" to "the British."
53. *To the People of Great Britain from the Delegates appointed by the Several English Colonies . . . to Consider their Grievances in General Congress* (London, 1775), 4, 13–16.

54. "The Declaration of Independence (1776)," in *Revolutionary America*, ed. Kierner, 137; Joseph E. Uscinski and Joseph M. Parent, *American Conspiracy Theories* (Oxford: Oxford University Press, 2014), 1–2. Concerned with modern conspiracy theories, these authors seem completely unaware of the anti-popish origins of the phenomenon they describe.
55. Clement Fatovic, "The Anti-Catholic Roots of Liberal and Republican Conceptions of Freedom in English Political Thought," *Journal of the History of Ideas* 66, no. 1 (January 2005): 37–58; Michael P. Winship, "Algernon Sidney's Calvinist Republicanism," *Journal of British Studies* 49, no. 4 (October 2010): 753–73.
56. This legal transformation can be followed in Curran, ed., *Catholics in Colonial Law*, 106–25. For the optimistic view, see Chris Beneke, "'Not by Force or Violence': Religious Violence, Anti-Catholicism, and Rights of Conscience in the Early National United States," in *Between Sovereignty and Anarchy*, ed. Griffin et al., 60–83.

A Deal with the Devil

REVOLUTIONARY ANTI-POPERY, FRANCOPHOBIA, AND THE DILEMMAS OF DIPLOMACY

Brendan McConville

BY EARLY 1777, AMERICA had been overtaken by the anarchy of war and revolution. The newly independent nation struggled for life as armies marched and local economies collapsed. And many feared that it would get worse still. North Carolina yeoman John Carter believed "that the French was coming in that the gentry was joining them to bring in the popish Religion." Another Carolinian, James Rollins, reported that "the Congress had given up the Country to the French to be governed by them, and then Popery would come into the Country."[1]

It is fair to say that most Americans today understand the Revolution's origins via a narrative that does not include seemingly paranoid fears of our French Catholic allies or outbursts against popery. In most tellings, one thing led to another until there was a revolution. After a troubled decade, the Boston Tea Party led Parliament to punish Massachusetts; that led to Lexington and Concord, Bunker Hill, and then independence. The French alliance made sense as a way to counter the British Empire's military might. Scholars' interpretations of the Revolution are nearly as settled and fixed in their natures. These suggest that the Imperial Crisis manifested thought about liberty and power derived from reading English oppositional ideology and the writings of the European Enlightenment; a clash of classes in a society transitioning to capitalism; or more recently, racial conflict. There is no room in such accounts for the Protestant-based political belief system most free British Americans shared or the anti-popish or Francophobic fears contained within that system acting as a driving force for change.[2]

These stories of national origins begin to dissolve when we view the period through the eyes of the many in the revolutionary generation who grew up fearing Catholics, France, and a French takeover. They lived an unrecognized revolution, filled with religiously grounded convictions and fears that seem paranoid now but were quite real to them. At independence, Americans continued to use beliefs derived from Protestant political culture to interpret events. These beliefs sometimes led them to uncomfortable conclusions about the revolutionary upheaval. In their worldview, the turmoil at independence and the military disasters that followed expressed the return of their hated enemies, Catholics generally and French Catholics specifically, who, they believed, had created the crisis as a means to enslave Protestant Americans body and soul. There is, from that perspective, no greater irony than the republic that emerged, or the French alliance that enabled its birth.

This essay argues that Protestant political idioms played a powerful, indeed central role in interpreting and driving change between 1774 and the early 1780s, but these beliefs were not fixed to one particular political community or political-ideological position. This persistence indicates a view of change in the period that contrasts sharply with national mythology, and with accepted scholarly views of revolutionary ideology. Colonial writers' appropriation and use of the anti-popish, anti-Catholic, and Francophobic idioms in 1774 and 1775 to indict the imperial administration and George III as politically popish and crypto-Catholic destroyed the empire's internal ideological logic and made a revolution possible. Those Protestant political beliefs remained current throughout the society on July 4, 1776, expressing a specifically Protestant revolutionary consciousness that continued to guide many people's understanding of events. Reaction to the Franco-American alliance in 1778 made apparent that these beliefs neither assured loyalty to the revolutionary governments nor was their survival and usage confined to those supporting American independence. The Franco-American treaty seemed to repudiate everything Protestant Anglo-Americans knew about history and politics. The alliance provoked anti-Catholic and anti-French outbursts throughout the English-speaking world's divided political communities; it encouraged constitutional conflict in the American states and rioting in the streets of London. In aligning themselves with Bourbon France, the revolutionary leaders made a deal with the devil, and went to war with their own spiritual-political history.[3]

A strong and distorting tendency exists among historians to understand the Revolution's ideological character as "republican." Republican and republicanism are terms packed with assumptions about change, and scholars who use them have privileged what is secular and related to the classical world. This approach has hidden much about ideological change in the eighteenth century. The most jarring of those unrecognized ideological transformations occurred in 1774, when American writers appropriated the idioms of Protestant political culture and used them to undermine London's control in the colonies. These writers explained to a still Protestant and British colonial population that the imperial ministry had been contaminated by popish tendencies.

Ironically, until 1774 anti-Catholic, anti-popish, and Francophobic language had been central to imperial political culture and institutional control in America. Profound fears about foreign Catholics and popish plots in Britain had served as the empire's central ideological strut since the Glorious Revolution of 1688–89, when William and Mary used the fear of political popery and Catholicism to legitimate their seizure of power from her Catholic father James II. The Convention Parliament called to legitimate the Glorious Revolution and legislation that followed then excluded Catholics from the throne and effectively proscribed them from public life in the empire. Anti-Catholic and anti-popish language that ran back to the English Reformation became institutionalized expressions of allegiance to a formally Protestant empire.[4]

This imperial worldview became entrenched in the colonies after 1690 as the empire became better integrated and an intermittent 120-year war against Bourbon France began. Eighteenth-century British America's biggest official holiday was November 5, Pope's Day, which involved the parading and destruction of giant pope effigies in remembrance of the foiling of Guy Fawkes's Catholic conspiracy against James I and Parliament in 1605. Anglo-American writers endlessly invoked the Roman Church's satanic goals, linking them to the French Bourbon monarchy's actions against Britain and Protestants generally; and to the French monarchy's tyrannical nature.[5]

The South Carolina politician and jurist William Henry Drayton defined this imperial-Protestant worldview in 1775. He described English liberty as a compounding of "the most generous civil liberty that ever existed; and the sacred Christian religion, released from the absurdities which are inculcated [by Catholicism]." Popish doctrines, he believed, lay at the foundation of any "cruel tyranny in church and state" wherever they took root. This tyranny had kept Europe in spiritual and political darkness for centuries. Liberty, property, and liberty of conscience could not be maintained "without our pious and unwearied endeavours." For Drayton and his peers, only a Protestant society could truly enjoy liberty and property. Catholicism promised only spiritual and political enslavement.[6]

Given this, it is little wonder that anti-popery became an important tool in British Americans' efforts to explain the Stamp Act crisis and what followed. Colonial writers attributed the crises to a conspiracy led by the deposed, Catholic, and pro-French Stuart dynasty (the heirs of the deposed Catholic king James II) and the Bishop of Rome. Boston minister Joseph Emerson preached that the Stamp Act would turn the colonies into "a tributary to the See of Rome." Even the supposedly enlightened Boston-area minister Jonathan Mayhew believed the Stamp Act's authors sought to aid the Catholic Stuart "Pretender," Bonnie Prince Charlie, the grandson of James II. Although largely ignored by modern scholars, this discourse played a powerful role in explaining the events of 1764 and 1765 to worried colonials.[7]

Even those we call the founders used these frameworks to justify resistance to imperial authority. "At a time," John Adams wrote in 1771, "when the barriers against popery, erected by our ancestors, are suffered to be destroyed, to the hazard even of the Protestant religion . . . it is not surprising that the great securities of the people should be invaded, and their fundamental rights drawn into question." Throughout his life Adams's writing, public and private, continued to reflect these values embedded in the British-American Protestant political culture he grew up in.[8]

Scholars have thus far failed to consider how these idioms went from pillar of empire to a central tool used by British-American writers to protest imperial control, and ultimately to destroy its internal ideological logic. This jarring rhetorical migration became fully evident in the year of revolt, 1774. Fears that a secret Catholic conspiracy had compromised the imperial ministry intensified when Parliament passed the Intolerable acts and the Quebec Act in that year. The Intolerable acts punished Boston and Massachusetts for the Boston Tea Party.

Virtual Representation, engraving, 1775. (© The Trustees of the British Museum; all rights reserved)

Saying "Deliver your Property," the Scottish Lord Bute, urged on by the Speaker of the House of Commons, a monk, and a Frenchman, aims a blunderbuss at an American backed by a British sailor. Britannia, blindfolded, stumbles into a pit while the "French Roman Catholick Town of Quebec" flourishes and the "English Protestant Town of Boston" burns.

The legislation closed the port of Boston, revoked the Massachusetts charter, and otherwise upended local institutions and customs. A military governor, Thomas Gage, replaced the much-hated royal civilian governor Thomas Hutchinson. The Quebec Act defined that province's institutions and place in the British Empire. The legislation protected the Catholic religion and allowed Catholics to take oaths to the empire without mentioning Protestantism or denouncing Roman Catholicism. This enfranchised French Canadians and allowed them to take part in government; put French civil law back in place and did away with trial by jury in some cases; joined much of the trans-Appalachian west to Quebec jurisdictionally; and made no allowance for an elected assembly like those that existed in the English-speaking colonies.[9]

All this seemed logical to the British ministry. Punish troublemakers; accommodate a local population's spiritual and ethnic differences. With the latter legislation, the imperial administration was trying to show cosmopolitan sensitivity in an empire becoming ever more sprawling and diverse. London administrators understandably believed they had to accommodate some portion of the existing social and spiritual order in their expanding domain in order to govern effectively. They could not afford to rule distant, and alien, provinces entirely by force, nor could they easily Anglicize them. But in Britain's North America provinces The Quebec Act spelled impending tyranny. The legislation established enough aspects of what British Americans understood as popish, arbitrary government for the colonists to believe that the empire would soon become a despotism. Provincial writers imaginatively melded the Intolerable acts and the Quebec Act together, portraying them as parts in one grand design to erode British liberty, seize private property, and corrupt Protestant souls.[10]

With that legislation, colonials turned (or more accurately returned) Protestant political discourse into a revolutionary ideology and began to use it to indict the ministry and the entire imperial structure. The claim that the London government had been compromised by a popish conspiracy initiated a cascading collapse that split the empire in a matter of months as the political beliefs that had held the empire together for a century began to tear it apart. The Protestant political idioms provided a historically legitimate logic for indicting the British government as popish at the core.

This made imperial governance impossible and open rebellion ever more likely. The Georgia assembly complained to the king that the Quebec Act had granted "little short of a full establishment, to a religion which is equally injurious to the rights of sovereign and of mankind." According to one Georgia minister, Parliament's efforts deprived colonists "of the enjoyment of their religion" and would lead to the establishment of "a hierarchy over them similar to that of the church of Rome in Canada." The South Carolina provincial congress denounced this act that denied

"English laws and a free government" to the people of Canada by restoring French legal practices. Connecticut gentleman Gurdon Saltonstall believed a Catholic-tainted conspiracy "was at the bottom of the Ministerial System" and accepted that an imperial rupture was becoming unavoidable. The act had become a dagger pointed at British Americans' spiritual and political hearts.[11]

By joining the trans-Appalachian interior administratively to the French-speaking colony, the London government seemed to colonials to reverse the great victory won in 1763 and threaten British Americans' future access to interior lands. South Carolina provincial congressmen complained bitterly that "the Roman Catholic Religion . . . and an absolute government are established in that province, and its limits extended . . . so as to border on the free Protestant English Settlements." They believed the act was designed to use "a whole people, differing in religious principles from the neighboring colonies, and subject to arbitrary power," to intimidate the English-speaking colonists into obedience.[12]

Young Alexander Hamilton argued that the Quebec Act and the linking of the western regions to Quebec administratively would lead to the establishment of arbitrary power and Catholicism in British America. The existing British-American colonies would be surrounded and their Protestant inhabitants at great risk. "How dangerous," he warned, "their situation would be, let every man of common-sense judge." Another New York writer summed up the long-term implications. An absolutist-minded London government had established the "Popish religion, as the national church, in the British dominions abroad [meaning Quebec], and will . . . in a few years establish the same at home." The western lands had become a "nursery of arbitrary power," which would ultimately spread its tentacles into the Protestant colonies.[13]

The belief that the home government had been corrupted led to adapting political rites that had until then supported imperial control. In 1774, new effigies were added to the Charleston, South Carolina, Pope's Day (November 5) procession that called into question the imperial order. Besides "the devil and the pope (effigies of which were traditionally carried through the streets), were exhibited the effigies of [British Prime Minister] Lord North, and that old traitor T[homas]. Hutchinson [last civilian royal governor of Massachusetts]" who they believed to be a ministerial minion. The mob burnt the effigies that evening, along with "a pamphlet with these words on the cover: 'Lord Dartmouth's pamphlet in justification of popery.'"[14]

Ominously, by early 1775 colonial writers began to implicate the king himself, and their views soon spread deep into the society. One North Carolina committeeman declared that George III "had established the Roman Catholick Religion in the Province of Quebeck." The king and Parliament intended "to establish Popery" throughout America. Another North Carolinian, a tavernkeeper, told all who would listen "that the King and Parliament had Established the Roman Catholick Religion in . . . Quebeck and did intend to bring in popish principles into America, and that the King had forfeited his Coronation Oath" by advancing this popish plot.[15]

The imperial contract cracked wide open as the belief that the king approved the offending acts spread. "What do you think," asked the South Carolinian Ralph Izard in a letter to his fellow Carolinian, the planter Edward Rutledge, "of the Boston Port Law—-the act for altering charters, juries &c. together with the Quebec law?" If, he continued on sarcastically, "the intentions of our most gracious sovereign are not clearly seen in these proceedings by every man in the British empire, the sight must be lost beyond the skill of any political occultist."[16] Many New Englanders believed that by signing the Quebec legislation, the monarch had violated his coronation oath and revealed his closeted Catholicism. A contemporary insisted that fear of popery led many New England families to send their children to the militias. "The common word then," a Connecticut man wrote, "was 'No King, No Popery.'" On receiving the news of Lexington and Concord, New York City committeeman and sometime crowd leader Isaac Low declared that George III had secretly converted to Catholicism. Low went on to say that the Stuart Pretender, Bonnie Prince Charlie, controlled the British ministry.[17]

For provincials, the monarch had bound the empire together symbolically and constitutionally. With the king corrupted, no power remained at the imperial core that might constitutionally halt the assault on liberty, property, and Protestantism. The spiritual-political logic of empire had birthed a historically legitimate rebellion. A British gentleman on board a warship in Boston Harbor explained to his brother at home how the monarch had come to be understood as a popish tyrant. Patriot leaders had implanted in people's minds that Parliament intended to establish "the Romish [Catholic religion]." This process had "begun in Canada" and the London ministry was determined to introduce Catholicism into every American colony. Many of what he called the country people claimed that George III had "turned Papist," and refused to warrant all evidence otherwise, citing the colonial newspapers' account of Catholic intrigue in Britain as evidence. With this perception, the empire began its astounding collapse, and within a year would be at war with itself.[18]

Seen this way, the relationship between the colonial past and the revolutionary crisis becomes more logically consistent with regard to the society's beliefs as a whole. This is not to claim that anti-popery caused the Revolution, nor that these ideological strands provided real answers to the myriad questions that faced a newly independent America. At the moment of crisis, though, the application of these idioms to imperial institutions and the London government's actions made a revolutionary alternative necessary. The empire's primary ideological structure had become cancerous in America. The empire there died of itself.

* * *

The power that Protestant political culture had over British Americans' worldview through the time of the Quebec Act creates a historical dilemma. How did secularized, enlightened, republicanism come to dominate the movement for independence so quickly after this spectacular outburst of anti-Catholicism and anti-popery? Or did it? Part of the answer is that scholars living in a secularized century too eagerly wrote off the empire's religiously charged political language, too readily celebrated the vaunted religious toleration that is one of the Revolution's grandest accomplishments as evidence of enlightened thinking, and overall too eagerly secularized the American Revolution. That upheaval was not a religious war, but those involved were intensely religious and had a Protestant political worldview.

For certain, by 1776 the Protestant political discourse being used in the nascent independent states had become diplomatically problematic. The urgent need for French military assistance became more apparent by the day as American forces suffered defeat after defeat in the disastrous fall of 1776. Necessity encouraged concerted efforts to silence those denouncing France, the Beast of Rome, and political popery. Writers sought to replace the older Protestant imperial rhetoric with enlightened proclamations of natural rights that would (it was believed) be more appealing to non-Britons. The empire's virulent anti-Catholic language would not do as Americans appealed first to Quebec's French-speaking Catholic population to join them in rebellion and shortly thereafter to the French monarchy itself for military and diplomatic aid.

The efforts to curtail public expression of anti-Catholicism and Francophobia are historically visible. George Washington issued a decree to the militia army besieging Boston in November 1775 warning against celebrations of Pope's Day (Guy Fawkes). Washington could not "help expressing his surprise" that some officers and men should be "so void of common sense as not to see the impropriety of such a step at this juncture." How could they be blowing up effigies of popes when "we are soliciting, . . . the friendship and alliance of the [Catholic and French-speaking] people of Canada, whom we ought to consider as brethren embarked in the same cause." To denigrate "their religion is so monstrous as not to be suffered or excused."[19]

Washington's proclamation was part of a concerted effort by revolutionary leaders to suppress their political culture's overt anti-popery and to portray the American cause as an enlightened one. Richard Montgomery and Benedict Arnold, two of the key American leaders of the assault into Canada in 1775, issued proclamations in support of universal religious toleration. The American commissioners sent to negotiate an alliance or union with Canada in 1775 and 1776 continued these efforts. They carried a declaration announcing, "we held sacred the rights of conscience, and should promise to the whole people . . . in the name of Congress, the free and undisturbed exercise of their religion." Of course, with an uninvited, Protestant, English-speaking army from the south on their soil, the Canadians showed little inclination to believe such statements. British officers fanned Quebeckers' doubts by reminding the population of the colonists' anti-Catholic responses to the Quebec Act just a year before.[20]

Hopes that French-speaking Canada would join them and that the French would sign an alliance led American leaders to suppress anti-popery and anti-Catholicism. And yet the reality of an alliance with the ancient enemy brought those feelings forcefully back into public life. After the Battle of Saratoga in 1777, America gained an ally against Great Britain, and in the process declared war against Anglophone history. In that strange geopolitical context, even the word Christian became a provocation to a population who still believed themselves a Protestant people.

In October 1778, one of the Revolution's most insightful chroniclers, Mercy Otis Warren, described to John Adams an astounding sight. "The squadrons of the House of Bourbon," she wrote, were "riding in the port of Boston and displaying the ensigns of harmony beside the Columbian shores." Their astonishing presence gave evidence of Britain's folly. As there had "not yet been time to prove the sincerity of either party—I think most of the officers who remember the late war, when we hugged ourselves in the Protection of Britain, look as if they wished, rather than believed" that the Franco-American alliance would hold. French officers, "half doubting our disinterested friendship," remained aloof and tentative. Only the younger generation, with no memories of the imperial wars, "extend their arms to embrace their new allies, an honest joy dances in their eye and every feature displays the wish of mutual confidence."[21]

There is indeed no grander historical disjuncture than to find ultra-Protestant Americans engaged in "Gen. rejoicing for the good news" of an alliance with Louis XIV's descendent, and welcoming French armies on American soil and French fleets into American ports.[22] The hope that Bourbon princes would protect American shores shaped political language then, and continues to guide, and distort, our understanding of the period now. Far from being universally accepted, the French alliance revealed deep anxieties within the American political community rooted in an anti-popish, Francophobic worldview shaped by Protestant political culture.

From the moment the war began, a foreign alliance seemed essential to many Americans. But even those who acknowledged that desired an alliance on very controlled terms. In Virginia, freeholders of Buckingham County expressed a widely held view when they urged their delegates to the state constitutional convention of 1776 to "beware of any other than commercial alliances with foreigners, and to keep their armies off your shores, if possible." While the need for French guns and gold was well understood, the traditional suspicion of what the Virginian Landon Carter called "the notorious Aims in France for universal monarchy" remained strong in 1776. The Pennsylvanian John Dickinson, famously opposed to independence in 1776, warned the Second Continental Congress that summer that France might use the crisis to regain Canada in order to control an independent America.[23]

Initially, the alliance failed miserably to live up to its advocates' hopes and more than realized skeptics' views. A Franco-American assault against British-occupied Newport, Rhode Island, in August 1778 turned into a minor disaster when a storm forced the French fleet to withdraw before they could either land troops or engage British warships. Left without naval support, the American troops retreated, and finger-pointing quickly broke out between the new allies. New Englander John Sullivan, who commanded the American forces, joined others in accusing the French of a lack of fortitude in prosecuting the campaign.[24]

The failure of Franco-American forces encouraged a revival of Protestant Americans' ancient fears about the Gallic power's true intentions, which had begun even before the debacle in Rhode Island. The American leadership expressed fears about French geopolitical designs on territory in North America. In a revealing private letter written shortly after the failed Rhode Island assault, George Washington asked the president of Congress, South Carolinian Henry Laurens, for absolute secrecy as he discussed "a point of the most delicate and important nature." French officers had proposed an expedition to capture Canada. Washington feared that the French, animated by "ties of blood, habits, manners, religion, and former connection" to the inhabitants of Quebec, would seize the province. The new United States would then be faced with the same situation that existed before 1763, "with Spain. . . . possessed of New Orleans, on our right, [French] Canada on our left, and seconded by numerous Tribes of Indians on our rear." France would be able "to give Law to these States." Washington believed this must be avoided at all costs. Washington expressed widely held fears. The Rhode Island campaign's failure resurrected fears about the "real" French intentions in the war. For many raised in the imperial period, France remained a rapacious power tainted by political popery in many minds.[25]

Perhaps the most surprising thoughts in Washington's letter to Henry Laurens concerned imperial reunion with the mother country. Washington told Laurens that if the French, joined by Catholic Spain, should begin to prevail at sea as well as by land and try to extend their domination to North America, "a reunion with England would avail very little." The British, "without men, without money, and inferior on her favorite element could give no effectual aid to oppose them." Washington knew, in a way that others could not admit to themselves or to others in public, that the French acted in the war entirely in their own interest. He even doubted his erstwhile protégé Marquis de Lafayette, who had suggested the French-led Canadian invasion to the commander-in-chief. Washington's words do not suggest the desire for imperial rapprochement as much as a shrewd understanding of geopolitics that demanded at least the possibility of reunion should the situation of international power turn against the American cause.[26]

Other American leaders shared Washington's position. The Franco-American alliance, John Jay realized, carried tremendous risks and emotional ambiguity. The alliance was a declaration of war against American society's imperial and spiritual past. "What the French treaty may be," he wrote, "I know not." If Great Britain "would acknowledge our independence, and enter into a liberal alliance with us, I should prefer a connexion with her to a league with any power on earth." He suspected, or perhaps hoped, that the British peace commissioners sent to the colonies in 1778 in response to the spread of the war to Europe would have the power to establish just such a peace and a firm alliance. He rejected a return to the empire vehemently, "but . . . I would give then advantageous commercial terms," much as the treaty that bears his name did in the mid-1790s. Jay continued that England's destruction "would hurt me . . . it afforded my [French Protestant] ancestors an asylum from persecution" after the Revocation of the Edict of Nantes expelled Protestants from Louis XIV's realm in 1685. Jay's views were not in essence much different from those of the North Carolinians who voiced their fears of popery and the French in 1777.[27]

In the difficult years between 1776 and the Yorktown victory, a spectrum of opinion about America's geopolitical future emerged. On the far end of the spectrum would be those like the Connecticut-born diplomat Silas Deane, whose personal bitterness at perceived and real mistreatment by the Continental Congress combined with his profound fear of French intentions to create a persona that seemed to be flirting with treason as he warned incessantly about the French pursuit of their own self-interest in the Franco-American alliance. From there the spectrum moved through those like Jay and Hamilton who loved Britain even as they sought independence; to those like Washington who realized that the geopolitical situation could change and reunion with Britain might become a necessary option; through to the likes of Patrick Henry and later Jefferson, who not only embraced the French alliance but admired French culture.

While many welcomed the French alliance, they also knew they were in league with the ancient enemy and at war with a Protestant people whose language and history they shared. This strange context helps explain why popular fears about the alliance continued to be expressed in a political-religious language very closely related to that used in the prerevolutionary empire. And it helps make comprehensible one of the revolutionary period's strangest (to modern eyes) ideological outbursts, the denunciations of the use of the inclusive term "Christian" in the debates over the Massachusetts constitutions of 1778 and 1779.

* * *

As state governments assumed authority under popular auspices in 1776 and 1777, many citizens and officials alike sought to make it clear that by government by the people they meant *Protestant* people. In their thinking, polities had a spiritual as well as institutional character that made them either free or unfree, balanced or absolute. Protestant states were free and their institutional powers somehow balanced. Examining the swirling debates around the creation of new state governments that raged in America between 1775 and 1780 reveals repeated calls for the creation of specifically Protestant polities. At times, the debates seemed to express resistance to the French alliance, and resistance to efforts to suppress anti Catholic and Francophobic rhetoric. Past norms would not die; they were indeed the very reason a revolution was necessary.

The tendency to demand a Protestant polity manifested in every region. Mecklenburg, North Carolina, yeomen instructed their delegates to the North Carolina state constitutional convention to push for formal exclusion of Catholics from all government posts. New Jersey's initial draft state constitution, calling for full civil rights for "all people professing a belief in God and our Lord Jesus Christ," was denounced by delegates who demanded it be rewritten: the wording would have included Catholics in the body politic. The draft probably had been written by Gloucester County Quaker John Cooper, who may well have been thinking of Quakers in using this wording; Friends had often faced political problems caused by their theologically based refusal to take oaths of allegiance. When the constitution that finally went into effect, New Jersey self-consciously restricted offices to Protestants.[28]

Even after years of war and the reality of the French alliance, received Protestant frameworks retained their power over the population. In Massachusetts, controversies erupted during state constitutional conventions in 1778 and then around a second convention in 1779–80. When conventioneers solicited responses to their constitutional drafts from all the towns and counties in the commonwealth, the inhabitants responded with specifically Protestant revolutionary expectations. The framers' effort to restrict office-holding to "Christians" provoked an outpouring of hostility. Townsmen from all parts of Massachusetts objected "to the Words Christian Religion" because it would have allowed "a Roman Catholic to be the first Magistrate in this State." Objections to the use of "Christian" ranged wide. There were those who wanted to make sure the Bay State's highest offices remained Catholic-free, those who wanted to make sure no papists became officials on any level, yet others who wanted Catholics effectively excluded from society, and those who wanted to create a specifically Protestant commonwealth. The preservation of a "free Government" demanded that the language be restructured and the term stricken. The new frame of government should at the very least ensure "that no Papist" should hold a judicial office or be elect to the legislature. Belchertown yeomen went further still, desiring that no man should hold *any* office "unless he be of the Protestant Religion," effectively proscribing Catholics from public life.[29]

As the Belchertown return suggests, it was not just fear of Catholics that shaped the reactions to the term "Christian" in the state constitution. Rather, it was their self-perception, the belief that Bay Staters "are a Protestant People," as the town of Colrain so forcefully put it. The Essex County convention, in its evaluation of the 1778 state's constitution, sought to explain its dissatisfaction by advocating for a different kind of constitution. The Essex scribes declared that when the people of Geneva in Switzerland, "perhaps the most virtuous republicans now existing," sought to create a political-religious order, "they called the celebrated Calvin to their assistance," to act as their guide and lawgiver.[30] Calvin as theologian, Calvin as lawgiver—in Essex County, Massachusetts, the distinction between the two roles blurred in the minds of those who sought to retain their traditional culture even as they stripped it of imperial meanings and tried to resituate it in a world made republican.

Many others shared this understanding of themselves as a specifically Protestant people whose revolution would lead to a Protestant polity. Berkshire County yeomen objected to the idea that a "Christian" might be governor because "it is a Community of Protestants that are Covenanting and emerging from a State of Nature . . . all executive Legislative Judicial and Military officers shall be of the Protestant Christian religion." These people believed that a stable social contract depended on their Protestantism, and they found the term Christian . . . too catholic.[31] The freemen in Dunstable, Middlesex County, seemed to hold even more militant views. They expressed their objections to the constitution's third article in the bill of rights because it seemed to open the door for a Catholic presence in the Bay State. The provision that "every denomination of Christian Demening them selves peasablely and as good subjects of the Common wealth shall be Equelly under the Protection of the law" seemed to them a dangerous innovation. The townspeople believed these sentences provided "full Protection to the Idalatrous worshippers of the Church of Rome." The state should not, they insisted, "give so much Incoragement to Idol worship as to Engage any full protection in their Idolatry for if the government should not Disturbe such in their pretended worship" it would be as much as they could reasonable expect.[32]

The particularly unhappy people of Dunstable believed the 1780 constitution failed to guard sufficiently against heresy generally. The sixteenth article of the bill of rights concerning a free press was objected to "as there being no restraint thereon it may be made use of to the Dishonor of God by printing herasy." The state's loyalty oath needed to be amended to "have the words by the living God added as is

Required in his word." They then went on to complain about another traditional enemy of the Bay State's Congregational order, the "the Denomination . . . Called Quakers" who the document allowed to be "admitted to office. . . . without taking the oath in manner and form as Required of others." Seen from Dunstable the document needed to be restructured to reflect the values found in their Protestant political culture and the state's Congregational establishment.[33]

The conceptual link of the American Revolution to the defense of European Protestantism intensified these townsmen's fears about the use of the term "Christian." Hampshire County yeomen thought that the use of the term in the 1780 constitution was unacceptable because of the possibility it created of a Catholic governor threatened "the preservation of a free Government and security of the Protestant Cause." The people of Williamsburg in the same county believed that the new commonwealth should follow "the Example . . . of All Protestant reformed Nations" in its political practices. As in the imperial period, these new Americans believed liberty and Protestantism were linked, and saw the continuation of both in the commonwealth as essential to the broader survival of their civil and religious rights.[34]

Constitutional architects in New Hampshire as well as Massachusetts knew that they lived in societies in which the fear of Catholics and political popery continued to run deep. Hoping to temper the anxieties produced by the French alliance, the authors of the proposed New Hampshire constitution of 1778–79 carefully delineated that not only elected officials but all *voters* should profess "the Protestant religion," as well as being of age, male, and paying taxes, effectively proscribing Catholics from politics. In the end, the state's yeomen rejected the constitution. Unease about the Franco-American alliance certainly encouraged this rejection. If the French reestablished themselves in Canada, New Hampshire would again be exposed to attack by French and Native American forces. This was sufficient reason to reject a new governing instrument that seemed too soft on the French presence in America. No friendly words about their French allies could change these anti-Catholic and Francophobic feelings.[35]

The American leadership realized the historical-political problems the French alliance created. These leaders also knew that without French help—guns, gold, ships, and troops—the war could well be lost. Thus, one official after another took up the pen to justify the ties to France in light of the Revolution's core values, and, paradoxically, the society's religious values as well. The concept of providential intervention helped these spokesmen explain how a Protestant God came to use a Catholic king for His holy aims. Massachusetts minister Samuel Cooper, himself a strong advocate of America as a new Protestant Israel, was aware of the alliance's problematic nature for Massachusetts's yeomen. Yet he also realized the necessity of French assistance and wrote to legitimate it. "France," he declared in his sermon celebrating the Massachusetts constitution of 1780, "tho' a monarchy, has been the nurse and protectress of free republics" for a long time. The Swiss, Cooper continued, "can attest to this . . . that during an alliance with France of more than three Hundred years, their liberties have been constantly befriended by that nation, and every part of the treaty for their support punctually performed." He went on to ask God to bless the kings of France and Spain, and give their arms success in the war they were engaged in.[36]

Such declarations, of course, flew in the face of everything Anglo-Americans had believed about the French before the war. These efforts at intellectual mediation are significant in and of themselves as they complicated the relationship between past and present, as well as between church and state, in revolutionary America. And they suggest why it has been difficult to see and understand this strain of thought historically. Those who created official records and much of the print culture understood the necessity of the French alliance, and their efforts masked the degree of suspicion present in the wider society about the French and popery.[37]

The outburst against the term "Christian" in constitutional debate and fears about the French alliance speak to a more ideologically complex Revolution than we have been comfortable with. And, when placed in the broader context of the by then fractured English-speaking world, a startling convergence emerges historically. By 1780, despite the opposition of leadership elements, the French alliance and the continuation of the war caused the imperial ideological substructure based in anti-popery and Franco-phobia to reassert itself simultaneously in all the politically fractured Anglophone political communities. What had supported the empire before the Revolution reemerged, even as its once united political communities remained locked in bloody warfare with each other.

The American alliance with France and the eruption of world war in 1778 went off like an ideological bomb in the Anglophone Atlantic. With that unlikely union, the first British Empire's history, ritual cycle, and political logic had been more thoroughly repudiated than it was on July 4, 1776. In all three primary political communities—American patriot, British-American loyalist, and in Britain itself—the French alliance exposed the persistence of Protestant political culture's interpretive frameworks. The common root stock of anti-popery, anti-Catholicism, and Francophobia inherited from the past remained politically alive, though used to very different ends in the distinctive communities.

The French alliance fundamentally altered loyalism's ideological tone. Early loyalist publications had celebrated the virtues of Britain and British liberties, and celebrated the king's military strength as well as his mercy for and love of his unruly subjects. Imperial fidelity had never made British-American loyalism ideologically static, however, and the French intervention brought a sudden shift in Loyalist writings toward anti-French, anti-popish political discourse. The *Pennsylvania Ledger*, a Loyalist paper published in Philadelphia during the British occupation of 1777–78, demonstrates this change. The paper scoffed at the French renunciation of its claims to Canada, and denounced the Continental Congress for rejecting "all possible offers of accommodation with Great Britain," a reference to the peace commissioners already preparing to depart for America in the spring of 1778. The writer claimed that this dismissal alarmed Americans, "who must be supposed to prefer a re-union with the Mother Country" than a risky intimacy with the ancient enemy.

These thoughts were startlingly close to those Washington expressed to Laurens in his November 1778 letter. They speak to the convergence of understanding brought on by the alliance. The Philadelphia writer accused the French, those unchangeable "enemies of the reformation," of trying to reestablish Catholicism throughout the western world. It was not an overt goal, as the writer admitted. France had improved its methods since the days of the "Saint Barthelmi massacres." The goal was now political popery as much as spiritual enslavement. In Loyalist eyes, the French alliance meant the American cause had married itself to a popish Bourbon tyranny. Shortly after switching sides in 1780, Benedict Arnold justified his betrayal of the American cause by invoking his disgust with an alliance with "the enemy of the Protestant faith" in his only public writing about his treason.[38]

In Britain, the Franco-American alliance led, indirectly, to a series of violent attacks that culminated in the Gordon Riots, an anti-Catholic, anti-popish, anti-French pogrom that held London in its grip for over a week in June 1780. Manpower shortages in the British armed forces, fear that Irish Catholics would follow the rebellious example of American Protestants, and the need to unify the British Isles in the face of renewed war with France led to the Catholic Relief Act of 1778. The act allowed Catholics to own property, encouraged an end to religious persecution, and permitted Irish Catholics to join the British Army without taking the traditional oath that demanded the recruit be opposed to the Bishop of Rome. Like the Quebec Act, the Relief Act reflected a period of liberalization of attitudes toward Catholics by the British leadership. George III, the first British-born Hanoverian king, believed himself an enlightened ruler who would bring in a new age of benevolence to a diverse and far-flung empire. Given, though, the international context and the traditional fears about Catholics and popery, it is little surprise that this further demonstration of enlightened sensitivity would be met with resistance, though it seems unlikely that anyone fully anticipated what happened.

The Relief Act led directly to a series of anti-Catholic outbursts that culminated in the infamous Gordon Riots. Unrest broke out in the streets in late 1778. In February 1779 Protestant mobs in Scotland attacked Catholics and Catholic chapels in Perth and Edinburgh. This unrest was connected to the rise of the Protestant Association,

"Freedom, Peace, Plenty," *Universal Magazine*, frontispiece, 1780. (Courtesy of the John Carter Brown Library at Brown University)

The poem laments that "Brittannia's Children" have forsaken the blessings of freedom to become "dupes to France." The "absurd" willingness of members of Congress to make "Popish Leagues" proves they are really "tyrants" who will "scourge the land."

a voluntary organization designed to protect the realm from popish infiltration. Its leader, Lord George Gordon, charged alternatively that Catholic army recruits would mutiny and join with the French, or that Catholics controlled elements in the British ministry.[39] In May 1780 the Protestant Association petitioned the House of Commons to repeal the Relief Act, a request the House promptly rejected. In the turmoil that followed, mobs destroyed Catholic chapels used by foreign embassies, sacked the homes of Relief Act supporters, destroyed Catholic-owned businesses, and assaulted several major prisons and government buildings. The mob, as Horace Walpole recounted in his diary, "extorted money from several persons and houses, on threats of burning them as Catholics." The government eventually quelled the disturbances with troops. Hundreds died, and the authorities hanged a number of rioters.[40]

While this brief account reveals nothing unknown about the Gordon Riots, when they are placed in the context of the entire English-speaking world in 1780, the unrest suggests that the ideological core created in the period 1688–1774 remained a potent political force across what had been the empire. The Franco-American alliance provoked the holders of that ideology into a series of anti-Catholic and

Sawneys Defence against the Beast, Whore, Pope, and Devil, etc., engraving, 1779. (© The Trustees of the British Museum; all rights reserved)

John Bull, symbol of the English people, lies prostrate and shackled. Only Sawney, an English nickname for ignorant Highlanders, can protect Britain's "Protestant Church and King" from the diabolical coalition of bishop, pope, and Lord North together with the Whore of Babylon and Beast from Revelations.

anti-French outbursts on both sides of the Atlantic. From challenging word usage in the new American state constitutions to murderous rioting in London's streets by a population fearing a French invasion and disgusted with a leadership that had seemingly become popish, the imperial culture of anti-Catholicism and anti-popery made itself felt.

The American Revolution placed a militantly Protestant people with a deep fear of France and the Church of Rome in alliance with Bourbon France and eventually Bourbon Spain as well. This historically shocking alteration reverberated through the entire Anglophone world. Americans, raised as they were to associate Protestantism with the assurance of liberty and property, feared the implications of their own greatest diplomatic triumph. It put them at war not only with Protestant Great Britain, but also with their own past and historical identity, as Loyalists and British commentators repeatedly pointed out to them. Britain's desperate embrace of Catholic toleration to defend the Protestant empire alienated those whose patriotism was rooted in the prerevolutionary, anti-popish consensus. The Protestant idioms did not have one political expression amid revolution and war, nor were they confined to any one political community. Rather, they remained current in all political communities, their continued usage indicative of their underlying power.

In signing an alliance with the French, American leaders repudiated ancient Protestant liberty. Anti-popery's reorientation in this period suggests that ideological developments were neither linear nor strictly whiggish; rather, war and revolution distorted received frameworks, which reemerged forcefully in different contexts at the end of the 1770s. However, the ideological positions associated with the old empire that reappeared in response to the French alliance were neither strong enough nor uniform enough across the fractured Anglophone political communities to reestablish the old empire. Too much blood had been spilled, and the former colonies had gone too deeply into a republican world, for fear of popery and the French to produce an imperial reconciliation.

Understanding the anti-Catholic and anti-popish outbursts of the late 1770s simply as the dying gasp of a failed belief system, though, is in error. Rather, these episodes should be seen as part of a longer process of change in the relationship of Protestant spirituality to the political. In America, that process did not reach its culmination until the 1830s, when a new church establishment, general and rhetorical rather than denominational and specific, was integrated into the emerging democratic order. Anti-popery and anti-Catholicism remained potent strains within America political culture well into the twentieth century. The American leaders who made a deal with the devil won independence but lost a history, helping to give the new order an antihistorical orientation that has masked the roots of beliefs and practices that have shaped behavior throughout the American past.

Notes

1. Deposition of Nathan Hallaway, 4th of July 1777, Oyer & Terminer Edenton District, September 1777, Edenton District Records of the Superior Court, 1774–1779, North Carolina State Archives; Deposition of David Taylor, 4th June 1777, Oyer & Terminer Edenton District, September 1777, Edenton District Records of the Superior Court, 1774–1779, North Carolina State Archives; Deposition of Joseph Taylor, 4th June 1777, Oyer & Terminer Edenton District, September 1777, Edenton District Records of the Superior Court, 1774–1779, North Carolina State Archives.
2. Suggestive and contrary to this tendency is Francis D. Cogliano, *No King, No Popery: Anti-Catholicism in Revolutionary New England* (Westport, CT: Greenwood, 1995), the first major study to take the rhetoric of anti-popery in revolutionary America seriously. Mary Ray's earlier study, *American Opinion of Roman Catholicism in the Eighteenth Century* (New York: Columbia University Press, 1936), began this process, although it receives scant attention today. The closest anyone has come to giving fear of popery causal primacy in bringing on the revolutionary crisis is Stephen J. Stein, "An Apocalyptic Rationale for the American Revolution," *Early American Literature* 9 (Winter 1975): 211–25. More recently, Vernon P. Creviston, writing in "'No King Unless It Be a Constitutional King': Rethinking the Place of the Quebec Act in the Coming of the American Revolution," *Historian* 73 no. 3 (2011): 463–79, has emphasized the importance of the Quebec Act in bringing the empire down. Other important and suggestive work in this vein includes Nathan O. Hatch, *The Sacred Cause of Liberty* (New Haven, CT: Yale University Press, 1977); Ruth Bloch, *Visionary Republic: Millennial Themes in American Thought, 1756–1800* (Cambridge: Cambridge University Press, 1988); Stephen A. Marini, *Radical Sects of Revolutionary New England* (Lincoln, NE: iUniverse, 1999); Thomas Kidd, *God of Liberty: A Religious History of the American Revolution* (New York: Basic Books, 2010).
3. Such an approach of course opposes the views put forth by Bernard Bailyn, *Ideological Origins of the American Revolution* (Cambridge, MA: Belknap Press of Harvard University Press, 1992).
4. For a discussion of the connections between Francophobia and anti-Catholicism generally, see Thomas S. Kidd, "Recovering 'The French Convert': Views of the French and the Uses of Anti-Catholicism in Early America," *Book History* 7 (2004): 97–111.
5. Brendan McConville, *The King's Three Faces: The Rise and Fall of Royal America* (Chapel Hill: University of North Carolina Press, 2006), examines this culture at length, 1–2, 56–63, 272–73, 301–2.
6. *The New York Journal; or, The General Advertiser,* February 2, 1775, Supplement page 1.
7. Joseph Emerson, *A Thanksgiving-Sermon Preach'd at Pepperrell, July 24th, 1766* . . . (Boston, 1766); Jonathan Mayhew, *[The Snare Broken], a Thanksgiving-Discourse Preached at the Desire of the West Church in Boston* . . . (Boston, 1766), 9; both are cited in McConville, *The King's Three Faces,* 261, 264.
8. Charles Francis Adams, ed., *The Works of John Adams, Second President of the United States: With a Life of the Author, Notes and Illustrations, by his Grandson, Charles Francis Adams,* 10 vols. (Boston, 1850), 2:252.

9. Creviston, "'No King Unless It Be a Constitutional King,'" 463–79; Cogliano, *No King, No Popery;* Charles H. Metzger, *The Quebec Act: A Primary Cause of the American Revolution* (New York: United States Catholic Historical Society, 1936), 204–5; Reginald Coupland, *The Quebec Act: A Study in Statesmanship* (Oxford: Clarendon Press, 1968); Philip Lawson, *The Imperial Challenge: Quebec and Britain in the Age of the American Revolution* (Montreal-Kingston: McGill-Queen's University Press, 1989); Victor Coffin, "The Province of Quebec and the Early American Revolution: A Study in English-American Colonial History," *Bulletin of the University of Wisconsin: Economics, Political Science, and History* ser. 1 (1896): 275–562; George M. Wrong, *Canada and the American Revolution: The Disruption of the First British Empire* (New York: Cooper Square Publishers, 1968), 257–58; Charles Hanson, *Necessary Virtue: The Pragmatic Origins of Religious Liberty in New England* (Charlottesville: University of Virginia Press, 1998), 11–12; Stein, "Apocalyptic Rationale," 211–25.
10. See Thomas Bernard, *An Appeal to the Public, Stating and Considering the Objections to the Quebec Bill* (London, 1774); Creviston, "'No King Unless It Be a Constitutional King,'" lays out the central issues.
11. "July 14, 1775 Georgia Assembly Petition to King George III," in *Georgia and the Revolution*, ed. Ronald G. Killion and Charles T. Waller (Atlanta: Cherokee Publishing Co., 1975), 152–53; John J. Zubly, D.D., *The Law Liberty. Sermon on American Affairs, preached at the opening of the Provincial Congress of Georgia. Addressed to the Right Honourable the Earl of Dartmouth. With an appendix, giving a concise account of the Struggles of Swisserland* [sic] *to Recover their liberty* (Philadelphia, 1775), vi; *South Carolina. In a Congress, begun and holden at Charles-Town, on Wednesday the first day of November one thousand seven hundred and seventy five, and continued, by divers adjournments, to Tuesday the twenty-six day of March, one thousand seven hundred and seventy six. A constitution or form of government, agreed to, and resolved upon, by the representatives of South Carolina* (Charles-Town, SC, 1776), 1–2; *Collections of the New-York Historical Society for the Year 1886* (Silas Deane Papers) (New York, 1887), 4.
12. *South Carolina. In a Congress, begun and holden at Charles-Town, on Wednesday the first day of November. . . ,* 1–2.
13. Richard B. Vernier, ed., *The Revolutionary Writings of Alexander Hamilton* (Indianapolis: Liberty Fund, 2008), 141, 151; *New York Journal; or, The General Advertiser,* October 13, 1774, Supplement page 2. George Washington and numerous members of the Virginia, New York, and Pennsylvania elite speculated in these western lands, and Benjamin Franklin and his soon-to-be Loyalist son William hoped to. The dreams of interior lands had now seemingly been crushed in one arbitrary move by a London focused on establishing popery, Nicholas B. Wainwright, *George Croghan, Wilderness Diplomat* (Chapel Hill: University of North Carolina Press, 1959), 296; for the best work on colonial interest in western lands and its implications for the revolutionary generation, see Marc Egnal, *A Mighty Empire: The Origins of the American Revolution* (Ithaca, NY: Cornell University Press, 2010). Also relevant is Colin G. Calloway, *The Scratch of a Pen: 1763 and the Transformation of North America* (Oxford: Oxford University Press, 2006).
14. *The New York Journal; or, The General Advertiser,* December 1, 1774, Supplement pages 1–2.
15. William L. Saunders, ed., *The Colonial Records of North Carolina,* Vol. 10, 1775–1776 (Raleigh, 1890), 126–27.
16. *Correspondence of Mr. Ralph Izard of South Carolina, From the Year 1774 to 1804; With a Short Memoir* (New York, 1844), 2, 28.
17. Martin I. J. Griffin, *Catholics and the American Revolution,* 3 vols. (Ridley Park, PA, 1907–11), 1:34–35; Thomas Jones, *History of New York during the Revolutionary War, and of the Leading Events in the Other Colonies at That Period,* 2 vols. (New York, 1879), 1:43.

18. Margaret Wheeler Willard, ed., *Letters on the American Revolution, 1774–1776* (Boston: Houghton Mifflin, 1925), 67.
19. Quoted in William Byrne, *History of the Catholic Church in the New England States* (Boston, 1899), 4.
20. J. Thomas Scharf, *History of Maryland from the Earliest Period to the Present Day* (Hatboro, PA: Tradition Press, 1967), 221–22; Jones, *History of New York during the Revolutionary War*, 1:92. Jones comments on the hypocrisy of Congress in denouncing the Quebec Act and then trying to enlist the Canadians in the rebellion. For a complete account of the way in which the efforts to bring Canada into the cause altered anti-popery's use in the colonies, see Amy Noel Ellison, "'Reverse of Fortune': The Invasion of Canada and the Coming of American Independence, 1774–1776" (PhD diss., Boston University, 2016).
21. Mercy Otis Warren to John Adams, Plymouth, October 15, 1778, Mercy Otis Warren Papers, microfilm, reel 1, Massachusetts Historical Society.
22. Caleb Gibbs Diary, April 6, 1778, American Antiquarian Society, Worcester, MA.
23. "Instructions of Buckingham County Freeholders to Delegates Charles Patterson and John Cabell," in *Revolutionary Virginia: The Road to Independence*, Vol. 7, pt. 1, *Independence and the Fifth Convention, 1776, A Documentary Record*, ed. Brent Tarter and Robert L. Scribner (Charlottesville: University of Virginia Press, 1983), 112; Jack P. Greene, *The Diary of Colonel Landon Carter of Sabine Hill, 1752–1778*, 2 vols. (Charlottesville: University of Virginia Press, 1965), 2:1032; David L. Jacobson, *John Dickinson and the Revolution in Pennsylvania, 1764–1776* (Berkeley: University of California Press, 1965), 113–14.
24. Piers Mackesy, *The War for America, 1775–1783* (Cambridge, MA: Harvard University Press, 1964), 218–19.
25. "To His Excellency Henry Laurens, Esq., Pres. of Congress, Fredricksburgh, Nov. 14th, 1778," George Washington Papers at the Library of Congress, 1741–1799, Series 3, Varick Transcripts, 184–188, George Washington Papers online, https://www.loc.gov/collections/george-washington-papers/?fa=partof:george+washington+papers:+series+3,+varick+transcripts,+1775-1785.
26. "To His Excellency Henry Laurens, Esq."
27. John Jay to Gouverneur Morris, Albany, April 19, 1778, in *The Correspondence and Public Papers of John Jay*, ed. Henry P. Johnston, A.M., 4 vols. (New York, 1890), 1:179–80.
28. Earle H. Ketcham, "The Sources of the North Carolina Constitution," *North Carolina Historical Review* 6, no. 3, (1929): 233; Irwin N. Gertzog, "The Author of New Jersey's 1776 Constitution," *New Jersey History* 110, no. 3–4 (1992): 8–9, 18. For the debate over related issues in New York, see E. Wilder Spaulding, "The State Government under the First Constitution," in *History of the State of New York*, Vol. 4, *The New State*, ed. Alexander C. Flick (New York, 1933), 158. John Jay attempted to effectively proscribe Catholics if they did not deny the spiritual and political authority of the pope. This failed, largely due to the diplomatic situation in 1777.
29. Oscar and Mary Handlin, eds., *The Popular Sources of Political Authority: Documents on the Massachusetts Constitution of 1780* (Cambridge, MA: Belknap Press of Harvard University Press, 1966), 561, 539. For accounts of the issues around the Massachusetts constitution of 1780, see Leonard L. Richards, *Shays's Rebellion: The American Revolution's Final Battle* (Philadelphia: University of Pennsylvania Press, 2003), 1–42; and Stephen E. Patterson, *Political Parties in Revolutionary Massachusetts* (Madison: University of Wisconsin Press, 1973).
30. Handlin and Handlin. eds., *Massachusetts Constitution*, 328–329.
31. Ibid., 491.
32. Ibid., 640–41.

33. Ibid.
34. Handlin and Handlin, eds., *Massachusetts Constitution*, 561, 625. For a study of eighteenth-century New Englanders' perception of their link to the Protestant Interest, see Thomas Kidd, *The Protestant Interest: New England after Puritanism* (New Haven, CT: Yale University Press, 2004).
35. John N. McClintock, *History of New Hampshire* (Boston, 1888), 402.
36. Samuel Cooper, *Sermon Preached before His Excellency John Hancock, Esq., the Honourable the Senate, and House of Representatives of the Commonwealth of Massachusetts, October 25, 1780, Being the Day of the Commencement of the Constitution and INAUGURATION on the New Government* (Boston, 1780), 42–43, 46.
37. For a study of eighteenth-century New Englanders' perception of their link to the Protestant Interest, see Kidd, *The Protestant Interest*.
38. *Pennsylvania Ledger*, published as *The Pennsylvania Ledger; or, The Philadelphia Market-Day Advertiser*, May 13, 1778, 3; Benedict Arnold, *To the Inhabitants of America. . . .* (New York, 1780). Arnold's use of the alias "Monck" references George Monck, a Cromwellian officer whose northern army enabled the Charles II's restoration to the English and Scottish thrones in 1660 at the end of the Interregnum.
39. There may well have been significant unease in the home islands about Catholic infiltration at the time of the Quebec Act, and it may have persisted, forming the substructure of the Protestant Association.
40. Christopher Hibbert, *King Mob: The Story of Lord George Gordon and the Riots of 1780* (1958; rpt. Stroud: Sutton, 2004); Peter Whiteley, *Lord North: The Prime Minister Who Lost America* (London: Hambledon Press, 1996), 185–86; H. M. Scott, *British Foreign Policy in the Age of the American Revolution* (Oxford: Oxford University Press, 1990), 294, 310; John Nicholson, *The Great Liberty Riot of 1789* (London: BM Bozo, 1985); A. Francis Steuart, ed., *The Last Journals of Horace Walpole during the Reign of George III from 1771–1783 with Notes by Dr. Doran* (London, 1910), 310. I am very grateful to Brad Jones for his comments in regard to the Gordon Riots. His work has focused on the unrest in other parts of Britain as well in the runup to these riots.

Tolerating Protestants

ANTI-POPERY, ANTI-PURITANISM, AND RELIGIOUS TOLERATION IN BRITAIN, 1776–1829

Peter W. Walker

THE GLORIOUS REVOLUTION, SIR John Nicholl declared in 1812, "taught our ancestors . . . that popery, on the one hand, and puritanism, on the other, were not very congenial with civil and religious liberty." Now, as MPs debated Irish Catholic demands for emancipation, Nicholl insisted that these lessons "should not be effaced from our recollection."[1] Nicholl's speech raises several interesting questions. First: for how long did anti-popery remain central to religious, political, and intellectual life in Britain? Nicholl's rhetoric will ring familiar to historians of the early modern period. That such rhetoric could still be employed in Parliament in the nineteenth century indicates its remarkable durability. Nevertheless, it did not prevent Catholic emancipation in 1829. Why not? Second: why did Nicholl distinguish liberty from *both* popery *and* puritanism? Anti-popery sometimes followed a Manichean logic—popery was bad, whatever was not popery was good—but at other times popery and extreme Protestantism were cast as equivalent, opposing extremes. What, then, was the relationship between anti-popery and resistance to extreme Protestantism—what we might call "anti-puritanism"—and how did that relationship affect the operations of each? Third: what was the relationship between anti-popery, anti-puritanism, and the collapse of the ecclesiastical constitution that Nicholl defended in 1812? This constitution, he believed, had been "settled" at the Glorious Revolution. Despite his best efforts, it would break apart with the repeal of the Test and Corporation Acts in 1828 and Catholic emancipation the following year. Why? What was the relationship between anti-popery, anti-puritanism, and religious toleration?

In addressing these questions, this essay draws on the methodologically innovative scholarship on sixteenth- and seventeenth-century anti-popery and applies its insights to the staler historiographical debates about eighteenth- and nineteenth-century "identity." Historians of eighteenth-century Britain agree that religion delimited the political community but disagree about where and how those limits were drawn. The key works remain those of Linda Colley, emphasizing a British Protestant "national identity" defined against Catholicism, and J.C.D. Clark, emphasizing an English Anglican "hegemony" defined against heterodoxy.[2] These approaches attribute overriding importance to either anti-Catholicism or anti-Dissent, leaving no room for understanding their coexistence or the relationship between them.[3] The complex interactivity between religion and politics in this period is better conveyed by Peter Lake's approach to the same problem in an earlier period.

Lake's approach treats "anti-popery" as simultaneously an ideology, a rhetorical tradition, and a source of identity. In 1989, Lake influentially argued that anti-popery was more than a "prejudice." It was a "long-standing ideological code" by which a Protestant "self-image" was defined against a half-imagined "anti-religion." Over time, anti-popery evolved into something more "rhetorically ambiguous," as the idea of popery became unmoored from Catholicism and instead became "available as a free-floating term of opprobrium."[4] More recently, reflecting on this methodological approach, Lake has emphasized that we are dealing with *rhetoric:* not with "coherent ideological positions," but rather with "constellations of ideas, attributes, and narratives" which could be arranged and articulated to advance a range of objectives. Anti-popish rhetoric was malleable but not vacuous. It created certain possibilities and foreclosed others, in ways that can only be understood through attention to context. This approach not only analyzes the ideological or identity work performed by anti-popish language at a given moment, but also the evolution over time of the resulting rhetorical tradition.[5]

Lake also raised the question of the relationship between anti-popery and its less-studied partner, anti-puritanism. Anti-puritanism was a competing rhetorical tradition that constructed an alternative religio-political program, defined against "puritanism." Just as anti-popery did not necessarily refer to Catholicism, anti-puritanism did not necessarily refer to real puritans. In the 1620s, Lake argued, anti-puritan rhetoric was used to link advocates of further reformation to a subversive plot against monarchy; by the 1660s, its tropes were used against Dissent.[6] Anti-puritanism and anti-popery competed with one another but were also intertwined, because puritanism and popery were both constructed with reference to one another. Puritanism was sometimes depicted as the opposite of popery, and alleged puritans were charged with carrying anti-popery to excess: anti-puritanism could thus provide a counterweight to anti-popery. At other times, popery and puritanism were depicted, not as opposites, but as twins resembling one another in their aversion to moderation.[7] Lake warned against "the simple endorsement of one rather than another of the available contemporary renditions of the key terms," an apposite criticism of both Colley and Clark. He instead proposed an analysis of the long-term evolution of both traditions as a way of making sense of Britain's "long post-Reformation haul," offering a research agenda to historians of the eighteenth century and beyond.[8]

In this spirit, this essay will follow the use of anti-popish and anti-puritan language in the toleration debate of the late eighteenth and early nineteenth century, revealing continuities and discontinuities with the historical context in which these languages first emerged.[9] The former had proven more consistent.[10] By contrast, the contours of Protestant belonging had been repeatedly renegotiated, first at the Restoration, at which "Dissent" was defined by the Clarendon Code, and then at the Glorious Revolution, at which (most) Dissenters were (partially) incorporated into a (largely) stable religious settlement.[11] Following these developments, there were neither "real" puritans nor legitimate grounds for fearing them. Nevertheless, old rhetorical habits endured. Tropes first used against puritans continued to be used against Protestants associated with excessive anti-popery: Dissenters, Methodists, "enthusiasts," and others. Attacks against these diverse constituencies shared certain family traits. They could all plausibly be cast as descendants of puritanism. They were all occasionally described as puritans. More importantly, they were all likened to papists and, paradoxically, criticized for their excessive anti-popery, just as puritans had been. Because puritanism was tied rhetorically to popery, the argumentative maneuvers and logics used against puritans outlived the puritan movement and remained present in some form for as long as anti-popery remained live. I am using the term "anti-puritanism" to refer to this capacious and flexible rhetorical tradition. Another possibility is Scott Sowerby's "anti-anti-popery," but I believe that "anti-puritanism" better emphasizes the synergy between resistance to anti-popery and resistance to extreme Protestants.[12] Understanding this synergy is crucial for understanding the extension of equal citizenship to Catholics and Dissenters in the late eighteenth and early nineteenth centuries.

The repeal of the anti-Catholic and anti-Dissenter penal laws in this period marked the end of a regime of legal privilege and exclusion that had operated since 1688–89, and with it, the symbolic collapse of the religio-political settlement bequeathed by the Glorious Revolution.[13] The eighteenth-century penal laws defined various tiers of legal privilege. By the 1689 Toleration Act, all the penal laws against Trinitarian Dissenters were suspended except the Test Acts.[14] These remained in force, but from mid-century they too were routinely suspended by annual Indemnity Acts.[15] Catholics, by contrast, remained subject to a far more severe assemblage of penal laws.[16] The anti-Catholic and anti-Unitarian penal laws were rarely enforced either; indeed, the non-enforcement or suspension of the various penal laws formed a policy of "connivance" by which the establishment's ascendancy was justified by its tolerance.[17] The entire apparatus of anti-Catholic, anti-Unitarian, and anti-Trinitarian penal laws were significant, then, less for their practical consequences than as symbols of national belonging, suggesting tiers of inclusion and marginalization while allowing room for ambiguity and negotiation.

The repeal of the penal laws was a process driven by the imperatives of nation-, state-, and empire-building in the Age of Revolutions, as imperial expansion and the threat of revolution made the old model of confessional citizenship unsustainable. The crisis began during the Seven Years' War, which brought large numbers of Catholics into the empire, and deepened with the American Revolutionary War, a civil war between Protestants. It deepened further with the political unrest associated with the French Revolution, particularly the United Irishmen rebellion and the consequent union between Great Britain and Ireland. In response to these pressures, the penal laws were repealed in fits and starts in a process beginning in the 1770s.[18] Catholic Relief Acts were passed in 1778 and again in 1791 and 1793. Government balanced concessions to Catholics with concessions to Dissenters, freeing their minsters from compulsory subscription to the Thirty-nine Articles in 1779, and repealing the anti-Unitarian statutes in 1813, though opposing a campaign for the repeal of the Test Acts between 1787 and 1790. The process hurried to completion in the late 1820s: the Test Acts were finally repealed in 1828 and Catholics admitted to Parliament in 1829, principally as a result of pressure from Ireland.

The crisis had different effects for Catholics and Dissenters. For Catholics, its effects were entirely salutary: the progressive repeal of the penal laws against them. In the context of the Age of Revolutions, their traditional association with oppression and arbitrary power was turned to their advantage, and they instead became associated with order, hierarchy, and political stability.[19] The same developments had the opposite effect on Dissenters. Once associated with liberty and resistance to tyranny, they now found themselves associated with radicalism, rebellion, and revolution. Although Dissenters did enjoy some small improvements in their legal status, they lost the *relatively* favored status they had enjoyed since the Glorious Revolution (as defined both by law and by the languages of citizenship and national identity). Their constitutional gains were less their own achievement than the result of the Catholic assault on the exclusionary constitution. Although Dissenters lost their relatively favored status, their legal position would never become inferior to that of Catholics. The anti-Dissenter laws were repealed when the exclusion of Catholics from citizenship finally became untenable.

Catholics and Dissenters achieved equal citizenship, then, not because religious prejudice had disappeared in the Age of Enlightenment, but because anti-popery and anti-puritanism together furnished a language of religious toleration able to justify repeal when it became unavoidable. A recurrent theme in anti-popish rhetoric was that Catholics were intolerant. Although this charge was supplied by anti-popery it was also leveled against Dissenters on the grounds that their extreme anti-popery made them like the papists they so opposed. Defenders of the establishment saw no contradiction in marginalizing Catholics and Dissenters because of their supposed intolerance. Nevertheless, their relentless insistence on the evils of persecution provided a mechanism for anti-popery to critique itself, if Catholics (and Dissenters) could be repositioned as the victims of intolerance rather than its perpetrators. This reorientation was driven by the pressures outlined above, but it was also the achievement of Catholics and Dissenters themselves, who learned to perform their tolerance by declaring their support for one another's increasingly effectual demands for citizenship. The languages of anti-popery and anti-puritanism were thus turned against themselves and refashioned as arguments for toleration. For this reason, Test Act repeal and Catholic emancipation did not spell the end of either rhetorical tradition, both of which continued to shape ongoing conflicts over the civil rights of religious minorities and continued to resonate into the twenty-first century.

Britain's religious freedom grew out of its imperial entanglements. Territorial expansion during the Seven Years' War posed the first serious challenge to the old model of confessional citizenship. The conquest of Bengal and Quebec undermined older conceptions of the empire as "Protestant, commercial, maritime and free" by vastly expanding its non-Protestant population.[20] The 1774 Quebec Act, which gave rights to the new Catholic subjects, was a turning point: a reluctant recognition that the application of the anti-papist laws there was simply impossible.[21] Many Protestants were alarmed by the increasingly authoritarian measures by which the expanding empire was governed and saw in the Quebec Act nothing less than the "establishment" of popery.[22] Such apprehensions helped mobilize the American Patriot movement.[23]

The subsequent outbreak of rebellion among the king's Protestant subjects in America further boosted the status of British Catholics. A set of Relief Bills were organized in order to better recruit Catholic soldiers, exempting Catholics who took an oath of allegiance from the worst of the penal laws.[24] English and Irish Acts passed with little controversy in 1778, but the proposed extension of relief to Scotland provoked no less than 347 hostile petitions as well as rioting in Edinburgh and Glasgow.[25] After the Scottish Bill was withdrawn, a "Protestant Association" was founded to campaign for the repeal of the English Act. Lord George Gordon, a leading Scottish opponent of relief, was elected president, an *Appeal from the Protestant Association* was widely distributed, and a repeal petition gathered 44,000 signatures.[26]

The language of anti-popery was used to criticize both Catholic relief and the government's American policy. The same constituencies tended to oppose both, as Gordon's parliamentary career demonstrates.[27] While relief enjoyed the unanimous support of the political establishment, opposition aligned with what Brad Jones has called an "aggressive and patriotic political culture" extending across the Atlantic.[28] To its opponents, the relief program—an effort to recruit Catholic soldiers in a war against fellow Protestants—evidenced a wider conspiracy against liberty.[29] The Protestant Association's *Appeal* urged Britons "to preserve our civil and religious liberties from the incroachments of Popery," which "not only enslaves the mind, but would bind nobles and people with the iron chains of despotism." These claims were supported by a litany of popish violence against Protestants—Queen Mary's persecutions, the Saint Bartholomew's Day Massacre, the 1641 Irish rebellion—motivated by such maxims as "no faith is to be kept with heretics" and "no obedience is due to an excommunicated Prince."[30] According to this logic, the American crisis and Catholic relief both threatened Protestant liberty.

To their opponents, however, the American colonists and the Protestant Association took Protestant principles to excess, providing a graver threat to liberty than the imagined threat of Catholicism. The association's supporters were denounced as "over zealous advocates for Protestancy," displaying "enthusiasm," "prejudices," "passions," "imagination," "phrenzy," "bigotry," and "fanaticism," terms that invoked a tradition of Protestant excess stretching back to the puritans.[31] Such historical parallels were often drawn explicitly, notably in the widespread claim that the American revolt was a "Presbyterian rebellion" resembling the seventeenth-century Civil Wars.[32] Such rhetoric also served to refute the use of anti-popish rhetoric, which was itself identified as a symptom of Protestant excess. Thus, Congress's opposition to the Quebec Act was dismissed as a hypocritical attempt "to kindle the flame of enthusiasm."[33] Likewise, the pamphleteer John Shebbeare attacked the Patriot movement ("those trans-Atlantic sectaries"), defended the Quebec Act ("*popery* and the *Roman Catholic religion* are not necessarily conjoined"), and refuted anti-popery's analysis of the imperial crisis (the "tale that has been assiduously propagated . . . that popery has, at all times, been attended with slavery").[34] These rhetorical habits bound support for Catholics to opposition to the colonists. The American crisis was thus closely tied to a British debate about religious toleration.

In this toleration debate, both sides claimed to oppose persecution. Perhaps unsurprisingly, the Protestant Association argued that it did not "desire to persecute," only "to secure ourselves . . . from Popish persecution." It warned that "to tolerate Popery, is to encourage what by Toleration itself we mean to destroy, a spirit of persecution and bigotry."[35] More surprisingly, advocates of relief used precisely the same language to suggest that the penal laws themselves manifested popery and persecution. The rational Dissenter Joseph Priestley asked, "shall we imitate that [Catholic] church in the very thing for which we most condemn it?"[36] A pseudonymous Protestant "Freethinker"—the Irish Catholic James Ussher—argued that the penal laws contradicted "Protestant Principles," especially, "*Liberty of Conscience.*" Ussher also argued that proponents of excessive anti-popery were more likely to commit persecution than Catholics were: "When a papist becomes a protestant, he may openly avow the deposing and king-killing doctrine with the late puritan writers . . . he may teach persecution as loudly as Calvin or Knox, and practice it with the Methodists . . . notwithstanding, he shall be free from the popery laws."[37] In different ways, both writers followed the anti-puritan tradition in suggesting that puritanical Protestants resembled the papists they opposed.

While supporters of relief did not contest the longstanding habit of equating "popery" with "persecution," disagreement instead turned on the question of whether Catholics were necessarily papists. To opponents of relief, it was absurd to argue that they could ever be anything but. They understood popery as the corruption of Christianity by the introduction of human authority into religious matters, making persecution inevitable. This understanding was fleshed out in the reams of anti-Catholic theological controversy published in the years 1778–81.[38] This literature asserted that the "system" of popery was grounded in "THE PERVERTING OF THE SACRED SCRIPTURES."[39] The Catholic clergy, in order to impose doctrines contrary to reason and scripture, claimed infallible authority and demanded blind submission of the laity, who "must swallow absurdity, blasphemy, and whatever the superiors of that religion choose to impose on them."[40] Catholic doctrines served "to exalt the ecclesiastical state" and "keep the civil state . . . in ignorance, superstition, implicit faith, and passive obedience."[41] Because Catholic teachings "need only be seen in order to be abhorred," the clergy "are careful to keep [the laity] in profound ignorance," using a variety of "arts" and "industries": the withholding of scripture, auricular confession, penance, absolution, the anathematization of heretics, and outright persecution.[42] Persecution was thus "an undoubted *mark and character of the beast.*"[43] Catholics' antichristian beliefs committed them to persecution: "intolerance and persecution cannot but follow popish principles."[44] Political tyranny was the inevitable consequence: "when men's minds are enslaved . . . they will make but a feeble resistance against other encroachments of a civil and worldly nature."[45] In short: falsehood was the root cause of persecution. Religious freedom meant freedom from error and the means used to enforce it. "Catholicism," "popery," and "persecution" were held to be inseparable.

Other anti-Catholic writers offered a more subtle argument, suggesting that the danger came not from Catholics' religious beliefs but from their political principles: not from Catholicism, in other words, but from popery. Because anti-Catholic polemic was grounded so heavily in Catholicism's alleged penchant for bigotry and persecution, anti-Catholic writers risked appearing hypocritical if they could not distinguish their anti-Catholicism from Catholics' alleged hatred of Protestants. Typical here was the reasoning employed by the Methodist leader John Wesley, who emphasized that he would tolerate the most absurd religious beliefs as long as they were harmless, but maintained that Catholics' political principles compelled them to overthrow the government and persecute Protestants.[46] Wesley here drew on a Lockean model of toleration that was widespread in the relief debate. John Locke's *Letter Concerning Toleration* argued that all religious beliefs should be tolerated except those that harmed the political community. As examples of intolerable beliefs, Locke cited such alleged Catholic doctrines as "promises to heretics need not be kept." Thus, Locke alleged that Catholics not only refused to accept the right of private judgment but also refused to submit to the superintending authority of the state over religious matters.[47] Opponents of relief echoed Locke's argument, as the heterodox churchman Francis Blackburne did when he explained that Protestant principles obliged the toleration of "doctrines merely religious" but not "political principles . . . obnoxious to our civil Government."[48] In this way, Blackburne, Wesley, and others claimed that they opposed popery rather than Catholicism while implying that Catholics would always and necessarily be papists.

The distinction between popery and Catholicism nevertheless provided a rhetorical opportunity for supporters of relief, who suggested that Catholics could in fact renounce popery and thus become eligible for toleration. The Irish Catholic priest Arthur O'Leary, again following Locke, demanded "impunity, safety and protection granted by the state to every sect that does not maintain doctrines inconsistent with the public peace."[49] In order to make Catholics tolerable according to the Lockean model, advocates of relief distinguished between Catholics' religious principles (Catholicism) and their political principles (popery). They sometimes claimed that Catholics were being reformed under the influence of "commerce, refinement, and philosophy."[50] The Catholic priest Joseph Berington published a history claiming that English Catholics, unlike those "found in the kingdoms of Italy, Spain, and Portugal," were not papists.[51] Alternatively, it was hoped that repeal would encourage such improvement, by allowing Catholics to "derive Advantages from their Commerce and Communication with their Protestant Neighbours."[52] Considerable erudition was devoted to the question of whether such intolerable maxims as "no faith is to be kept with heretics" were "established doctrines" of the Catholic Church, or whether Catholics could renounce them and remain Catholic.[53] Indeed the new Oath of Allegiance required Catholics to abjure precisely these popish maxims.[54] Skeptics maintained that popery was unchangeable: Catholics could not take the oath without renouncing their principles, and those who did so must have been insincere; indeed, the principle that "no faith is to be kept with heretics" made any oath logically redundant.[55] While the identification of "popery" with "persecution" remained commonsensical, then, the identification of "Catholicism" with "popery" was widely—and inconclusively—debated.

Matters stood thus until the summer of 1780, when the Gordon Riots fundamentally changed the terms of the debate. On June 2, the Protestant Association called a public meeting to deliver the repeal petition to Parliament. Its rejection sparked a week of rioting that targeted Catholic property, the embassy chapels, pro-Catholic politicians, the Bank of England, and the London prisons. The riots profoundly unsettled polite opinion.[56] With the credibility of the British friends of America already jeopardized after 1778 by the Franco-American alliance, the riots wholly discredited opponents of relief: henceforth they would be seen as advocating persecution, not defending Protestants from it. The riots not only demonstrated that Catholics could indeed be the victims of persecution. They also suggested that Dissenters, Methodists, and other "puritanical" Protestants embodied the perpetration of anti-Catholic intolerance, with lasting implications for both Catholics' and Dissenters' subsequent efforts to obtain toleration.

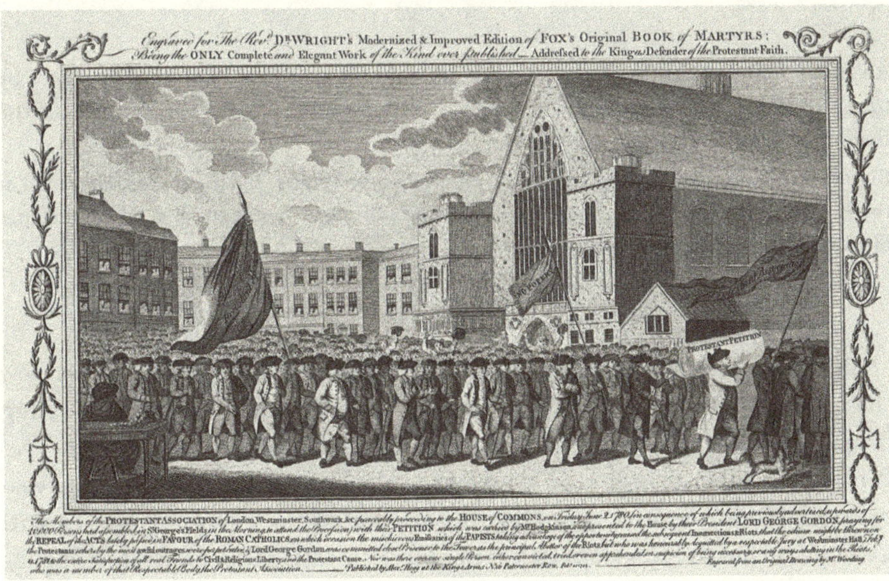

The Members of the Protestant Association, Engraved for The Rev[d]*. D*[r]*. Wright's Modernized & Improved Edition of Fox's Original Book of Martyrs; Being the* ONLY *Complete and Elegant Work of the Kind ever published. Addressed to the King as Defender of the Protestant Faith,* engraving, 1784. (© The Trustees of the British Museum; all rights reserved)

This orderly procession highlights the respectable quality of the Protestant Association that presented their "Protestant Petition" to popular acclaim. The text below claims "the Papists" took "advantage of the opportunity" to provoke "the subsequent Insurrections & Riots" and blame them on the Lord George Gordon.

An Exact Representation of the Burning, Plundering and Destruction of Newgate by the Rioters, on the memorable 7th of June 1780, engraving, 1781. (© The Trustees of the British Museum; all rights reserved)

Rioters, women and men, burn the prison and free its prisoners. The lower-class character of the Protestant Association is suggested by the promiscuous, drunken, mix, which includes black men and political pamphleteers.

The riots were quickly identified with the excesses of anti-popery. In this view, the rioters were provoked by the Protestant Association's "artful, insinuating, dangerous language," demonstrating "the real power of that popular cry—'No Papists! No Popery!'"[57] Similar claims had followed the Scottish riots the year before.[58] Moreover, a range of figures attributed the riots not just to anti-Catholicism but to Protestant excess in general, blaming Dissenters, Methodists, and other "enthusiasts."[59] Thomas Holcroft suggested that Gordon had "the manners and air of a modern Puritan."[60] The deist philosopher David Williams believed that Gordon was supported by "those Scotch Presbyterians, and those Methodists in England, who are of the same intolerant complexion."[61] The Whig clergyman Thomas Lewis O'Beirne described the association's supporters as "religious enthusiasts and visionaries," "bigoted sectaries," "methodist preachers," "the frequenters of tabernacles, and nightly conventicles," "fanatic followers of Wesley," and "the scum of the Scotch fanatics." He added that the rioters were "as intolerant, as persecuting, and as sanguinary as ever the Papists were in the days of the bigot Mary."[62] These various writers simultaneously attributed the riots to excessive anti-popery and to a vaguely defined "puritanism," which had stolen popery's clothes.

The profound impact of the Gordon Riots was due not only to their violence but also to the wider contexts, which made social, political, and religious disorder particularly unsettling. The imperial context was most important: the reaction against the Gordon Riots was amplified by the wider British reaction against the American Revolution. The Protestant Association's opponents held that the riots were the natural consequence of antigovernment politics. One author blamed the riots on the Patriot party, which supported the American rebels and introduced relief in order to inflame popular prejudices.[63] The Dissenter John Stevenson initially opposed the Quebec Act, but condemned the Protestant Association's "pretended zeal for the constitution," having grown disillusioned with the colonies' "daring rebellion," particularly their alliance with Catholic France and Spain.[64] While this "unnatural alliance" embarrassed the colonists' British supporters, advocates of relief stressed Catholics' loyalty during the crisis.[65] Mounting opposition to the Protestant Association was thus closely tied to the shift in British perceptions of the colonists: "From fellow-nationals to foreigners," in Stephen Conway's phrase.[66] The social context was also important. The rioters were represented as a drunken, plebian mob (see illustration page 266). The riots, one pamphleteer wrote, had shown that "there is not a capitol in Europe under worse police than London," provoking a debate about public order in the expanding metropolis.[67] Different lines of criticism bled into one another: attacks on "methodist" opposition to relief, the disreputable associators, and the rioting mob who drank themselves to death in the streets.[68] But it was the American rebellion that made questions of social and religious order paramount.

The riots discredited Gordon, the Protestant Association, and the potentially violent excesses of anti-popery. Gordon's supporters continued to represent themselves as respectable, orderly Protestant patriots (see illustration page 265), but they became newly vulnerable to accusations of intolerance. For example, after Parliament freed Dissenting ministers from compulsory subscription to the Thirty-nine Articles in 1779, instead requiring an oath affirming the divine inspiration of the scriptures,[69] an anonymous author published a petition condemning the oath as an ongoing infringement of liberty of conscience. The *Monthly Review* judged the petition to be "in the true spirit of Voltaire." It was republished the following year alongside a letter from the author justifying the exclusion of Catholicism from "universal toleration," and praising Gordon—who had voted against the oath—for "Being at the Head of the Protestants against the Papists." That was before the riots. Afterward, the publication was condemned as "insane" by the *Westminster Magazine* and disowned by associates of Williams's congregation.[70] The incident indicates what Colin Haydon has called a "parting of the ways" after 1780 between popular xenophobia and a polite culture of tolerance.[71] The American Revolution and the Gordon Riots had rendered opposition to government-sponsored Catholic relief suspect. Opponents of relief lost their credibility when they claimed to be defending Protestants from persecution by Catholics. Instead, it became increasingly possible to see their anti-Catholicism as persecuting, intolerant, and itself "popish." Anti-popish rhetoric was used to negate itself.

The American Revolution and Gordon Riots allowed Catholics to claim a larger measure of religious freedom but hampered Dissenters' ability to do the same for themselves. Catholic success, though incomplete, prompted Dissenters to launch their own campaign for the repeal of the Test Acts in the late 1780s. The Dissenting deputies, the traditional political representatives of Dissent, brought closely fought motions to Parliament in 1787 and 1789, but a third motion was resoundingly defeated in 1790 amid growing alarm at the unfolding Revolution in France.[72] The campaign reveals the difficulties Dissenters had in claiming toleration in an age of revolution and counterrevolution. The same reorientations that discredited excessive anti-Catholicism also discredited, by extension, Dissenter's demands for toleration. Dissenters lost what had once been the principal argument in their favor: that the true danger came from Catholicism whereas they stood at the forefront of anti-popery. When they attempted to use such arguments, they appeared as champions of persecution rather than religious liberty. They discovered—haltingly and with considerable disagreement among themselves—that supporting the toleration of Catholics was a more effective way of making themselves tolerable. Their response to this strategic dilemma was complicated by a developing rift between their "evangelical" and "rational" wings.[73] Evangelical Dissenters generally remained opposed to further Catholic relief, but heterodox "rational" Dissenters proved more willing to join with Catholics in demanding equal citizenship for all, adding their voices to the emerging idea that the principles of anti-popery demanded the toleration of Catholics.

The American Revolution was crucial in prompting Dissenters to contest their exclusion from full citizenship. Since the Glorious Revolution, Dissenters had generally been willing to celebrate their pan-Protestant, anti-Catholic alliance with English churchmen.[74] Yet Dissenters had always been subordinate partners in this alliance. The American Revolution made them more vulnerable by making their traditional association with oppositional politics suspicious, and ultimately removing a vast Dissenting constituency in the colonies that had allowed them to hold their own as an influential pressure group.[75] At the same time, many Dissenters had been radicalized by the Revolution. Rational Dissenters enjoyed a close relationship with the leaders of the new United States. Thomas Jefferson's 1785 Virginia Statute for Religious Freedom, republished in London by Richard Price, was the critical precedent for the repeal campaign.[76] On balance, however, Dissenters' campaign for repeal was driven not by bullishness but by a loss of status.

That the repeal campaign was launched at all indicated an emerging division between rational and evangelical Dissenters. The deputies were drawn from the London elite, where rational Dissenters played a leading role unrepresentative of Dissent as a whole. Test Act repeal held particular interest for rational Dissenters, who were most disadvantaged by the prevailing legal regime notwithstanding their wealth, social status, and position as an intellectual elite. Many of the supporters of the repeal campaign had also been involved in the antisubscription petitioning of the 1770s, which benefited rational Dissenters and which many orthodox Dissenters had opposed.[77] Despite their reassurances that "a common interest must dictate similar feelings," the deputies' campaign was disowned by a number of orthodox Dissenters.[78] Orthodox Dissenters' attacks on the campaign's Unitarian leadership chimed with the sentiments of High Churchmen such as Bishop Samuel Horsley, who believed the Test Acts were necessary to guard against heterodoxy.[79] One writer suspected that the whole venture was the work of Unitarians, "*Infidels and Blasphemers*" beyond the pale of Christianity.[80] The repeal campaign, then, drew its strength from the most vulnerable of the increasingly vulnerable Dissenters.

Dissenters argued that they should be tolerated because they—and the nation at large—were Protestant. The deputies argued that Test Act repeal would advance "the honour of Religion . . . the security and strength of the Protestant interest . . . [and] the welfare of the Nation."[81] In response, defenders of the Test Acts charged Dissenters with taking Protestant principles to excess. They recalled how the "glorious benefits" of the Reformation "overcame the weak and unsettled judgment of some unenlightened Followers of the Protestant Faith, and hurried them to an ungovernable Enthusiasm." The same writer described "Independency" as "an extreme form of Puritanism" consisting "of the same hypocrisy refined, and of the same intemperance unrestrained."[82] Another writer thought that Dissenters were "thoroughly *soured* by the remains of the old puritanical *leven*."[83] Despite their best efforts Dissenters could only draw so much capital from the simple fact of their Protestantism, reflecting their ambiguous and indeterminate status, neither simple insiders (*pace* Colley) nor simple outsiders (*pace* Clark).

Dissenters ran into the same problem when they attempted to advance their claims by emphasizing their anti-Catholic credentials. One sympathetic churchman acknowledged that Dissenters "have given the strongest proof of their attachment to the constitution, and their detestation of Popery."[84] In response, opponents of Test Act repeal compared Dissenters to Catholics or suggested that repeal would benefit Catholics. One writer urged Dissenters to quietly accept the Test Acts and instead unite around "that bulwark of Protestantism, the Church of England."[85] Despite Colley's emphasis on its unifying effects, appeals to anti-Catholicism did not get Dissenters far. Moreover, this was not just a rhetorical problem.

The deputies were faced with a strategic dilemma when they had to decide whether to support or oppose further concessions to Catholics. In 1787, a "Catholic Committee" began lobbying for further relief, achieving a second Relief Act in 1791.[86] Comparisons between Dissenters' and Catholics' legal status were unavoidable. Should the deputies argue that Dissenters should be tolerated because they were not Catholic? Or should they demand toleration for all nonconformists, whether Protestant or Catholic? As one anti-Dissenter pamphlet gleefully pointed out, "Dissenters cannot mean to argue for the admission of Catholicks . . . for if they do, they contradict the Principles, which they have always maintained; and if they do not, their favourite Argument, the Injustice of a Disqualification upon the account of Nonconformity, is instantly done away."[87] Comparisons with Catholic relief placed Dissenters in a catch-22.

Whichever strategy the deputies pursued they were accused of intolerance: of siding with intolerant papists or refusing to tolerate Catholics. If they supported Catholic relief, they were accused of supporting popery (as, according to a long tradition of anti-puritan rhetoric, extreme Protestants were wont to do). One writer argued that repeal would open the door to "a complete Toleration . . . including even Popery itself!"[88] Yet if they opposed Catholic relief, they were accused of manifesting the intolerant, hypocritical, and persecuting qualities deemed typical of "puritanical" Protestants. Under the Test Acts, it was claimed, Dissenters enjoyed "perfect freedom from persecution . . . which was by no means the case when the . . . sectaries overturned the constitution of this kingdom in the last century."[89] Dissenters' supposed intolerance of Catholics was held to be an indicator of their willingness to persecute the Church of England also. One pamphlet asked, "what chance can members of the Church have against those two cries, which have so often maddened this nation, *Popery* and *Slavery*," with which Dissenters had recently provoked "Lord George Gordon's tumult."[90] As this pamphlet indicates, the Gordon Riots remained an important influence limiting Dissenters' ability to exploit anti-popery.

The deputies began their campaign by circulating a pamphlet, *The Case of the Protestant Dissenters*, which appealed almost exclusively to anti-Catholic arguments. It argued that the Test Act "was made wholly against Papists, and not to prevent any danger which could happen to the Nation or Church from the Dissenters." Dissenters "willingly subject[ed] themselves to the disabilities created by it rather than obstruct what was deemed so necessary to the common welfare." The sacramental test "can be no real or effectual security" for Protestants anyway, since it "may be received by many Papists, because many of them hold the Church of England to be no Church."[91] Catholics, in short, were the real enemy.

However, assumptions about anti-Catholicism were changing in the aftermath of the American Revolution and the Gordon Riots, wrong-footing the deputies and their anti-Catholic strategy. Catholic relief was now a respectable cause, Horsley suggested, contrasting the "moderate and gentle" spirit of English Catholics with Price's "impassioned fondness for the democratic form" and praise for the American Revolution.[92] Catholic writers quickly retaliated against the deputies. Berington asked how they "could be so inconsistent, as . . . to profess *intolerance*, when they complain of its injustice." He wished to see Dissenters and Catholics "united in a common petition to Parliament," but Dissenters refused to reciprocate.[93] The deputies backed down, carefully and deliberately removing such passages from subsequent publications.[94] Having discovered that by opposing Catholic relief they risked appearing intolerant, the deputies went silent on the Catholic question. Subsequent pro-repeal pamphlets cautiously suggested that the "religious liberty" Dissenters demanded would extend to Catholics if adequate "securities" could be obtained, thereby avoiding precisely the contested issue.[95] The deputies were not yet willing to support Catholic relief—that was still a losing strategy—but they no longer stood to gain by directly opposing it.

The contrast with the strategy adopted by English Catholics is striking. The Catholic Committee sought to disown popery, publishing a declaration renouncing popish principles, and assimilating themselves rhetorically to Protestant Dissenters by calling themselves "Protesting Catholic Dissenters."[96] One committee member declared that there was not "one single external mark to distinguish us from other Dissenters."[97] The committee made their support for Test Act repeal well known. One newspaper reported that "The Roman Catholicks are keen sticklers for the abolition of restraints on [Protestant] Dissenters."[98] Supporting the toleration of Dissenters served to distinguish Catholicism from "popery" by refuting the accusation that Catholics were intolerant, and by likening Catholics to Dissenters and thus positioning Catholicism as nothing more than a matter of religious belief. These contrasting strategies—the Catholic Committee supported Test Act repeal while the deputies ignored Catholic relief—reflected the asymmetrical status of Catholics and Dissenters: Catholics had more to gain and Dissenters had more to lose from what contemporaries called "universal toleration."

Yet this question also divided rational Dissenters—who had more to gain—from orthodox Dissenters—who had more to lose from "universal toleration." Priestley's support for relief in 1778 had been exceptional, but a decade later many rational Dissenters advocated further concessions to Catholics. The realignment was bolstered by the secession of "liberal Anglicans" from the Church: Theophilus Lindsey reversed his opposition to Catholic relief after he formed a Unitarian congregation outside the protection of the Toleration Act.[99] Conversely, some Dissenters remained opposed to both Catholic relief and the repeal campaign. In the 1770s the Protestant Association had appealed to the ideal of Protestant unity, but in 1790 it condemned the deputies, warning that "Price and Priestley" were seeking "the Repeal of the Penal Laws against Popery."[100] Dissenting opponents of the deputies agreed it was "opening a door" that might assist "the Papists."[101] The deputies avoided the Catholic question in order to disguise these divisions, which significantly hindered their campaign.

The principal reason for the deputies' failure, however, was the strength of the British reaction against the threat of revolution, first from America and then from France. For their opponents, Dissenters' attempt to contest their marginalization was evidence of the qualities that necessitated it in the first place. In soliciting popular support for a third application, the deputies unleashed a wave of petitions, publications, and public meetings.[102] Opposition intensified correspondingly. Churchmen held their own public meetings, lamenting "that the national tranquility should be disturbed by the malevolent Resolutions which are daily printed and industriously dispersed."[103] Examples of Dissenting radicalism were seized upon and condemned. In March 1790, the third repeal bill was overwhelmingly defeated in Parliament.[104] The conservative reaction to the French Revolution made Test Act repeal a dead letter for the rest of the 1790s. Aware that further agitation risked attracting hostility, the deputies' "repeal committee" disbanded.[105] Unitarians became particularly suspect. As many continued to oppose the war in the colonies, their early expressions of support for the Revolution were used against them, most influentially by Burke.[106] Government repression and rioting mobs drove a Unitarian diaspora into exile in France or the United States.[107] If the British counterrevolution targeted Dissenters in general and Unitarians in particular, this was not just due to these constituencies' support for reforming causes. The logic of anti-popery and anti-puritanism was also crucial, representing Dissenters as opponents of tyranny in one context but opponents of all order in another.

Likewise, the traditional association of popery with despotism was turned to Catholics' advantage in the early 1790s. The deputies' failure contrasts with Catholic success in obtaining further Relief Acts for England in 1791 and Scotland in 1793 to a startling absence of opposition.[108] While Dissenters suffered from their association with revolution, British Catholics benefitted from sympathy with the persecuted Catholic Church in France. In 1791, Berington refused to join Priestley's "Revolution Dinner" in Birmingham, thereby escaping the subsequent riots.[109] The incident indicates the extent to which Catholics' stock had risen and Dissenters' fallen in the early 1790s. However, the significance of Catholic relief should not be overstated. Relief only meant a more expansive and generous toleration for Catholics, comparable to what Dissenters already enjoyed. By contrast, Test Act repeal meant political equality for Dissenters. It therefore challenged the confessional identity of the state in a way that Catholic relief did not. Both Catholics and

Dissenters would have to wait until the second quarter of the nineteenth century before the old model of confessional citizenship was abandoned.

The final unravelling of the confessional state began with the Union between Britain and Ireland. A response to the prospect of an alliance between Irish radicals and French revolutionaries, the Union galvanized Irish Catholics' demands for admission to the Westminster Parliament, generating massive popular support for Daniel O'Connell's Catholic Association. Resistance proved intractable, sustained by the king's fidelity to the Coronation Oath and Lord Liverpool's government (1812–27). The resulting impasse was eventually broken in the moment of political instability following Liverpool's stroke in 1827.[110] As well as making Catholic emancipation all but inevitable, the Union also ushered in Test Act repeal, because the former was unthinkable without the latter. Parliament repealed the Test Acts in the spring of 1828, principally as a result of the changing fortunes of pro- and anti-emancipation forces in Parliament after Liverpool's incapacity.[111] The final blow against the Protestant constitution was struck by O'Connell's illegal election as MP for County Clare in June that year, which conclusively demonstrated that the exclusion of Ireland's aggrieved Catholic majority was unsustainable and led the duke of Wellington and Robert Peel to abandon their opposition.[112]

The controversy over Catholic emancipation demonstrated that the French Revolution had not put an end to anti-popery. Colley has suggested that, after the Revolution, radicals, atheists, and Jacobins replaced Catholics as the new enemies to the Protestant nation.[113] Yet traditional sources of anti-Catholic anxiety reemerged with the 1798 United Irishmen uprising, a second uprising in 1803, Napoleon's Concordat with the papacy in 1801, the reinstatement of the Jesuits in 1814, and the persecution of French Protestants at the Bourbon Restoration.[114] Nevertheless, remembering the Gordon Riots, the elite defenders of the Protestant constitution were reluctant to embrace the disorderly and disreputable forces of popular anti-Catholicism.[115] The French Revolution made anti-popery not irrelevant, but more dangerous than ever.

Arguments for and against emancipation took shape along well-established lines. Opponents claimed that Catholics' allegiance to a foreign prince was incompatible with subjecthood.[116] Both High Churchmen and evangelicals argued that Ireland should be assimilated by a "second reformation" rather than the extension of citizenship to Catholics.[117] Their opponents were not necessarily more sympathetic to Catholicism, but they were more optimistic about the effects of emancipation. The *Evangelical Magazine* warned that Ireland will remain "a Catholic country . . . if she is not *conciliated,*" declaring that "true Protestantism will show itself more in endeavouring to liberate the Catholic mind from the galling yoke of superstition, than in seeking to perpetuate political restrictions."[118] Playing to this view, the Catholic Association appealed to the principle that "EVERY HUMAN BEING SHOULD WORSHIP GOD ACCORDING TO THE SINCERE DICTATES OF HIS CONSCIENTIOUS BELIEF."[119] Both supporters and opponents of emancipation thus continued to speak the language of Protestant nationhood, and Catholics took their demands for religious freedom from this same language.

There was a consensus that the Catholic question was more important than Test Act repeal. While the former remained unresolved, any further concessions to Dissenters were unlikely. True, beside the Catholic threat, Dissenters appeared harmless. Parliament received over 3,000 petitions against emancipation, but only 28 against Test Act repeal.[120] However, repeal was discussed in terms of its unknowable effects on the Catholic question: the Catholics' opponents feared that repeal would open the door to emancipation, while the Catholics' supporters feared that the admission of Dissenters would reinforce the Catholics' exclusion.[121] Moreover, the prospect of Catholic emancipation led many Anglicans to redouble their insistence that the Test Acts were necessary to protect the established Church.[122] One Anglican pamphleteer acknowledged, "Protestant Dissenters are rather like fellow-subjects who are of a different party; but Papists are nothing less than avowed enemies," while maintaining that both "Protestant and Popish Dissenters" should be excluded from power.[123] Another writer thought that Dissenters were "Anarchical," "Anti-social," "Un-peaceable," "Un-patriotic," "Uneconomical," "Un-seemly," "Unlearned," and "Un-Scriptural," but ought nevertheless "to ally themselves to our Church" against the papists' "bold front."[124] High Churchmen took the opposite approach, arguing that Dissenters were more dangerous than Catholics. Herbert Marsh, bishop of Peterborough, opposed emancipation because its "first and necessary consequence would be a repeal of the Corporation and Test Acts."[125] If emancipation was considered more important than Test Act repeal it did not make it more likely. As in the 1780s, a prevailing discourse of Protestant nationhood did not benefit Dissenters in a straightforward way.

When Dissenters launched a new repeal campaign in 1827, it faced similar challenges to those applying before the French Revolution. As Richard W. Davis has shown, Dissenters sought to avoid any entanglement with the divisive Catholic question.[126] A letter from the deputies' secretary to Lord John Russell explicated this strategy: the campaign would "abstain from noticing that great Question upon which all parties are so much divided."[127] Yet the widening rift between evangelicals and Unitarians made it increasingly difficult for Dissenters to maintain a united front. This rift became institutionalized after 1811, when the deputies' lukewarm response to an attempt to restrict the licensing of itinerant preachers led evangelical Dissenters to set up their own Protestant Society for the Protection of Religious Liberty. Meanwhile, the repeal of the anti-Unitarian laws in 1813 permitted the establishment of a Unitarian Association six years later.[128] The Protestant Society was reluctant to agitate for Test Act repeal for fear of assisting Catholic emancipation, while the Unitarian Association impatiently called for an alliance with the Catholic Association.[129] It was not until 1827 that the divided institutional representatives of Dissent settled their differences to demand Test Act repeal. That year, the "General Body of Dissenting Ministers," Dissenting deputies, Unitarian Association, and Protestant Society formed a United Committee, resolving to "petition against the statutes which oppressed them . . . on the broad and general ground, leaving it to others to determine to what other bodies, besides their own, those principles would apply."[130] The United Committee carefully ignored the Catholic question.[131] As in the 1780s, the Catholic question presented Dissenters with a catch-22: either supporting or opposing the toleration of Catholics would jeopardize their Protestant credentials. Ignoring the elephant in the room was the only option.

During the campaign, the old fault line between rational and orthodox Dissenters widened into a rift between pro-Catholic Unitarians and anti-Catholic evangelicals. The Unitarian Association petitioned in favor of emancipation the day the Sacramental Test Act became law. Robert Aspland, the founder of the Unitarian Association, announced his hope that "the three great religious divisions of the country [Anglicans, Dissenters, and Catholics] . . . will be bound together in the bond of peace and charity, and form the triple cord that cannot be broken."[132] By contrast, evangelical Dissenters were decidedly unenthusiastic about Test Act repeal. They were more concerned with the defense of the foreign and domestic missionary movement, where they cooperated closely with Anglican evangelicals.[133] Some historians have suggested that their religious fervor disposed them to anti-Catholic prejudice. Others have argued that the denominational division coincided with the all-important class division.[134] Yet tactical considerations were more important here than belief or class. Compared to Unitarians, evangelicals had less to gain and more to lose from attacking the status quo.

Evangelicals gained little from opposing Catholic emancipation: as we have already seen, the rhetoric of anti-popery rarely benefited Dissenters in a straightforward way. We might expect to find Dissenters advancing a similar argument to that which the deputies had briefly offered in 1787: if the true danger came from Catholicism then the threat of emancipation made Test Act repeal all the more urgent. Yet this argument was almost entirely absent from the printed debate, and those few Dissenters who advanced it ran into tremendous difficulties. Joseph Ivimey, the secretary to the Baptist Irish Society, was the most prominent anti-emancipation Dissenter. He opposed Dissenters' efforts against the Test Acts for fear of inadvertently assisting the Catholics. In 1813, he resigned from the Ministers after they petitioned "for the repeal of all penal Statutes now in Force on the Subject of Religion."[135] After the Test Acts were repealed, the Ministers again petitioned in the Catholics' favor, and Ivimey resigned a second time, attempting to lead a Trinitarian secession.[136] Yet Ivimey struggled to justify the exclusion of Catholics. "I have not opposed the Roman Catholics, sir, by signing any petition against them, lest I should recognize a principle which I do not believe, namely, that civil governments have a right to legislation on the subject of religion!" he explained, "But while I have done nothing to oppose the Catholics, I most certainly will do nothing to promote their wishes." Ivimey's opposition to emancipation even muted his criticism of the anti-Dissenter laws. He considered the Test Acts "a foul blot on our fair and excellent Constitution," but opposed any political agitation for their repeal, suggesting that the question be left to Parliament.[137] He broke his own injunction to neutrality in 1821, when he anonymously published a letter to Lord Liverpool, who was rumored to be considering emancipation, arguing that *if* Catholics were emancipated *then* the Test Acts should also be repealed.[138] In short, Ivimey tied himself in knots trying to square his anti-Catholicism with his commitment to Dissenters' rights, while grappling with the reality that repeal without emancipation was unlikely. As Ivimey's efforts demonstrate, Dissenters were better served by performing their tolerance of Catholicism than by flaunting their anti-Catholic credentials.

In contrast to the United Committee's efforts to avoid the Catholic question, the Catholic Association was outspoken in its support for Test Act repeal. It proposed a joint campaign with the Dissenters, but the United Committee rebuffed the idea.[139] The association organized petitions for Test Act repeal that were signed by as many as 100,000 Irish Catholics.[140] These petitions supported the Catholic Association's efforts to disown popery by promising that "the Catholic Religion is friendly to civil liberty" and "favourable to freedom of conscience."[141] One Catholic petition sought to "claim on behalf of the Protestant Dissenters of England, the benefit of the Protestant principle of the right . . . of private interpretation and private judgment in matters of religion."[142] Supporting Dissenters gave Catholics an opportunity to perform their tolerance and disown popery, just as supporting Catholics gave Unitarians an opportunity to perform their tolerance. In doing so both groups took the old exclusionary language of Protestant nationhood and used it to insist that Protestant principles demanded universal toleration.

Any attempt to provide a rhetorical analysis of the toleration debate must grapple with the fact that, much of the time, contemporaries were simply hurling the same set of insults at one another. A rough grammar of religio-political argument is nevertheless visible. Catholics and extreme Protestants were represented as mirror images of one another—both opposites and twins—meaning that many of the arguments and terms of abuse used against Catholics were also applied

The Battle of the Petitions, a Farce now performing with great applause at both Houses, engraving, 1829. ()

Parliamentary supporters of Catholic Emancipation, armed with favorable petitions, attack the defenders of "No Popery" sheltering behind a barricade of contrary petitions. Irish Catholic nationalists and the devil delight to see the "Protestant Succession," "Rights of Englishmen," and "Magna Charta" trampled.

to Dissenters. The language of anti-popery could thus be used not only against Dissenters but also against itself: extreme anti-popery was held to be much the same thing as popery.

The key terms here were "persecution" and "toleration." These terms had long justified the marginalization of (intolerant) Catholics and Dissenters and the ascendancy of the (tolerant) establishment. In the half-century following the American Revolution, however, Catholics and Dissenters were able to use these terms to demand toleration for themselves. Eventually, the anti-Catholic and anti-Dissenter penal laws came to be seen as manifestations of "popery" rather than defenses against it. This realignment tracked the British reaction against first the American and then the French Revolutions. While Catholics were increasingly seen as supporters not of tyranny but of the social order, Dissenters were increasingly seen as supporters not of liberty but of revolution. Faced with this loss of status, they gradually began pursuing their civil rights by supporting rather than opposing Catholic rights.

If the languages of anti-popery and anti-puritanism operated everywhere in the toleration debate, we cannot assume that the penal laws were repealed thanks to the march of tolerance, enlightenment, and progress. Repeal was driven less by intellectual change than by the problems of governing an expanding and religiously diverse empire. These problems became insurmountable in the Age of Revolutions. The position of Catholics and Dissenters was never symmetrical, and this was therefore a process driven by concessions to Catholics rather than concessions to Dissenters. The forms of exclusion which upheld the established Church in England proved unworkable in Quebec and Ireland. The sheer number of Catholics was also crucially important. Compared to Dissenters, they could offer many more bodies to the war effort, while the political unrest O'Connell generated in Ireland overshadowed anything Dissenters achieved. In this period between the loss of the American colonies and the expansion of evangelical Dissent in the Victorian age, the Dissenting constituency was at its smallest. Even though Dissenters continued to enjoy a relatively favored status compared to Catholics, the American Revolution left them in a newly vulnerable position. For this reason, it was primarily the heterodox Unitarians who resurrected the Test Acts as a symbol of Dissenters' inequality and fought for redress in the name of the entire Dissenting interest.

Treating anti-popery and anti-puritanism as rhetorical traditions (rather than manifestations of static structures of national "identity" or ideological "hegemony") also helps to account for their afterlives beyond the "constitutional revolution" of 1828–29. The language used to defend the old model of confessional citizenship was also used to attack it, and could therefore be retained after that model was abandoned. Anti-Catholicism did not become embarrassing after Catholic emancipation. Throughout the remainder of the nineteenth century, ongoing conflicts among Dissenters, Catholics, and Anglicans about the limits, conditions, and tensions of toleration continued to be debated in familiar terms.[143] But to note the endurance of these languages into the modern period is not to argue that they remained unchanged. The anti-popish tradition was fractured in the Age of Revolutions. For Gordon's Protestant Association, "Protestant principles" fused patriotism, religious liberty, resistance to tyranny, and political opposition to foreign and domestic Catholicism. Victorian anti-Catholicism—associated with evangelical Anglicanism, conservative politics, and anti-Irish sentiment—was heir to one branch of this tradition. The other was represented by the popular liberalism that advocated free trade and political reform alongside disestablishmentarianism, attacks on Anglican-controlled education, opposition to European Ultramontanism, and support for the rights of Irish Catholics.[144] Though we might find the latter more sympathetic, both are indebted to early modern anti-popery, whose dialectic has produced both modernity and antimodernity.

Notes

I would like to thank the two anonymous reviewers for their insightful comments and suggestions on this essay, as well as Evan Haefeli, Simon Skinner, Bob Harris, Joanna Innes, Chris Brown, and Melissa Morris.

1. *Hansard's Parliamentary Debates,* vol. 21, column 503 (https://hansard.parliament.uk/Commons/1812-02-03).
2. Linda Colley, *Britons: Forging the Nation, 1707–1837,* 3rd ed. (New Haven, CT: Yale University Press, 2009); J.C.D. Clark, *English Society, 1660–1832: Religion, Ideology, and Politics during the Ancien Régime,* 2nd ed. (Cambridge: Cambridge University Press, 2000); J.C.D. Clark, "Protestantism, Nationalism, and National Identity, 1660–1832," *Historical Journal* 43, no. 1 (2000): 249–76.
3. Tony Claydon and Ian McBride, eds., *Protestantism and National Identity: Britain and Ireland, c. 1650–c. 1850* (Cambridge: Cambridge University Press, 1998); Grayson Ditchfield, "Church, Parliament, and National Identity, c. 1770–c. 1830," in *Parliaments, Nations, and Identities in Britain and Ireland, 1660–1850,* ed. Julian Hoppit (Manchester: Manchester University Press, 2003), 64–82.
4. Peter Lake, "Antipopery: The Structure of a Prejudice," in *Conflict in Early Stuart England: Studies in Religion and Politics, 1603–1642,* ed. Ann Hughes and Richard P. Cust (London: Longman, 1989), 72–106, quotes on 74, 75, 79, 96.
5. Peter Lake, "Anti-Puritanism: The Structure of a Prejudice," in *Religious Politics in Post-Reformation England,* ed. Kenneth Fincham and Peter Lake (Woodbridge: Boydell, 2006), 80–97, quotes on 96.
6. Lake, "Anti-Puritanism," 82.
7. For a different approach to "moderation," coercion, and toleration, see Ethan H. Shagan, *The Rule of Moderation: Violence, Religion, and the Politics of Restraint in Early Modern England* (Cambridge: Cambridge University Press, 2011), esp. 73–186, 288–325.
8. Lake, "Anti-Puritanism," 84, 90.
9. For another essay applying Lake's methodology to the eighteenth century, see Mark Knights, "Occasional Conformity and the Representation of Dissent: Hypocrisy, Sincerity, Moderation and Zeal," *Parliamentary History* 24, no. 1 (2005): 41–57.
10. Colin Haydon, *Anti-Catholicism in Eighteenth-Century England: A Political and Social Study* (Manchester: Manchester University Press, 1993); Jan Albers, "'Papist Traitors' and 'Presbyterian Rogues': Religious Identities in Eighteenth-Century Lancashire," in *The Church of England, c. 1689–c. 1833: From Toleration to Tractarianism,* ed. John Walsh, Colin Haydon, and Stephen Taylor (Cambridge: Cambridge University Press, 1993), 317–33; Robert G. Ingram, "'Popish Cutthroats against Us': Papists, Protestants, and the Problem of Allegiance in Eighteenth-Century Ireland," in *From the Reformation to the Permissive Society: A Miscellany in Celebration of the 400th Anniversary of Lambeth Palace Library,* ed. Melanie Barber and Stephen Taylor (Woodbridge: Boydell, 2010), 151–209.
11. E. Payne, "Toleration and Establishment: 1. A Historical Outline" and E. Carpenter, "Toleration and Establishment: 2. Studies in a Relationship," in *From Uniformity to Unity, 1662–1962,* ed. Geoffrey F. Nuttall and Owen Chadwick (London: SPCK, 1962), 257–342.
12. Scott Sowerby, "Opposition to Anti-Popery in Restoration England," *Journal of British Studies* 51 (2012): 26–49.

13. G.F.A. Best, "The Constitutional Revolution, 1828–1832, and Its Consequences for the Established Church," *Theology* 62 (1959): 226–34; Colley, *Britons*, 320–63; Clark, *English Society*, 26–34, 501–64.
14. I.e., the 1673 Test Act and the 1661 Corporation Act.
15. James E. Bradley, *Religion, Revolution, and English Radicalism: Nonconformity in Eighteenth-Century Politics and Society* (Cambridge: Cambridge University Press, 1990), 49–90; Martin Fitzpatrick, "Natural Law, Natural Rights, and the Toleration Act in England, 1688–1829," in *Naturrecht und Staat: politische Funktionen des europäischen Naturrechts (17.-19. Jahrhundert)*, ed. Diethelm Klippel (Munich: Oldenbourg, 2006), 35–58; K.R.M. Short, "The English Indemnity Acts, 1726–1867," *Church History* 42 (1973): 366–76.
16. Colin Haydon, "Parliament and Popery in England, 1700–1780," *Parliamentary History* 19 (2000): 49–63.
17. For the concept of "connivance" in the European context, see Benjamin J. Kaplan, *Divided by Faith: Religious Conflict and the Practice of Toleration in Early Modern Europe* (Cambridge, MA: Belknap Press, 2007), 195–97. For an example of the workings of "connivance" in Britain, see Joanna Innes, *Inferior Politics: Social Problems and Social Policies in Eighteenth-Century Britain* (Oxford: Oxford University Press, 2009), 279–341.
18. Richard W. Davis, *Dissent in Politics, 1780–1830: The Political Life of William Smith, M.P.* (London: Epworth Press, 1971); Ursula Henriques, *Religious Toleration in England, 1787–1833* (London: Routledge and Kegan Paul, 1961); R. B. Barlow, *Citizenship and Conscience: A Study in the Theory and Practice of Religious Toleration in England during the Eighteenth Century* (Philadelphia: University of Pennsylvania Press, 1962).
19. Luca Codignola, "Roman Catholic Conservatism in a New North Atlantic World, 1760–1829," *William and Mary Quarterly*, 3rd ser., 64, no. 4 (2007): 717–56.
20. David Armitage, *The Ideological Origins of the British Empire* (Cambridge: Cambridge University Press, 2000), 8; Peter W. Walker, "The Bishop Controversy, the Imperial Crisis, and Religious Radicalism in New England, 1763–74," *New England Quarterly* 40, no. 3 (2017): 306–43; Jessica Harland-Jacobs, "Incorporation the King's New Subjects: Accommodation and Anti-Catholicism in the British Empire, 1763–1815," *Journal of Religious History* 39 (2015): 202–23.
21. P. J. Marshall, *The Making and Unmaking of Empires: Britain, India, and America, c. 1750–1783* (Oxford: Oxford University Press, 2005), 182–206; Jacqueline R. Hill, "Religious Toleration and the Relaxation of the Penal Laws: An Imperial Perspective, 1763–1780," *Archivium Hibernicum* 44 (1989): 101–7; Mary Louise Sanderson, "'Our Own Catholic Countrymen': Religion, Loyalism, and Subjecthood in Britain and Its Empire, 1755–1829" (PhD diss., Vanderbilt University, 2010), 65–141.
22. Thomas S. Kidd, *God of Liberty: A Religious History of the American Revolution* (New York: Basic Books, 2010), 57–74; James B. Bell, *A War of Religion: Dissenters, Anglicans, and the American Revolution* (Basingstoke: Palgrave Macmillan, 2008), 91–106; Colin C. Bonwick, *English Radicals and the American Revolution* (Chapel Hill: University of North Carolina Press, 1977), 114–49.
23. See the essays by Evan Haefeli and Brendan McConville in this volume; Charles H. Metzger, *The Quebec Act: A Primary Cause of the American Revolution* (New York: United States Catholic Historical Society, 1936).
24. Robert Kent Donovan, *No Popery and Radicalism: Opposition to Roman Catholic Relief in Scotland, 1778–1782* (New York: Garland, 1987), 111–48.
25. *Scotland's Opposition to the Popish Bill. . . .* (Edinburgh, 1780).
26. Eugene Charlton Black, *The Association: British Extraparliamentary Political Organization, 1769–1793* (Cambridge, MA: Harvard University Press, 1963), 131–73.

27. Robert Kent Donovan, "The Popular Party of the Church of Scotland and the American Revolution," in *Scotland and America in the Age of Enlightenment*, ed. Jeffrey R. Smitten and Richard B. Sher (Edinburgh: Edinburgh University Press, 1990), 83–94; Donovan, *No Popery and Radicalism*, 272–82. For the similar situation in Newcastle-upon-Tyne, see Kathleen Wilson, *The Sense of the People: Politics, Culture, and Imperialism in England, 1715–1785* (Cambridge: Cambridge University Press, 1995), 365–70.
28. Brad Jones, "'In Favour of Popery': Patriotism, Protestantism, and the Gordon Riots in the Revolutionary British Atlantic," *Journal of British Studies* 52, no. 1 (2013): 79–102, quote on 95; Stephen Conway, *The British Isles and the American War of Independence* (Oxford: Oxford University Press, 2000), 246–59.
29. *The Protestant Magazine; or, Christian Treasury*, vol. 1 (London: R. Denham, 1781), 157; Donovan, *No Popery and Radicalism*, 147–48; John Seed, "'The Fall of Romish Babylon Anticipated': Plebian Dissenters and Anti-Popery in the Gordon Riots," in *The Gordon Riots: Politics, Culture, and Insurrection in Late Eighteenth-Century Britain*, ed. John Seed and Ian Haywood (Cambridge: Cambridge University Press, 2012), 79–83.
30. *Appeal from the Protestant Association to the People of Great Britain Concerning the Probable Tendency of the Late Act of Parliament in Favour of the Papists* (London, 1779), 5, 7–11, 15–17.
31. R. B. Coghlan, *An Apology for the Catholic Faith, Morality and Loyalty. . . .* (London, 1779), 13; [Joseph Berington], *A Letter to Dr. Fordyce, in Answer to His Sermon on the Delusive and Persecuting Spirit of Popery* (London, 1779), 16, 35, 40, 43, 60; [Joseph Berington], *The State and Behaviour of English Catholics, from the Reformation to the Year 1780. With a View to Their Present Number, Wealth, Character, &c. in Two Parts* (London, 1780), 4; [James Ussher], *A Free Examination of the Common Methods Employed to Prevent the Growth of Popery. In which Are Pointed Out Their Defects and Errors, and the Advantages They Give Papists* (London, 1766), 51.
32. Richard Gardiner, "The Presbyterian Rebellion: An Analysis of the Perception That the American Revolution Was a Presbyterian War" (PhD diss., Marquette University, 2005).
33. *Hypocrisy Unmasked; or, a Short Inquiry into the Religious Complaints of our American Colonies. . . .*, 3rd ed. (London: W. Nicoll, 1776), 4.
34. John Shebbeare, *An Answer to the Queries, Contained in a Letter to Dr. Shebbeare. . . .*, 2nd ed. (London, 1775), 111, 120, 137.
35. *Appeal from the Protestant Association*, 5, 56.
36. [Joseph Priestley], *A Free Address to those who have Petitioned for the Repeal of the Late Act of Parliament, in Favour of the Roman Catholics. . . .* (London, 1780), 6.
37. Ussher, *Free Examination*, iii, 4, 209.
38. For a sample of this diverse literature, see John Fellows, *The Protestant Alarm; or, Popish Cruelty Fully Displayed. . . .* (London, [1778]); John Towers, *The Church of Rome Proved to Be the Mother of Harlots. . . .* (London, 1779); James Fordyce, *The Delusive and Persecuting Spirit of Popery. . . .* (London, 1779); Benjamin Bennet, *A View of the Whole System of Popery. . . .* (London, 1781); Hugh Worthington, *Christianity, an Easy and Liberal System; that of Popery, Absurd and Burdensome. . . .* (London, 1778); Abraham Rees, *The Obligation and Importance of Searching the Scripture, as a Preservative from Popery. . . .* (London, [1779]); James Smith, *The Errors of the Church of Rome Detected. . . .*, 2nd ed. (London, 1778); Henry Venn, *Popery a Perfect Contrast to the Religion of Christ. . . .* (London, 1778); Charles Edward de Coetlogon, *A Seasonable Caution against the Abominations of the Church of Rome* (London, 1779); John Wesley, *Popery Calmly Considered*, 3rd ed. (London, 1779); *A Protestant's Resolution: Shewing his Reasons why he will not be a Papist. . . .*, 32nd ed. (London, 1780); [Anthony Horneck], *Questions and Answers Concerning the Two Religions, Viz. that of the Church of England, and the other, of the Church of Rome*, 7th ed. (London, 1781); Beilby Porteus, *Brief Confutation*

of the Errors of the Church of Rome. Extracted from Archbishop Secker's Five Sermons against Popery.. . . (London, 1781).

39. Towers, *Church of Rome,* 38.
40. Fellows, *Protestant Alarm,* 109.
41. *Strictures on a Pamphlet, Entitled, "The State and Behaviour of English Catholics, from the Reformation to the Year 1780"* (London, 1782), 71.
42. Fellows, *Protestant Alarm,* xi; Fordyce, *Delusive and Persecuting Spirit,* 10; Smith, *Errors of the Church of Rome,* 361–63.
43. Bennet, *View of the Whole System,* 296.
44. *An Antidote to Popery; or, The Protestant's Memory Jogg'd in Season.*. . . (London, 1778), 2.
45. Rees, *Obligation and Importance,* 29.
46. John Wesley, *Letter to the Printer of the Public Advertiser, Occasioned by the Late Act, Passed in Favour of Popery.*. . . (London, 1781), 3–4.
47. Mark Goldie, introduction to *The Reception of Locke's Politics,* ed. Mark Goldie, 6 vols. (London: Pickering & Chatto, 1999), xliii–xliv; Jakob De Roover and S. N. Balagangadhara, "John Locke, Christian Liberty, and the Predicament of Liberal Toleration," *Political Theory* 36, no. 4 (2008): 523–49.
48. Francis Blackburne, *Considerations on the Present State of the Controversy between the Protestants and Papists of Great Britain and Ireland; Particularly on the Question of How Far the Latter are Entitled to a Toleration upon Protestant Principles.*. . . (London, 1768), 71–78, quotes on 72, 103.
49. Arthur O'Leary, *Loyalty Asserted; or, The New Test Oath, Vindicated.*. . . (Cork, 1776), 7–8; Arthur O'Leary, "An Essay on Toleration; or, Mr. O'Leary's Plea for Liberty of Conscience," in *Miscellaneous Tracts: By the Rev. Arthur O'Leary* (Dublin, 1781), 314–93.
50. [Thomas Lloyd], *An Essay on the Toleration of Papists* (London, 1779), 8.
51. Berington, *State and Behaviour,* vi.
52. *Inquiry into the Policy of the Laws, Affecting the Popish Inhabitants of Ireland.*. . . (Dublin, 1775), 78–79.
53. *Letters on Popery: Being a Vindication of the Civil Principles of Papists.*. . . (Dublin, 1775), 8–12, 29–35, 42–46; [William Abernathy Drummond], *The Lawfulness of Breaking Faith with Heretics Proved to Be an Established Doctrine of the Church of Rome. In a Letter to Mr G.H.* (Edinburgh, 1778); *Historical Remarks on the Pope's Temporal and Deposing Power.*. . . (Dublin, 1778); *The Question Fairly Stated, Whether It Is Prudent to Repeal All the Popery Laws of This Kingdom.*. . . (Dublin, 1778); [George Hay], *An Answer to Mr. W.A.D.'s Letter to G. H., in which the Conduct of Government, in Mitigating the Penal Laws against Papists, Is Justified.*. . . (Edinburgh, 1778); [Henry Peckwell], *Interesting Facts Concerning Popery, by Way of Question and Answer; Showing that it has no Claim to Antiquity; is a Gross Corruption of Christianity; and Enjoins Principles Subversive of Civil Government in a Protestant State.*. . . , 4th ed. (Edinburgh, 1779); *An Impartial Inquiry, Whether the Two Propositions, to Be Abjured by the Oath of Abjuration, Are Doctrines of the Church of Rome* (Dublin, 1780); Wesley, *Letter to the Printer of the Public Advertiser,* 14–22.
54. 18 Geo. III, c. 60.
55. Towers, *Church of Rome,* 29–30; *Appeal from the Protestant Association,* 37.
56. Haydon, *Anti-Catholicism,* 213–33; Ian Haywood, "'A Metropolis in Flames and a Nation in Ruins': The Gordon Riots as Sublime Spectacle," in *Gordon Riots,* ed. Seed and Haywood, 117–43.
57. *Fanaticism and Treason; or, A Dispassionate History of the Rise, Progress, and Suppression, of the Rebellious Insurrections in June 1780.*. . . (London, 1780), 3, 30.

58. [George Hay], *A Memorial to the Public, in Behalf of the Roman Catholics of Edinburgh and Glasgow. . . .* (London, 1779), 41–43.
59. John Seed, *Dissenting Histories: Religious Division and the Politics of Memory in 18th Century England* (Edinburgh: Edinburgh University Press, 2008), 175–79.
60. [Thomas Holcroft], *Plain and Succinct Narrative of the Late Riots and Disturbances in the Cities of London and Westminster, and Borough of Southwark. . . .* (London, 1780), 11.
61. David Williams, *A Plan of Association, on Constitutional Principles, for Parishes, Tithings, Hundreds, and Counties of Great Britain; by which the Outrages of Mobs, and the Necessity of Military Government will be Prevented. . . .* (London, 1780), 10.
62. [Thomas Lewis O'Beirne], *Considerations on the Late Disturbances, by a Consistent Whig* (London, 1780), 7, 13, 14, 15, 22.
63. *History of the Roman Catholics*, 5–7, 11, 14, 58–59, 74.
64. [John Stevenson], *A Letter to a Dissenting Minister, Containing Remarks on the Late Act for the Relief of His Majesty's Subjects Professing the Popish Religion. . . .* (London, 1780), 1–2, 4–5, 6, 7.
65. Burke, *Speech of Edmund Burke*, 39–42.
66. Stephen Conway, "From Fellow-Nationals to Foreigners: British Perceptions of the Americans, circa 1739–1783," *William and Mary Quarterly*, 3rd ser., 59, no. 1 (2002): 94–100.
67. *The History of the Roman Catholics. . . .* (London, 1780), 71; Black, *The Association* (1963), 183–84; Matthew White, "'For the Safety of the City': The Geography and Social Politics of Public Execution after the Gordon Riots," in *Gordon Riots*, ed. Seed and Haywood, 204–25.
68. *History of the Roman Catholics*, 33; Holcroft, *Plain and Succinct Narrative*, 36; Susan Matthews, "'Mad Misrule': The Gordon Riots in Conservative Memory," in *Gordon Riots*, ed. Seed and Haywood, 226–42; Iain McCalman, "Mad Lord George and Madame La Motte: Riot and Sexuality in the Genesis of Burke's Reflections on the Revolution in France," *Journal of British Studies* 35, no. 3 (1996): 343–67.
69. Grayson Ditchfield, "The Subscription Issue in British Parliamentary Politics, 1771–1779," *Parliamentary History* 7, no. 1 (1988): 61–66; Conway, *British Isles*, 259–63.
70. *A Petition Written with the Intention that it should be Presented to the House of Lords, Concerning Freedom in Religion. . . .* (London, 1781), v, vii–ix, xiii, 75–94; *Monthly Review; or, Literary Journal* 61 (September 1779): 238; *Westminster Magazine* (June 1780), 327.
71. Haydon, *Anti-Catholicism*, 237–44, quote on 164; Eliga H. Gould, "American Independence and Britain's Counter-Revolution," *Past and Present* 154 (1997): 134–41; Marshall, *Making and Unmaking*, 377–79.
72. Davis, *Dissent in Politics*, 28–52; Thomas W. Davis, introduction to *Committees for Repeal of the Test and Corporation Acts: Minutes 1786–90 and 1827–8*, ed. Thomas W. Davis (London: London Record Society, 1978), x–xvii.
73. Deryck W. Lovegrove, *Established Church, Sectarian People: Itinerancy and the Transformation of English Dissent, 1780–1830* (Cambridge: Cambridge University Press, 1988); John Seed, "'A Set of Men Powerful Enough in Many Things': Rational Dissent and Political Opposition in England, 1770–1790," in *Enlightenment and Religion: Rational Dissent in Eighteenth-Century Britain*, ed. Knud Haakonssen (Cambridge: Cambridge University Press, 1997), 140–68; Martin Fitzpatrick, "Joseph Priestley and the Cause of Universal Toleration," *Price-Priestley Newsletter* 1 (1977): 3–30; Grayson Ditchfield, "'Incompatible with the Very Name of Christian': English Catholics and Unitarians in the Age of Milner," *Recusant History* 25, no. 1 (2000): 52–73.
74. Scott Sowerby, "Forgetting the Repealers: Religious Toleration and Historical Amnesia in Later Stuart England," *Past and Present* 215, no. 1 (2012): 114–15; Scott Sowerby, *Making*

Toleration: The Repealers and the Glorious Revolution (Cambridge, MA: Harvard University Press, 2013), 261.

75. Alison G. Olson, "The Eighteenth Century Empire: The London Dissenters' Lobbies and the American Colonies," *Journal of American Studies* 26, no. 1 (1992): 41–54; Carl Bridenbaugh, *Mitre and Sceptre: Transatlantic Faiths, Ideas, Personalities, and Politics, 1689–1775* (Oxford: Oxford University Press, 1962), 43–45, 50–53, 83–115; Stephen Taylor, "Whigs, Bishops, and America: The Politics of Church Reform in Mid Eighteenth-Century England," *Historical Journal* 36, no. 2 (1993): 344–51.
76. Bradley, *Religion, Revolution, and English Radicalism*, 147–58; Bonwick, *English Radicals*, 188–215.
77. [John Disney], *An Arranged Catalogue of the Several Publications Which Have Appeared, Relating to the Enlargement of the Toleration of Protestant-Dissenting-Ministers, and the Repeal of the Corporation and Test Acts* (London, 1790), 3–16; John Stephens, "The London Ministers and Subscription, 1772–79," *Enlightenment and Dissent* 1 (1982): 43–71.
78. *Committees for Repeal*, 24, 107–10; Stephen Addington, *A Letter to the Deputies, of Protestant Dissenting Congregations, in and about the Cities of London and Westminster* (London, 1787); James Martin, *A Speech on the Repeal of Such Parts of the Corporation and Test Acts as Affect Conscientious Dissenters. . . .* (London, 1790).
79. F. C. Mather, *High Church Prophet: Bishop Samuel Horsley (1733–1806) and the Caroline Tradition in the Later Georgian Church* (Oxford: Clarendon Press, 1992), 53–63; Peter B. Nockles, *The Oxford Movement in Context: Anglican High Churchmanship, 1760–1857* (Cambridge: Cambridge University Press, 1994), 53–63.
80. *Remarks on Dr. Priestly's Letter to the Right Honourable Mr. Pitt* (London, 1787), 13.
81. *The Case of the Protestant Dissenters, with Reference to the Test and Corporation Acts* ([London?], 1787), 3.
82. *An Essay on the Origin, Character, and Views of the Protestant Dissenters* (Oxford, 1790), v–vi, 3.
83. *Caricature Anticipations and Enlargements; Occasioned by a Late Pious Proclamation* (London, 1787), 18–19.
84. William Bristow, *Cursory Reflections on the Policy, Justice, and Expediency of Repealing the Test and Corporation Acts, Addressed to the Nation* (London, 1790), 8.
85. *Dangers of Repealing the Test-Act: in a Letter to a Member of Parliament* (London 1790), 9, 11.
86. Sanderson, "Our Own Catholic Countrymen," 149–59.
87. *Essay on the Origin, Character, and Views*, 15.
88. *Collection of the Resolutions*, 8.
89. Thomas Sherlock, *Bishop Sherlock's Arguments against a Repeal of the Corporation and Test Acts. . . .* (London, 1787).
90. *Dangers of Repealing the Test-Act*, 41.
91. *Case of the Protestant Dissenters*, 1, 3.
92. [Samuel Horsley], *A Review of the Case of the Protestant Dissenters; with Reference to the Test and Corporation Acts* (London, 1790), 12, 13, 31; Mather, *High Church Prophet*, 64–115.
93. Joseph Berington, *An Address to the Protestant Dissenters, who have lately Petitioned for a Repeal of the Test and Corporation Acts* (London, 1787), 3, 44; [Alexander Geddes], *Letter to a Member of Parliament, on the Case of the Protestant Dissenters; and the Expediency of a General Repeal of all Penal Statutes that Regard Religious Opinions* (London, 1787).
94. [Samuel Heywood], *The Right of Protestant Dissenters to a Compleat Toleration, Asserted . . .*, 2nd ed. (London, 1789), iv–v, 13–16; compare Heywood, *Right of Protestant Dissenters* (London, 1787), preface [unpaginated] and 20–23.

95. George Walker, *The Dissenter's Plea; or, The Appeal of the Dissenters to the Justice, the Honour, and the Religion of the Kingdom, Against the Test Laws* (Birmingham, [1790?]), 29–30; Heywood, *Right of Protestant Dissenters* (1787), preface [unpaginated]; Heywood, *Right of Protestant Dissenters* (1789), iv.
96. [Robert Edward Petre], *Letter from the Right Honourable Lord Petre, to the Right Reverend Doctor Horsley, Bishop of St. David's* (London, 1790), 27–33.
97. Harry Englefield, *A Letter to the Author of the Review of the Case of the Protestant Dissenters* (London, 1790), 23–24.
98. *Public Advertiser*, March 27, 1787.
99. Ditchfield, "Incompatible with the Very Name of Christian," 52–59; Fitzpatrick, "Joseph Priestley," 3–30.
100. *Appeal from the Protestant Association*, 59; *Public Advertiser*, February 19, 1790.
101. Addington, *Letter to the Deputies*, 28; Barlow, *Citizenship and Conscience*, 255–56.
102. *Committees for Repeal*, 34; Disney, *Arranged Catalogue*, 16–31; Davis, *Dissent in Politics*, 49–50, 59–60.
103. *A Collection of the Resolutions Passed at the Meetings of the Clergy of the Church of England* (London, 1790), 33.
104. Samuel Fletcher, *To Thomas Plumbe, Esq; Chairman of the Bolton Committee* ([Manchester?], 1790); *Test against Test; or, a View of the Measures Proposed in the Resolutions of the Dissenters, to Remove All Tests by Imposing One of their Own Upon Every Candidate for a Seat in the House of Commons, at the Next General Election* (London, 1790).
105. Grayson Ditchfield, "The Parliamentary Struggle over the Repeal of the Test and Corporation Acts, 1787–1790," *English Historical Review* 89, no. 352 (1974): 551–77; *Committees for Repeal*, 50, 59–61; Davis, *Dissent in Politics*, 77–88.
106. *Some Strictures on a Late Publication, Entitled Reasons for Seeking a Repeal of the Corporation and Test Acts* (London, [1791?]), 21; Stuart Andrews, *Unitarian Radicalism: Political Rhetoric, 1770–1814* (Basingstoke: Palgrave, 2003), 85–94.
107. David L. Wykes, "'The Spirit of Persecutors Exemplified': The Priestley Riots and the Victims of the Church and King Mobs," *Transactions of the Unitarian Historical Society* 20, no. 1 (1991–92): 17–39; Michael Durey, *Transatlantic Radicals and the Early American Republic* (Lawrence: University Press of Kansas, 1997), 9, 134–73.
108. James Sack, *From Jacobite to Conservative: Reaction and Orthodoxy in Britain, c. 1760–1832* (Cambridge: Cambridge University Press, 1993), 227–30; Stephen Conway, "Christians, Catholics, Protestants: The Religious Links of Britain and Ireland with Continental Europe, c. 1689–1800," *English Historical Review* 74, no. 509 (2009): 853–61; Dominic Aidan Bellenger, *The French Exiled Clergy in the British Isles after 1789: An Historical Introduction and Working List* (Bath: Downside Abbey, 1986), 11–34.
109. Robert Hole, *Pulpits, Politics, and Public Order in England, 1760–1832* (Cambridge: Cambridge University Press, 1989), 106.
110. Fergus O'Ferrall, *Catholic Emancipation: Daniel O'Connell and the Birth of Irish Democracy, 1820–30* (Dublin: Gill & Macmillan, 1985); Thomas Bartlett, *The Fall and Rise of the Irish Nation: The Catholic Question, 1690–1830* (Dublin: Gill & Macmillan, 1992), 228–342; G.I.T. Machin, *The Catholic Question in English Politics, 1820 to 1830* (Oxford: Clarendon Press, 1964).
111. Brown, *National Churches*, 139–40; Davis, *Dissent in Politics*, 244–55.
112. Boyd Hilton, *A Mad, Bad, and Dangerous People? England, 1783–1846* (Oxford: Oxford University Press, 2006), 372–492.
113. Colley, *Britons*, 326–71.

114. James Kelly, *Sir Richard Musgrave, 1746–1818: Ultra-Protestant Ideologue* (Dublin: Four Courts Press, 2009), 90–150; Joseph Ivimey, *Neutrality the Proper Ground for Protestant Dissenters Respecting the Roman Catholic Claims. . . .* (London, 1813), 14; Joseph Ivimey, *The Supremacy of the Pope Contrary to Scripture, and Dangerous to the Safety of Protestant Governments* (London, 1819), viii–xiii.
115. G.I.T. Machin, "The No-Popery Movement in Britain in 1828–9," *Historical Journal* 6, no. 2 (1963): 193–211, especially 210–11.
116. "Report from the Select Committee Appointed to Report the Nature and Substance of the Laws and Ordinances Existing in Foreign States, Respecting the Regulation of their Roman Catholic Subjects, in Ecclesiastical Matters, and their Intercourse with the See of Rome, or any other Foreign Ecclesiastical Jurisdiction," *House of Commons Papers: Reports of Committees* 501 (1816).
117. Stewart J. Brown, *The National Churches of England, Ireland, and Scotland, 1801–1846* (Oxford: Oxford University Press, 2001), 93–136; Irene Whelan, *The Bible War in Ireland: The "Second Reformation" and the Polarization of Protestant-Catholic Relations, 1800–1840* (Dublin: Lilliput Press, 2005), 152–91; David Hempton, *Methodism and Politics in British Society, 1750–1850* (London: Hutchinson, 1985), 120–23.
118. *Evangelical Magazine and Missionary Chronicle*, n.s., 6 (April 1829): 154.
119. *Christian Reformer; or, New Evangelical Miscellany* 14, no. 158 (February 1828): 75.
120. Colley, *Britons*, 336; Davis, introduction, xxi.
121. G.I.T. Machin, "Resistance to Repeal of the Test and Corporation Acts, 1828," *Historical Journal* 22 (1979): 115–20; Davis, *Dissent in Politics*, 218–20.
122. Davis, *Dissent in Politics*, 218–20.
123. Robert Morres, *Reflections on the Claims of Protestant and Popish Dissenters, Especially of the Latter, to an Equality in Civil Privileges with the Members of the Established Church* (Salisbury, [1824?]), 31–33.
124. Francis Merewether, *The Case between the Church and the Dissenters Impartially and Practically Considered* (London, 1827), 2–3, 150.
125. Herbert Marsh, *Charge Delivered to the Clergy of the Diocese of Peterborough in July MDCCCXXVII, on the Influence of the Roman Catholic Question on the Established Church* (London, 1827), 11.
126. Richard W. Davis, "The Strategy of 'Dissent' in the Repeal Campaign, 1820–28," *Journal of Modern History* 38, no. 4 (1966): 374–93.
127. Robert Winter to Lord John Russell, January 10, 1828, Protestant Dissenting Deputies, Secretary's Out-Letter Book, pp. 57–58, London Metropolitan Archives, CLC/181/MS03085.
128. Michael A. Rutz, *The British Zion: Congregationalism, Politics, and Empire, 1790–1850* (Waco, TX: Baylor University Press, 2011), 31–51; Lovegrove, *Established Church, Sectarian People*, 121–41; Davis, *Dissent in Politics*, 148–211.
129. Davis, "Strategy of Dissent," 378–84.
130. *Monthly Repository of Theology and General Literature* 1, no. 5 (May 1827): 379.
131. Davis, *Dissent in Politics*, 239–48; Davis, introduction, xvii–xxvi.
132. *Monthly Repository* 2, no. 19 (July 1828): 497; no. 20 (August 1828): 574.
133. Rutz, *British Zion*.
134. Henriques, *Religious Toleration*, 147; Machin, *Catholic Question*, 7; Davis, *Dissent in Politics*, 229–35.
135. Three Denominations, Minute Books, vol. 3 (1798–1827), 77–85, Doctor Williams's Library, MS.38.106; Ivimey, *Neutrality the Proper Ground*, 15–16, 22, 40.

136. Joseph Ivimey, *Dr. Williams's Library, and the Debate on the Roman Catholic Claims: A Letter Addressed to the Trinitarian Members of the General Body of Dissenting Ministers of the Three Denominations, on the Above Subject* (London, 1829), 3–9; *Christian Reformer* 15, no. 172 (April 1829): 191–95.
137. Ivimey, *Neutrality the Proper Ground,* 8, 14.
138. [Joseph Ivimey], *A Letter to the Right Honourable the Earl of Liverpool, on the Dissimilarity Existing between the Cases of Protestant and Roman Catholic Dissenters. . . .* (London, 1821), ii; for Ivimey's authorship, see George Pritchard, *Memoir of the Life and Writings of the Rev. Joseph Ivimey, Late Pastor of the Church in Eagle Street, London; and Twenty Years Gratuitous Secretary to the Baptist Irish Society* (London, 1835), 135–36.
139. *Committees for Repeal,* 86
140. [Edward Blount], *Corporation and Test Acts* ([London?], [1828?]); O'Ferrall, *Catholic Emancipation,* 181–82.
141. *Christian Reformer* 14, no. 158 (February 1828): 77.
142. *Congregational Magazine,* n.s., 39, no. 9 (March 1828): 164.
143. Brown, *National Churches;* Whelan, *Bible War;* John Wolffe, *The Protestant Crusade in Great Britain, 1829–1860* (Oxford: Oxford University Press, 1991); Timothy Larsen, *Friends of Religious Equality: Nonconformist Politics in Mid-Victorian England* (Woodbridge: Boydell, 1999).
144. Eugenio F. Biagini, *Liberty, Retrenchment, and Reform: Popular Liberalism in the Age of Gladstone, 1860–1880* (Cambridge: Cambridge University Press, 1992).

CONCLUSION

History, Polemic, and Analysis

Evan Haefeli

MAY THE PROTESTANT RELIGION prevail & flourish through all nations!" So toasted the residents of Northampton, Massachusetts, the news of peace with Britain that brought independence to the United States in 1783. The American Revolution had altered the circumstances of British-American anti-popery but not its ambitions. On the contrary, just a few months earlier, Ezra Stiles, Congregational minister and president of Yale, had proclaimed, "American ideas of toleration and religious liberty . . . will become the fashionable system of Europe very soon." Building on the old anti-Catholic trope that conflated Protestantism with reason, Stiles targeted France and Spain as among the nations that would break with the ancient hegemony of the Catholic Church and permit the growth of "wisdom and enlightened politics." He also looked forward to the day when the "United States will embosom all the religious sects and denominations in Christendom," a vision of religious liberty that of course would be dominated by Protestants like him.[1]

This volume has demonstrated how pervasive and vital anti-Catholicism was in the British-American world. The contributors have also emphasized that it varied in degree, character, and form from place to place and over time—not least because it did not always apply to actual Roman Catholics. To fill in that gap, we have suggested adopting the concept of anti-popery as developed by historians of early modern England to bridge the spheres of politics and religion, which the concept of anti-Catholicism tends to keep separate. Anti-popery captures the occasionally contradictory consequences of what was, in the end, more than just an irrational religious prejudice. Occasionally a force for Protestant unity, it also deserves credit for sometimes advancing the cause of reason, for example in early criticisms of witchcraft beliefs and trials. As the essays in this volume illustrate, one can see these ideologies change, adapt, and fracture even while seeming to preserve the same basic values. From the perspective of the British-American world, anti-popery and anti-Catholicism can look rather different depending on the local context.[2]

The upheavals following the outbreak of the French Revolution set the world on a rather different track from what Stiles had anticipated. However, the anti-popish framework of the former revolutionaries in America still influenced how they understood their place in the world. Watching the Age of Revolutions sputter in the 1810s, Thomas McKean, born in Delaware to Presbyterian parents from Ulster, agreed with John Adams that "a democratic form in France, in the present age, was preposterous." McKean predicted that moves toward liberalism in Spain "will be attacked and resisted by the inquisitors, Jesuits, monks, and all the bigots and petty tyrants." For his part, Adams believed the "present question before the human race, that great democratical tribunal, is whether the *jus divinum* is in men or in magistrates." It was, he believed, a struggle that could be dated back to "the death of Abel," or maybe its origins lay "with Constantine and the council of Nice? With Clovis? With the Crusades? With the wars of the Hussites? With Luther? With Charles V, Louis XIV? Shall we recollect the Waldenses, the powder plot, the Irish massacre, St. Bartholomew's day, Robespierre, or Equality, the Duke of Orleans, or his predecessor, the Regent of France, and his Mississippi?" The French Revolution fit smoothly into the anti-popish Anglo-American chronology of the struggle for liberty.[3]

Modern, democratic British Americans would continue to draw on the anti-popish ideas and artifacts of their ancestors as they confronted the challenges of the nineteenth century. By 1897, the anti-Catholic (and pro-Huguenot) colonial classic *The French Convert,* published first in England and then in Boston in 1708, had gone through at least twenty-one American and twenty-five British editions. It told the story of an aristocratic French Catholic woman who, left home alone while her husband fought in a war, was converted to Protestantism by the devout piety of her Huguenot gardener. In classically anti-Catholic fashion, the Catholic figures in the story, her priest and household steward, are lecherous and corrupt: after she converts they seek to have her raped and murdered (instead, they are the ones who die). In the colonial period, the book had often appeared in conjunction with a brief account of the persecution of the Huguenots. In the early republic it appeared with *Signs of the Times; or, The Overthrow of Papal Tranny in France, the Prelude of the Destruction to Popery and Despotism, but of Peace to Mankind* by the English Baptist minister James Bicheno. Printed nine times between 1793 and 1795 in Boston, New London, and New York, *The French Convert* saw additional printings in New Hampshire, Connecticut, Baltimore, and Philadelphia by 1798. In 1812 it apparently became the first book published in Buffalo, New York. New editions continued to appear in New York and New Hampshire in the 1830s. Its (mostly) anti-French and (certainly) anti-Catholic publishing career closely mirrored that of the famous captivity narrative *The Redeemed Captive Returning to Zion.* Written by the early eighteenth-century minister of Deerfield, Massachusetts, John Williams, it described the sufferings of his devout congregation, men and especially women, at the hands of French and Indigenous Catholic captors and became a timely reminder of local anti-Catholic patriotism. Up through the 1840s, New England presses often reprinted it in tandem with popish crises. Only thereafter did it sink into the realm of antiquarian interest.[4]

Anti-Catholic "religious animosity" may have been less in evidence during the early years of the republic, but anti-popery did not fade away.[5] When Catholic immigration surged in the 1830s, Americans were well primed to see it as a threat to their liberty and religion. New texts, like *Confessions of a French Catholic Priest, to which are added Warnings to the People of the United States,* discredited the immigrants' religion. Edited and published in 1837 by Samuel F. B. Morse, painter, university professor, inventor of the telegraph, and avid anti-Catholic spokesman, *Confessions* was just one of a number of tell-all accounts by former Catholic priests and other converts to Protestantism that described Roman Catholicism in lurid, sexually titillating ways.[6] Such accounts, together with a spate of novels, fed the longstanding Protestant fascination with Catholic convents and other secret spaces that allowed the sexes to interact outside the sphere of the Protestant patriarchal household. But they were not new. One of the most frequently republished works of anti-popery in the 1830s and 1850s was *The Great Red Dragon; or, The Master Key to Popery* (a reference to the Book of Revelations chapters twelve and thirteen), a text that has appeared in editions as recently as 2003–10. Written in 1724 by Antonio Gavin, a former Spanish priest who ended his days as an Anglican minister in Virginia, it claimed that the practice of auricular confession, whereby women confessed their most intimate sins to priests, led to illicit and even perverse sex, and set the tone for a number of nineteenth-century accounts.[7]

Old and new anti-popish texts continued to pass back and forth across the Atlantic, published and republished in a still largely shared culture of anti-popery. Ingram Cobbin, a Congregational minister from London who had been active in various missionary societies before poor health compelled him to focus on writing, produced a number of influential school textbooks and a few anti-popish tracts that appealed to Americans. In 1840, the Presbyterian Board of Publications published his *Book of Popery,* a self-proclaimed *Manual for Protestants,* which offered a *Description of the Origin, Progress, Doctrines, Rites, and Ceremonies of the Papal Church.* This author of *Scripture Light on Popish Darkness* also released a new edition of *Foxe's Book of Martyrs* (the "cheapest" currently available) shortly before his death in 1851 to prove that "Popery is but paganism under a mask" and that "persecution is not inherent in Protestantism, while in Popery it is an essential ingredient."[8]

Old texts remained relevant because popery "was not 'one thing in Naples and another in New York,'" as a writer in *Putnam's Monthly Magazine of American*

Literature, Science, and Art insisted in 1869. The "Church in America today . . . is as the Church in Rome in the sixteenth century." As historian Timothy Verhoeven points out, Catholicism was essentially considered "a medieval remnant."[9] The axiomatic conflation of Roman Catholics across time and space into the catchall category of popery served many purposes, both old and new. Obviously, it justified continuing hostility to Roman Catholics and their religion. As a book written in New Jersey in 1871, but published across the country, affirmed, popery remained "the foe of the true Church and of Republicanism, the determined enemy of liberty, civil and ecclesiastical, personal and national" just as "it has always been."[10] At the same time, this comfortably static image of popery also helped make sense of the new corners of the world coming to people's attention. The "Idol Worship" of Roman Catholicism featured in a brief essay for *Harper's Weekly* in April 1866 that juxtaposed pictures of the "Cardinal Archbishop of Toledo conveying the image of the Virgin of Olvido to the Royal Palace, Madrid" with the "Annual procession of the Dragon at Saigon" as equivalent examples of "human nature." Each revealed "the essential features of human superstition" that was "very much the same all the world over."[11] Anti-popery continued to adapt and expand along with the Anglo-American empires.

Present at the foundation of Anglo-American liberalism, anti-popery has never disappeared. It has continued to intervene in the evolution of Anglo-American democracy on both sides of the Atlantic down to the present. One historian has recently traced back the origins of the modern evangelical political movement to Protestant fundamentalists' reactions against the election of Franklin D. Roosevelt, whom they despised as a "Dictator-President" elected by Jews and Catholics. Combined with the rise of dictatorships in Europe, this election stoked apocalyptic hopes and fears that led some to wonder whether the reign of Antichrist was at hand.[12] Examining mid-twentieth-century American liberalism, the Roman Catholic scholar John McGreevy has found "that discussion of Catholicism, along with criticism of racial segregation and opposition to fascism and Communism, helped define" its terms, including "the insistence that religion, as an entirely private matter, must be separated from the state, that religious loyalties must not threaten national unity, and that only an emphasis on individual autonomy, thinking on one's own, would sustain American democracy." These beliefs "inevitably clashed with Catholic understandings."[13] Looking at post–World War II Britain, Clive Field sees anti-Catholicism moving toward apparently favorable views of individual Catholics but increasingly negative views of the leadership of the Church.[14]

This ongoing history is difficult to separate from the study of anti-Catholicism and anti-popery. Indeed, it is one reason the relationship between these scholarly categories is still up for debate. There is still no complete agreement on their meaning or proper use. Some scholars use anti-Catholicism and anti-popery interchangeably. Others, like Tim Harris, insist on a clear distinction between the

252 HARPER'S WEEKLY. [APRIL 21, 1866.

IDOL WORSHIP IN SPAIN—THE CARDINAL ARCHBISHOP OF TOLEDO CONVEYING THE IMAGE OF THE VIRGIN OF OLVIDO TO THE ROYAL PALACE, MADRID.

ception of the little Royal stranger, the Archbishop of Toledo, Cardinal Father TIRILO, set out by special train to fetch the Virgin from the convent of San Pascual, at Aranjuez, and was accompanied by a priest, whose sacred duty it was to carry the image, as though he were bearing a doll. Our illustration is taken from a sketch representing the entrance of the Archbishop to the railway station, where, as usual, a number of the faithful had assembled to witness the deportation of the image whose presence in Madrid was expected to be so serviceable to the Queen in her hour of trouble.

IDOL WORSHIP IN COCHIN CHINA—ANNUAL PROCESSION OF THE DRAGON AT SAIGON.

"Idol Worship," *Harper's Weekly,* engraving, April 21, 1866. (Image courtesy of HarpWeek)

The illustration equates a Spanish priest carrying the image of the Virgin "as though he were bearing a doll" to the Chinese "Annual Procession of the Dragon" in Saigon.

two. Still others, like Jeffrey Collins, deny that one can make a meaningful distinction between them. Collins argues that the very idea that one can distinguish between the religious and political aspects of Roman Catholicism is anti-Catholic. He makes this case by pointing to the failed attempt by the so-called "Blackloist" faction of English Catholics (named after the pseudonym for their leading thinker, Thomas White, a k a Blacklo) to exploit "the distinction of political Romanism" from "religious Catholicism" to achieve toleration for Roman Catholics during the revolutionary years of the 1640s and 1650s. Drawing on the philosophy of Thomas Hobbes, the Blackloists proclaimed their loyalty to the revolutionary regime and disavowed the political authority of the papacy. In short, they did all they could to disarm anti-popish criticisms short of taking the final step of converting to Protestantism. Nonetheless, Protestants like Oliver Cromwell were not persuaded. Then, after the Restoration, the Blackloists' ties to the Cromwellian regime were held against them to justify continuing to deny them toleration. For Collins, the Blackloists' failure to find religious and political equality in seventeenth-century England demonstrates the fundamental anti-Catholicism of the Protestant anti-popery, which culminated with John Locke, by showing Protestants' inability to accept the Blackloists' distinction between anti-popery and anti-Catholicism. This anti-Catholicism, which excluded Catholics from toleration because they acknowledged papal—and thus foreign—authority, lies at the root of modern Lockean liberalism, giving it a clear Protestant bias.[15]

Collins has a point: it is not easy to separate anti-Catholicism from anti-popery. Nevertheless, we should at least recognize that attempting to do so has been an integral part of anti-popery's history, which, as he shows, has never been exclusively Protestant. The Christian tradition of hostility to the papacy dates back to the Middle Ages.[16] English Roman Catholic hostility to papal influence led to the passage of various anti-papal statutes between 1351 and 1393, most notably those of *praemunire,* which restricted the authority of any foreign power or agents of a foreign power (i.e., the papacy) within the king's territories by outlawing "*imperium in imperio.*" The last, or Great Statute of *Praemunire,* raised questions about the relationship between secular and spiritual jurisdiction that persisted into the Protestant Reformation and beyond, figuring, for example, in the Parliamentary Militia Ordinance of 1642 that gave Parliament the right to raise an army to fight against the overreaching claims its king.[17]

In sum, anti-Catholicism and anti-popery remain fascinatingly diverse, occasionally contentious, and vibrant topics meriting much more attention than they have received thus far. In an effort to impose some order on future scholarship, John Wolffe has proposed a taxonomic model of four distinct strands of anti-Catholicism to facilitate analysis and discussion. Although designed for studies of nineteenth- and twentieth-century anti-Catholicism, it is worth considering for the earlier period as well as it captures some of the variety evident in this volume. It also agrees with our point that anti-popery and anti-Catholicism have a history worth tracking over time.

Wolffe's first variant of anti-Catholicism is the constitutional/national. Considering the Roman Catholic Church to be an extraterritorial power striving for global political supremacy, it generally focuses on the machinations of the papacy and Jesuits. Powerful in the early modern period, it waned in the late eighteenth century as the papacy became less threatening. The suppression of the Jesuit order in 1773, and then the capture and humiliation of the pope by Napoleon's troops in 1798 revealed the papacy's inability to even defend itself, much less attack others.[18]

Wolffe's second strand, theological anti-Catholicism, attacks the "perceived doctrinal errors of the Roman Catholic Church." In its more extreme manifestations, it portrays "Romanism" and "Popery" as "soul-destroying counterfeits of true Christianity." Since its primary goal was to convert Catholics, theological anti-Catholicism could encourage tolerant stances toward Catholic individuals, for example by distinguishing "theological polemic from personal hostility." It too started strong but receded in the Age of Revolutions, although it returned in force with the resurgence of Roman Catholicism after 1815. While theological anti-Catholicism could prompt positive expressions of Protestant religion by affirming doctrines of faith over works, as attitudes toward Catholics became more liberal and their place in Protestant society secure, it became increasingly associated with sectarianism and fundamentalism. Works of "premillennial historicist eschatology," like that of a 1933 Australian pamphlet warning of an upcoming Armageddon pitting the United States, the British Empire, and Japan against the rest of world, including a Soviet Union "controlled and corrupted by the pope and the Jesuits in alliance with the forces of Islam and 'heathenism,'" continued to be published. However, Wolffe sees such views as becoming increasingly marginal, especially after the Roman Catholic Church modernized itself in the Vatican II reforms of the 1960s.[19]

Sociocultural anti-Catholicism, Wolffe's third variant, is less obviously attached to religion. Instead, it focuses on the real or alleged sexual immorality associated with Roman Catholic practices. Its prurient nature links it to the history of pornography. Obsessed with the sexual conduct of priests and nuns and stories of young people held captive in nunneries, it is nevertheless not exclusively about sex. It also involved controversies over issues like schooling and the dissemination of allegedly false teachings. It also blamed "popery" for a variety of social ills, including (above and beyond sexual perversion) credulity, hypocrisy, criminality, poverty, ignorance, persecution, and deceit. These dimensions are especially evident in discussions of the Irish, where conversion to Protestantism was linked to the civilizing of that rude and barbarous people. Sociocultural anti-Catholicism emphasized the "obscurantist nature of the Catholic sub-culture, perpetuated by segregated education, censorship, and hostility to scientific and scholarly advances." It too was largely rendered redundant by Vatican II in the 1960s. However, it persists around questions of birth control and sexuality and has gained new life thanks to the recent pedophilia and other sexual scandals in the Church. What some recent writers have labeled the new anti-Catholicism is merely the resurgence of this once dormant variety of anti-Catholicism.[20]

The fourth and final form of anti-Catholicism Wolffe identifies is the popular strain, "shaped and expressed primarily by oral rather than by print culture." Popular anti-Catholicism has "produced organisational structures largely independent of control by political, religious, or social elites." Often linked to ethnic antagonisms, whether against the Irish in Britain or the French in colonial America, it manifests itself most obviously in outbreaks of riots and physical violence against people, buildings, or things. Public celebrations like Guy Fawkes / Pope's Day fall within this category. Popular violence could be encouraged by any of the previous three categories of anti-Catholicism, which "could both provoke attacks from Catholics themselves and give Protestants a sense of ideological legitimacy for their more visceral sectarian antagonisms." Where it has persisted most tenaciously, as in Northern Ireland, it is often tied to local identity and civic pride. Anti-Catholic parades and celebrations serve a variety of community functions above and beyond anti-Catholicism, but even in Ulster those functions are fading away, as they have most everywhere else in the English-speaking world during the twentieth century.[21]

Wolffe admits that the boundaries between his categories can blur. Still, they help impose some order on studies of anti-Catholicism if not anti-popery. As he notes, their undeniable historical significance demands "some definitional precision if the concept is not to become too diffuse to be useful." Using his schema to chart "ebbs and flows in anti-Catholicism over the last few centuries," Wolffe identifies a particular high tide in the 1850s when all four strands were strongly resurgent, then an uneven decline in the twentieth century. Theologically marginalized, anti-Catholicism's popular base has also been substantially weakened, except in certain local contexts like Belfast. He believes the constitutional-national and sociocultural aspects have proven most resilient because they are easily adaptable to secular, rather than just Protestant, discourse. One could question just this distinction between the secular and the Protestant, or perhaps bridge it by noting anti-popery's ability to target individuals, institutions, and phenomena not directly part of Roman Catholicism. Nevertheless, Wolffe's point about the "sheer diversity of manifestations of anti-Catholicism" is important. Indeed, as he points out, "the inherent diversity of anti-Catholicism and the factors giving rise to it" do "much to explain its pervasiveness and persistence."[22]

In the end, it is clear that anti-popery and anti-Catholicism are much more complex and important phenomena than is commonly thought. Far more than an unpleasant prejudice, they represent closely related ideologies premised on a rejection of the Roman Catholic papacy, its actual practices and imagined policies, that have figured in various aspects of British-American culture and history and have been absorbed into modern liberalism around the world.[23] Although there still is no consensus on the distinction (if any) between anti-Catholicism and anti-popery, it is clearly impossible to discuss the major political or social ideals of the British-American world without some reference to them. There is certainly more work to be done, but we hope this book has demonstrated at least a few key points: first, that anti-popery was an inextricable part of Britain's civil and religious legacy to the United States; second, that for all the similarities, anti-popery and anti-Catholicism were diverse forces that varied over time and space and demand interdisciplinary attention; and finally, that we have much to gain by overcoming the division between the fields of English, Scottish, Irish, and American studies. Certainly before 1783 these were different corners of a common worldview and experience—united and ultimately divided by anti-popery.

Notes

1. *Maryland Gazette*, June 12, 1783, cited in William C. Stinchcombe, *The American Revolution and the French Alliance* (Syracuse, NY: Syracuse University Press, 1969), 103; Ezra Stiles, *The United States Elevated to Glory and Honor: A Sermon* (New Haven, 1783), 52–54.
2. Vera Hoorens, "Why Did Johann Weyer Write *De praetigiis daemonum?* How Anti-Catholicism Inspired the Landmark Plea for Witches," *BMGN: The Low Countries Historical Review* 129, no. 1 (2014): 3–24.
3. Thomas McKean to John Adams, August 20, 1813, and John Adams to Thomas McKean, July 6, 1815, in John Adams, *The Works of John Adams, Second President of the United States: With a Life of the Author, Notes and Illustrations*, 10 vols. (Boston, 1850–56), 10:61, 167.
4. Thomas S. Kidd, "Recovering 'The French Convert': Views of the French and the Uses of Anti-Catholicism in Early America," *Book History* 7 (2004): 97–111; Evan Haefeli and Kevin Sweeney, "*The Redeemed Captive* as Recurrent Seller: Politics and Publication, 1707–1854," *New England Quarterly* 77, no. 3 (2004): 341–67.
5. Maura Jane Farrelly, *Anti-Catholicism in America, 1620–1860* (Cambridge: Cambridge University Press, 2018), xiv–xv and chap. 4, argues that this era of tolerance for Roman Catholics allowed Catholics to get caught up in internal disputes, while chap. 5 examines "Anti-Catholicism in the Age of Immigration."
6. Samuel F. B. Morse, ed., *Confessions of a French Catholic Priest, to which are added Warnings to the People of the United States* (New York, 1837). Timothy Verhoeven examines the links between French and American opponents of the Roman Catholic Church in the years 1830–1870 in *Transatlantic Anti-Catholicism: France and the United States in the Nineteenth Century* (New York: Palgrave Macmillan, 2010).
7. Patrick W. Carey, "The Confessional and Ex-Catholic Priests in Nineteenth-Century Protestant America," *United States Catholic Historian* 33, no. 3 (Summer 2015): 1–26; Sandra Frink, "Women, the Family, and the Fate of the Nation in American Anti-Catholic Narratives,

1830–1860," *Journal of the History of Sexuality* 18, no. 2 (May 2009): 237–64; Rodney Hessinger, "'A Base and Unmanly Conspiracy': Catholicism and the Hogan Schism in the Gendered Religious Marketplace of Philadelphia," *Journal of the Early Republic* 31, no. 3 (Fall 2011): 357–96; and Cassandra Yacovazzi, "'Are You Allowed to Read the Bible in a Convent?': Protestant Perspectives on the Catholic Approach to Scripture in Convent Narratives, 1830–1860," *United States Catholic Historian* 31, no. 3 (Summer 2013): 23–46. For British parallels, see Rene Kollar, "Foreign and Catholic: A Plea to Protestant Parents on the Dangers of Convent Education in Victorian England," *History of Education* 31, no. 4 (July 2002): 335–50; Rene Kollar, "*Punch* and the Nuns: Anti-Catholicism and Satire in Mid-Nineteenth-Century England," *Downside Review* 130 (July 2012): 1–26; Rene Kollar, "Convents, the Bible, and English Anti-Catholicism in the Nineteenth Century," *Women's History Magazine* 74 (Spring 2014): 11–18; Allison Giffen, "Suffering Girls: The Work of Anti-Catholicism in Martha Finley's Novels," *Children's Literature Association Quarterly* 41, no. 1 (Spring 2016): 3–23; Diane Long Hoeveler, *The Gothic Ideology: Religious Hysteria and Anti-Catholicism in British Popular Fiction, 1780–1880* (Cardiff: University of Wales Press, 2014). See also the annotated bibliography by Carol Herringer, "Catholicism and Anti-Catholicism," in *Victorian Literature: Oxford Bibliographies Online* (2012) DOI: 10.1093/OBO/9780199799558-0102.

8. Ingram Cobbin, *The Book of Popery: A Manual for Protestants; Description of the Origin, Progress, Doctrines, Rites, and Ceremonies of the Papal Church* (Philadelphia, 1840); John Foxe, *Foxe's Book of Martyrs: A Complete and Authentic Account of the Lives, Sufferings, and Triumphant Deaths of the Primitive and Protestant Martyrs, in All Parts of the World, with Notes, Comments, and Illustrations,* ed. Rev. John Milner, *A New and Corrected Edition, with an Essay on Popery, and Additions to the Present Time* by Ingram Cobbin (London, 1851), iii–iv; Thompson Cooper, "Cobbin, Ingram (1777–1851)," rev. David Huddleston, *ODNB*.
9. Timothy Verhoeven, "Transatlantic Connections: American Anti-Catholicism and the First Vatican Council (1869–70)," *Catholic Historical Review* 100, no. 4 (Autumn 2014): 698.
10. Joseph S. Van Dyke, *Popery: The Foe of the Church, and of the Republic* (Philadelphia, 1871), 4.
11. "Idol Worship," *Harper's Weekly,* April 21, 1866, 251–52.
12. Matthew Avery Sutton, "Was FDR the Antichrist? The Birth of Fundamentalist Antiliberalism in a Global Age," *Journal of American History* 98, no. 4 (March 2012): 1052–74, quote on 1067. Sutton does not discuss anti-popery or anti-Catholicism as such, but the apocalyptic thinking he describes has deep roots within anti-popery.
13. John T. McGreevy, "Thinking on One's Own: Catholicism and the American Intellectual Imagination, 1928–1960," *Journal of American History* 84, no. 1 (June 1997): 97–131, quotes on 98.
14. Clive D. Field, "No Popery's Ghost: Does Popular Anti-Catholicism Survive in Contemporary Britain?" *Journal of Religion in Europe* 7, no. 2 (2014): 116–49.
15. Jeffrey Collins, "Restoration Anti-Catholicism: A Prejudice in Motion," in *England's Wars of Religion, Revisited,* ed. Charles A. W. Prior and Glenn Burgess (Burlington, VT: Ashgate, 2011), 281–306, quote on 286.
16. For a study of an anti-papal image dating back to the late fifteenth century that was used by Protestants and Catholics alike, see Lawrence P. Buck, *Roman Monster: An Icon of the Papal Antichrist in Reformation Polemics* (Kirksville, MI: Truman State University Press, 2014).
17. W. T. Waugh, "The Great Statute of Praemunire," *English Historical Review* 37, no. 146 (April 1922): 173–205; P. R. Cavill, "'The Enemy of God and His Church': James Hobart, Praemunire, and the Clergy of Norwich Diocese," *Journal of Legal History* 32, no. 2 (August 2011): 127–50; J. A. Guy, "Henry VIII and the Praemunire Manoeuvres of 1530–1531," *English Historical Review* 97, no. 384 (July 1982): 481–503; Warren E. Spehar, "The Militia Ordinance of 1642

and the 14th-Century Great Statute of *Praemunire*," *Parliamentary History* 35, pt. 2 (June 2016): 111–31. For examples of *praemunire* in early seventeenth-century religious debates, see Charles W. A. Prior, *A Confusion of Tongues: Britain's Wars of Reformation, 1625–1642* (Oxford: Oxford University Press, 2012), 25, 52–54, 207–8. See also the discussion of *imperium* in David Armitage, *The Ideological Origins of the British Empire* (Cambridge: Cambridge University Press, 2000), passim.

18. John Wolffe, "A Comparative Historical Categorisation of Anti-Catholicism," *Journal of Religious History* 39, no. 2 (June 2015): 182–202.
19. Wolffe, "Comparative Historical Categorisation," 189, 193.
20. Wolffe, "Comparative Historical Categorisation," 197.
21. Wolffe, "Comparative Historical Categorisation," 197–98.
22. Wolffe, "Comparative Historical Categorisation," 201–2.
23. Works pointing to the anti-Catholic roots of modern liberalism include Danilo Raponi, "An 'Anti-Catholicism of Free Trade?' Religion and the Anglo-Italian Negotiations of 1863," *European History Quarterly* 39, no. 4 (2009): 633–52; and Young-Chan Choi, "Rhee Syngman's Protestant Theory of Liberty, 1894–1910," *Global Intellectual History* (2019): DOI: 10.1080/23801883.2019.1633677.

EPILOGUE

Words, Deeds, and Ambiguities in Early Modern Anti-Catholicism

Anthony Milton

I VIVIDLY REMEMBER WHEN I made my first purchase of anti-Catholic literature in a local second-hand bookshop. The works in question were two short books that had clearly been collected by a single individual, as one could tell from their often splenetic annotations in a firm ink pen. Both books had the same virulently anti-Catholic content, with which the owner had clearly been in vehement agreement. But these were not early modern texts, affording an antiquarian glimpse of a strange forgotten world of primordial confessional allegiance and prejudice. They had actually been written and published during the Second World War. One was H. G. Wells's *Crux Ansata: An Indictment of the Roman Catholic Church* (published by Penguin, and written just a year after his book *Phoenix* had called for reimposing the Test Act on Catholics). The other was *The Papacy in Politics Today* by the ex-priest and freethinker Joseph McCabe. The Wells book might be familiar to some readers, although it rarely features much in discussions of his writings, and certainly not in the latest *DNB* life, and is notably absent from some copyright libraries, such as that of Cambridge University. The first chapter is entitled "Why Do We Not Bomb Rome?" Another, entitled "Shinto Catholicism" claims to identify a deliberate attempted assimilation of Catholicism and the Shintoism of Japan, while at the end, the book declares "Before mankind gets rid of it, the Papacy may be drowning our hopes for the coming generation in a welter of blood—in an attempt to achieve a final world-wide St Bartholemew's Eve." The subtitle of McCabe's work, "The Guilt of the Roman Church in the World War," indicates its contents.[1]

What immediately struck me were some remarkable similarities with the seventeenth-century anti-Catholicism that I had been studying. There was the same association of Roman Catholicism, and of the papacy in particular, with the nation's military enemy (although in these cases this was Fascism and the Axis powers rather than the early modern forces of France and the Habsburgs) and also the alliance of Roman Catholicism with a fundamental hostility to justice and truth (although in these cases the truths were democracy, socialism, and modernity rather than Protestantism). Many of the staples of anti-Catholic discourse were virtually unchanged—the insistence that the Roman court upheld a perverse religion for purely cynical and mercenary reasons, the horror stories of rape and sexual deviance in monasteries, the papal tyranny over conscience and its dangerous political implications, the claim that Roman Catholicism was an alien body that would promote treason wherever it could gain a foothold, its allegedly deliberate fostering of ignorance to maximize control over the laity, the cynical trickery of miracles, and so on.

Of course, some similarities were to be expected: anti-Catholicism always draws to some extent on past events and earlier traditions, which are assumed to have direct relevance to the present. Certain anti-Catholic arguments and images have proved remarkably resilient—not least the myth of Pope Joan. But for all the echoes and borrowings, and the sense that the elements of a familiar story or set of associations are simply being reordered, the reformulations in Wells's and McCabe's works are themselves equally significant: there are different inflections, and different assumptions about how the papacy worked and to what end, a different selection of features of conventional anti-popery being deployed toward different ends beyond the simple desire to create an alien "other" of Roman Catholicism (and sometimes that "othering" is not self-evident).

I would like in this essay to ponder a little such manifestations of continuity and change—this shifting body of thoughts, ideas, and assumptions in different countries over different centuries that may appear misleadingly uniform. I wish to raise the question of whether historians of anti-Catholicism in different countries and different centuries are really looking at the same thing, but also to problematize some of the ways in which we tend to approach and interpret anti-Catholic ideas and activities. My aim is not to propose a single unifying interpretation, but hopefully to prompt some further reflection on how we use this material. I will begin with anti-Catholic ideas, and then move on to discuss overt actions toward Roman Catholics. While obviously the question of how the one relates to the other is crucial, it is the ways in which historians tend to conceptualize anti-Catholicism as a body of ideas that has often had a decisive influence upon how they then read anti-Catholic behavior, and this impact has not always been a useful or fruitful one.

In recent years, there has been a greater recognition among historians of the importance of anti-Catholicism in early modern Protestant thought. Indeed, in some recent work it seems to loom as the only coherent element of Protestantism. It is certainly true of course that Protestantism emerged in opposition to the Roman

Church and its doctrines, and that many Protestant doctrines were essentially formulated in disagreement with, and thus partly defined by, the Catholic position that they were opposing. Elements of this position were most famously and effectively described in Peter Lake's 1989 essay "Anti-Popery—The Structure of a Prejudice." Lake saw anti-popery as occupying a fundamental position in the English Protestant mind-set, as popery was perceived "through a series of binary oppositions" in which "every negative characteristic imputed to Rome implied a positive, cultural, political, or religious value which Protestants claimed as their own exclusive property." In this way, anti-popery was "a rational response to situations in which values central to that [Protestant] self-image came under threat." If anti-popery was simply seen by contemporaries as an expression of Protestantism, so Roman Catholicism was represented by them as essentially an antireligion: the pope was Antichrist and Rome Babylon; its faith was a form of paganism, its doctrines a form of blasphemy and atheism. Rome was the absolute antithesis of godliness; the doctrine of the two churches (in which everyone was understood to belong to either the church of good or the church of evil) was sometimes converted into the conviction that Rome was the church of evil opposing Protestantism, the true church.[2]

Lake's essay has been a very influential analysis: it is compellingly written and brilliantly argued. But an important point to remember is that Lake was concentrating on the very specific political usage of a form of anti-popery at a very particular time. Ultimately he was exploring how anti-Catholic ideas were specifically deployed as a political ideology—a harbinger of the way that anti-popery would serve as a language of opposition to royal tyranny later in the seventeenth century. What Lake was *not* seeking to do was to place this discourse in the context of how contemporaries variously viewed Roman Catholics—the range of representations and polemical constructions of Roman Catholics and of their Church. Nor was he setting out to contextualize it within the shifting policies that governments adopted toward Roman Catholics, or the ways in which Roman Catholics themselves behaved, wrote, and in some ways shaped both the agenda of confessional polemic and the policies that were adopted toward them.[3] But arguably one way to understand and analyze how anti-Catholicism worked, to comprehend its meaning and resonance for contemporaries, involves situating it precisely in this broader range of Protestant representations of, and interactions with, Catholics and Catholicism.

As Lake agrees, and as I have argued elsewhere, this representation of Rome as an antireligion was only one mode of anti-Catholic writing and thinking. He and Robin Clifton chose to focus on pamphlets written by converts from Roman Catholicism (dubbed elsewhere as "deconversion narratives") when constructing this model of anti-popery, and yet these represent only one narrow genre of anti-Catholic writing that was not particularly widely read (certainly, none of these works went through more than one edition).[4] In fact, the depiction of Rome as an antireligion was only one of many modes of oppositional representation and thought about Rome. Anti-Catholic polemical writing was actually very wide-ranging and flexible in scope and argument, experimenting with a variety of approaches. It *had* to be flexible in order to be able to respond effectively to the resourcefulness and flexibility of Roman Catholic polemical arguments (one basic point here being that the Roman Catholic position was *not* monolithic). As a result, anti-Catholic polemic often presented a far more complex and potentially ambiguous picture of Roman Catholicism. Even puritans deployed multiple modes of anti-Catholic polemic, and recognized the tactical value of appearing more moderate and irenical than their Roman Catholic opponents. A great many doctrines were discussed where the division between Roman Catholics and Protestants was not always presented as a simple inversion (including whether Rome was a true church and a branch of the universal catholic church, the possibility of salvation within its communion, the qualified and potentially temporary nature of the Protestant separation from Rome, the degree to which both churches essentially taught the same basic Christian doctrines, and so on). As well as reflecting the need to respond to Roman Catholic polemical tactics, a more strategically qualified assessment of Rome was also driven by inter-Protestant and even inter-puritan divisions. Thus, when English Presbyterians found their ordination attacked by Independents and sectaries in the 1640s and 1650s as deriving from antichristian Rome, they were forced to argue that Rome was "truly a church" (albeit a corrupt one).[5]

In these many representations and arguments Roman Catholicism was not then presented as an "other," as a simple inversion of Protestant values. There were multiple modes of discourse regarding Roman Catholicism, presenting what was often a complex and ambiguous picture.[6] Noting this range of anti-Catholic responses does not merely help us to contextualize the "binary inversion" style of anti-Catholicism as merely one narrow genre (and therefore its aggressive political deployment against individual Roman Catholics as only one of the ways in which anti-popery might be used). This wide variety of forms of anti-Catholicism can also explain the shape and range of ways in which anti-popery was used, and its use in disputes between Protestants. As I have argued elsewhere, the very fact that representations of Roman Catholicism were diverse and sometimes ambiguous meant that, whenever a particular individual Protestant was suspected of doctrinal heterodoxy and hence of potential complicity with Rome, it was very easy to find apparent supporting evidence in their possession of "popish" books or friends, or in their expressing apparently moderate opinions regarding Rome.[7] And here it is interesting to note parallels between how English and Dutch Arminians were attacked in the early decades of the seventeenth century. Arminius, just like William Laud, was accused of having accepted a cardinal's hat from Rome and of being a Jesuit agent. Similarly, just like Laud and his English Arminian colleague Richard

Montagu, Arminius himself and his followers Adolphus Venator and Petrus Bertius were attacked for granting that Rome was a true though corrupt church (which God had not yet granted a bill of divorce), for distinguishing between the Church of Rome and the Court of Rome, and for maintaining that Protestants had not departed from Rome in those doctrines which Rome shared with Protestants.[8] These were all points that were also maintained by unimpeachably orthodox Calvinists, but could look suspicious in the writings of divines who were already suspected of heterodoxy.

Of course, attacks on these sorts of moderate remarks concerning Roman Catholicism can imply (misleadingly) that only rigid and crude stereotypes of Roman Catholicism were seen as orthodox—unless we note the flexibility of even puritan writers on many of these positions. And this leads me to a more fundamental point: that Protestants were not trapped in an anti-Catholic ideological straitjacket. They *could* perform the mental gymnastics involved in moving between different forms and representations of the Roman Church and of its religion. And here I think that a recognition of the flexibility of early modern Protestants' usage of anti-Catholicism is absolutely crucial. We need to be careful to avoid talking about anti-Catholicism as a mere reflex. We can all agree perhaps that anti-Catholicism should not be depicted simply as an irrational prejudice (while leaving the door open that in some cases it was and still manifestly is), but we need to tackle the so-called "rationality" of anti-Catholicism in a flexible way. In art history, Clare Haynes has provided some striking examples of how Protestant writing on art juggled between different modes of anti-Catholicism and negotiated some tricky inconsistencies, employing a highly selective anti-popery, laying aside elements that presented obstacles to preferred modes of thought while (for example) seeking to justify the appreciation of Raphael's religious art.[9] I would also argue more broadly here that we need to have a sense of the potential inconsistency of people's thought patterns, then and now.

Historians should undoubtedly show a sensitivity toward the ways in which people in the past may have thought and behaved in a manner very different to our own. But there is a danger that in estranging the past we can also end up orientalizing it—that is, that we create static, timeless bodies of exotic ideas that form a neat coherent whole, which our ancestors were trapped in, and where the very exoticism of the ideas convinces us both of the accuracy of our rendering of it, and of the potency that we then attribute to it in the early modern world in overwhelming all other opinions, imperatives, and practices. The stranger the idea, the more we can congratulate ourselves that by emphasizing it we are avoiding anachronism, and are displaying our capacity to absorb the alien spirit of the age. And if the idea seems exotic, so is the temptation all the greater to assume that its very exoticism must have made it all the more powerful in a premodern society. Arguably, historians need instead to develop a keener sense of how early modern people could free themselves from the ideological straitjackets in which we seek to confine them.

That being said, the challenge is to restore to early modern individuals a sense of agency in belief without implying that they simply picked up and discarded ideas in a utilitarian, Machiavellian fashion (which is not of course to say that this did not also sometimes happen). Lyndal Roper has written of early modern belief in witchcraft that "like all belief, it consisted in a morass of images, half-articulated convictions," which often lay "dormant in the mind, the contents of which . . . [were] . . . very far from being a set of coherent arguments." She uses this partly to explain how demonology—a set of arguments for witchcraft belief that could lead to horrific witch-hunts trials and executions—could also contribute to a literature of entertainment, of titillation and humor.[10] The same is arguably true of anti-Catholicism—there could be levels of belief and assumption, views that could be both believed and (in a sense) not believed, apocalyptic ideas (that the pope was Antichrist) that need not feed directly into anti-Catholic conduct. This could turn anti-Catholicism in the individual mind into a mélange of potentially inconsistent ideas.

This inconsistency can partly explain the extraordinary levels of intellectual co-existence of Protestants and Catholics—the puritan libraries with shelves groaning with Roman Catholic tomes; the Protestant galleries filled with Roman Catholic art; the affable scholarly correspondence between scions of anti-popery such as Archbishop Ussher and Franciscans and Catholic bishops.[11] It is of course a challenge to try to understand how these levels of belief worked; to decode precisely how violently anti-Catholic writers read their huge collections of Roman Catholic philosophy, biblical exegesis, and devotional literature (which was manifestly not read in the manner of the old Republican who attended Democrat party rallies "so 's to keep my disgust fresh").[12] Perhaps one could argue that it should be possible for us to understand such selective beliefs when we live in a culture where people smoke cigarettes, which they extract from a packet that bears the apparently unambiguous message "Smoking kills."

One explanation for much of this confusion and inconsistency, of course, is that Roman Catholicism and Protestantism were not binary opposite bodies of belief, however much it may have suited polemicists occasionally to depict them as such. Even if "popery" was merely a Protestant "construct," it only had meaning through its claim to portray the Roman Catholic religion, and as soon as Protestant observers engaged with the actual writings and practices of the Roman Church they ran the risk of discovering that these did not match the polemical construct of Rome as an "antireligion."

However, there may also be a broader sense that people are generally able to cope with a remarkable degree of cognitive dissonance—perhaps more so than historians of ideas tend to assume. Neat binary oppositions may characterize a particular genre of writing, but they rarely typify how the human mind works. People will often be happiest when the inconsistencies in their thought patterns appear fewest, but minds can accommodate far more inconsistencies than we often allow.

Jason Slone, in an intriguing little book entitled *Theological Incorrectness*, has argued that the sociocultural approach to religion has failed to account for the many ways in which religious people do not think "properly" but instead maintain instinctive views (for example, regarding "luck") that are inconsistent with the more orthodox, received theologies, which they will sometimes use in a more reflective way. Individual humans are not cultural sponges (their minds a blank slate that learn what to think from "culture") and religious cultures are not necessarily homogeneous. Rather than seeing so-called "theological incorrectness" as "sloppy thinking," Slone argues that it is actually entirely natural and coherent behavior—these are examples of people thinking "abductively" rather than deducing their thoughts from given theological premises (indeed, "theological incorrectness" may be embraced precisely because it violates a smaller number of intuitive ontological expectations), and are thus a natural byproduct of cognition, of intuitive ontology. The key, he suggests, is to see religion not as a special irreducible feature of human life, but as dependent on the cognitive organs of the human brain, so that religious behavior is seen as constrained by the cognitive mechanisms involved in everyday nonreligious behavior. Similarly, the anthropologist Benson Saler has complained of scholars' tendency to talk loosely of "belief systems" and to create a "misconstrued order" in their accounts of religious traditions—a tendency to exaggerate the systematicity of religious beliefs, which on the ground may prove to be more context-dependent, unstable, and disconnected. Apparently stable intellectual systems can in practice be "a more or less pragmatically successful aggregate of ideas" that are applied to immediate social situations.[13]

This also means that all forms of religious identity tend to be more diverse, contested, and fluid than outsiders or committed insiders tend to imagine. We need to bear this in mind when we look at the different ways in which anti-Catholic ideas may be used. But even before then, we need to raise a further caveat, and that is of people's capacity for immunity to anti-popery. There is a danger in always assuming (as some early modern historians have tended to do) that it was a hegemonic discourse. As I have argued elsewhere, not only were there people who could resist this discourse, but there was indeed an alternative discourse that specifically attacked the political deployment of anti-Catholicism—which Scott Sowerby, studying this phenomenon in the Exclusion Crisis and the 1680s, has dubbed "anti-anti-popery."[14]

We can find "anti-anti-popery" even at times of the supposed high-water mark of officially sanctioned anti-popery, in Elizabethan and Jacobean England, especially in poetry and on the stage. An unhealthy obsession with anti-Catholic apocalyptic in particular is ridiculed in the figures of Ananias, Tribulation Wholesome, and Zeal-of-the-land Busy in Ben Jonson's *The Alchemist* and *Bartholomew Fair*, or in Richard Corbett's poem "The Distracted Puritane" who boasts that he has met the great red dragon and "of the Beasts ten hornes (God blesse us) / I have knock't of three allready . . . I unhorst the whore of Babel / With a Launce of Inspirations: / I made her stinke / And spill her drinck / in the Cupp of Abominations."[15] The English Civil War and Interregnum immeasurably strengthened attacks on anti-popery, which could now be depicted as a cloak for attacks on church and state—anti-papal language could be not just ridiculed, but presented as inherently treasonous (at least in some hands, and especially in the aftermath of the Exclusion Crisis and then in the reign of James II). Tories such as Samuel Parker, Denis Granville, and John Dryden, but also Dissenters and erstwhile anti-Catholic firebrands such as Henry Care, all condemned the evils of anti-popery, even though they did this with varying motives, as Tories seeking to criticize factious Dissenters, or as Dissenters seeking royal protection. But some of those who attacked anti-popery were also capable of deploying it themselves.[16] Anti-popery and anti-anti-popery were not inherently incompatible—it depended on who was using it, in what context, for what purpose, and also (perhaps) what sort of anti-popery was being deployed. One thinks of the example of Lord John Russell even in the nineteenth century, condemning anti-popery, but then embracing it in the face of the so-called "Papal Aggression" of 1850.[17] The immediate political context could be crucial—indeed decisive—in determining the attitudes of Anglicans or Dissenters toward anti-popery. They might either condemn anti-popery, or enthusiastically embrace it.

The uses of anti-Catholicism could of course be very diverse. It could unify Protestants in the face of a common enemy—giving Puritans a way of sharing common ground with Elizabethan and Jacobean bishops and showing their loyalty to the established church.[18] Or it could be used to denigrate opponents, to attack the orthodoxy of fellow Protestants, to articulate constitutional fears,[19] or to explain political conflict. It could be used to attack surviving Roman Catholicism in the Church of England's liturgy, or to condemn persecution, or to condemn toleration.

Anti-popery's potential usage also expanded as its meanings and applications became more diverse. In his seminal article, Lake emphasized that "popery" had a limited meaning in the period before 1642, tied to the specific polemical usage that he outlined. But the English Civil War hugely complicated matters, polemics changed, and the old antitype was used for different purposes so that it was "made available as a free-floating term of opprobrium."[20] Not the least of these migrations was manifested in the fear that the radical religious groups emerging in the 1640s and 1650s were in alliance with subversive papists. One of the most baffling (to modern eyes) was the association of popery with Quakers, but this need not have been a mere smear tactic or arbitrary connection based on the fact that both groups refused the Oath of Allegiance. Their common defense of free will and veneration of poverty and visions, as well as their common denial of the sufficiency of scripture, gave critics plenty to work with. Early Methodists would of course be branded "papistical Methodists," their leaders accused of taking Spanish money to raise a Jacobite army, and their meetings depicted as mere cover for papist plotting. Again, this need not have been just a matter of smearing opponents: as John Walsh has noted, there were "just enough catholic elements" in the Wesley brothers' theology to raise suspicions that they were "popishly inclined."[21] Tory anti-popery, as Tim Harris has demonstrated, could convict a range of Dissenters of either implicit or direct popery. Similarly, William Bulman has demonstrated how "popery" in the later seventeenth century and beyond could become "universalized," and could be used to categorize universal forms of religious power, imposture, corruption, piety, ritual, and belief, acting as a means of understanding and explaining Judaism, Islam, and paganism, while also enabling depictions of these other religions to have an implicit application to events back in England.[22]

Now, the flexible meaning of "popery" might have frustrated some contemporaries, and it is vital to grasp the range of its use (there is sometimes a problem that Lake's delineation of a more polemically limited form is exported wholesale into the study of later periods). But nevertheless, it must be emphasized that these were supplementary modes of discussion and analysis. Moreover, the emergence of what other historians have identified as so-called "civil" notions of popery does not mean that that was now all it was, or that (as Steven Pincus has argued) "popery was now a civil *rather than* a spiritual issue," with ideas of secular, economic interest ideologically dominant, and "popery" a mere catch-all term for civil opponents.[23] There was undoubtedly an increasing *range* of anti-papal discourses present in the later seventeenth century. But there is a danger in assuming the hegemony of one particular type of anti-papal discourse. There is a tendency in some historical scholarship to assume that the emergence of a different usage of the term created a new hegemonic discourse, and that there can only be one dominant form of anti-Catholicism at any one time. It might be more useful to think instead of the coexistence of multiple forms of anti-Catholicism, with the emergence of a new genre or mode of application simply adding to those on offer. After all, the content of Protestant opposition to Roman Catholicism was constantly changing anyway.

A related danger is occasional allusions that historians sometimes tend to make to anti-Catholicism as "evolving," as if it is a single thing in its own right that changes and adapts. As I have stressed already, there were multiple forms of anti-Catholicism, which were deployed in different ways by different people. It was a tool and a weapon that was adapted and appropriated; it was not an organism. Moreover, if it did "evolve," there was plainly an element of irrational survivalism, of vestigial limbs still clinging to the anti-Catholic physiognomy. For example,

Thomas Freeman has strikingly demonstrated that the myth of "Bloody Mary" (Mary Tudor) began in the Exclusion Crisis. Earlier accounts had blamed the bishops and clergy for the persecutions of her reign—it was only with the conversion of James, duke of York that Mary was increasingly blamed for events, and progressively came to be accused of acting tyrannically and thus providing a warning of what the country could expect from a Roman Catholic monarch. It is difficult to see the rationale for the perpetuation of this element of anti-Catholicism given the disappearance of the Stuart threat after 1745, and yet if anything the myth of Bloody Mary intensified after this, especially in the nineteenth century.[24]

But what of the relationship of anti-popery as an ideology to the practical policies adopted by the Protestant authorities toward Roman Catholics? When we look at forms of official persecution, it is certainly possible to find some of the more aggressive motifs of anti-popery being deployed to explain and justify it. Thus, prominent English clergymen wrote tracts on the identity of the pope as Antichrist at the beginning of James I's reign specifically to counter suggestions that the king might grant toleration to Roman Catholics. And when, after the Gunpowder Plot, Roman Catholics were invited to take an Oath of Allegiance to affirm their political loyalty, for many aghast Protestants this simply made no sense. A politically loyal Roman Catholic was a contradiction in terms, and there was a real fear that many Roman Catholics might actually take the oath, and that anti-Catholic laws would be suspended as a result.[25]

Mention of the Oath of Allegiance and parliamentary concerns at the lax enforcement of anti-Catholic legislation, however, reminds us that state policy could often dictate the toleration, rather than the persecution, of Roman Catholics. Political stability enabled governments to ignore the siren calls of anti-Catholicism. After the Treaty of Paris in 1763, British colonial governors wanted to pursue more tolerant policies toward their new Catholic subjects in Quebec in order to win their loyalty. When the resulting Quebec Act of 1774 granted toleration to Catholics, including the right of the clergy to collect tithes, New Englanders (John Adams among them) were outraged. Yet with the coming of the Revolutionary War, members of the Continental Congress soon changed their own attitude toward Catholics for strategic reasons, even to the extent of attending a Catholic mass. Political expediency dictated that the colonies should accept the religious provisions of the Quebec Act; the ideological justification came later.[26] The granting of toleration to Roman Catholics was not therefore a simple index of the decline of anti-Catholicism. It was the need to recruit more soldiers, rather than a sudden decline in anti-Catholicism, that prompted plans among England's governing elites in the 1770s to promote Roman Catholic toleration.[27] Moreover, the same British Empire that granted limited toleration to Roman Catholics in Quebec in 1774 denied it at the same time to Roman Catholics in Grenada, where the Test Acts were imposed.[28]

What was going on when early modern Protestants were deciding not to persecute Roman Catholics? Just as this did not necessarily reflect an embracing of tolerationist principles, so we need not see it as a simple disregard of confessional imperatives. To understand what was happening, we might find it useful to recall our earlier observations regarding "theological inconsistency," and also to adapt and appropriate the distinction that the historian of anti-Semitism Gavin Langmuir has made between religion and religiosity. In Langmuir's rendering, "religion" is defined as the approved confessional identity and specified forms of belief and behavior promulgated and prescribed by churches and their confessions; and "religiosity" as that messier reality of what individuals actually feel and think—not a simple conformity to a prescribed religion, but rather the distinctive property of particular individuals, in which they make an often highly idiosyncratic contact with an ultra-empirical reality. Here, a mix of patterns of experience, and varying social, emotional, and cultural imperatives and priorities creates a very personalized response to confessional imperatives. An individual's religiosity therefore does not represent the simple suspension of a confessional identity, but rather the manner in which a religious identity carries a jumble of often inconsistent ideas, associations, and notions of compatibility and incompatibility.[29]

When we are looking at anti-Catholic religious ideas and their impact in a profoundly confessionalized early modern Protestant culture, therefore, we arguably have to allow for the fact that those ideas are subject to the interpretation, appropriation, and manipulation (often unconscious) of each individual's religiosity. And this is the way in which the clash between socioreligious exclusivism and the practical forms of social, political, and intellectual coexistence is managed. Each individual religiosity may aspire to a coherent and continuous identity, and will be happiest when it comes closest to achieving this coherence, but each religiosity can also find a way of managing intellectual dissonance and inconsistency. An apparent rejection or suspension of a confessional imperative need not therefore indicate that the individual concerned has consciously renounced his or her confessional identity.

Toleration of Roman Catholics need not therefore be seen as evidence that anti-Catholicism is dead. In fact, contemporaries might argue that more anti-Catholicism was required precisely because Roman Catholics were being granted a pragmatic degree of toleration: that is certainly how the puritan Richard Sheldon reasoned in a Paul's Cross sermon in 1622, and the same logic was rehearsed in Victorian sermons.[30] Of course, there is plenty of evidence of elite hostility to Roman Catholicism being maintained in a range of genres of elite writing right through the nineteenth century. If elites were supposedly more tolerant of Roman

Catholics, it did not mean that they liked them very much. Even someone like William Gladstone robustly defended the civil rights of Roman Catholics, but in a famous pamphlet attacked the papal statement on infallibility of 1870 as subversive of the civil obedience of Roman Catholics, claiming the existence of a papal conspiracy to overthrow civil independence and to embrace a "policy of violence."[31] When looking at those who lobbied for the toleration of Roman Catholics, we should of course remember that the meaning of "toleration," after all, is a forced forbearance from persecuting something that is still disliked.[32]

Similarly, in foreign policy, pragmatism could often dictate a policy that was not built upon crude confessional binary opposites. An anti-Habsburg foreign policy could rarely be implemented as a purely anti-Catholic alliance, as it usually required the support of the Catholic French. But England's alliance with Henri IV's France in the 1590s was not seen as a denial in ideological terms of the assumed unitary force of Catholicism under the power of the pope. And for much of the Jacobean period even those of profoundly anti-Catholic views were capable of adopting reasonably positive views of Anglo-Spanish relations. All of this need not be construed as a rejection of the idea of a confessional foreign policy, or of more sophisticated forms of anti-Catholicism. The suggestion that ideologies of foreign policy were essentially deconfessionalized by the later seventeenth century tends to ignore both the ambiguities in earlier "confessional" foreign policy, and also the degree to which confessional concerns continued to be strongly aired and invoked in the second half of the seventeenth century and well beyond, even if they were now competing with other ideological forces such as political economy and the perceived "balance of power."[33]

But what about the world beyond government policy? Was this an arena of lingering, simple-minded anti-Catholic bigotry remote from the more sophisticated liberalism of intellectual and governing elites? Or was it the haven of practical everyday coexistence between individuals within the broader local community—what the Dutch historian Willem Frijhoff has dubbed "the ecumenicity of everyday life"? It used to be suggested that practical toleration emerged with secularization and official toleration; but now in the work of Benjamin Kaplan in particular the suggestion is that actually this coexistence was the norm within confessional Europe. "Honour, loyalty, friendship, kinship, civic duty, devotion to the commonweal" could "complicate an individual's confessional allegiance," rather than simply reinforcing it. Again, we need not assume that this reflected a conscious rejection of confessional identities, or a principled, conscious preference of other values over those of religion. These may just be flexible religiosities at work. This degree of flexibility on a personal level would parallel what has been suggested above about intellectual coexistence among elite groups. Certainly, as the work of both Kaplan and Frijhoff has made very clear, this coexistence was not free of significant tensions, and it is notable that where Kaplan still dubs this coexistence "toleration," Frijhoff explicitly refrains from using this term as its associations are "loaded with positive values."[34] In fact, the treatment of Roman Catholics in local society in Protestant countries would seem to oscillate between coexistence and occasional violent attacks and panics. Coexistence might indeed make attacks *more* likely rather than less, creating an endless series of tense stand-offs.

But how should we approach those famous examples of anti-Catholic religious riots and panics—in England in 1640–42, 1678–81, 1688–89, 1715, and 1745, when domestic upheaval, threats of foreign invasion, and fears of Roman Catholic restoration led to waves of "panic fears" sweeping the country? Wild rumors, typically of Irishmen and Roman Catholics "who burn, kill, and destroy all they meet with," prompted Protestant crowds to attack recusants, to search homes for arms, to vandalize shops and destroy clandestine chapels.[35] We may if anything have underestimated the number of anti-Catholic panics that could seize local communities. I have found it relatively easy to uncover new poems and letters that describe local panics about a feared Spanish invasion and Catholic uprising in the 1610s and 1620s that led to sudden raisings of the local militia and flights of local communities.[36] These events certainly seem to be dramatic manifestations of anti-Catholicism. But is there a problem in our tendency to see these events as somehow the "purest" form of anti-Catholicism, with the anti-Catholic riot or panic as "echt" anti-popery?

We need not presuppose that these panics necessarily represent the fast-flowing river of anti-Catholicism finally swelling over its banks. Roper talks of beliefs in witchcraft as "half-articulated" fragments of ideas that could occasionally come together "in searing clarity" in an accusation of witchcraft; as lying dormant and triggering aggression only when they fit in with other anxieties and conditions. The same would seem to be true of these anti-Catholic panics. As Kaplan has observed, "ideological fuel" was not sufficient in itself to provoke popular religious violence unless there was a "specific trigger."[37] Fears of papist activity could dissipate as rapidly as they arose. Just thirteen years after the Gunpowder Plot, one notable London parish (Saint Botolph Aldgate) decided to cease having sermons on the 5th of November, even though the parishioners also decided a few months later to appoint and pay for a parish lecturer (so it wasn't that they had anything against godly sermons per se). It is remarkable that the weeks following the Gunpowder Plot did not witness anti-Catholic panics on anything like the scale of 1641–42. While the apparent threat from Roman Catholics might objectively have seemed greater in November 1605, it was the political crisis in the early 1640s which seems to have done more to create the anti-Catholic paranoia.[38]

When we look at these anti-Catholic panics, it is worth flagging the problematic terminology regarding whether these panics were "popular." It is sometimes suggested that in the eighteenth and nineteenth centuries elite anti-popery disappeared and only popular fears remained. But there is ample evidence of the involvement of elites in these panics (which also helps to explain the mass mobilization involved in many of them). Even the later riots—in Glasgow in 1778–79, in the Gordon Riots, and even in the popular anti-Catholic agitation in 1829 and 1850—political elites were very closely involved in whipping up anti-Catholic hostility and providing it with targets.[39] Elite and popular, local and national, political and religious were closely intertwined in most if not all of these panics. Here was no mere primordial popular aggression.

In England at least, political fears and instability often had a major role in triggering these panics. In what is by far the most subtle reading available of an outbreak of popular violence against Catholics, John Walter's interpretation of the Stour Valley riots of 1642 has pointed to a combination of economic distress, class hostility, and pro-parliamentary popular political mobilization in which anti-Catholic language and action had a vital role to play in helping to construct and articulate an understanding of events and a legitimating of certain responses. Such actions *could* be read as a confessional purging, but this would be to highlight only one aspect of crowd activity and motivation. Anti-Catholicism may have provided some rationales and targets, but it was not necessarily the engine driving events or the sole ideological influence directing people's anger and hostility.[40] As Roper has pointed out, the ideas may trigger physical aggression only when they fit into other anxieties and conditions.

Just as we have questioned whether there was a single continuous body of anti-Catholic ideas, so we may need to resist the temptation to see so-called anti-Catholic riots and panics as the same phenomena. Historians' occasional tendency to talk of particular anti-Catholic riots as being "carbon copies" of other anti-Catholic riots seems potentially dangerous.[41] It is true, of course, that some forms of ritualized aggression and fear may take some culturally standardized forms of expression, but there will often be uniquely local triggers to the behavior, and local targets of the fears (as Walter's work suggests). There may be many different elements to these riots and protests: social tensions, local and national politics, gender, economic problems could all play an important role. Anti-popery may help to give a particular incident of unrest its form, focus, and edge, but this does not mean that religious issues were foremost in its agitation (and this is perhaps another reason why these riots might not be regarded as the purest form of anti-Catholicism).[42]

We might also ponder the importance of Roman Catholic behavior in provoking some of these panics. As several scholars have noted, various levels of de facto toleration would often be possible for Roman Catholics as long as they played the game and kept their confessional heads down. An absence of public processions by Roman Catholics could have been the key to securing tolerance: Kaplan has noted that in mixed-religion communities on the continent it was almost always these forms of overt, public confessional behavior that prompted religious riots.[43] On the other hand, however, Victor Stater has noted that it was precisely the degree to which the minority Roman Catholic population in Restoration England developed forms of discreet, underground networks of organization and worship that made them seem all the more threatening and ubiquitous when political anxieties led to the uncovering of these hidden networks. Discreet activities behind closed doors can easily appear as conspiracy if the political climate changes.[44] As I have argued more generally, if political crises led to a sudden desire to reassert and intensify confessional boundaries, amid fears that these boundaries were being broached, then it was usually very easy for contemporaries to find evidence of such worrying transgressions because these were often the norm in coexistential practice. Given that these boundaries were being covertly or even explicitly disregarded on a day-to-day basis, it was relatively simple to find apparent evidence to confirm the worst fears both of Roman Catholic conspiracy and also of the complicit involvement of fellow Protestants. It was confessional coexistence that provided the evidence needed for more violent anti-Catholicism: rather than being incompatible phenomena, the one actually fed upon the other.[45]

Sometimes, Roman Catholic overconfidence and more public forms of confessional activity could prompt a Protestant panic. This is certainly observable in the early years of James I's reign, at the time of the Spanish Match in the early 1620s, and in the later 1630s. At times of political tension, a Roman Catholic walking round with a broad smile on his face was enough to prompt serious apprehensions among Protestants. But sometimes a confidence born of despair could be equally dangerous. Frijhoff has written a fascinating analysis of the anti-Catholic fear in the Netherlands in 1734. The panic was prompted by rumors that the Roman Catholics intended to massacre the Protestants, but as Frijhoff notes, there were Roman Catholic prophesies circulating at the time that foretold precisely this event. These were "prophecies of hope," but they played an important role in generating the panic, which was not simply a mass Protestant fear caused by the influx of seasonal migrant Roman Catholic laborers.[46]

To conclude: I think that we can all agree that there was a great deal of anti-Catholicism around throughout the Atlantic world in the early modern period, and that it certainly had many consistent features. And if we study anti-Catholic discourse in nineteenth-century England and New England we can find many of the same themes that are evident in Elizabethan anti-Catholicism: the use of the confessional as a means of exercising power, the Roman Catholic insistence on absolute obedience, the impiety and sexual aberrations in monasteries, the dangerous emphasis on secrecy, the political danger of Roman Catholic views of obedience, the dangerously compelling and seductive power of Roman Catholic priests, the identification of the pope as Antichrist, and so on. "Deconversion narratives" remained a notable genre of anti-Catholic writing, although anti-Catholic ideas were also disseminated more widely than ever through the new media of novels, magazines, and children's literature.[47] Anti-Catholicism did not simply disappear, or become merely a "popular" primordial superstition manifested in spasmodic irrational religious riots. Nor did it cease to exist with the granting of civil rights and religious toleration to Roman Catholics (Roman Catholic emancipation in England was manifestly against the wishes of most of the population). Anti-Catholic polemic was a prominent feature of public discourse—elite and popular—from the 1830s through to at least the 1870s in England and the United States, and arguably right through to the early twentieth century.[48]

When we write about early modern anti-Catholicism, then, it is important that we should not feel compelled to create a modernizing teleology, whereby the anti-Catholicism of the sixteenth and seventeenth centuries appears as an exotic prejudice destined to expire in the wake of the march toward modernity in the eighteenth and nineteenth centuries. The authors with whom I began—Wells and McCabe—demonstrate that you did not have to be an evangelical Protestant, or even a Christian, to embrace anti-Catholicism with many of its traditional tropes, in very public writings right into the 1940s and beyond. Some secularist organizations have also more recently shown a tendency to revive some very old anti-Catholic chestnuts. Wells's *Crux Ansata* is back in print, and, of course, among some evangelical groups virulent anti-Catholicism has never really gone away. The Free Church of Scotland minister Alexander Hislop's *The Two Babylons; or, The Papal Worship Proved to Be the Worship of Nimrod and His Wife*—first published in the 1850s, was still being republished in hardback in 1976, and now has had a massive revival online. The comic-book evangelist Jack Chick has a large following for his anti-Catholic ravings, which include the familiar claim that the Roman Church is the Whore of Babylon, and the (hopefully less familiar) claims that the Church of Rome has used Islam to lure people from Christianity and that it masterminded the Holocaust.

Nevertheless, while over the centuries a remarkably resilient body of anti-Catholic fears and beliefs have been endlessly rehearsed and repeated, they have not necessarily had a constant configuration or meaning. There are real dangers in assuming that anti-Catholicism was constant from Elizabeth to Victoria, that John Foxe and William Hogarth had the same worldview, and that anti-Catholic ideas everywhere had the same resonance, or constituted the same call to action. There were vital changes in the exact nature of the perceived Roman Catholic threat, and in its supposed agents and their objectives. Even theological polemic underwent constant change, development, and adaptation. Not only has anti-Catholicism changed over time, but its content and focus has often varied considerably in the same time period, and even within the duration of a single anti-Catholic panic (and sometimes indeed even within a single anti-Catholic text). Moreover, as I have argued, even the same body of anti-Catholic ideas could have a very different meaning and resonance for different individuals and different religiosities.

It is vital for historians, then, that they situate every incident or example of anti-Catholicism—whether written or acted—in the immediate context of broader belief systems, polemical circumstances, political developments, the religiosities of the individuals concerned, and the treatment and behavior of Roman Catholics themselves. Most of all, we need to be flexible in our reading and interpretation of what can appear extreme and inflammatory ideas. A piece of anti-Catholic writing needs to be situated within a contemporary spectrum of ideas of and attitudes toward Roman Catholics. We should not assume that the ideas were normative and hegemonic, and must always be ready to leave interpretative space for people who did not agree with these ideas, or who reserved the right to vary in how they applied them. We might also, perhaps, need to distinguish between the political, theological, social, moral, and even aesthetic elements within any single piece of anti-Catholic polemic or action.

The crucial thing, I would argue, is to avoid the temptation to invoke a body of anti-Catholic ideas and associations as being simply hard-wired into the Protestant mind-set, so that early modern Protestants can be seen as simple automatons in the grip of an anti-Catholic intellectual straitjacket. When we identify anti-Catholic ideas or actions being expressed, this should herald the beginning of our research, and not—as it so often is—the end of it.

Notes

A version of this paper was first delivered as a keynote lecture at the conference "Antipopery: The Trans-Atlantic Experience c. 1530–1850," at Philadelphia in September 2008. I am grateful to the audience on that occasion, and to various other audiences who have heard versions of the paper subsequently, for their helpful comments, and most of all to Evan Haefeli for first inviting me to give the paper, and for encouraging me to revisit it for publication here.

1. H. G. Wells, *Crux Ansata: An Indictment of the Roman Catholic Church* (Harmondsworth: Penguin, 1943); Joseph McCabe, *The Papacy in Politics To-day: The Guilt of the Roman Church in the World War*, 4th ed. (London: Watts, 1943).
2. Peter Lake, "Anti-Popery: The Structure of a Prejudice," in *Conflict in Early Stuart England*, ed. Richard Cust and Ann Hughes (London: Longman, 1989), 73–74, 75–80. On the two churches see Richard J. Bauckham, *Tudor Apocalypse* (Abingdon: Sutton Courtenay Press, 1978), chap. 3.

3. Lake is much clearer about the diverse nature of anti-Catholicism in his later work, notably his "Anti-Puritanism: The Structure of a Prejudice," in *Religious Politics in Post-Reformation England,* ed. Kenneth Fincham and Peter Lake (Woodbridge: Boydell Press, 2006).
4. Robin Clifton, "Fear of Popery," in *The Origins of the English Civil War,* ed. Conrad Russell (London: Macmillan, 1973), 148–49; Lake, "Anti-Popery," 74–79, 98n6.
5. E.g., John Brinsley, *The Araignment of the Present Schism* (London, 1646), 26–27; Daniel Cawdrey, *Independencie a Great Schism Proved against Dr. Owen* (London, 1657), 102, 115–16.
6. Anthony Milton, "A Qualified Intolerance: The Limits and Ambiguities of Early Stuart anti-Catholicism," in *Catholicism and Anti-Catholicism in Early Modern English Texts,* ed. Arthur F. Marotti (Basingstoke: Macmillan, 1999), 88–91; Anthony Milton, *Catholic and Reformed: The Roman and Protestant Churches in English Protestant Thought 1600–1640* (Cambridge: Cambridge University Press, 1995), 40–42.
7. Milton, "Qualified Intolerance," 109–10.
8. Carl Bangs, *Arminius: A Study in the Dutch Reformation* (Nashville: Abington Press, 1971), 287, 295, 303–4, 319, 322–23; R. B. Evenhuis, *Ook dat was Amsterdam,* 5 vols. (Amsterdam: Uitgeverij W. Ten Have N.V., 1965–78), 5:245–46.
9. See Clare Haynes's essay in this volume.
10. Lyndal Roper, "Witchcraft and the Western Imagination," *Transactions of the Royal Historical Society* 16 (2006): 117–41, quotes on 120, 141
11. See Milton, "Qualified Intolerance," 91–95; Milton, *Catholic and Reformed,* 234–35.
12. H. C. Porter, *Reformation and Reaction in Tudor Cambridge* (Cambridge: Cambridge University Press, 1958), 277.
13. D. Jason Slone, *Theological Incorrectness: Why Religious People Believe What They Shouldn't* (Oxford: Oxford University Press, 2004); Benson Saler, "Finding Wayu Religion," *Historical Reflections* 31, no. 2 (2005): 255–57.
14. Milton, *Catholic and Reformed,* 46–55, 63–72; Scott Sowerby, "Opposition to Anti-Popery in Restoration England," *Journal of British Studies* 51 no. 1 (2012): 26–49.
15. Richard Corbett, *Poems,* ed. J.A.W. Bennett and H. R. Trevor-Roper (Oxford: Clarendon Press, 1955), 57–58; Peter Lake, *The Antichrist's Lewd Hat* (New Haven, CT: Yale University Press, 2002), 602–5, 608.
16. Sowerby, "Opposition," 34–43.
17. Walter Ralls, "The Papal Aggression of 1850: A Study in Victorian anti-Catholicism," *Church History* 43 (1974): 242–43.
18. Peter Lake, *Moderate Puritans and the Elizabethan Church* (Cambridge: Cambridge University Press, 1982), 57; and passim; Milton, *Catholic and Reformed,* 31–37.
19. Michael P. Winship, "Freeborn (Puritan) Englishmen and Slavish Subjection: Popish Tyranny and Puritan Constitutionalism, c. 1570–1606," *English Historical Review* 124, no. 510 (2009): 1050–74.
20. Lake, "Anti-Popery," 96; Tim Harris, *London Crowds in the Reign of Charles II* (Cambridge: Cambridge University Press, 1987), 33.
21. Barry Reay, *The Quakers and the English Revolution* (London: Palgrave Macmillan, 1985), 59–60, 65, 96; Paul Chang-Ha Lim, *In Pursuit of Purity, Unity, and Liberty: Richard Baxter's Puritan Ecclesiology in Its Seventeenth-Century Context* (Leiden: Brill, 2004), 141–43; Colin Haydon, *Anti-Catholicism in Eighteenth-Century England* (Manchester: Manchester University Press, 1993), 10, 63–64, 127, 248–49; John Walsh, "Methodism and the Mob in the Eighteenth Century," in *Popular Belief and Practice,* ed. G. J. Cuming and Derek Baker, Studies in Church History 8 (Cambridge: Cambridge University Press, 1972), 226.

22. Harris, *London Crowds,* 139–44; Tim Harris, *Restoration: Charles II and His Kingdoms, 1660–1685* (New York: Penguin, 2005), 247; William J. Bulman, "From Anti-Popery and Anti-Puritanism to Orientalism," in *Making the British Empire 1660–1800,* ed. Jason Peacey (Manchester: Manchester University Press, 2020). I am very grateful to Professor Bulman for allowing me to read his article in advance of publication.
23. Steven C. A. Pincus, *Protestantism and Patriotism* (Cambridge: Cambridge University Press, 1996), 448 (emphasis mine).
24. Thomas S. Freeman, "Inventing Bloody Mary: Perceptions of Mary Tudor from the Reformation to the Twentieth Century," in *Mary Tudor: Old and New Perspectives,* ed. Susan Doran and Thomas S. Freeman (Basingstoke: Palgrave Macmillan, 2011), 78–100.
25. Milton, *Catholic and Reformed,* 100–101; Milton, "Qualified Intolerance," 105–6.
26. Haydon, *Anti-Catholicism,* 171–72; Charles P. Hanson, *Necessary Virtue: The Pragmatic Origins of Religious Liberty in New England* (Charlottesville: University of Virginia Press, 1998), 11, 61–65, 77–78, 85–91, 97.
27. R. K. Donovan, "The Military Origins of the Roman Catholic Relief Programme of 1778," *Historical Journal* 28 (1985): 81–84.
28. H. W. Muller, "Bonds of Belonging: Subjecthood and British Empire," *Journal of British Studies* 53, no. 1 (2014): 29–58.
29. Gavin I. Langmuir, *History, Religion and Anti-Semitism* (Berkeley: University of California Press, 1990), 158–76.
30. Richard Sheldon, *A Sermon Preached at Paules Crosse* (London, 1625), 31, 41–43, 45; Milton, "Qualified Intolerance," 97–98; Miriam Elizabeth Burstein, "Anti-Catholic Sermons in Victorian Britain," in *A New History of the Sermon: The Nineteenth Century,* ed. Richard H. Ellison (Leiden: Brill, 2010), 261–62; Alexandra Walsham, *Charitable Hatred: Tolerance and Intolerance in England, 1500–1700* (Manchester: Manchester University Press, 2006), 316.
31. E. R. Norman, *Anti-Catholicism in Victorian England* (London: Routledge, 1968), 90–96.
32. John Coffey, *Persecution and Toleration in Protestant England, 1558–1689* (London: Longman, 2000), 10–11.
33. Julian Lock, "'How Many Tercios Has the Pope?' The Spanish War and the Sublimation of Elizabethan Anti-Popery," *History* 81 (1996): 197–214; Katherine S. van Eerde, "The Spanish Match through an English Protestant's Eyes," *Huntington Library Quarterly* 32 (1968): 59–75; Pincus, *Protestantism and Patriotism;* Heinz Schilling, "Konfessionalisierung und Formierung eines internationalen Systems wahrend der frühen Neuzeit," in *Die Reformation in Deutschland und Europa: Interpretationen und Debatten,* ed. H. Guggisberg and G. Krodel (Gütersloh: Gütersloher Verlagshaus, 1993), 597–613; *Konfessionalisierung und Staatsinteressen 1559–1660,* ed. H. Guggisberg and G. Krodel (Leiden: Brill, 2007); Heinz Schilling, *Early Modern European Civilization and Its Political and Cultural Dynamism* (Lebanon, NH: University Press of New England, 2008), 67–86; David Onnekink and Gijs Rommelse, eds., *Ideology and Foreign Policy in Early Modern Europe (1650–1750)* (Farnham: Routledge, 2011); Tony Claydon, *Europe and the Making of England 1660–1760* (Cambridge: Cambridge University Press, 2007); A. C. Thompson, "Early Eighteenth-Century Britain as a Confessional State," in *Protestantism and National Identity: Britain and Ireland, c. 1650–c. 1850,* ed. Tony Claydon and Ian McBride (Cambridge: Cambridge University Press, 1998), 96–106.
34. Willem Frijhoff, *Embodied Belief: Ten Essays on Religious Culture in Dutch History* (Hilversum: Uitgeverij Verloren, 2002), 48; Benjamin J. Kaplan, *Divided by Faith: Religious Conflict and the Practice of Toleration in Early Modern Europe* (Cambridge, MA: Belknap Press of Harvard University Press, 2007), 9, 11; Benjamin J. Kaplan, "Religiously Mixed Marriage in Dutch Society," in *Catholic Communities in Protestant States: Britain and the Netherlands, c. 1570–1720,*

ed. Benjamin J. Kaplan, Bob Moore, Henk van Nierop, and Judith Pollmann (Manchester: Manchester University Press, 2009), 50.

35. Clifton, "Fear of Popery," 157–63.
36. For two hitherto unmentioned early Stuart examples, picked up virtually at random, see British Library, Add MS 46885A, fols. 9v–10v; *Wentworth Papers 1597–1628*, ed. J. P. Cooper, Camden Society 4th ser. 12 (1973): 263.
37. Roper, "Witchcraft," 141; Kaplan, *Divided*, 73–98.
38. London Metropolitan Archives, [GL] MS 9236/1, fol. 61v. I am grateful to Dr Julia Merritt for this reference. On anti-Catholicism in 1640–42 see the important new analysis in J. F. Merritt, *Westminster 1640–1660: A Royal City in a Time of Revolution* (Manchester: Manchester University Press, 2013), chap. 1.
39. Haydon, *Anti-Catholicism*, 207–13; D. G. Paz, *Popular anti-Catholicism in Mid-Victorian England* (Stanford, CA: Stanford University Press, 1992), 280–90.
40. John Walter, *Understanding Popular Violence in the English Revolution* (Cambridge: Cambridge University Press, 1999), 318–30, 342–43, and passim.
41. E.g., Haydon, *Anti-Catholicism*, 260.
42. Paz, *Popular Anti-Catholicism*, 225–65; Walsham, *Charitable Hatred*, 129–33.
43. Kaplan, *Divided*, 73–86. Note also his discussion of semi-clandestine *schuilkerken* (172–97).
44. Victor Stater, "The Popish Iceberg" (Paper presented to the conference "Antipopery: The Transatlantic Experience c. 1530–1850," Philadelphia, September 2008).
45. Milton, "Qualified Intolerance," 109.
46. Willem Frijhoff, "The Panic of June 1734," in Frijhoff, *Embodied Belief*, 181–213.
47. Paz, *Popular Anti-Catholicism*, 59–66; Burstein, "Anti-Catholic Sermons," 233–48; Paul Misner, "Newman and the Tradition Concerning the Papal Antichrist," *Church History* 42 (1973): 377–95; Robert J. Klaus, *The Pope, the Protestants, and the Irish: Papal Aggression and Anti-Catholicism in Mid-Nineteenth-Century England* (London: Garland, 1987), 219–37; Susan M. Griffin, *Anti-Catholicism in Nineteenth-Century Fiction* (Cambridge: Cambridge University Press, 2004).
48. Paz, *Popular anti-Catholicism*, 225–65, 299; G.F.A. Best, "Popular Protestantism in Victorian Britain," in *Ideas and Institutions of Victorian Britain*, ed. Robert Robson (London: G. Bell and Sons, 1967), 115. For later: Erik Sidenvall, *After Anti-Catholicism? John Henry Newman and Protestant Britain 1845–c. 1890* (London: T. and T. Clark, 2006).

CONTRIBUTORS

CRAIG GALLAGHER is a lecturer in Early American history at New England College, and holds a Ph.D. in history from Boston College. He is currently completing his first book manuscript, entitled “Imperial Zealots: Scots and the Rise and Fall of British North America,” which offers the first comprehensive treatment of the critical role played by Scottish colonists in the coming of the American Revolution. He also has a forthcoming article in the *Journal of British Studies,* titled “British Caledonia: English America and the Scottish Darien Project,” that is due out in 2020.

EVAN HAEFELI is an associate professor of colonial American and Atlantic history at Texas A&M University. He is the author of a number of works including *New Netherland and the Dutch Origins of American Religious Liberty* and, most recently, *Accidental Pluralism: America and the Religious Politics of English Expansion, 1497–1662.* He is currently completing a manuscript on the politics of religion in England's Restoration colonies.

TIM HARRIS is the Munro, Goodwin, Wilkinson Professor of European History at Brown University. He has written and edited eleven books on early modern British history, most recently *Rebellion: Britain's First Stuart Kings, 1567–1642* (2014) and *Politics, Religion, and Ideas in Seventeenth- and Eighteenth-Century Britain: Essays in Honour of Mark Goldie* (2019, coedited with Justin Champion, John Coffey, and John Marshall). He is currently working on a study of Britain's century of revolutions, 1603–1691.

CLARE HAYNES, FSA, is currently an independent researcher. In 2013 and 2015 she was Rita and William H. Bell Visiting Professor of Anglican and Ecumenical Studies at the University of Tulsa. She is the author of *Pictures and Popery: Art and Religion in England, 1660–1760* (2006), and most recently contributed chapters on “Anglicanism and Art” in *Establishment and Empire: the Development of Anglicanism, 1662–1829,* edited by J. Gregory (2017), and “A Space Set

Aside: St. Peter Hungate as Church, as Museum, as Gallery" in *Management of Religion, Sacralisation of Heritage*, edited by Ernst van der Hemel and Irene Stengs (2020).

SUSAN P. LIEBELL is an associate professor of political science at Saint Joseph's University. She is the author of *Democracy, Intelligent Design, and Evolution: Science for Citizenship* and is currently writing a book on citizenship and the Second Amendment.

BRENDAN MCCONVILLE is a professor of early American history at Boston University and the author, most recently, of *The King's Three Faces: The Rise and Fall of Royal America, 1688 to 1776* (2006). He is currently completing a microhistory on the revolutionary period, *The Brethren: Heresy, Conspiracy, and the Creation of the Revolutionary American State*, and is working on a manuscript on the transformation of American politics from 1774 to 1794 entitled *In the Season of Revolution*.

ANTHONY MILTON is a professor of history at the University of Sheffield. His publications include *Catholic and Reformed: The Roman and Protestant Churches in English Protestant Thought, The British Delegation and the Synod of Dort (1618–19), Laudian and Royalist Polemic in Seventeenth-Century England*, and (most recently) *England's Second Reformation: The Battle for the Church of England 1625–62*. He also edited volume 1 of *The Oxford History of Anglicanism*.

ANDREW R. MURPHY is a professor of political science at Virginia Commonwealth University. His research focuses on the intersections between religion and politics in the Anglo-American political tradition. His most recent works are *William Penn: A Life*, and *Liberty, Conscience, and Toleration: The Political Thought of William Penn*.

GREGORY SMULEWICZ-ZUCKER is a PhD candidate in political science at Rutgers University, New Brunswick. He is the editor of eight books. His most recent is *Anti-Science and the Assault on Democracy* (2018). His current research focuses on nineteenth-century German, American, and British theories of the state and their influence on institutional change.

LAURA M. STEVENS is Chapman Professor of English at the University of Tulsa. A former editor of *Tulsa Studies in Women's Literature* and past president of the Society of Early Americanists, she is the author of *The Poor Indians: British Missionaries, Native Americans, and Colonial Sensibility* (2004) and *Friday's Tribe: Eighteenth-Century English Missionary Fantasies* (forthcoming 2021).

CYNTHIA J. VAN ZANDT is an associate professor of colonial American and Atlantic history at the University of New Hampshire. Most recently the author of *Brothers among Nations: The Pursuit of Intercultural Alliance in Early America, 1580–1660* (2008), she is currently working on a study of the regicides Whalley and Goffe, and the radical puritan underground during the Restoration.

PETER W. WALKER is an assistant professor of history at the University of Wyoming. The author of "The Bishop Controversy, the Imperial Crisis, and Religious Radicalism in New England, 1763–74," *New England Quarterly* (2017), he is currently coediting a collection of American Loyalist correspondence and working on a book titled *The Church Militant: Loyalism, the Church of England, and the American Revolution.*

INDEX

Page numbers in *italics* indicate illustrations and associated captions. Page numbers with an "n" appended indicate a page number in the notes section.

Recent books in the series

Early American Histories

Conceived in Crisis: The Revolutionary Creation of an American State
CHRISTOPHER R. PEARL

Redemption from Tyranny: Herman Husband's American Revolution
BRUCE E. STEWART

Experiencing Empire: Power, People, and Revolution in Early America
PATRICK GRIFFIN, EDITOR

Citizens of Convenience: The Imperial Origins of American Nationhood on the U.S.-Canadian Border
LAWRENCE B. A. HATTER

"Esteemed Bookes of Lawe" and the Legal Culture of Early Virginia
WARREN M. BILLINGS AND BRENT TARTER, EDITORS

Settler Jamaica in the 1750s: A Social Portrait
JACK P. GREENE

Loyal Protestants and Dangerous Papists: Maryland and the Politics of Religion in the English Atlantic, 1630–1690
ANTOINETTE SUTTO

The Road to Black Ned's Forge: A Story of Race, Sex, and Trade on the Colonial American Frontier
TURK MCCLESKEY

Dunmore's New World: The Extraordinary Life of a Royal Governor in Revolutionary America—with Jacobites, Counterfeiters, Land Schemes, Shipwrecks, Scalping, Indian Politics, Runaway Slaves, and Two Illegal Royal Weddings
JAMES CORBETT DAVID

Creating the British Atlantic: Essays on Transplantation, Adaptation, and Continuity
JACK P. GREENE

The Evil Necessity: British Naval Impressment in the Eighteenth-Century Atlantic World
DENVER BRUNSMAN